...eg, MB. R3B 2E9 Canada

Landlords and Tenants on the Prairie Frontier

STUDIES IN AMERICAN LAND POLICY

By the same author

The Illinois Central Railroad and Its Colonization Work (1934)

The Wisconsin Pine Lands of Cornell University: A Study in Land Policy and Absentee Ownership (1943)

Fifty Million Acres: Conflicts over Kansas Land Policy, 1854–1890 (1954)

The Farmer's Age: Agriculture, 1815–1860 (1960)

Agriculture and the Civil War (1965)

California Ranchos and Farms, 1846–1862 (1967)

History of Public Land Law Development (with a chapter by Robert W. Swenson) (1968)

Landlords and Tenants
on the Prairie Frontier

STUDIES IN AMERICAN LAND POLICY

by Paul W. Gates

Cornell University Press

ITHACA AND LONDON

First published 1973 by Cornell University Press.
Published in the United Kingdom by Cornell University Press Ltd., 2-4 Brook Street, London W1Y 1AA.

International Standard Book Number 0-8014-0763-X
Library of Congress Catalog Card Number 72-12403

Printed in the United States of America by Vail-Ballou Press, Inc.

Librarians: Library of Congress cataloging information appears on the last page of the book.

Preface

These nine essays, with an introduction, written over the course of thirty-three years, offer an intensive examination of segments of the story of the development and operation of the public land system; they focus mostly on the prairie states of the Upper Mississippi Valley. I have been at pains to show some of the obstacles in the path of westward-moving migrants looking for "cheap" government land, which was cheap only in relation to the price of land in well-established communities enjoying the benefits of roads, schools, and local government. In doing so, I have drawn attention to the roles of the speculators in land, the early cattle kings and bonanza farmers, and the landlords with estates as large as those of the most opulent cotton and sugar planters of Louisiana and Mississippi. These developments were occurring in the years when government policy, as expressed in Congress by the framers of the land laws, was moving away from Alexander Hamilton's plan of selling the public lands to produce the greatest possible revenue at the least cost to the government, to one of reducing the price and ultimately offering free land. Revenue became less important; the publicly stated purpose of land policy was to make farm ownership easily accessible to all willing to engage in the farm-making process on the frontier.

Fundamental to western history is the story of the development of policies for the administration and alienation of the public lands of the United States, the kinds of ownership patterns that emerged, and the exploitation and use of these lands.

[v]

That story has been greatly complicated by thousands of laws and administrative orders interpreting these laws, by the differing attitudes of various elements toward the lands, and by the differences in the types of land to which the laws and administrative regulations applied.

The essays, originally designed to focus on a particular facet of the subject, have been revised somewhat to make them more up to date, but have been permitted to remain as units. They are offered here in the hope of providing a better understanding of the functioning of our national land system in the prairie states prior to the adoption of the Homestead Act.

Following each essay is a bibliographical note indicating the important studies that have appeared since the essays were first published. For a connected narrative of the development and operation of the public land system I refer the reader to Gates and Swenson's *History of Public Land Law Development* (Washington, D.C., 1968). Further references, including numerous studies in manuscript, are in the bibliography of that book.

For permission to reprint these essays I am grateful to the publishers and editors: "Tenants of the Log Cabin," *Mississippi Valley Historical Review*, XLIX (June, 1962), 3–31; "The Role of the Land Speculator in Western Development," *Pennsylvania Magazine of History and Biography*, LXVI (July, 1942), 314–333; "Southern Investments in Northern Lands before the Civil War," *Journal of Southern History*, V (May, 1939), 155–185, copyright 1939 by the Southern Historical Association, reprinted by permission of the Managing Editor; "Land Policy and Tenancy in the Prairie Counties of Indiana," *Indiana Magazine of History*, XXXV (March, 1939), 1–26; "Land Policy and Tenancy in the Prairie States," *Journal of Economic History*, I (May, 1941), 60–82; "Hoosier Cattle Kings," *Indiana Magazine of History*, XLIV (March, 1948), 1–24; "Cattle Kings in the Prairies," *Mississippi Valley Historical Review*, XXXV (December, 1948), 379–412; "Frontier

Landlords and Pioneer Tenants," *Journal of the Illinois State Historical Society*, XXXVIII (June, 1945), 143–206; "Frontier Estate Builders and Farm Laborers," in Clifton B. Kroeber and Walker D. Wyman, editors, *The Frontier in Perspective* (Madison: The University of Wisconsin Press; © 1957 by the Regents of the University of Wisconsin), 143–163.

PAUL W. GATES

Ithaca, New York

Contents

Landlords and Tenants on the Prairie Frontier

STUDIES IN AMERICAN LAND POLICY

Introduction

As late as 1924 the history of the transfer of the public lands
of the United States to private ownership was an almost untouched field of investigation. True, Payson J. Treat, George M.
Stephenson, Amelia C. Ford, Lewis H. Haney, John B. San-
born, and Raynor G. Wellington had produced useful studies of
the political background of land legislation. More important,
Benjamin H. Hibbard had just brought out his *History of Public Land Policies,* in which he discussed objectives and some of
the results of land legislation; Roy Robbins was to start his
Our Landed Heritage: The Public Domain, 1776–1936 in 1926.
These were milestones in public land history because of their
comprehensive coverage and realistic treatment of the major
legislation of the past. Neither author examined to any considerable degree the manuscript records of land entries, and
both had to rely on Thomas Donaldson's *The Public Domain*
(1884), the annual reports of the General Land Office, and
other congressional documents, including the reports of the three
public land commissions, for information concerning the transfer of lands to private ownership. Their studies, therefore, excellent as they are, left the reader uncertain about the basis
for their many generalizations. How well, for example, did the
various settlement laws achieve their purposes? Who were the
beneficiaries of measures said to be badly administered by inept
and sometimes corrupt officers? What methods were used to
establish the great holdings of timber, mining, grazing, and
agricultural lands that have long troubled Populists, Progres-

sives, trust busters, antimonopolists, conservationists, and advocates of single-family farms?

These and other questions came prominently to mind when I began my study of the first land grant railroad, the Illinois Central. It became clear that I could not deal properly with the land and settlement policies of this railroad until I had investigated how and to whom the alternate sections reserved by the government within the primary area—within the six-mile limit —of the line and, indeed, the odd sections between the six- and fifteen-mile limits had been conveyed. Were the original purchasers of these odd sections actually farm makers, were they land speculators hopeful of quick profits from resales to others, or were they primarily concerned with town promotion, an activity in which it seemed at times that most Illinoisians were engaged?

Examination of the abstracts of entries and registers of receipts of the eight land districts of Illinois, fortunately preserved in excellent condition in the Illinois state archives, revealed that the disposal of the public lands was a great uncharted area of study that promised to yield answers to many questions about western American history and to bring history to the real grass roots of man's attempts to master the new West.

Prior to the establishment of the National Archives and the construction of the new headquarters of the Department of the Interior, the central archive of the General Land Office was in a huge barnlike hall in the old Nineteenth and F Street building in Washington. There were to be found duplicates of the record books showing the entries of land made with cash, scrip, or warrants in the twenty-nine public land states. They showed that many hundreds of people in the eastern and southern states had invested capital in western lands in anticipation of a future rise in value. In the expansive days of the 1830s and 1850s writers, doctors, lawyers, and businessmen great and small bought land for investment, as did politicians like Daniel Webster, Caleb Cushing, Stephen A. Douglas, William J. Grayson, and John

Slidell, who did not draw a sharp line between their personal interests and the public policies they favored, and bankers like Elisha Riggs, William W. Corcoran, members of the Biddle family, August Belmont, and Jay Cooke. In Illinois alone, the remaining public lands were grabbed by settlers and speculators after the grant for the railroad had been made and while its construction was being hurried to completion. Yet by 1860, 14,000,000 acres had not been converted into farms. Of this number, 3,000,000 acres were never to be divided into farms, since they consisted of urban, mining, and forest property; 1,000,000 were held by the state for sale; and approximately 1,000,000 were still held by the railroad. This left 9,000,000 acres that were held by speculators, large and small. In addition, more than 6,000,000 acres of land included within farms were not improved—that is, fenced or cultivated, and probably not even pastured. Forty percent of the state's land was thus held for speculation or future development. In all the other states the hand of the speculator was similarly evident.

Clearly, the speculator, whether absentee or local resident, was an important person on the frontier, where he was ubiquitous. Together with the money lender or loan shark, the note shaver, the town promoter, the land agent, and the land looker or timber cruiser—all these types shaded into one another—he did much to shape the development of new communities for good or evil. Years of intermittent research in the land office records and in many collections of speculators' papers and supplementary investigation of the deed records of numerous counties in Indiana, Illinois, Wisconsin, Iowa, and Kansas enabled me to summarize my findings in "The Role of the Land Speculator in Western Development," the second chapter of this collection.

In the cash, warrant, and scrip volumes listing all entries for public lands in the Upper Mississippi Valley were the names of prominent southerners. The best known of these southern investors in western lands were John Slidell of Louisiana, Eli Shorter of Alabama, Williamson R. W. Cobb of Alabama, Wade

Hampton of South Carolina, and John C. Breckinridge of Kentucky. Least known, except in the West, was the most extensive investor, the firm of Easley & Willingham of Halifax County, Virginia. This firm entered over 400,000 acres, mostly for settlers, charging the usual frontier interest rates. These and other intersectional investments raised interesting questions: Why should residents of an underdeveloped region, lacking sufficient capital to exploit its own resources fully, invest funds in remote areas? Were some of these numerous southerners with northern investments sufficiently unionist-minded to be hedging against the possibility of civil war by acquiring resources in territories and states closed to slavery? One great Natchez planter and banker, Stephen Duncan, surely was hedging, for he invested hundreds of thousands of dollars in northern securities; in the Civil War he was a unionist. Dozens of southerners from Maryland to Georgia and even from Mississippi, Alabama, and Louisiana invested in public lands in the Upper Mississippi Valley, buying mostly wild lands but also acquiring lots in promising communities like Leavenworth, Kansas, and Superior, Wisconsin. Chapter 3, "Southern Investments in Northern Lands before the Civil War," tells the story of some of these investments.

Investigation among the records of the General Land Office subsequent to my original search has turned up information about other holdings by southerners, indicating a greater total acreage and dollar-value investment by residents of the South in northern states. To this degree and in some other details, my original article has here been altered to conform with later findings. For example, John Slidell's ownership with Elisha Riggs and August Belmont of 45,000 acres in Wisconsin and Iowa was noted in the original article, but the quantity now seems small in comparison to his extensive land holdings in Louisiana.

Early critics of the federal land system predicted that the unlimited right to buy public land for investment would result in the emergence of farm tenancy and a pattern of ownership and use similar to that in the Old World. They were troubled by the sale and pricing policies of the federal government, the tolerance and actual encouragement of large-scale speculative purchasing by individuals and land companies, and the huge grants to railroads and canal companies, which were naturally concerned to sell their land at the highest possible prices. The intrusion of speculators and land companies between the government and the actual settlers substantially increased the cost of farm-making to the pioneers. Loan sharks came to new communities almost with the first surveyors and settlers, prepared to lend to the latter, at frontier interest rates ranging as high as 10 percent a month, the two hundred dollars with which they could enter their quarter-section pre-emption claims. Thus a debtor-creditor relationship was established that many a pioneer farmer found difficult to end.

Some large purchasers of land started out with the intention of creating landlord-managed and tenant-farmed estates; among them were Daniel Webster, Matthew T. Scott, Caleb Cushing, Henry L. Ellsworth, Arthur Bronson, William Scully, William W. Corcoran, Romulus Riggs, Thomas L. L. Brent, and two prominent land-owning families of the Genesee Valley of New York, the Wadsworths and the Carrolls. Most of these new estates were in Illinois, Indiana, Iowa, Michigan, and Wisconsin.

Two chapters on land policy and tenancy in the Prairie States discuss these developments in Illinois and Indiana. They show that whether or not they had originally planned to do so, landholders who found it impossible to resell their land at a profit as early as they had hoped and moneylenders unable to collect on their mortgages were, not uncommonly, compelled to rent the lands with the understanding that the tenants would pay the taxes and make certain improvements. In this way the speculator enhanced the value of his land and at the same time protected himself from squatters and the danger of occupancy and other adverse possession claims being established. In those counties where speculation was extensive, tenancy appeared early and increased rapidly in the 1850s and thereafter. It is no mere accident that counties most affected by speculative buying in the thirties and fifties had the highest percentage of tenant farms in 1880.

Another aspect of frontier agricultural development is treated in two chapters describing the activities of the cattle kings in Indiana and Illinois. They were of two types: Some, like Isaac Funk, from their first settlement in the prairies, concentrated upon buying, raising, and fattening cattle and hogs. Shrewd judges of stock, which they purchased cheaply from frontiersmen, these men grazed their animals on the wide-open public lands, then assembled them at a central location and fattened them on the cheap and superabundant corn raised in their states. Over the years they accumulated from their operations large profits, which they invested in land, as settlers moved in and threatened to break up their ranges. The second type of cattle king consisted of men who had acquired their wealth from the operation of railroads, grain elevators, or slaughterhouses or from land transactions or a law practice. They invested their gains in great tracts of swampland or poorly drained prairie lands that came into the market in the early fifties at a few cents an acre. Their holdings of 10,000 to 40,000 acres in northwestern Indiana and central Illinois, their large herds of livestock, gradually improved by the introduction of purebred Herefords, and the huge fields of corn they raised for their livestock were the wonder of the West before the appearance of the bonanza farmer of the Red River Valley of the North or the cattle kings of the Colorado and Wyoming frontier. The Sumners, Fowlers, Funks, and Gilletts as cattle kings were as transitory as the later bonanza farmers, but both left a legacy of tenancy and absentee-owned estates.

As farming on the wide-open prairies of Indiana, Illinois, and Iowa prepared settlers for pioneering on the treeless plains of Kansas, Nebraska, and Dakota territory, so the development of the cattle industry in Indiana and Illinois pointed the way to larger-scale operations east and west of the 98th meridian. The prairie cattle kings of the 1850s and 1860s were prototypes of the later cattle kings of the Great Plains. To understand the latter, one should first be familiar with the practices of their predecessors, their methods of accumulating land, their handling of fencing problems, their use of tenant farmers to raise the necessary grain for their operations, and their similar political objectives.

The chapter "Frontier Landlords and Pioneer Tenants" traces the creation of several large landed estates that have lasted to the present day. These prairie properties were developed by tenants and by the extensive use of hired labor. Excessive demands by the more greedy landlords and their unwillingness to sell to their tenants aroused ill-feeling against them, particularly against William Scully, who with his 220,000 acres of land in the prairies of Illinois, Missouri, Kansas, and Nebraska farmed by 1,100 to 1,200 tenants, was America's greatest landlord. Scully was an Irish landowner who was acquiring prairie lands right and left and introducing on them some of the more objectionable features of the Irish land system just at the time when agrarian radicals were complaining about the extent to which British capitalists were buying up major American cattle companies and the extensive lands they owned or claimed on the Great Plains. The rush to acquire land by Scully and other British investors led to a successful demand for the adoption of anti-alien landowning laws, which were enacted by a number of states and by the United States.

For the last chapter, "Frontier Estate Builders and Farm Laborers," the original census schedules were used to determine how many farm laborers, as well as tenants, were to be found in the better agricultural counties of the Corn Belt, particularly in Illinois and Iowa. Swiftly rising land values made it difficult, if not impossible, for a man to climb the ladder of ownership from laborer or tenant to part owner and full owner—a fact that agricultural economists and some historians took long years to learn. Disillusioned by their lack of success, these laborers and tenants were attracted to the Great Plains, where the transcontinental railroads were promoting settlement and where free homesteads were available after 1862. Corn Belt farm workers and tenants embarked for the new frontier by the trainload in the seventies and eighties. Their places were taken by new immigrants from central and eastern Europe who found American tenancy on good land superior to anything they had known in the Old World. The displacement of unsuccessful and discontented farm workers and tenants and their migration to the great plains were partly responsible for the weakness of the Populist movement in the Corn Belt.

Occupancy or occupying tenants' laws were as important as pre-emption laws in giving protection to the frontier settler as he moved into unsurveyed areas of Kentucky or Tennessee, where large land claims had been shingled over each other in succession as the same land was mistakenly acquired by two, three, four, and more owners in a system not requiring advanced survey and title registration. They were also important in areas where the United States land system had permitted two or more titles or claims to titles to be issued to the same land, as in the Half Breed Tract or on the Des Moines River and Navigation Co. lands in Iowa. Settlers who mistakenly took up unimproved land owned by others and developed it and paid taxes on it were entitled, when the first owner challenged their right to it in court, either to be paid the value of their improvements, as determined by local juries, or to buy the title of the land at its value minus the value of all improvements they had put on it. Occupancy laws were designed to mitigate the harshness of the common law's treatment of land rights. Colonial Virginia early resorted to them; they were later adopted as major features of remedial or relief legislation by Kentucky and Tennessee. These laws were challenged in the courts, and the Kentucky law was struck down by the United States Supreme Court in a decision that few lawyers then or later could accept. Kentucky denied its relevance and enacted an even tighter measure; its example was followed by at least fourteen other western and southern states and territories. Eventually, the United States actually provided for the protection of occupying claimants with a color of title in the territories. Logically, and chronologically, "Tenants of the Log Cabin" belongs first in this book.

If, as has been suggested, my writings reflect a bias against the speculator, I have not been blind to the promotional work land buyers did in directing emigration to communities, in providing credit for settlers in the absence of government loans to pioneers, in building up towns and bringing in railroads. It is true the capitalist-investor in western lands did provide credit to his buyers, otherwise he never could have expected to get his price. Also, the money lender did provide the means for impecunious squatters to enter their land. In rebuttal the settlers would have responded that they should be allowed sufficient time, before their claims were put up for sale, to enable them to earn from crops both the cost of creating their farms and the government's charge of $1.25 an acre.

Some historians have suggested that there was little or no connection between the development of tenancy and speculative buying of land, land grants to railroads, and other factors that intruded capitalists between the government and the actual farm makers. I have placed the emphasis upon the difficulties met by actual settlers in gaining ownership of public land; my concern has been to examine the intent of the framers of the laws, as shown by their public utterances and their private actions (which were sometimes at variance with each other), to determine whether the legislation was carried out as intended, and to determine the effect of the legislation and the administrative interpretations on the development of the West. The constantly stated purpose of the land system was to make land available to the "actual settler," other than in the early years, when the need for revenue counted heavily; I have tried to keep this purpose in mind and to weigh the successes and failures according to the degree in which they contributed to that end.

By adopting the Act of 1946 to provide for the creation of the

Indian Claims Commission and by authorizing identifiable Indian groups to sue the United States for having made improper compensation for land they had once surrendered, Congress contributed to the establishment of two schools of thought concerning the value of wild and unimproved land on the frontier. In the 605 claims brought against the government under this law, calling for the payment of many hundreds of millions of dollars, a host of land appraisers, agricultural economists, and historians have been employed by attorneys for the Indians, and perhaps an equal number have been marshaled for the defense by the Department of Justice. Not since the days of Henry George and his single tax theory have so many people been absorbed in arguing for either a high or a low valuation for unimproved wild land in remote areas. Whatever their views on land values, most people would doubtless be glad to have the Indians obtain more compensation, no matter how delayed, that might improve the lot of America's most depressed ethnic group. The evidence presented about land values by the two sides was so disparate that it was difficult to realize that both groups were talking about the same lands.

One cession in Arkansas, for example, that included some first-rate alluvial land suitable for cotton but much more land that was never to attract buyers in one hundred years, even at $.125 an acre, was appraised at $.05 an acre by the government witness and at $2.00 by the witness for the Indians. Another tract, surrendered in 1833 in what later became Iowa and Nebraska territories, was hundreds of miles from any settlement and was not to attract any attention from buyers for a generation; it was appraised by the government expert at $.15 but by the expert for the Indians at $1.50 an acre. To arrive at decisions, members of the Commission, who were appointed because of their political influence rather than because of familiarity with frontier land values of a century before, had to work through a vast array of data, old documents, and detailed arguments, as well as the testimony of anthropologists concerning aboriginal occupancy. Whether they felt that the Indians had something coming to them or whether the briefs of the appraisers and historians that favored high land values were more persuasive, the members of the Commission have been generous in their awards, accepting values not in accord with the views of the nineteenth century. Opinions of the historians who favor high valuation appear in their scholarly writings.

The welter of litigation, accompanied by the most intensive research by consultants and appraisers, has resulted in the revisionist theory of some historians, who contend that the minimum price set by the government for all public lands was well below the actual value of the better lands. Indeed, the revisionists imply that the government was engaged in a great giveaway, disposing of its major resource at little more than cost instead of trying to obtain the actual going value for it. Thus speculators and settlers alike were assured of a favorable and sometimes a quick return on their investments. That both investors and settlers tried to gain as much land as their funds and consciences permitted lends credibility to this argument.

Without attempting to determine whether $1.25 an acre was a fair price for *all* public lands at *all* times, I have generally agreed with the commonly expressed western view that unimproved wild land remote from settlements, transportation facilities, and the amenities of schools, churches, and local government had little or no value. It was the pioneer who gave value to land in his vicinity by the improvements he made, by the road work he was required to perform, by the taxes he paid for schools and local government, by his support of churches. The coming of the railroads added value to adjacent lands, but it was the settler who, by buying the high-priced railroad lands and assuring the railroads' freight, made possible their construction. This view was expressed by Congressman Wayne Aspinall of Colorado speaking in Lincoln, Nebraska, in 1962 at the celebration of the hundredth anniversary of the adoption of the Homestead Act: "Let us stop referring to these lands as free lands; let us nail down the fact that this was no 'give away.' Over 1,600,000 people have gained title to over 270,000,000 acres of public lands by paying in hard work and by donating to the United States a farm production capability greater than that existing elsewhere." [1]

This book is largely devoted to the malfunctioning of an intended democratic system of land disposal. It does not attempt to provide a picture of the relative success of those who settled on public land; that is another story. The system that resulted in the creation of 967,697 farms in the public land states and territories by 1860, and 2,185,492 by 1880, of which 76.2 percent were owner-operated, was clearly an outstanding success. It even justified some of the hyperbole that Congressmen employed in their more optimistic moments. If Jefferson could have seen the results of the public land system, he would have been convinced that despite the compromises he had been obliged to make (sales instead of free grants) with his pure agrarian preferences, the policy had worked reasonably well. Yet these statistics do not reveal the hardships of pioneering, the failures of many who never acquired full ownership or even the status of tenants but who remained as farm laborers, the incessant worry over meeting mortgage payments and taxes, the fear of the loss of equities in land by foreclosure, by tax sale, or by controversies over titles. Much malfunctioning of the land system might have been prevented by more careful drafting of legislation, by congresses more sensitive to the problems of the pioneers, by administrators and judges more concerned with the intent of the land laws and less willing to recognize every loophole in them, and by land seekers less ready to perjure themselves in their greed.

[1] Wayne N. Aspinall, "Making Policy for Land Use," in Howard W. Ottoson, ed., *Land Use Policy and Problems in the United States* (Lincoln, Neb., 1963), 463.

1. Tenants of the Log Cabin

Some of the harshness of American land law, built on the common law of England and strengthened by the rigidities of the courts, was ameliorated by equity jurisdiction and a variety of colonial and state remedial measures. Such measures brought the state legislatures into conflict with both state and federal courts and in one notable instance involved Kentucky in an acrimonious dispute with the Supreme Court of the United States. In this delightful interlude in American constitutional practice, when the Court declared a Kentucky statute in violation of the contract clause of the Constitution, the offending state not only refused to accept the verdict but tightened the allegedly defective measure and made it stick. What is more, the principle of that law was thereafter widely adopted by western states and by the federal government itself at a later time. Kentucky's efforts to soften the effects of Virginia land law and, indeed, common law thus had an influence in shaping and ameliorating legislation elsewhere.

Virginia's method of distributing its public lands was notorious for its wasteful inefficiency. Prodigal conveyances that greatly exceeded the area of land available, looseness of entry procedure, and absence of the rectangular system of survey permitted extensive frauds, duplicating and overlapping boundaries, huge and multiple grants to the same persons, concentration of holdings, and a large amount of absentee ownership. By 1784, when the Kentucky country had only a few thousand widely scattered

[13]

settlers, more rights to land had been granted than there was land available. After attaining statehood Kentucky displayed equally lavish generosity in dispensing its public lands, and when the granting process came to an end sufficient land had been promised to cover the state four times over.

Humphrey Marshall, a cousin of the more illustrious John, emigrated to Kentucky in 1782, where, as deputy surveyor and highly successful land agent, he became "immensely wealthy." In writing later of the effects of the Virginia land system on Kentucky when separation took place, he said: "The face of Kentucky was covered, and disfigured by a complication of adverse claims to land, not less on an average than four fold. Such had been the effects of the laws of Virginia. Such was the calamitous situation of Kentucky that she was to go through the toil of adjusting them." Marshall spoke of the "infinitude of conflicting claims . . . the face of the earth, was covered, again—and again —and again; with locations of the one, or the other description; containing quantities, for one hundred acres, to one hundred and fifty thousand; and even more of such acres." All this "retarded her population—obstructed her improvement—distracted her people—impaired her morals—and depreciated the value of her rich soil, throughout the country." [1] Marshall spoke from experience, for he was at the time involved in litigation over 12,311 acres with the heirs of Charles Willing, a wealthy Philadelphia merchant.[2] Henry Clay maintained that the "same identical tract was frequently shingled over by a dozen claims," while George M. Bibb, certainly one of the men most familiar with the title

---

[1] Humphrey Marshall, *History of Kentucky* (2 vols.; Frankfort, 1824), I, 150–153. See also the statement of George M. Bibb in the Richmond *Enquirer*, copied in the Frankfort *Commentator*, March 6, 1822. Marshall was the author of a series of articles on the case of *Green v. Biddle* in the United States Supreme Court that appeared under the caption "I, By Itself," in the Frankfort *Commentator*, beginning August 23, 1821 (Anderson O. Quisenberry, *Life and Times of Hon. Humphrey Marshall* [Winchester, Va., 1892], 15).

[2] Marshall's interest in the land dated from 1813. The case reached the Supreme Court of the United States in 1831 but was remanded to the circuit court for further adjudication (*Lewis v. Marshall*, 5 Peters 469 [1831]).

confusion in Kentucky, said that thousands more land warrants had been issued by Virginia than there was land available.[3]

Lacking prior surveys on the rectangular system, such as the United States introduced for its land in Ohio, the Virginia system in Kentucky had left the surveys to be run by the locators, the land hunters, who, as Marshall contended, "were generally illiterate, and ignorant of what the law required to constitute a good location. They nevertheless proceeded to make entries, urged by their employers, with all the avidity of men, fearful of loss, and intent upon gain. Hence, they strewed the locations over the face of the country, as autumn distributes its falling leaves; heedless of those which had previously fallen; and almost as destitute of intelligent design, as they were ignorant of the legal consequences." [4] Out of this reckless piling of grant upon grant, crudely surveyed and marked, if marked at all, subsequently further confused by settlement rights, tax titles, liens, estate difficulties, mortgage foreclosures, was to come endless litigation, "a labyrinth of judicial perplexities," cluttered court dockets, "the breaking up of favorite homes . . . wide spread discontent and distress . . . a litigious spirit, and in some instances, a disregard of legal right in general." [5]

The millions of acres included in the distress sales of the Kentucky Court of Appeals are clear evidence of the instability and

---

[3] *Richmond Enquirer*, quoted in the *Commentator*, March 6, 1822. For examples of the extraordinary difficulties through which the Kentucky courts had to wade in determining between rival contenders for ownership of land and the complex claims that grew out of the indiscriminate grants and surveys, see James Hughes, *Report of the Causes Determined by the Late Supreme Court for the District of Kentucky, and by the Court of Appeals* (Lexington, 1803), *passim*.

[4] Marshall, *History of Kentucky*, I, 150.

[5] Mann Butler, *History of the Commonwealth of Kentucky* (Cincinnati, 1836), 138; Godfrey T. Vigne, *Six Months in America* (2 vols.; London, 1832), II, 28–29; Lewis N. Dembitz, *Kentucky Jurisprudence* (Louisville, 1890), 185. Dembitz wrote: "Neither the county surveyor nor the Register of the Land Office can know officially whether land of which the survey or grant is asked has not been patented before." His estimate of the duplication of patents was that "much of the land was patented more than once, and more than twice."

confusion of titles. Ever growing costs of litigation to clear
titles, eject persons with rival claims, and protect land from intrusion and plunder, together with the court fees and the high
interest on borrowed capital, were all a constant threat to the
security of investments and kept litigants in continued turmoil. The very abundance of untilled, absentee-owned land encouraged intrusions, and squatters were almost impossible to
expel. John Rowan, Kentucky judge and congressman, declared that the land laws of Virginia and Kentucky were responsible for encumbering and cursing Kentucky "with a triple layer
of adversary claims" that were as harsh in their effects as "the
infliction of savage warfare" with which Kentuckians were quite
familiar.[6]

Settlers looking for land fell into this Pandora's box of evils.
They usually found not one but several owners with whom they
had to negotiate for the title and even after they had purchased
the land and made their improvements they were likely to be
faced with ejectment proceedings brought by persons having
prior rights to their tracts. Harassed by attorneys and agents of
absentee landlords, or by swindlers with defective titles, the
settlers were compelled to buy their land again and again and to
pay not only the value of raw unimproved land but also the
value of all the improvements they themselves had put on the
land. Those who refused to pay were threatened not only with
ejectment but also with suits and distraint for back rent from the
time they took up the land. It is small wonder that many settlers
were driven to despair by this insecurity of tenure in Kentucky,
which was worse than in any other state. François André Michaux, who toured Kentucky in 1802, declared that the occupant
of every house at which he stopped expressed doubts as to the
soundness of his neighbors' titles.[7] Many Kentucky owners per-

[6] Zachariah F. Smith, *History of Kentucky* (Louisville, 1886), 344; Charles
William Janson, *The Stranger in America* (London, 1807), 389.

[7] François A. Michaux, *Travels to the Westward of the Alleghany Mountains* (London, 1805), 198–201.

mitted their taxes to become delinquent and paid the penalties in order to obtain tax titles for the purpose of strengthening their own claims against which there were adverse interests. Some settlers, having been defeated several times in their effort to acquire ownership of their claims, migrated elsewhere in the hope of finding better luck. Others became tenants on the property of such landlords as the Marshalls, who gave four years free rent and then charged yearly rent of twelve dollars per hundred acres.[8]

"The infinitude of conflicting claims" is illustrated by the huge number of claims of the first two official surveyors of Kentucky. George May and Humphrey Marshall, whose family holdings exceeded 1,100,000 and 405,000 acres, respectively, were surely entitled to be called "Barons of the Bluegrass," to use Thomas Perkins Abernethy's fetching term. One quarter of the entire state was claimed by twenty-one extensive speculators.[9] Marshall's unpopularity in Kentucky in his later life is understandable. Like other great landlords he doubtless had controversies with squatters, tenants, delinquent-land buyers, timber thieves, assessors and tax collectors, and Democratic officials. Yet, throughout these controversies he was a stout supporter and defender of land reform legislation.

Kentucky's speculators expected early profits from their holdings, and indeed the rush of settlers into the state and reports of the rapid rise in land prices seemed to justify their expectations. One potential English investor who was in Kentucky in 1795 looking for promising land deals commented on the 100

[8] Dembitz, *Kentucky Jurisprudence*, 185; Representative Robert P. Letcher of Kentucky, in *Annals of Congress*, 18 Cong., 1 Sess., 2515–2516 (May 3, 1824); Marion Tinling and Godfrey Davies, eds., *The Western Country in 1793: Reports on Kentucky and Virginia by Harry Toulmin* (San Marino, Calif., 1948), 76. J. J. Marshall advertised several farms for rent near Frankfort in the *Argus of Western America*, March 22, 1821.

[9] Thomas P. Abernethy, *Three Virginia Frontiers* (Baton Rouge, 1940), 67. For information on the claims, see Willard R. Jillson, *Kentucky Land Grants*, Filson Club Publications, XXXIII (Louisville, 1925).

percent rise in land values of the previous two years and added
that in many instances values had risen from 300 to 500 percent.
He warned his fellow countrymen, however, to beware of the
American land jobbers who might offer them tracts in question-
able areas or with dubious titles. Another foreign traveler spoke
of the stock-jobber who, seizing upon the "infatuation" for land
speculation, practices "a multiplicity of illicit means . . . to
make these lands sell to advantage," fabricating false plans,
inserting imaginary rivers, and presenting their tracts as ideal
lots.[10] Henry Clay described well some of the hazards of land
ownership by absentee investors in 1814:

You have no doubt heard that our lands in Kentucky are frequently
covered by two or three or more original patents granted by the
State. When that is the case (and it is almost always so in the quarter
of the Country in which these lands are situated) one can only form
a satisfactory judgment after a view of all the papers, and obtaining
much local knowledge of facts connected with them. In the case of
these lands the patents I observe are late, which is unfavorable. I do
not much like the character of the persons through whose hands the
titles have passed; most of them being Land Speculators. Besides the
inherent difficulties attending original titles, many embarrassments
have grown out of sales made for taxes. If these lands were entered
for taxes (as they ought to have been) it is more than probable that
the taxes have not been regularly paid, and in that case they have
been sold, and very probably twice sold, once for the State, and once
for the direct tax formerly imposed by the General Government.[11]

Commenting on the seven-year adverse possession law, enacted
by the Kentucky legislature in 1809, Clay said: "If therefore
the lands . . . are occupied by others, and there are ten chances
to one that they are, you will see that they are in much danger
from this law." He added that his "greatest fear is that the

[10] Harry Toulmin, "Comments on America and Kentucky, 1793–1802,"
Kentucky Historical Society, *Register* (Frankfort), XLVII (April, 1949),
101–103; Michaux, *Travels*, 197.

[11] Henry Clay to William H. Crawford, May 10, 1814; James F. Hopkins,
ed., *The Papers of Henry Clay* (4 vols. to date; Lexington, 1959——), I, 898.

title will be found insecure," and he urged that the lands be sold for what they would bring without regard to any expected price.

As Clay suggested, large investors in land became timid about the vulnerability of their commitments in Kentucky and were inclined to sell before gaining their hoped-for returns, lest they lose all. Fear of adverse possession claims, settlement rights, tax titles, or loss of land through failure to have it registered for taxes caused many to liquidate their holdings but not always before liens had been placed on the property. Owners of large but unsurveyed tracts sometimes sold a few hundred acres, likewise unsurveyed. Subsequent buyers from either the original grantees or from secondary purchasers were certain to run into boundary disputes and title controversies. The shingling character of the early grants was, therefore, compounded by additional title and boundary questions which could only be determined by court action. Advertisements of large tracts of Kentucky land for sale again and again illustrate the uncertainty and insecurity of titles.[12] By 1821 a third of Kentucky had been conveyed to banks and other nonresident capitalists through foreclosures, tax sales, and other forced sales.[13] Whether the numerous forced sales put land into firmer hands is not clear, but one fact is certain: they did not contribute to easing title questions in the Bluegrass country.

Fear that the land system would "cause very unequal distribution of land by giving enormous Quantities to those who could

[12] See, for example, a long advertisement by Henry Banks in the Frankfort *Commentator*, November 14, 1821, listing twenty-one tracts, containing some 123,000 acres he had acquired from Gilbert Imlay, John Holder, Thomas Lewis, and others, which he sought to sell. He conceded that some tracts had defective surveys, were involved in pending suits, or were claimed by others. For other advertisements of holders having doubt of their titles see Robert Triplett, *ibid.*, July 5, 1822, and R. H. L. Mosby, *ibid.*, March 15, 1823.

[13] Compiled from abstracts of the "Court of Appeals Deeds-Grantees," in Willard R. Jillson, *Old Kentucky Entries and Deeds*, Filson Club Publications, XXXIV (Louisville, 1924), 393–464. I have attempted to eliminate duplications in this compilation.

advance most money" was expressed as early as 1782 by the "Inhabitants of three Counties of Kentuckey [*sic*]." Sad experience proved, said the petitioners, that "without further compulsory acts, the Engrosser will neither settle himself, nor dispose of it to those who will." They urged that absentee owners be subjected to legislation requiring cultivation and improvement of their land. Another petition of 1782 praying for the revival of the "antient Cultivation Law" referred to the injurious effects of the purchase without cultivation principle, particularly reduced immigration and the movement of population elsewhere.[14]

Two years later the concentration of ownership of land in Kentucky again came in for consideration, this time at the first convention called to consider statehood. Since most Kentuckians were non-landowners living in the midst of enormous tracts held by absentees, "tenants of the log cabin" they were called,[15] they naturally hoped that separation from Virginia might be followed by a land policy more favorable to local interests.[16] The convention held that larger grants than the owner could properly utilize were "subversive of the fundamental principles of a free republican Government" and would produce "innumerable evils" to the less opulent inhabitants.[17] That this action may not

[14] James R. Robertson, ed., *Petitions of the Early Inhabitants of Kentucky to the General Assembly, 1769 to 1792*, Filson Club Publications, XXVII (Louisville, 1914), 63, 67–68.

[15] Senator Clement C. Clay of Alabama used this term, not critically, in 1841, in a discussion of pre-emption (*Cong. Globe*, 23 Cong., 2 Sess., Appendix, 18 [Jan. 4, 1841]).

[16] Thomas P. Abernethy, *Western Lands and the American Revolution* (New York, 1937), 326. Much earlier, in 1778, "Destressed Inhabitants" of Kentucky enumerated the many difficulties through which they were passing in the Revolution, including the loss of their property, and petitioned for land grants without which they must migrate to the Spanish country or suffer the indignity of "becoming tennants to private gentlemen who have men employed at this junction in this country at one hundred pounds per Thousand for, running round the land, which is too rough a medicine ever to be dejested [*sic*] by any set of people that have suffered as we have" (Robertson, ed., *Petitions of Early Inhabitants*, 45–46).

[17] Thomas P. Abernethy, ed., "Journal of the First Kentucky Convention,

have been very meaningful is suggested by another action of the same convention protesting against a higher tax on holdings in excess of 1,500 acres than on small holdings. Also, the fact that Kentucky, when it came into the control of its public lands, continued the same reckless and extravagant largess suggests that human nature was the same on both sides of the mountains.

Notwithstanding its reckless prodigality in disposing of its land, Kentucky moved early to protect the thousands of settlers who had tried to make pre-emption claims on land they assumed to be vacant and unclaimed or had bought a right from one of the numerous land agents, all unaware of adverse interests and defective titles. They were threatened with complete loss of the years of labor they had devoted to improving their farms when they were faced with ejectment suits by absentee owners whose rights may have been previously unknown in the region and who sought to establish their equities now that the lands were acquiring value. The legislature of Kentucky, though dominated by resident landlords, was not unmindful of the interests of actual settlers. It tried to aid those who were defeated in ejectment suits but who had color of title to their claims by securing to them the value of their improvements and freeing them from rent for past use of the land. A bill embodying these features passed the lower house in 1794 but was defeated in the more conservative upper house, whose members felt it to be contrary to the compact made between Virginia and Kentucky at the time of the latter's admission to statehood.[18] By the third condition of this compact "all private rights and interests in lands . . .

Dec. 27, 1784–Jan. 5, 1785," *Journal of Southern History*, I (Feb., 1935), 76.

[18] Humphrey Marshall, who claimed authorship of the bill, acquired rights to 96,000 acres of land in Kentucky. Leadership in the opposition to the occupying claimants bill in 1794 Marshall attributed to James Hughes, who may have been the same man who acquired 80,000 acres from Kentucky in seventeen patents and had conveyed to him an interest in 272,000 acres in Court of Appeals deeds (compiled from Jillson, *Old Kentucky Deeds*, and Jillson, *Kentucky Land Grant*). See Marshall, *History of Kentucky*, II, 210 ff.

derived from the laws of Virginia prior to such separation, shall remain valid and secure . . . and shall be determined by the laws now existing" in Virginia.[19] Never has a state entered the Union with a more dangerous limitation on its rights than this.

The occupying claimants bill, as introduced in the Kentucky legislature, was in no sense a radical innovation. Amelia C. Ford's analysis of the colonial statutes of Virginia led her to conclude that the practice was common of conceding to settlers with color of title, who were defeated in ejectment suits, the right to the value of all improvements they had put on the land. For example, in 1642–1643 Virginia was sufficiently bothered by "diverse suits" over conflicting land claims "to the great trouble and molestation of the whole colony" to provide for judgment in an ejectment suit in favor of the occupant for the assessed value of his improvements.[20] This statute was broad enough to cover squatters' rights, whereas the later Virginia and Kentucky statutes only covered improvements of settlers having color of title to their claims. Miss Ford also found precedents for such legislation in other colonies and in the policies of the English Board of Trade.[21]

Humphrey Marshall, the great Kentucky speculator, Federalist politician, historian, and author of the first occupying claimants bill, punctured the arguments of those who defended a rigid interpretation of the Virginia-Kentucky compact. He held that the third condition of the compact had already been breached by a series of measures and declared that if the compact was binding on Kentucky it would deny her the right to

[19] William W. Hening, ed., *The Statutes at Large: Being a Collection of All the Laws of Virginia* (13 vols.; Philadelphia and New York, 1810–1823), XII, 789; XIII, 19.

[20] *Ibid.*, I, 260, 349, 443; II, 96. The occupying claimants law of 1661 was still on the statute books in 1737 (John Mercer, *An Exact Abridgment of the Public Acts of Assembly of Virginia* [Williamsburg, Va., 1737], 137).

[21] Amelia C. Ford, *Colonial Precedents of Our National Land System as It Existed in 1800, Bulletin,* University of Wisconsin, History Series, II, No. 2 (Madison, 1908), 124.

legislate on lands; it would, in fact, make her subject to Virginia law and thus deny her the equality with other states that she so cherished. Marshall's reasoning prevailed in 1797, the Senate having been "imbued with much of the popular feeling on this subject," as he quaintly said.[22]

The purpose of the occupying claimants law of February 27, 1797, was essentially to extend the principles of equity to eviction by ejectment. Its preamble is instructive:

Whereas from the frequency of interfering claims to land, and the unsettled state of the country, it often happens that titles lay a long time dormant, and many persons deducing a fair title from the record, settle themselves on land supposing it to be their own, from which they may be afterwards evicted by a title paramount thereto; and it is just that the proprietor of the better title shall pay the occupying claimant of the land for all valuable improvements made thereon; and also that the occupying claimant shall satisfy the real owner of the same, for all damages that may have been done to the land by the commission of waste or otherwise during the occupancy.[23]

Previously, as Marshall pointed out, occupants of the land in litigation which was proved to be owned by others were compelled to pay rent for the years they had used the land and the damages they may have done to it. The occupant might, it is true, bring suit in chancery for the value of the improvements he had made as an offset to the payments required of him and might obtain an injunction against ejectment until the court passed judgment on his rights. But the method of redress open to the occupant was "circuitous, dilatory, expensive, and troublesome," and doubtful of success.[24]

Under the new measure, occupants of land to which they had a color of title, if defeated in ejectment action by someone with

---

[22] Marshall, *History of Kentucky*, II, 208–211. Marshall had been elected to the United States Senate in 1795 and was not in the Kentucky legislature when the occupying claimants law was adopted.

[23] *Acts of Kentucky*, 5th General Assembly, 1797, p. 143.

[24] Marshall, *History of Kentucky*, II, 209.

a better title, were entitled to have a local jury assess the value of their improvements—house, outbuildings, fences, cost of clearing. After a similar assessment of any damages or waste they had committed on the land and after rent for the land since the initiation of the action had been deducted, they could have the balance declared a judgment against the successful litigant. A jury was also to assess the value of the land without the improvements, and if it was less than the assessed value of improvement, the successful litigant had the option of conveying his better title to the occupying claimant and having a judgment for the assessed value of the land alone. If he did so he might get little for his title, since local juries would likely favor the occupant against an absentee landlord. Michaux observed this tendency in his travels in Kentucky. "Many of the inhabitants," he said, "derive the security of their estates from this confusion; for the law, which is very favourable to agriculture, provides that the cost of clearing and of improvements shall be paid by him who succeeds in ejecting the first occupier: and, as the valuation, on account of the extreme high price of labour, is always made in favour of the cultivators, it follows that many dare not assert their rights, from a fear of being obliged to pay considerable indemnifications." [25]

Two years later the Kentucky legislature enacted a law which provided that the state should have a perpetual lien on every tract of land for the amount of its tax and interest thereon and authorized speedy sale of all land on which the taxes were not promptly paid. Persons who paid taxes and were later defeated in ejectment because of a better title were allowed a lien on the land and right to possession until their payment with interest was reimbursed by the owner. Also, if the settler had a tax title, which was a color of title under the Act of 1797, he could have a lien on the land and possession until the owner had reimbursed him for the tax and the improvements he had made.[26]

[25] Michaux, *Travels*, 201.

[26] Acts of Feb. 28, 1797, and Dec. 21, 1799, *Laws of Kentucky* (2 vols.; Lexington, 1799–1807), I, 401 ff.; II, 27.

In 1801 nonresidents were compelled to list their lands for taxes or suffer the penalty of forfeiture. Extensions of time were later granted in which to list their lands, but delinquent taxes were to carry a 50 percent penalty; in 1806 the penalty was made 100 percent.[27]

The next step taken by Kentucky in its effort to unravel title controversies was made in 1809, when an act was passed "to compel the speedy adjustment of Land Claims." This act, which barred bills in equity after 1816 to recover possession from an occupant who had color of title and had been in possession of the land for seven years, established an unusually short period of possession as necessary to a good title in lawsuit with an adversary. Again, the preamble is meaningful:

Whereas the prosperity of this commonwealth, hath been greatly checked, its improvement and settlement retarded, and its citizens continually alarmed, and often ruined in their fortunes, by reason of the interference of land claims founded or alledged to be founded on the land laws of Virginia or of this state; as claims dormant and utterly unknown to the neighbourhood of a disputed tract of land, are often brought up, not only to alarm, but eventually to cast out naked on the world, numerous well settled and industrious families; as late and inferior claims to land are held up and concealed until the witnesses to establish the elder and superior title, shall be dead or removed to remote places, or until the property may have fallen into the hands of persons ignorant of the sources of proof respecting it; and as these evils instead of passing away as was once hoped with the lapse of time, are still increasing . . .[28]

In 1812, in a second occupying claimants law, Kentucky materially strengthened the position of the occupant by freeing him from responsibility for rents or profits from the land prior to the judgment or decree as the first act had freed occupants

---

[27] Act of Dec. 12, 1801, *ibid.*, II, 137; Act of Nov. 28, 1806, *ibid.*, II, 419.

[28] *Acts of Kentucky*, 17th General Assembly, 1809, p. 85. Settlers having tax titles on their claims after seven years of unchallenged occupancy would under the statute of 1809 acquire full ownership. Thus absentee owners who neglected to act were faced with loss of their equity.

from liability for rents and profits prior to the initiation of the suit. The occupant was allowed to retain possession during litigation unless the claimant gave bond for the value of the improvements. The new statute allowed the judgment to be on the land, not on the claimant. A clause that proved obnoxious to absentee landlords required that if the commissioners of award found the value of the improvements to exceed three fourths of the value of the land without improvements, the occupant could choose a judgment against the claimant for the value of his improvements, or he could have the land and give security to pay the assessed value of it without improvements. On the other hand, if the value of the improvements was found to be less than three fourths of the value of the land alone the rightful owner had the choice.[29]

A further liberalizing change in the occupancy laws was made in 1819. This measure provided that if the successful claimant elected to pay the occupant for his improvements the latter was entitled to harvest the growing crops on the land.[30] And finally, an act of December 12, 1820 once more extended the remedial features of land law by providing that persons contending with a successful claimant under the same title and evicted should be entitled to all the rights of occupants. The measure defined the procedure for determining occupants' rights against those of claimants, disallowed rents after judgments and gave the occupant possession, rent free, until judgment for his improvements had been met.[31]

---

[29] Act of Jan. 31, 1812, *Acts of Kentucky*, 20th General Assembly, 1812, p. 117. Justice Bushrod Washington's summary of the differences, slightly exaggerated, between the acts of 1797 and 1812 may be seen in *Green v. Biddle*, 8 Wheaton 70 (1823).

[30] Act of Feb. 9, 1819, *Acts of Kentucky*, 27th General Assembly, 1818–1819, p. 761.

[31] Act of Dec. 20, 1820, *Acts of Kentucky*, 29th General Assembly, 1820–1821, pp. 148–51. It was this rent-free provision of the Act of 1820 that Chief Justice George M. Bibb of the Court of Appeals of Kentucky called "harsh, rigorous and unequal," unfavorable to successful claimants, and advantageous to occupants. Bibb was no opponent of the occupying claimants'

Kentucky had thus enacted the two great principles of equity into statutory law: the right of occupants with a color of title to their improvements and the right of settlers on privately owned land, unchallenged for seven years and paying taxes thereon, to a firm and clear title to their land no matter what adverse titles might be outstanding. In this series of measures passed between 1797 and 1820 the legislature had attempted to protect the rights of innocent parties from the demoralizing effects of the system under which the lands had been unwisely distributed. Kentucky had pioneered in enacting land-title legislation that was to have a profound effect on title and settler legislation in other states.

It should be noted that none of the laws conceded rights to squatters having no color of title. This was taken care of to some degree, however, by equity. In 1820 the Kentucky Court of Appeals held that persons having no connected title in law or equity, and therefore not entitled to relief under the occupying claimants laws, were on equitable principles entitled to compensation for all improvements made prior to the commencement of the suit, minus rents, profits, waste, and deterioration of soil.[32] But a case in equity would involve the employment of a lawyer and payment of court fees, expenses heavy enough to discourage a landless person with poor improvements from entering into a suit to recover the value of the investment he had made in the land.

Kentucky's occupancy laws contained no deliberate discrimination against the absentee speculator or non-improving owner. True, such an owner, already beset by taxes on unproductive land, penalties, timber thieves, and squatters whose rights might with adverse possession become paramount, was now faced with additional litigation to maintain his title and with the prob-

---

legislation, but he felt that this statute had gone too far. His opinion was delivered as a dissent (*Fisher v. Higgins*, 21 Kentucky Reports 147 [1827]). The Act of 1820 was repealed on January 7, 1824.

[32] *Parker v. Stephens*, 10 Kentucky Reports 202 (1820).

ability of further expenses for occupants' improvements. Also, he might have to share the unearned increment on his land with the occupant. But improvements on and around his land added to the value of his equity, to which he contributed nothing.

The year 1821 was a fateful year in the constitutional annals of both Kentucky and the federal government because of the variety of issues that came to the attention of the courts and the stand they took upon them. It was in this year that the Supreme Court of the United States attempted to strike down the occupancy laws of Kentucky and rendered a decision in the Cohens lottery case that greatly angered Virginia, and the Kentucky Court of Appeals came into conflict with the legislature over stay or replevin measures. These issues produced bitter attacks upon the judiciary and led to moves to abolish the Superior Court of Kentucky and to create a new one more sensitive to popular will, to permit the Supreme Court of the United States to strike down state legislation only when the decision was unanimous, and to give appellate jurisdiction to the United States Senate in matters affecting state legislation.[33]

Economic issues were in the background of the tensions producing these constitutional difficulties. The Panic of 1819, which followed a period of unparalleled inflation, speculation in land, and banking experiments of dubious character, brought many banks to destruction and led to the foreclosure of many properties, some of which were sold in execution for less than the costs of suit or sale, the creditors gaining nothing. Efforts to collect debts that ended thus disastrously produced a clamor for relief legislation. Kentuckians divided sharply on the way to deal with the debilitating contraction. The Relief party consisted of debtors, several eminent lawyers, and a large majority of the population; the strength of the Anti-Relief party was in

[33] Charles Warren, *The Supreme Court in United States History* (3 vols.; Boston, 1922), II, chaps. 16 and 17.

the mercantile class, the lawyers and judges, and the larger farmers. Among the relief proposals were measures to provide for additional state banks with extensive note issuing powers, stay or replevin laws to postpone foreclosures, property laws to limit the loss debtors might suffer from foreclosure of their homes and farms, bankruptcy laws, and measures to abolish imprisonment for debt.[34] Kentucky, in the vanguard of the movement to provide relief, adopted measures to add greatly to bank notes in circulation, to abolish imprisonment for debt, to prevent the sale of property taken in execution at less than three-fourths of appraised value, and to stay collections for as much as two and a half years. When the replevin law was struck down by the Court of Appeals, the legislature proceeded to abolish the court and create a new court which the governor filled with members friendly to the relief legislation.[35]

Other states were experimenting with similar legislation to such an extent that Thomas Hart Benton later remarked in contemplating the era:

No price for property, or produce. No sales but those of the sheriff and the marshall. No purchasers at execution sales but the creditor, or some hoarder of money. . . . Stop laws—property laws—replevin laws—stay laws—loan office laws—the intervention of the legislature between the creditor and the debtor: this was the business of legislation in three-fourths of the States of the Union—of all south and

[34] Louisville *Public Advertiser,* Sept. 13, 1821; Timothy S. Arthur and William H. Carpenter, *History of Kentucky* (Philadelphia, 1852), 300.

[35] Acts of Dec. 11 and 21, 1821, *Laws of Kentucky,* 30th General Assembly, 1821, pp. 340, 415; *Niles Register* (Baltimore), XVII (Sept. 11, 1820), 19, and XX (April 7, 1821), 85; Lexington *Western Monitor,* June 11, 18, 25, Aug. 18, 1822; Frankfort *Argus of Western America,* Jan. 11, 1826. For the Panic of 1819 and resulting depression and relief problems in Kentucky and Missouri, see Samuel Rezneck, "The Depression of 1819–1822: A Social History," *American Historical Review* XXXIX (Oct., 1933), 28 ff.; Thomas D. Clark, *A History of Kentucky* (New York, 1937), 196 ff.; W. J. Hamilton, "The Relief Movement in Missouri, 1819–1822," *Missouri Historical Review,* XXII (Oct., 1927), 51 ff.

west of New England. . . . DISTRESS the universal cry of the people: RELIEF, the universal demand thundered at the doors of all legislatures.[36]

It was in such trying times, when vested interests were under serious attack and agrarians were urging radical relief, that the occupancy laws of Kentucky came up for consideration before the court of John Marshall in the case of *Green v. Biddle*. When the case reached the Supreme Court, only the claimant's side, antagonistic to the rights of occupants, was presented— regrettably, said Justice Joseph Story.[37] Story's decision showed little or no effort to meet possible arguments in behalf of the laws, no awareness that the case did not belong in the Federal Court until the states of Virginia and Kentucky had utilized the device provided in the compact for the adjudication of mutual problems, no concern about the inferior position in the Union in which the decision placed Kentucky, and no consideration of land problems in Kentucky.[38] Story held that the laws "materially impair the rights and interests of the rightful owner in the land itself. They are part of a system, the object of which is to compel the rightful owner to relinquish his lands, or pay for all lasting improvements made upon them, without

[36] Thomas H. Benton, *Thirty Years' View* (2 vols.; New York, 1858), I, 5–6.

[37] 8 Wheaton 11 (1823). The legislature of Kentucky was convinced that neither Green nor Biddle had any interest in the land involved in the case of *Green v. Biddle* and maintained that the object of the litigation was to obtain a decision voiding this law (*Acts of Kentucky*, 30th General Assembly, 1821, p. 457). On the other hand, the Lexington *Western Monitor* contended that the case was not fictitious, that both parties were favorable to getting it before the Supreme Court, and that the occupant wanted to get a clear title but did not contest the case because he wanted the legislature to do so.

[38] Henry Clay emphasized the point that "although the court had jurisdiction between the parties . . . it was doubtful if it had over the subject; because by the compact a stipulation is expressly made for the case of any violation of it, by the appointment of a tribunal, and until there had been a refusal, by one of the parties to the compact to constitute that tribunal," no federal court could take jurisdiction (speech of Clay before the Virginia Assembly, Lexington *Kentucky Reporter*, March 4, 1822).

his consent or default; and in many cases those improvements may greatly exceed the original cost and value of the lands in his hands." They diminish the "beneficial interests of the rightful owner in the lands." With a firm belief in the sanctity of property rights Story and his colleagues, perhaps swayed by him, unanimously found the statutes in violation of Article Seven of the Virginia-Kentucky compact which sought to assure to Virginia's grantees rights and interests which, as Story put it, "shall be exclusively determined by the laws of Virginia, and that their security and validity shall not be in any way impaired by the laws of Kentucky." [39]

Kentuckians had reason to be appalled when news of the action of the Supreme Court in voiding the occupancy laws reached the state. A writer in the Frankfort *Commentator* spoke of the "treacherous conduct" of those Kentuckians who had pressed the case before the Supreme Court, one of whom was a member of the state legislature and attorney for the commonwealth. The writer called the laws a bulwark against the "exterminating litigation of nonresidents and aliens." It was said that ownership of a third of the property of the state would be jeopardized and thrown into litigation by the decision.[40] Richard M. Johnson declared in Congress that the decision "would overturn the deliberate policy of the State for a period of about twenty-four years . . . and, if persisted in, would produce the most disastrous consequences in giving rise to much litigation where questions had been settled for years, and put everything respecting landed property into the greatest confusion." [41]

Some questions concerning the constitutionality of the occupancy laws had been raised by leading conservatives in the Kentucky legislature and by Governor Charles Scott, who had

[39] 8 Wheaton 13, 15–16.
[40] Frankfort *Commentator*, April 19, 1821; Louisville *Public Advertiser*, Feb. 6, 1822.
[41] *Annuals of Congress*, 17 Cong., 1 Sess., 23 (Dec. 12, 1821), 67–91, 95–114 (Jan. 14, 15, 1822).

vetoed the measure of 1812 only to have it passed over his veto. Though Humphrey Marshall, a staunch Kentucky Federalist, was a strong supporter of its principles (he had some difficulty in accepting the Act of 1812 in its entirety), many large property owners took the other side of the question. Opponents were called together in 1822 by a notice in the *Kentucky Gazette* of November 28, to urge Virginia not to compromise on rights assured land owners in the compact. The Lexington *Western Monitor* expressed approval of the decision in *Green v. Biddle*, despite the fact that its hero, Henry Clay, led the fight in behalf of the laws.[42] On the other hand, a writer in the Frankfort *Commentator* of August 9, 1821 declared that the laws had been of major benefit to Kentuckians in providing machinery for determining rights and had brought about a "lasting cessation from suits about right of soil." Virginia and Virginians also seem not to have raised questions concerning the constitutionality of the measures. The Kentucky Court of Appeals had consistently upheld the laws and determined knotty questions in thirty-eight cases coming before it by 1820. No case had been appealed to the federal courts prior to 1819.[43]

Both the governor and the legislature of Kentucky expressed strong views in opposition to the decision of Justice Story. Certainly the resolution of the Kentucky legislature presented the view that would be sustained today. The compact, it held, was no contract binding upon and making the state of Kentucky

[42] Lexington *Western Monitor*, May 6, Aug. 22, 1823. Interestingly, a writer in the *Kentucky Gazette*, January 31, 1822, declared that the land jobbers had been well pleased until 1821 with the occupancy laws, for under the Act of 1797 the occupant was subjected to back rent until the value of his improvements was offered and under the Act of 1812 he was compelled to pay more for the land than it would bring without improvements, as a result of the improvements on land in the vicinity or the location of the land with relation to towns that may have sprung up.

[43] The Frankfort *Commentator*, June 1, 1825, extra and following issues, devoted many columns of involved argument in support of the laws and condemning the Supreme Court while at the same time denouncing the State Court of Appeals for its action in voiding the stay laws of Kentucky.

subject to Virginia as much as thirty-two years after its admission into the Union. "To each state is guaranteed, a republican form of government, and each ought to have an equal share of sovereignty." Property rights were not absolute, above limitation. Laws imposing taxes, requiring improvement of waste lands, limiting actions, forfeiting lands not listed for taxes, or requiring road work were as unconstitutional as the occupancy laws for they "impair the rights and interests of the owner," to use Story's phrase. Regardless of the unusual way in which the case was considered by the Court, the reasoning and history on which it was based was a "mistaken view of the principles and justice of our laws, and the true intent and meaning of the compact," said the legislature.[44]

Kentucky hoped to have Virginia join it in opposing the exercise of judicial review in matters predominantly state in character and had some reason to believe such aid would be forthcoming, for John Marshall in the Cohens case [45] had angered Virginians by broadly emphasizing the supremacy of the federal government over state governments, as the Green case angered Kentucky. But the Virginia anger had begun to subside when the Green case created the storm in Kentucky. Furthermore, Virginia had grievances against Kentucky and, when the latter sought its aid in the move for the preservation of state powers, Virginia could think only of its grievances, not of its constitutional principles.

Kentucky first sought relief from the damage the Green decision might do by requesting through Henry Clay a rehearing, which was granted.[46] The additional time enabled Kentucky to send commissioners to Richmond to persuade the Virginia government to join her in maintaining that the occupancy laws were not violations of the compact and therefore not unconstitutional. Henry Clay and George M. Bibb, two of Kentucky's most out-

---

[44] *Laws of Kentucky*, 30th General Assembly, 1821, pp. 456–469.

[45] *Cohens v. Virginia*, 6 Wheaton 265 (1821).

[46] Frankfort *Commentator*, Aug. 9, 1821.

spoken defenders of the occupancy laws, were appointed as commissioners. Their presentation before the Virginia House of
Delegates was widely advertised; the gallery was thronged with
ladies and the floor of the House filled to its utmost capacity
with an expectant crowd to hear the two protagonists of Kentucky. Their long addresses, well reported in the Richmond
Enquirer and copied in the Frankfort and Lexington papers,
were devoted to the multitude of conflicting claims resulting
from Virginia's land policies, the uncertainty of the location of
the entries, and the tremendous costs of litigation prior to the
adoption of the occupancy laws, without which, it was said, the
tormented people of Kentucky would migrate elsewhere. Clay
cited Virginia's experiences toward occupants and the favorable
court decisions concerning them as late as 1794. He held that
Kentucky, when admitted into the Union, entered with complete
equality, and maintained that the compact—the Act of December
18, 1789, he called it—was not designed to put her into an inferior position and did not restrict her from adopting occupancy
laws. If there were any real difference between the two states,
Clay said, they should be settled between themselves, not
through appeal to the federal courts. In a "masterly and eloquent" address of three hours Clay urged that the Virginia
legislature declare the occupancy laws of 1797 and 1812 not in
violation of the Act of December 18, 1789. Bibb also took three
hours, in which he pulled all the stops in a "powerful, pathetic
and touching" appeal for generosity by Virginia.[47]

The task of Clay and Bibb was not easy, despite their favorable reception, for they had to answer charges that Kentucky had
denied holders of certain military warrants, amounting to approximately a third of a million acres, the right to locate them.[48]
Whatever the rights of Kentucky in this matter, Virginia thought

[47] Richmond *Enquirer;* copied with editorial comments in Lexington *Western Monitor,* Jan. 19, 31, Feb. 19, 26, March 5, 12, 1822, and in Frankfort
Commentator, March 6, 1822.

[48] Washington *National Intelligencer,* Dec. 16, 1822.

it had a grievance, insisted upon redress, and was not inclined to listen sympathetically to calls for aid unless its demands were met.

After the Virginia side had been presented, in turn, to the Kentucky legislature, the two states appointed commissioners to meet together and work out a compromise of the issues separating them. Clay and John Rowan were counsellors of the Kentucky commissioners. It was charged that they were outmaneuvered by the commissioners of Virginia, but whatever the facts, the Virginia legislature refused to ratify the results and Kentucky had no support from the Old Dominion in the rehearing of the Green case.[49] Typical of the reaction to the obstinacy of Virginia was the statement of the Louisville *Public Advertiser* of March 13, 1822: "In this affair Virginia accurately personates the waspish, hysterical mother who, while she is proclaiming us 'bone of her bone and flesh of her flesh,' rebukes us because we have dared to consult the prosperity and tranquility of our own household, in preference to sacrificing both, that we might retain the affection of the good old lady."

On the second hearing of the Green case before the Supreme Court, Clay and Bibb argued for upholding the constitutionality of the occupancy laws and Benjamin Hardin, long an opponent, urged the Court to stand by its original decision—an act which doubtless contributed to his retirement from Congress that year. One of the points made in defense of the acts was that anything in the compact which subordinated Kentucky law to that of Virginia was unconstitutional. As Clay later expressed it: "What-

[49] Clay and Benjamin W. Leigh of Virginia met together and amicably drew up a convention to submit to their respective states. Possibly Clay was bested in the deliberations, but he was aware that some real concessions had to be made to win Virginia's aid. Virginia refused to ratify the convention on February 6, 1823 (*National Intelligencer*, Feb. 7, 1823). The views of Clay and Leigh on the convention and its rejection by Virginia may be seen in letters of Clay to Francis Brooke, January 31, March 9, August 28, 1823; and Leigh to Clay, February 12, 1823 (Calvin Colton, ed., *The Private Correspondence of Henry Clay* [Boston, 1856], 71–83).

ever sovereign powers one has, each and all have. . . . Whatever one State can do, all can do." [50]

A minority of three of the seven judges, with Bushrod Washington speaking for the Court, reaffirmed the Story decision. John Marshall, though he had concurred in the earlier decision, did not participate. Possibly, on reconsideration, he was bothered by the fact that his cousin was not only the author of one of the laws but also a major supporter of both. Thomas Todd, a Kentuckian, and Brockholst Livingston were too ill to participate, and William Johnson dissented. [51] Like Story, Washington was mostly concerned with the owners of land, whose rights he sought to protect. That they were commonly remiss about paying their taxes, had done nothing to improve the land, and, in fact, by their neglect and failure to mark out boundaries and clearly establish their rights had practically invited settlement and improvement by others did not matter. Nor did it appear significant that it was the improvements of settlers, of occupants, that induced the owner finally to look to his title and attempt recovery from the occupant. The occupancy laws, said Washington, deprived "the rightful owner of the land, of the rents and profits received by the occupants." The judge held that "the common law of England was . . . the law" of Virginia; hence, he searched common law, with its bias against debtors, mortgagors, and occupying claimants, and its equally marked property bias, for precedents to support his view that nothing could properly deprive the owner of rent from his land. [52]

Though Virginia had in the past, when a colony, adopted occupancy measures giving greater rights to the occupant than the

---

[50] Frankfort *Commentator*, Oct. 4, 1823.

[51] All three of these had been members of the Court which unanimously supported the Story decision in 1821.

[52] Lewis N. Dembitz, *Treatise on Land Titles in the United States* (2 vols.; St. Paul, 1895), I, 782; Charles Warren, *History of the American Bar* (Boston, 1911), 232; John A. Krout and Dixon Ryan Fox, *The Completion of Independence* (New York, 1944), 288. Kentucky had actually tried to bar judges and lawyers from invoking common law in state courts.

two Kentucky laws gave, those measures were not mentioned. Instead, Justice Washington held that since successful claimants could recover rents in action of trespass in Virginia, and they could not in Kentucky, the Kentucky laws were suspect. By denying the successful claimant the value of the rents during the time the occupant had held the land, the occupancy laws were in violation of the compact between Virginia and Kentucky and therefore were in violation of the contract clause of the Constitution. He disregarded the eighth section of the compact which provided that lands of nonresidents should neither be taxed higher than those of residents nor be forfeited for failure to cultivate or improve for a period of six years after admission. If both sections of the compact are considered together—and the rule of construing a law requires that all parts be examined together—the meaning of the limitation of Section Seven becomes clearer: that is, for six years Kentucky was not to declare titles forfeit; and what is more drastic than to declare titles forfeit? Surely not occupancy laws.[53]

By thus applying the harsh doctrines of common law to the occupancy statutes of Kentucky, the Court threatened to destroy all equity in improvements settlers had made on land having prior claimants. It was a frightening decision, "most ruinous" and causing "great alarm" for Kentuckians, but its dangers were not limited to Kentucky.[54] Though the Court struck down only Kentucky's occupancy laws in the Green case, it may be assumed that Washington's reasoning might also have been sufficient to invalidate similar laws of other states. Rarely, if ever, has the Supreme Court so threatened property rights long since secured to the less privileged by legislative and judicial action.

The fact that only three judges could be brought to concur in the decision and that William Johnson was to give a dissenting

[53] This point was made by Representative Robert P. Letcher in discussing the case in Congress. See *Annals of Congress*, 18 Cong., 1 Sess., 2514–2527 (May 3, 1824).

[54] *Ibid.*, 2515; Dembitz, *Treatise on Land Titles*, I, 782.

opinion bothered the Court, and the decision was put off for a year, perhaps in the hope that the ill judges might be able to participate or that Marshall might be persuaded to lend his great prestige as he had in the original decision; but the postponement was to no avail.[55] The decision, called both "pedantic" and "unworkable" by Professor Edward S. Corwin, and the "most far-fetched extension of the contract clause" rendered by the Marshall Court "out of an excess of zeal for broadening the scope of the contract clause," by Benjamin F. Wright, had to stand as the judgment of a minority of the Court.[56]

The year's delay did nothing to soften the attack upon the Court by Kentuckians. Humphrey Marshall, old Federalist as he was, spoke of the "erroneous and alarming decision of the court which went to overturn the foundation of a large portion of our legislative power." He felt that the judges' perceptions were confused, their minds bewildered. He feared that if the decision were not reversed an insurrection would follow. Another speaker said that the decision "disposed of the rights of half a million people with as little ceremony as a Frenchman eats a frog"; and John Rowan maintained that "it disfranchises Kentucky, and deprived her of her sovereign power over her own soil." [57] In a second remonstrance against the decision the Kentucky legislature condemned the erroneous and degrading doctrines which reduced Kentucky to a province of Virginia.[58]

[55] Warren, *Supreme Court in United States History*, II, 99, and *passim*. Story spoke of the "peculiar opinions" of William Johnson. "He was against the laws, and yet willing to give them a partial operation through the medium of a jury instead of commissioners" (Story to Justice Thomas Todd, March 14, 1823, in William W. Story, ed., *Life and Letters of Joseph Story* [2 vols.; Boston, 1851], I, 422).

[56] Edward S. Corwin, *John Marshall and the Constitution* (New Haven, 1920), 188; Benjamin F. Wright, *The Contract Clause of the Constitution* (Cambridge, 1938), 47, 214. Corwin assumes that Marshall was responsible for the position of the Court in the Green case.

[57] Frankfort *Commentator*, Nov. 15, 1823; Lexington *Western Monitor*, Dec. 2, 1823.

[58] *Acts of Kentucky*, 32d General Assembly, 1823–1824, pp. 520–527. A petition of Clay and Rowan for a second rehearing was rejected. For the

Kentucky had no intention of accepting the action of the Supreme Court in declaring the occupancy laws unconstitutional. In a decision of 1824 the Court of Appeals declared the occupancy law of 1812 not inconsistent with the compact and the constitutions of Kentucky and the United States, recalled that the validity of the act had been uniformly upheld in the state courts and its provisions enforced, noted that the Green case had been decided by a minority of the Supreme Court, and flatly rejected it as binding on Kentucky courts.[59] Two years later the Court of Appeals declared that the constitutionality of the Act of 1812 was no longer open to question; "this *act* is *constitutional* until some tribunal, capable of controlling this court" shall determine otherwise; and so it remained.[60]

Not only were the Kentucky legislators angry at the perversity of the members of the Supreme Court and at absentee speculators for bringing the issue to the Court, but they were indignant that Virginia had not supported their position before the Court.[61] In the preamble of an act of January 7, 1824, which

petition see *A Remonstrance to the Congress of the United States on the Subject of the Decision of the Supreme Court of the United States on the Occupying Claimant Laws of Kentucky* (n.d., n.p.), 31–54.

[59] *Bodley v. Gaither*, 19 Kentucky Reports 60 (1825).

[60] *Sanders' Heirs v. Norton*, 20 Kentucky Reports 465 (1827); *McKinney v. Carroll*, 21 Kentucky Reports 97 (1827).

[61] Henry Clay seems to have been more deeply troubled at his failure to induce Virginia to support Kentucky on the constitutionality of the occupancy laws than he was at his defeat before the Supreme Court. For his reactions to the decision of Virginia, see his letters to Francis Brooke of January 31 and August 28, 1823 (Colton, ed., *Private Correspondence of Clay*, 71–83). Writing from Washington, December 22, 1823, to Benjamin W. Leigh about the angry message of Governor John Adair to the Kentucky legislature, Clay said: "The Governor was ill advised in his message. It was the occasion of some warm conversation between us. My late information continues to assure me that nothing extravagant will be done in regard to the General Government. They may possibly send us a memorial here with some intemperate paragraphs; but you know all that is mere expression. The mouth and the pen are happy conductors to let off bad humors. Not that I do not really think that we have much justly to complain of in respect to the fate of our Occupying claimant laws. But then I do not think that we ought to make any Civil war about

was designed to undo the possible effects of the Green case, they reviewed the lamentable evils resulting from the land policy of Virginia, deplored Virginia's refusal to uphold the occupancy laws, and justified the harshness of the measure. The principal objective of the measure was to compel absentee owners of land to abide by the occupancy laws in ejectment proceedings or suffer the consequences. Owners who did not abide by the occupancy laws were compelled to improve, clear, fence, and cultivate five acres for each one hundred and girdle ten acres in each thousand they owned, or suffer forfeiture.[62] Actually, there was little necessity for such a broad measure, for the occupancy laws were enforced in the state courts without any deviation. Nevertheless, a case did reach the Kentucky Court of Appeals in 1833 that involved the statute of 1824 and enabled the court to render a very broad decision on the inviolable sanctity of contracts and the inability of the states to adopt measures that would in any way modify absolute ownership of land by private individuals. That states were and long since had been modifying that absolute ownership by means of tax laws, lien laws, and other measures received no consideration, but the court was careful to cast no doubt on the occupancy laws.[63] These had been further strengthened in 1825 by a measure that declared that occupants were to have possession of their land free of rent when defeated in ejectment proceedings and to have a lien on the land until the judgments in their favor were paid.[64]

Senator Richard M. Johnson's statement that the Green case "prostrates the deliberate policy" of Kentucky and threatens to "produce the most disastrous consequences" was not mere hyperbole. Wherever possible, large holders of land, troubled by

---

them." A copy of this letter, the original of which is in Miscellaneous Papers, Series I, Vol. II (1789–1830), North Carolina Department of Archives and History (Raleigh), was kindly furnished by Mary Wilma Massey Hargreaves, of the staff of the Henry Clay Papers, University of Kentucky.

[62] *Acts of Kentucky*, 32d General Assembly, 1823–1824, pp. 443–450.

[63] *Gaines v. Buford*, 31 Kentucky Reports 481 (1833).

[64] Act of Jan. 12, 1825, *Acts of Kentucky*, 33d General Assembly, 1824–1825, pp. 206–211.

the occupancy laws, the limited action law, and the seven-year adverse possession law, either threatened court action or took their cases into the federal courts and were said, possibly with some exaggeration, to have "swept thousands of families into ruin, and induced thousands of others to abandon the state." [65] The Louisville *Public Advertiser* blamed the "liberal, patriotic and enlightened citizens of Virginia" for this "unparalleled distress." For their resistance to the position of the Supreme Court, "speculators, fools, and knaves called the people of Kentucky disorganizers, factionists and land stealers." But the federal courts had difficulty in accepting the possible meaning of the Green case. In 1826, Robert Trimble, federal district judge of Kentucky and later promoted to the Supreme Court, greatly narrowed it by holding that appeal to the compact in cases in federal courts could only be made by persons to whom the patent had been issued. For this boon the *Advertiser* called Judge Trimble an "angel of light." [66]

Clay, Bibb, Rowan, Marshall, and other supporters of the occupancy laws had good reason to feel vindicated in 1831 when the United States Supreme Court, in a decision upholding the seven-year and twenty-year adverse possession laws, took over the arguments they had presented to it a decade earlier. It was Justice William Johnson, who had dissented in the Green case, who now spoke for a unanimous court in a decision reflective of a philosophy markedly different from that found in the Story and Washington decisions. Kentucky would not have accepted the compact, Johnson maintained, had it meant a "limited and crippled sovereignty: nor is it doing justice to Virginia to believe that she would have wished to reduce Kentucky to a state of vassalage." A literal interpretation of the compact, which the justice flatly rejected, would leave Kentucky a dependent of Virginia. He even implied that forfeiture for non-improvement was constitutional, though the Kentucky Court of Appeals at that very time was voiding such a law. A sentence that would

---

[65] *Annals of Congress*, 17 Cong., 1 Sess., 23 (Dec. 12, 1821).
[66] Louisville *Public Advertiser*, Dec. 13, 1826.

not have appeared in a decision by Story or Washington is worthy of note: "And no class of laws is more universally sanctioned by the practice of nations, and the consent of mankind, than laws which give peace and confidence to the actual possessor of the soil." [67] Story, though making no public opposition to the Johnson decision, seems not to have changed his opinion on the constitutionality of the Kentucky occupancy laws, for in his *Commentaries*, first published in 1833, he stubbornly held to the views he had enunciated in 1821.[68]

Meanwhile, occupancy laws were being introduced into other states where land titles were in serious confusion, and, it may be added, no state was without conditions that produced much confusion. Vermont, badgered by the conflict between New York and New Hampshire as to ownership, had two sets of titles to much of its acreage, in addition to other title difficulties arising from large-scale speculative activity. To protect squatters on land to which they had nothing but settlement claims, the state provided that if they were on land prior to 1780 and were defeated in ejectment proceedings they could recover from the legal owner the value of their improvements but not the rise in value of the land, thus edging farther than Kentucky was later prepared to go in conceding occupants' rights in the improvements they put on land to which they had no color of title.[69]

The beginnings of Tennessee were marked by all the diffi-

----

[67] *Hawkins v. Barney's Lessee*, 5 Peters 466 (1831). Compare this sentence with Washington's "Nothing . . . can be more clear . . . than that a law which denies to the owner of land a remedy to recover the possession of it . . . or to recover the profits received from it . . . or which clogs his recovery of such possession and profits . . . impairs his right to, and interest in, the property" (8 Wheaton 78). Washington, it should be noted, was no longer on the Court when Johnson rendered his decision.

[68] Joseph Story, *Commentaries on the Constitution of the United States* (3d ed.; 2 vols.; Boston, 1858), II, 300 ff., especially 305. Cf. Story's deviation from common law in *Van Ness v. Picard*, 2 Peters 137 (1829), in which he conceded a tenant's right to remove buildings constructed for business purposes.

[69] *Laws of Vermont to 1807* (2 vols.; Randolph, Vt., 1808), I, 204–208.

culties over titles that had racked Kentuckians, and its leaders moved in the same way to secure relief. The new state was scarcely a year old when it adopted its first occupancy law, giving to occupants having color of title to their tracts the right to recover the value of their improvements if they were defeated in ejectment proceedings. Persons having a deed of conveyance and seven years residence on their tracts were assured of a perfect title, unchallengeable by others whose title might antedate theirs. Squatters having no title were assured the value of their improvements if defeated in ejectment, minus the value of the profits after commencement of the action. Thus Tennessee, like Vermont, went farther than Kentucky in protecting squatters in the value of their improvements.[70] Like Kentucky, Tennessee had difficulty in reconciling its occupancy laws with the compact it had made with its mother state, North Carolina, but that trouble did not reach the same proportions.[71]

Title confusion in Kentucky was commonly related to the fact that grants were made before survey and that persons locating them could run their lines as they wished. The rectangular system of survey before location, it was held, would have avoided much of the confusion and litigation. Yet litigation early appeared in the rectangularly surveyed public land states between settlers having a color of title or squatters on the one hand and legitimate claimants having the patent on the other. Indeed, controversies between conflicting claimants reached heights of excitement and open warfare in Iowa, Kansas, and California that exceeded anything witnessed in Kentucky. Some

[70] Act of Oct. 28, 1797, *Laws of Tennessee, Including Those of North Carolina, 1715–1820* (2 vols.; Knoxville, 1821), I, 612–615; *Laws of Tennessee,* 10th Assembly, 1813, 33–34. Thomas P. Abernethy, *From Frontier to Plantation in Tennessee* (Chapel Hill, 1932), 262 ff., deals with Andrew Jackson's opposition to the occupying claimants law of Tennessee. See also Joseph H. Parks, *Felix Grundy, Champion of Democracy* (Baton Rouge, 1940), 155 ff.

[71] *Bass v. Dinwiddie,* 3 Tennessee Reports 97 (1812); *Carson's Lessee v. Gordon, ibid.,* 112; *Bristoe v. Evans and M'Campbell,* 2 Overton's Tennessee Reports 341–352 (1815).

of the issues that produced this excitement and called for the adoption of occupancy laws were the common practice of issuing tax titles on delinquent land year after year; foreclosures and forfeitures that were not always conducted according to the letter of the law or which did not cut off the rights of all heirs; loosely framed laws that were susceptible of varying interpretations, such as whether swamp or railroad selections had priority; Indian allotments; and the slowness with which the private land claims were adjudicated.

To the new states across the Ohio and Mississippi rivers, Kentucky contributed largely of its population, political principles, and institutions, folkways, and law, especially its occupancy and possession laws. North, west, and south of Kentucky extensive speculation in public lands and large absentee ownerships were, if not common, numerous. This was particularly true of the military tracts of Ohio, Illinois, Missouri, and Arkansas. Much of this speculation was unstable, as it had been earlier in Kentucky, for capitalists persisted in investing beyond their means to carry their property the length of time necessary to obtain satisfactory returns. In consequence tax titles issued against the property and other liens of agents or attorneys, and of probate courts, cluttered up the conveyance records. One has only to look at the abstracts of properties of these areas to realize how litigious landowners were and how imperfect the land system was that caused so much difficulty and created so many costs for farm-makers. To protect the innocent holders of secondary titles who were making farms on land they assumed they owned in fee, these states adopted occupancy laws based on those of Kentucky, borrowing the language, procedures, and assurances. Ohio, in which there was almost twice as much land owned by absentees as by residents in 1810, adopted general occupancy laws in 1810 and 1816 and went farther in 1843 in providing that settlers on the canal lands, on which they were squatting, were to have the value of their improvements, if their claims were bought by others.[72] Illinois Territory adopted its first occupancy law in 1810,[73] Indiana in 1818, Missouri in 1834, Alabama in 1836, and Arkansas and Michigan in 1838.[74]

Occupancy laws followed the westward movement of settlers into the new states and territories. Iowa Territory took action in 1839 for the areas of its greatest title confusion—the Half Breed Tract—and in 1851 the state adopted a general occupancy law.[75] Mississippi followed in 1846, Wisconsin in 1849, Minnesota in 1851, Oregon in 1854, Kansas Territory in 1855, and California in 1856.[76] Kansas and California tried to assure squatters who had no other right to their claims than a settlement right that in the event of ejectment they could recover the value of their improvements. Strangely, the state that was to produce America's greatest critic of Anglo-Saxon principles of land tenure was

[72] William T. Utter, *History of the State of Ohio*, II: *The Frontier State* (Columbus, 1942), 131; *Laws of Ohio*, 8th Assembly, 1810, pp. 116–118; *ibid.*, 14th Assembly, 1815–1817, pp. 128–131; *ibid.*, 41st Assembly, 1842–1843, p. 25. The last reference was furnished by Harry Scheiber.

[73] Francis S. Philbrick, ed., *Laws of Illinois Territory, 1809–1818*, Collections of the Illinois State Historical Library, XXV (Springfield, 1950), 41–45. Illinois made clearer its occupancy law in 1819 and 1845 (*Revised Code of Laws of Illinois, 1829* [Cincinnati, 1829], 98–102; *Revised Statutes of Illinois, 1845* [Springfield, 1845], 204 ff). There is much on the confusion of titles in the Military Tract of Illinois and mention of the seven-year adverse possession law of 1839 in Theodore L. Carlson, *The Illinois Military Tract: A Study of Land Occupation, Utilization, and Tenure* (Urbana, Ill., 1951).

[74] *Revised Laws of Indiana, 1824* (Corydon, 1824), 269; *Revised Statutes of Missouri, 1835* (St. Louis, 1835), 236; *Laws of Alabama, 1835–1836* (Tuscaloosa, 1836), 20–21; *Laws of Arkansas*, 3d General Assembly, 1840 (Little Rock, 1840), 60; *Revised Statutes of Michigan, 1838* (Detroit, 1838), 478.

[75] *Laws of Iowa Territory, 1839*, p. 19; Code of Iowa (Iowa City, 1851), 196.

[76] A. Hutchison, comp., *Code of Mississippi* (Jackson, 1848), 656; *Revised Statutes of Wisconsin, 1858* (Chicago, 1858), 842; *Laws of Wisconsin, 1861* (Madison, 1861), 295; *Revised Statutes of Minnesota Territory, 1851* (St. Paul, 1851), 389; *Statutes of Oregon Territory, 1853–1854*, p. 130; *Statutes of the Territory of Kansas, 1855* (Shawnee, 1855), 328–329; *General Laws of the State of Kansas, 1862* (Topeka, 1862), 121–125; *Statutes of California*, 7 Sess., 1856, p. 56.

to be the only state whose high court struck down its state's occupancy law. What makes that act of the California Supreme Court most striking is that the court went back to the discredited and almost entirely abandoned decision of *Green v. Biddle* for justification and precedent.[77] True, the invalidated California statute had conceded occupancy rights to settlers on claims to which they had no color of title other than a settlement right, as did the Tennessee law, but the settlers' improvements might be, and were in many instances, as substantial as those made elsewhere by persons having some color of title. In other instances the settlers' improvements exceeded the value of those of the owners. The California statute, which had shown some promise of resolving by judicial procedure the bitter conflict between Mexican grantees and their assignees on the one hand and the swarming settlers on the other, and of contributing to breaking up the huge and slightly utilized estates, the product of the Mexican land system, was thus defeated, though almost everywhere else in the western states occupancy laws prevailed.

General reliance on occupancy laws had become so common that in 1873 a measure was introduced into Congress to give occupants found not to be rightful owners the same privileges in the federal courts that the statutes of the states and territories had given them in their courts. It received its principal support from representatives of Kansas and Iowa. A Kansas representative said in its support that all over his state settlers had taken up public lands, made their improvements, paid their fees, and were later ordered off the land without redress by decisions of the Secretary of the Interior, for one reason or another. An Iowa representative declared that homesteaders with patents for their lands on which they had lived for as much as twenty years had their titles voided by action of the Supreme Court on demand of the Des Moines River Navigation Company and again without redress for their improvements. The measure quickly passed and

[77] *Billings* v. *Hall*, 7 California Reports 1–26 (1857).

became law on June 1, 1874.[78] Congress thus reversed the principle of the Green case, though it had long been a dead letter, so far as occupancy rights were concerned.

The move from the common law doctrine of property rights, as expounded by Story and Washington, to the view that the rights of occupants to the value of their improvements were paramount if they could prove some color of title was thus won generally by tenants of the log cabin outside of California. Their victory roughly coincided with the success of the land reformers in gradually liberalizing the public land system and finally securing enactment of the Homestead Law. The right of occupancy stands with the pre-emption and homestead rights as major victories won by tenants of the log cabin.

Tax liens, tax titles, and occupying tenants' or occupancy rights have been studied but little by historians. Theodore L. Carlson, in *The Illinois Military Tract: A Study in Land Occupation, Utilization and Tenure* (Urbana, Illinois, 1951), discusses occupancy or possession laws as used in an area largely acquired by speculators. Paul W. Gates, in "California's Embattled Settlers," California Historical Society *Quarterly*, XLI (June, 1962), 99–130, treats the unsuccessful efforts of the settler element in California to secure legislation in both Washington and Sacramento that would assure occupying tenants either title to the land they had improved or the value of their improvements; the same author, in "Land and Credit Problems in Underdeveloped Kansas," *Kansas Historical Quarterly*, XXXI (Spring, 1965), 41–61, deals with the adoption of occupancy legislation in Kansas. Robert P. Swierenga's "The Tax Buyer as a Frontier Investor Type," *Explorations in Economic History* VII (Spring, 1970), 257–292, and his "Land Speculation and Frontier Tax Assessments," *Agricultural History*, XLIV (July, 1970), 253–266, are concerned with the investment possibilities and the credit provided the delinquent owner.

[78] *Cong. Record*, 43 Cong., 1 Sess., 1603 (Feb. 18, 1874); 4118 (May 21, 1874).

2. The Role of the Land Speculator in Western Development

The land use pattern of the twenty-nine public land states of the South, the Middle West and the Far West is the result of a long process of development and adaptation in which such factors as speculation, absentee ownership, credit, usury, farm mechanization, transportation and government controls have played important roles.[1] Not until the depression of the 1930s did the United States realize the errors it permitted to develop in this land use pattern. Only then did it become apparent that this pattern is the product in part of mistaken land policies which were once thought to be establishing a democratic system of land ownership. Wishful thinking, unwillingness to face the facts, and political oratory combined to obscure the appearance of ominous signs that a democratic pattern of ownership was not wholly achieved. A few notable spokesmen protested against policies which permitted concentration of land ownership; but Americans, big and little, were too much concerned with the accumulation of wealth through land speculation to listen to their Cassandra-like predictions.

From the seventeenth to the nineteenth centuries European immigrants, many of them from classes to which actual land ownership was denied, brought with them to America a craving for land. Land for a home and a competence was first desired; then land to assure wealth and social position was wanted. This

[1] The data concerning land entries was compiled from the abstracts of land entries in the General Land Office, now in the National Archives.

craving for land explains much in American history and is one of its central themes. It was the motivating force which sent hordes of settlers into the expanding frontier, and it drew forth large sums of money for investment in America's unsettled areas. Until the modern corporation came to be the dominant factor in American economic life, the principle opportunity for investment was in real estate. All persons seeking land for investment rather than for a farm home have been called land speculators, and the term, loose as it may be, has an important position in our terminology.

The term "land speculator" meant different things to different people and different sections. To a frontiersman it meant an eastern capitalist who bought large quantities of newly offered land in anticipation of settlers to come; or it meant a railroad or canal construction company to which had been given alternate sections of land in a strip ten or twenty miles wide paralleling the line of the improvement; or it meant a pineland baron who acquired 5,000, 10,000, or 50,000 acres of rich timberland. The frontiersman distinguished between resident and absentee speculators. Only nonresident owners of land who were not contributing to the development of the West by making improvements upon their lands were regarded by him as speculators and were the object of his resentment. Land grants for internal improvements were strongly favored by the frontier, which thirsted for connections with the outside world, but the frontiersman expected these lands to be sold promptly and on the pre-emption system.

To an urban worker the term "speculator" meant some one who laid out towns or additions to them, donated lots for churches and schools, attracted industries or state institutions to the new communities, and peddled out building lots at high prices to newcomers. To Horace Greeley the term meant, in addition the thousands of persons settling the West who sought a stake in the land greater than they could expect to use personally. Greeley also applied it scornfully to those westerners of means who purchased wild lands as an investment, as did their eastern associates. All were speculators; all contributed their share to the pattern of ownership which exists today.

Although frontiersmen, as a rule, possessed little or no capital, they were anxious to own as much land as possible. The first wave of settlers who followed the fur trader squatted upon choice locations, made rude improvements, and, when new arrivals came in, sold their claims and moved on to a new frontier before the government auction took place. These squatters were in a sense speculators. They sought to engross a half section or more and established claim associations to protect their rights. Henceforth these quasi-legal claims were bought and sold just like patent titles.

The second wave of settlers remained on the land until the the auction sale on which occasion they borrowed to the hilt to buy as much land as possible. The more successful, who had brought considerable money with them, or who had accumulated something from land and barter exchanges on the frontier, might have sufficient credit at the western banks to enable them to purchase 320, 480, or 640 acres. Loose banking policies made credit easy to secure and everyone attempted to borrow for land speculation. Rosy dreams of profits to be made distracted the attention of frontiersmen from the business of making farms in the wilderness. An English observer shrewdly remarked: "Speculation in real estate . . . has been the ruling idea and occupation of the Western mind. Clerks, labourers, farmers, storekeepers, merely followed their callings for a living, while they were speculating for their fortunes. . . . The people of the West became dealers in land, rather than its cultivators." [2] Calvin Fletcher, an Indianapolis banker and large landlord heavily involved in speculating in public lands, deplored the granting of credit for speculative purchases of land. "The consequence is," he said in 1838, "that for the last 4 years say 6 years there has

[2] D. W. Mitchell, *Ten Years in the United States: Being an Englishman's Views of Men and Things in the North and South* (London, 1862), 325–328.

scarcely been the extension of a farm. No new fields opened &
at the same time an enormous increase of consumers—What
Son will go to work or what farmer will draw out the energies
of his family where they can dress them, clothe them & feed
them on the glorious anticipations of a years accidents which
may or may not pay the debt without an effort." [3]

On every frontier the settler-speculator was present. He
rarely learned from experience. By claiming 320 acres instead
of 160 he separated himself that much more from his neighbor.
He had to bear a heavier proportion of the cost of road construction and maintenance; his school costs were increased or the
establishment of schools was delayed and his children were
denied educational opportunities; the expense of county and
state government, in a period when the land tax was the principal source of government income, was burdensome. Other social
institutions like churches, granges, and libraries came more
slowly because the population was so dispersed. Furthermore,
railroads, which all settlers wanted in their vicinity, could not
be pushed into sparsely settled areas without large subsidies.
State and county subsidies required special assessments upon
the already overburdened taxpaying farmers, and land grants,
whether by federal or state governments, created a near land
monopoly. Careful observers like Greeley saw many of these
results and urged settlers to be content with smaller tracts which
they could conveniently cultivate.

The chance of making a fortune in wild lands or town lots in
the rapidly expanding communities of the West was an allure-
ment difficult to resist. Fantastic stories of the profits others had
won were printed in the newspapers and retold in letters from
the West. Here, in 1816–1819, 1834–1837, or 1854–1857 was
the lodestone to quick wealth. Touched by the fever of land
speculation, excited people throughout the country borrowed to
the extent of their credit for such investments. Men from all

[3] Entry of Aug. 22, 1838, manuscript diary of Calvin Fletcher, Indiana
Historical Society, Indiana State Library, Indianapolis.

walks of life permitted their dreams to overcome their better judgment. Politicians, bankers, writers, ministers, planters, and poets, everyone, it seemed, who had any resources at all undertook to invest in western land. Levi Beardsley, a prominent New Yorker who went West in 1836 to invest some $20,000 in wild land, has left an interesting description of the speculative excitement of that year:

Every one was imbued with a reckless spirit of speculation. The mania, for such it undoubtedly was, did not confine itself to one particular class, but extended to all. Even the reverend clergy doffed their sacerdotals, and eagerly entered into competition with mammon's votaries, for the acquisition of this world's goods, and tested their sagacity against the shrewdness and more practiced skill of the professed sharper.[4]

The existence of a class of professional land agents facilitated land purchases by absentee capitalists. Eastern papers with a wide circulation among the wealthy contained numerous advertisements of these land agents during the years from 1830 to 1857. In every enterprising community on the frontier were agents who were prepared to buy or enter land for others with cash or warrants.[5] For a commission of 5 percent or a share in the transaction, generally from a third to a quarter, they would select land, sometimes by personal investigation, sometimes by a superficial search of the entry books, and make purchases for their principals.

Some of the more important of these land agents were Henry W. Ellsworth of Lafayette, Indiana; Cook & Sargent of Davenport, Iowa; and Henry C. Putnam of Eau Claire, Wisconsin. Ellsworth published a booklet, *Valley of the Upper Wabash*,[6] to attract attention to western Indiana and eastern

[4] Levi Beardsley, *Reminiscences: Personal and Other Incidents* . . . (New York, 1852), 252.

[5] A writer in Janesville, Wisconsin, in 1855, speaks of the "hundreds of land agents and dealers watching to show some new comer . . . and all manner of tricks to gull the unsuspicious" (Rutland [Vermont] *Herald*, Nov. 16, 1855).

[6] New York, 1838.

Illinois, and he and his father, Henry L. Ellsworth, Federal Commissioner of Patents, were able to induce hundreds of easterners, mostly New Englanders, to invest in the West. Cook & Sargent maintained offices in each of the eight land-office towns in Iowa where they entered nearly 200,000 acres.[7] Putnam's entries in Wisconsin exceeded a half million acres.[8]

These western land agents rank with the registers and receivers of the land offices as among the most important people on the frontier. They dealt in land warrants and scrip, ran a local note-shaving business, purchased exchange, sometimes operated a bank of issue with funds provided by eastern capitalists, loaned eastern funds to squatters at frontier rates ranging from twenty to sixty per cent, bought and sold land, paid taxes for absentee owners and undertook to protect their lands against depredations. At a later date, they arranged for renting land, made collections, and sold produce received in payment of rent. Small investors in the East were obliged to work through these agents, to submit to their exactions, and to suffer from their careless attention to details and could not effectually protest against their obvious neglect. The agent could take his commission from rents or sales before any money was remitted to the owner, could sell his own land to prospective purchasers, rather than that of the owners he represented, could neglect tax payments and get the title involved, or could pay taxes on the wrong land. In numerous cases western agents took advantage of their clients, used the prestige which their contacts provided for personal interests, and constantly minimized the value of the land they represented in order to increase sales and thereby commissions. In this way absentee investors whose eastern responsibilities did not permit them to give personal attention to their possessions in the West were imposed upon and victimized.

[7] For advertisements of Cook & Sargent, see *Iowa Sun* (Davenport), May 16, 1840; Davenport *Democratic Banner*, Feb. 10, May 5, 1854; Davenport *Democrat and News*, Nov. 2, 1859. Circulars of Cook & Sargent dated October 15, 1847, and October 15, 1850, are in the Corcoran and Riggs Papers, Library of Congress.

[8] The Woodward-Putnam letters are in Olin Library, Cornell University.

A case in point is that of Senator Henry H. Hubbard of New Hampshire, who, in association with Daniel Webster and other Yankees, invested well over $50,000 in western lands. Hubbard sent Moses B. Strong of Vermont to Wisconsin Territory in 1836 to invest a part of this money. Land was acquired and some sales were made by Strong before the crash of 1837 put a stop to the business. Thereafter the investment went from bad to worse. Strong's charges for the slight services he rendered after the actual purchase were so heavy that Hubbard was forced to sell part of the land at distress prices. When sales declined Strong neglected the business for politics and Hubbard was obliged to supplant him.[9]

An analogous case is that of Cyrus Woodman who represented a group of New England capitalists organized as the Boston and Western Land Company. This company invested $100,000 in 60,000 acres of wild land and in numerous embryo towns in Illinois, Wisconsin and Missouri in 1835 and 1836. The crash of 1837 broke the market; lands could scarcely be sold at any price, and interest, taxes, and agents' costs further discouraged the Boston promoters. Woodman, who was sent to the West to retrieve something from the wreck of the company's ambitious scheme, made no effort to put the investment in its best light but, from the first, filled his letters with pessimistic forebodings of ever greater contraction in prices accompanied by rising taxes. It is small wonder then that the owners became discouraged and sold their property to Woodman for a fraction of its cost. The land was that good prairie and timberland which in the fifties was to bring prices that almost justified the optimistic hopes of the thirties; but the original purchasers were not to share in the prosperity.[10]

[9] The papers of Moses Strong in the Wisconsin Historical Society Library contain the story of the Hubbard-Strong land business. Joseph Schafer used them in the preparation of an article entitled "A Yankee Land Speculator in Wisconsin," *Wisconsin Magazine of History*, VIII (1925), 377–392.

[10] Cyrus Woodman was a methodical businessman who kept his papers, including impression copies of letters he wrote. They are now in the Wisconsin

One of the most successful agent-speculator relationships was that of William A. Woodward and Henry C. Putnam who were natives of New York State. Both were shrewd judges of land values and both knew thoroughly the techniques of the land business. Putnam went to Wisconsin in the fifties where he invested funds of Woodward and other New Yorkers in short term loans to settlers and in timber and prairie land. The fees Putnam received for the numerous services performed for his eastern principals made him a leading businessman in the rising town of Eau Claire. He aided in selecting the university, school, and swamp land, became land agent for a land-grant railroad, was elected register of deeds and county surveyor, was appointed deputy United States assessor, and with others founded the leading bank in Eau Claire. When Ezra Cornell was looking for someone to help him locate the million acres in land scrip which New York State had received under the Agricultural College Act, Woodward and Putnam persuaded him to let them make the selections in the Chippewa Valley where, Cornell was assured, Putnam virtually controlled all land entries by means of his position in the United States land office at Eau Claire. Cornell gave them the agency and from it they both made substantial profits.[11]

A great impetus was given to land speculation in the mid-thirties by federal and state banking policies. The failure to recharter the Second Bank of the United States removed the curbs on state bank policy while the lure of federal deposits led to a scramble for such easy funds and to a mushroomlike growth of new banks in the South and West. Loans on real estate at inflated valuations were easily secured. Rising land values and easy credit attracted unprecedented quantities of capital from the East for investment in wild lands and corner lots. The federal surplus produced by increased land sales was distributed among

---

Historical Society Library and comprise one of the most valuable extant collections on the land business.

[11] See note 8.

the states, thereby providing funds for elaborate schemes of internal improvements. Canals, railroads, highways were projected throughout the newer states, regardless of their feasibility. This combination of an easy banking policy with large government expenditures on public works came at a time when emigration to the western country was greatly accelerated. The total purchases of the hordes of immigrants and the speculators who were attempting to anticipate settlers' needs made the public land sales of these years the largest in American history.

Between 1835 and 1837, 38,000,000 acres of public lands were sold, 29,000,000 of which were acquired for speculation. A minimum speculative investment of $36,000,000—exclusive of agents' costs, interest and taxes—was thus tied up in unimproved lands. To this figure should be added perhaps as large an amount for investments in towns and city lots.

Much of this land purchasing was done by banks or bankers. For example, Isaac Bronson and his sons Frederick and Arthur, prominent bankers of New York, together with Charles Butler, brother of the attorney general of the United States, and a group of New York capitalists, used funds of the New York Life Insurance & Trust Company and other banks with which they had connections to buy a third of a million acres in eight states and territories. The prominence of the promoters and the fact that some of them were closely identified with an administration which favored land reform and denounced land speculators gave the Whigs an opportunity of showing how hollow were the pretensions of some Jacksonians.[12]

Another group whose purchases of land were made with credit of banks it controlled consisted of such well-known Massa-

---

[12] Aside from the publications and advertisements of the American Land Company and the numerus attacks upon it which may be found in the *United States Telegraph,* quoted in the *Indiana* (Indianapolis) *Journal,* July 23, 1836; *Havanna Republican* (New York), Nov. 27, July 31, 1839; and *Chicago American,* Aug. 12, 1839, the William B. Ogden Papers in the Chicago Historical Society Library, and the Butler Papers in the Library of Congress are important.

chusetts financiers as John Tillson, Jr., John Shaw Hayward, Charles Holmes, Jr., Winthrop Gilman, and Griggs, Weld & Company. These men controlled the state bank of Illinois from which they were able to borrow for their extensive land speculations. When the bank itself undertook to loan funds to squatters and to buy large quantities of land, it came to be regarded as the great financial octopus of Illinois and Iowa against which numerous antimonopoly tirades were directed.[13]

A group whose operations in banks, land, and railroads was scarcely to be matched consisted of Alvah Buckingham and Solomon Sturges of Zanesville, Ohio, and their numerous children. They acquired or established banks of issue in Ohio, Indiana and Illinois, some of which received federal deposits. The banks made it possible for them to pyramid their land purchases until they ultimately reached 276,000 acres, or the equivalent of 1,725 quarter section farms. Railroads, grain elevators, and lumber yards were added to this princely estate. Neither the panic of 1837 nor that of 1857 destroyed the economic power of Buckingham and Sturges, and for a generation their names were widely known from Ohio to Nebraska.[14]

Throughout the East and, indeed, to a somewhat less degree in the old South, other banks, directors and customers of banks were using their credit to buy public lands. For years thereafter these banks or their receivers were engaged in disposing of quantities of wild land they had bought directly or acquired through mortgage foreclosures.

Squatters upon the public lands did not benefit from the easy banking policies of the thirties. Since they had no property to mortgage, credit was available to them only on the most usurious terms.

---

[13] *Iowa News* (Dubuque), May 18, Sept. 7, 14, Nov. 23, 1839; *Iowa Territorial Gazette and Burlington Advertiser*, May 4, Jan. 26, Feb. 2, 1839, Nov. 21, 1838; *Burlington Hawkeye and Iowa Patriot*, Aug. 12, 1841.

[14] *Prairie Farmer*, May 20, 1858; *History of Muskingum County, Ohio* (Columbus, 1882), two pages and photograph inserted after p. 72.

When newly surveyed lands were first announced for sale the squatters had to arrange for the purchase of their lands—made valuable by their improvements—before the opening of the auction or run the risk of losing them to speculators. Claim clubs and special pre-emption laws gave them protection against speculators only to the date of the sale. Squatters were inclined to put their meager capital into livestock, housing, fencing, and clearing, which seemed the most essential for the moment, and to hope that the land sale would be postponed until they could accumulate money with which to purchase their claims. The sale, although announced in advance by advertisement, seemed always to catch the settlers unprepared and obliged them to borrow from the nearest "loan shark."

These moneylenders were the representatives of western banks and eastern capitalists. Their charges were 5 percent for arranging loans and from 2.50 to 5 percent for making collections. Such eminent westerners as William B. Ogden,[15] James W. Grimes and Lucius Lyon,[16] later to become respectively president of the Chicago and Northwestern Railroad, and United States Senators from Iowa and Michigan, made their start by lending eastern funds on such a basis.

Loan sharks were present at every public land auction, and their agents were stationed in every land-office town, prepared to buy claims for squatters. The 10 or 12 percent allowed by the usury laws did not satisfy these moneylenders who found it possible to evade such restrictions. They would buy claims on which squatters had their improvements, according to previous agreements, and would then resell the land to them for an advance of $30 above cost on a quarter section. The squatter would agree to pay at the end of one or two years the maximum interest allowed by law. If the legal interest was 12 percent and the debt

[15] Ogden Manuscripts, Chicago Historical Society Library.

[16] There are many Lyon letters in the Ogden collection; others are published in Michigan Pioneer and Historical Society, *Historical Collections*, XXVII (Lansing, 1897), 414–604.

was paid in one year the lender would net 28 percent on his investment. The loan agents always denied that they were violating the usury laws, but they were exceedingly loath to have cases involving their transactions taken into the courts. Thousands of desperate squatters throughout the West snatched at the aid offered by the moneylenders who personally or through land agents invested many millions of dollars in this lucrative business. When later the squatters had difficulty in meeting their obligations they turned against their creditors and raised the cry of usury.

Jackson's specie circular of 1836 struck squarely at the rapidly expanding volume of land purchases. It showed that the chief executive, unlike many of his followers such as Butler, Kendall, Walker, and Ellsworth, did not at this time approve of the operations of land speculators and moneylenders. The president's purpose in issuing the circular was to "repress alleged frauds, and to withhold any countenance or facilities in the power of the Government from the monopoly of the public lands in the hands of speculators and capitalists, to the injury of the actual settlers in the new States, and of emigrants in search of new homes." Jackson further explained his purpose in his annual message of December, 1836, wherein he said the circular was intended to "save the new States from a nonresident proprietorship, one of the greatest obstacles to the advancement of a new country and the prosperity of an old one." He declared that the circular had "tended to keep open the public lands for entry by emigrants at Government prices instead of their being compelled to purchase of speculators at double or treble prices." [17] Except for Jefferson, Jackson was the only American president who seriously deplored that feature of public land policy which permitted speculators to buy land in unlimited amounts.

[17] *American State Papers, Public Lands*, VIII, 910; James D. Richardson, ed., *Compilation of the Messages and Papers of the Presidents, 1789–1902* (n.p., 1907), III, 249–250.

The specie circular required that only gold or silver be accepted from purchasers of land, except actual settlers who were permitted to use bank notes for the remainder of the year. The order brought down the whole bloated structure which had been erected by unsound banking practices, the deposit of federal funds in the state banks, and the elaborate programs of internal improvements undertaken by the states. Land purchases by speculators stopped immediately; only the business of lending money to squatters remained.

The federal government's need of revenue caused the money-lending business to thrive for a time after the crash of 1837. Quantities of land were ordered into the market when it was clear that squatters could raise the purchase price of their claims only with the greatest difficulty. Despite pleas for postponement the sales were held. Western banks were now closed; only gold or silver was accepted at the sales and only eastern bankers could furnish it. In 1838 and 1839 Ogden found it possible to lend eastern funds to squatters to net 30 percent a year before the deduction of commissions. Such usurious interest rates continued into the forties and, indeed, were increased in the fifties when it was possible for brokers to use in place of cash the military land warrants then in wide circulation at prices ranging downward to fifty cents an acre. By this means returns of 40, 50, and even 60 percent could be secured from squatters.

Ogden, Grimes and Lyon had assured their principals that there was no risk in lending money to squatters to buy their claims, since their improvements had already raised the value of the land above the government minimum price, and since they would make every possible effort to pay their debts and secure title to land on which they had expended years of toil. These men did not foresee the deplorable situation into which the West was plunged after 1837. Squatters, now attempting to meet their payments under the most trying circumstances, fought a losing battle. Payments were delayed and then completely suspended.

Many settlers became discouraged and moved on to another frontier to try once more to gain ownership of a piece of land.

Moneylenders, land speculators, and gamblers in town lots now found themselves loaded with financial burdens which they could not carry. Their land was unsaleable, yet their taxes continued to mount as did also the interest on the money they had borrowed. Having invested everything in property not easily liquidated they now were forced to surrender much of their land to the banks when these institutions began to call in their loans. The abstracts of conveyances for the years following the panic of 1837 show a tremendous volume of mortgage foreclosures of large estates.[18]

These foreclosures, the suspension of most of the wildcat banks and the bankruptcy of many financial institutions in the East all combined to keep land titles in the West in a state of chaos. Taxes were paid tardily, if at all, tax titles of a dubious nature were annually issued, and the difficulties of an already complex situation were thereby increased. During the period of stress settlers accumulated grievances against the absentee owners which seemed to justify stealing their timber, despoiling their fences and buildings, and using their land for pasture. New settlers moved on the absentee-owned land, sometimes bought a tax title, and set up a claim of ownership by right of possession and the tax deed. Absentee owners were powerless to deal with such a problem unless their property investment was sufficiently large to enable them to maintain a local agent employed on a full-time basis to watch over their interests.

During the bleak years of the early forties the equity of absentees was gradually eaten up by tax titles, agents' costs, interest, and depredations. Ultimately the burden became too

[18] The conveyance records of the following counties have been used: Vermilion, Champaign, Iroquois, McLean, Logan, Sangamon, and Christian, in Illinois; Benton, Newton, White, and Carroll, in Indiana; and Iowa, La-Fayette, and Sauk, in Wisconsin.

great and many sold their holdings for less than the original cost, disregarding interest, fees, and taxes. It was this situation that induced Dr. Joseph Schafer, for years a careful student of land problems and policies, to conclude that land speculation was on the whole an unprofitable business.[19]

The career of Calvin Fletcher, a cautious Hoosier from New England reared in an atmosphere of conservative finance, sheds much light on this era of unbridled land speculation. The craze for speculation overcame Fletcher's better judgment, and with Nicholas McCarty, likewise a Hoosier, he engaged in a joint speculation with $40,000 borrowed from the state bank of Indiana of which Fletcher was a director. The mental torture Fletcher went through during the following years as a result of this "hazardous" investment is recorded in his diary. Unlike the majority of settler-speculators, who lost their land when the depression years set in, Fletcher was able to carry his investment until it began to produce returns. In 1846, when the banks had foreclosed many mortgages and thousands of farmers having lost their homes had either gone elsewhere to make another attempt at securing ownership of land or had sunk to the position of tenants upon their old claims, Fletcher stated that one-third of the voters of Indiana were then "tenants or day laborers or young men who have acquired no property." [20]

On the frontier the fog of depression is quickly dissipated by rising commodity prices, quickened immigration, and a new influx of capital. In the middle forties these factors were again at work and there followed a new era of land speculation in which old residents and new settlers participated equally. The curve of

[19] Joseph Schafer, *Wisconsin Domesday Book, Town Studies* (Madison, 1924), I, 10, and note; Schafer, *The Wisconsin Lead Region, Wisconsin Domesday Book, General Studies* (Madison, 1932), III, 153.

[20] Diary of Calvin Fletcher, entry of March 23, 1846. A first volume of this valuable diary, with the title *The Diary of Calvin Fletcher Including Letters of Calvin Fletcher and Diaries and Letters of His Wife Sarah Hill Fletcher, 1817–1838*, edited by Gayle Thornbrough, was published in Indianapolis in 1972.

land purchases shot upward as people in all occupations once more neglected their routine work to buy raw prairie land or corner lots in newly platted cities. Eastern capitalists again established banks of issue in the West and South under the lax systems still prevailing there and used the funds to purchase land. Land agents, professional locators, loan sharks, town-site promoters flourished. Few seemed to have learned from experience.

The peak years of speculative purchasing were 1854 to 1858, when a total of 65,000,000 acres of public domain were disposed of to purchasers or holders of land warrants. To this figure should be added an equal or greater amount of land which was granted to the states for canals, railroads, swamp drainage, and education and sold by them, mostly to speculators, large and small. A comparison of the census figures of land in farms with the land-office figures of land sold shows a tremendous concentration of speculator-owned land in all public land states, especially in the newer states like Iowa, Wisconsin, Illinois, Missouri and Arkansas.

The speculators' contributions to the present day pattern of land ownership and land use are most important. For a generation agricultural economists have said that tenancy was an inevitable result of the commercialization of farming and rising land values. This is true, but tenancy got its start in the Middle West as a result of the activities of land speculators and money-lenders. Squatters who could not meet their usurious demands had their contracts cancelled and their equity confiscated. They might, however, remain on their old claims as tenants and pay rent for the land or they might make a new contract for the land but at a higher valuation. In either case, the farmer found ownership difficult to attain. Elsewhere speculators, dismayed at the cost of carrying their projects, sought relief by inducing land seekers to settle on their holdings, the sole condition being that they must pay taxes. If land was scarce it was not difficult to persuade immigrants to settle upon speculators' tracts, per-

suade immigrants to settle upon speculators' tracts, perhaps with
the understanding that they might be able to buy later. The
farmers' improvements raised the value of the property but did
not bring in immediate cash income sufficient to enable them
to make payments upon the land. As the value went up the
owners' price increased; ownership proved unattainable to many.
Tenancy thus had come to stay in the first generation of settlement in Illinois, Indiana, Iowa, Kansas, and Nebraska. Furthermore, owners of small farms had borrowed heavily to secure
title, and from their debts many were never to be free. Some
were ultimately depressed to the state of tenancy.

Speculator ownership and tenancy did not always result in
the best use of the land. It has already been seen that speculator
ownership forced widespread dispersion of population and placed
heavy tax burdens upon farmers whose improved lands could be
more heavily assessed than the speculators' unimproved land.
Furthermore, speculators were slow to pay taxes. They resisted
increased levies, secured injunctions against expenditures for
buildings and roads, and sometimes simple refused to pay taxes.
Heavy interest penalties and tax titles did not trouble them
particularly since they knew they could later make a compromise
settlement with the hardpressed county boards, or could have
the tax titles set aside by the courts. All of this meant that the
tillers of the soil, if they were to enjoy the benefits of schools,
roads and local railroads had to dig down into their own jeans
more deeply because the speculators were not carrying their
share of the burden. Taxes continued to climb and rarely or
never declined, even in a period of depression. They are one of
the rigid costs which trouble the farmers deeply when their own
income is sharply declining. Heavy tax burdens forced farm
practices which depleted the soil, produced erosion, and diminished land values.

Speculators left their mark on the West in areas other than
land ownership. The nationalizing influence of their investments
in western lands should not be neglected. Speculators were

naturally inclined to favor internal improvements in the vicinity of their land. The Wabash Canal, the Illinois and Michigan Canal, the Des Moines River Navigation and Improvement Company, and the Fox and Wisconsin Canal were all the work of speculators who sought to increase the value of their holdings by bringing transportation facilities to them at government expense. The investments of Daniel Webster of Massachusetts and John Rockwell of Connecticut in central Illinois made them keenly aware of the need for internal improvements in the prairie state and led them to support the movement for railroad land grants for that area.[21]

The land and town lot speculators were also influential in securing state, county, and municipal subsidies for local railroads. Many railroad enterprises were in themselves as much land speculations as transportation developments. The pinery railroads of northern Wisconsin promised few or no profits from operations, but the land grants included valuable stands of white pine from which large returns might be secured. Some of the other railroads for which there now seems little justification were doubtless chartered for the sake of the land grant.

Land and town lot speculators had much to do with railroad strategy in the West. During the territorial period of Kansas and in the first decade of statehood the struggle between the supporters of rival routes for land grants for their railroad enterprises is one of the chief issues, transcending in importance the slavery and union issues. Out of the melee certain groups emerged triumphant such as that which revolved around one of the most notorious corruptionists in American history, Samuel C. Pomeroy. Two railroads of which he was an officer and stockholder received land grants, one was permitted to buy a valu-

---

[21] Webster and Rockwell were both warm supporters of the measure to grant land for the aid of the Illinois Central Railroad. Rockwell is said to have received for his share in securing the land grant 2.50 percent of the land or its equivalent (Fitz Henry Warner, Washington, D.C., Dec. 1, 1852, to Charles Mason, Burlington, Iowa, Mason MSS., Iowa State Department of History and Archives, Des Moines).

able ceded Indian reservation for less than its current value, and three were required to converge on his own town of Atchison. The struggle over the location of the eastern terminus of the Union Pacific Railroad, the efforts of Cairo, Illinois, promoters to require the Illinois Central to locate its southern terminus at that point, the desire of the Northern Pacific to build up its own town on Puget Sound are illustrations of how speculators, whether operating within or without the railroad companies, have influenced the location of railroad routes and their terminal points. Another factor which tended to prevent railroads from selecting the shortest line between two points was the desire of their promoters to secure the largest possible land grants.

The petty fights over the location of county seats, territorial and state capitals, land offices, state universities, agricultural colleges and normal schools, and institutions for the insane, the blind, and the criminal comprise no small part of the political controversies of the time. That some of these institutions were located in remote, inaccessible places wholly unsuited to the functions they were to perform may be blamed upon speculators who succeeded in having them established in the vicinity of their lands.

Westerners were united in their demand that the federal government should donate to the states the land within their boundaries. This demand was never attained in full but it was achieved in part through a piece-meal system of securing special grants for education, canals, river improvements, and the drainage of swamp lands. As successive states entered the union they were given larger proportions of their land, the proportion running as high as one-third in the case of Arkansas, Louisiana, Michigan and Minnesota, to two-thirds in the case of Florida. The states were expected to sell these lands for the best possible price, and the proceeds, if derived from education grants, were to provide endowments. Speculator influence in the state capitals and county seats tended to break down the effective utilization of these grants.

Numerous scandals marked the sale of state lands and indicate that state and local governments were even more subject to speculator influence than was Congress and the General Land Office. The two-township grant for state universities brought in little return, the common school sections were in many cases wastefully administered, the agricultural college lands or their scrip equivalent were sold for a pittance by Rhode Island, Massachusetts, Indiana, Ohio and other states, and the river improvement grants were wasted away. Worst managed of all were the swamp lands, of which 64,000,000 acres were patented to the states. Some were sold as low as ten cents an acre; others were given to railroad companies to aid in construction; still others were granted to drainage companies for the improvements they contracted to make. Little or no security was ever required by the local officials for the performance of the contracts and in few cases were the improvements actually made. One prairie county of Illinois permitted its judge to contract 47,000 acres to a Utica, New York, resident on the understanding that he would drain the lands. The latter were conveyed but no improvements were made; later it was found that the judge had an interest in the business.[22]

Indian lands were fair game for speculators who used both legal and illegal means to secure them. Traders and speculators devised a method by which treaties of cession would include 640-acre allotments of the choicer lands to chiefs and half-breeds. They could easily be induced to sign away their allotments for an extra portion of whisky. By this means most of the desirable land along the upper Wabash Valley in Indiana and other valuable tracts in Illinois, Mississippi, Alabama and Wisconsin passed into the hands of speculators including the great trading firm of W. G. & G. W. Ewing of Fort Wayne, Senator John Tipton of Indiana, and Simon Cameron of Pennsylvania.[23]

[22] H. H. Beckwith, *History of Iroquois County*. . . (Chicago, 1880), 372–389; Iroquois County Deeds, 27:37.

[23] I have described this method of land disposal in the introduction to *The*

In Kansas speculator influence carried this method of land acquisition even farther. Here Indian tribes such as the Potawatomi (whose members had already been victimized by the Wabash traders), the Kickapoo, the Delawares, the Cherokees, and the Osage were induced to cede over 9,000,0000 acres of land in trust, to be sold for their benefit. Such lands were not to become part of the public domain and were, therefore, not subject to the general land laws. Until Congress woke up to what was going on these tracts were being rapidly conveyed to groups and individuals close to the Indian Office for distinctly less than their actual market value at the time.

Speculators pressed for the general allotment system, which was adopted in 1887. They also cooperated with the lumbermen of Wisconsin and Minnesota in securing the opening of reservations containing valuable stands of white pine.

To gain their objectives the speculators were forced to enter politics. Whether from the East or West, they opposed a free homestead policy which, they feared, would reduce the value of their holdings. They favored grants for railroads and measures to make easier land accumulation. They were influential in local and state governments which they warped to suit their interests. Thus one sees Wisconsin in the seventies and eighties controlled by a tight little group of lumbermen-speculators including Cadwallader Washburn, Jim Thorp, Nelson Luddington, Philetus Sawyer, William Price, and Isaac Stephenson. Elsewhere the story is the same. These men opposed land reform, fought other agrarian legislation, championed protective tariff duties, and condemned monetary heresies. They represented the creditor, the large property owners, the railroads, and the rising industrialists.

John Tipton Papers, ed. Nellie A. Robertson and Dorothy Riker, Indiana Historical Collections (Indianapolis, 1942); and in "Indian Allotments Preceding the Dawes Act," in *The Frontier Challenge: Responses to the Trans-Mississippi West,* ed. John G. Clark (Lawrence, Kan., 1971), chap. 6, pp. 141–170.

Not until 1888 and 1889, by which time the best of the public land was gone, were they ready to abandon their long struggle to prevent the public domain from being reserved for actual settlers only, a recommendation long since made by Jefferson and Jackson.

The successful land dealer of one generation became the banker, the local political oracle and office holder, or the country squire of the next. Scarcely a city or country town in the West but had its first family whose fortune had been made by shrewd selection of lands and their subsequent sale or rental to later comers. Wealth which had come easily to them through their speculations had become a vested interest which they sought to protect against the demagogues who demanded the ten-hour day in the saw mills, or the imposition of an income tax, or the regulation of railroads.

The influence of the speculator may also be noted in the cultural field. The owners of western lands were not only responsible for a flood of pamphlets, booklets, guidebooks, and emigrant gazettes advertising their projects, but also for many travel books published for the same purpose. It is well known that Samuel Augustus Mitchell's *Illinois in 1837* was published to aid the sale of the 124,000 acres of land purchased in 1836 and 1837 by John Grigg, Mitchell, and other Philadelphians. Similarly, none can doubt that Henry W. Ellsworth's *Valley of the Upper Wabash* is a real estate advertisement and not a careful appraisal of the Grand Prairie of Indiana and Illinois. William Ferguson, J. G. Kohl, and Richard Cobden also wrote accounts primarily to aid the sale of lands in Illinois. James Caird, an English agricultural journalist, on the other hand, disguised his land promotion propaganda so effectively that reputable historians have continued to borrow from his *Prairie Farming in America*, little realizing how prejudiced and distorted it is. Even Charles Dickens, whose investment in Cairo real estate proved disastrous to him, was attracted to America, in part, out of curiosity to see the investment which had repaid him so poorly.[24] The productions of numerous other writers who were interested in western lands were widely read at the time of their publication and for years were drawn upon by subsequent travelers and compilers of guide books.

For better or for worse the speculator, whether absentee or resident, squatter or banker, local politician or eastern senator, was present on every frontier. He affected every phase of western development and left in all places his indelible mark. His motives and his deeds one may deplore, but so characteristically American was he, so dynamic a part did he play in shaping land and cultural patterns, that it is difficult to imagine an American frontier without him.

Speculation in public lands has long interested historians, but in recent years they have studied its aspects more intensively. One group has been primarily concerned with the profits and losses, ignoring the economic and social effects of the intrusion of the speculator between the government and the actual settler. Examples are James A. Silver, "Land Speculation Profits in the Chickasaw Cession," *Journal of Southern History*, X (February, 1944), 84–92; Allan G. and Margaret B. Bogue, "Profits and Frontier Land Speculation," *Journal of Economic History*, XVII (March, 1957), 1–24; and Robert P. Swierenga, *Pioneers and Profits: Land Speculation on the Iowa Frontier* (Ames, Iowa, 1968). Another group has been interested in land speculation as a business: Larry Gara, *Westernized Yankee: The Story of Cyrus Woodman* (Madison, Wisconsin, 1956); Kenneth W. Duckett, *Frontiersman of Fortune: Moses M. Strong of Mineral Point* (Madison, Wisconsin, 1955); Alice E. Smith, *James Duane Doty: Frontier Promoter* (Madison, Wisconsin, 1954); Allan G. Bogue, *Money at Interest: The Farm Mortgage On the Middle Border* (Ithaca, New York, 1955); and Paul W. Gates, *The Wisconsin Pine Lands of Cornell University: A Study in Land*

---

[24] For Ferguson, Cobden, Caird, and Dickens, see Paul Wallace Gates, *The Ilinois Central Railroad and Its Colonization Work* (Cambridge, 1934), *passim*.

Policy and Absentee Ownership (Ithaca, New York, 1943), and "Frontier Land Business in Wisconsin," *Wisconsin Magazine of History,* LIII (Summer, 1969), 306–327.

Irene D. Neu, in *Erastus Corning: Merchant and Financier, 1794–1872* (Ithaca, New York, 1960), deals more with speculation in town sites. Mary E. Young, in *Redskins, Ruffleshirts and Rednecks: Indian Allotments in Mississippi and Alabama, 1830–1860* (Norman, Oklahoma, 1961), shows how a number of well-financed land companies secured control of most of the Chickasaw and Choctaw allotments. E. Louise Peffer considers why the large speculative holdings did not result in latifundia instead of being gradually broken up into small farms of 50 to 160 acres, in "The Family Farm and the Land Speculator," *Journal of Farm Economics,* XL (May, 1958), 330–343.

Two book-length studies of land policies and problems bear heavily on speculation: Malcolm J. Rohrbaugh, *The Land Business: The Settlement and Administration of the American Public Lands, 1789–1837* (New York, 1968); and Everett Dick, *The Lure of the Land: A Social History of the Public Lands from the Articles of Confederation to the New Deal* (Lincoln, Nebraska, 1970).

3. Southern Investments in Northern Lands before the Civil War

Investments by the people of one section of the United States in the enterprises of other sections is a phase of American economic history that has been little studied. Northern investments in southern and western states have received some attention, but they deserve further examination. That southern [1] capital in considerable amounts was invested in public lands in the Upper Mississippi Valley before 1860 will come to many as a surprise. The amount of this investment and the fact that it was made by the people of a section ordinarily thought to have no surplus capital should warrant some study. [2]

The ante-bellum South could easily have absorbed all the

---

[1] The terms "South" and "southern" as used in this chapter refer to that section below the Mason and Dixon Line.

[2] Southern investments in northern securities—except securities of land companies—are not considered in this study, but it is only fair to point out that such investments were made. Southerners in 1820 owned over one half the stock in the second United States Bank which was held privately in the United States. In 1832 the South's share in the Bank was valued at $10,000,000 (Ralph C. H. Catterall, *Second Bank of the United States* [Chicago, 1903], 508). Representative Thomas H. Bayley of Virginia and Corcoran and Riggs of Washington held considerable blocks of Illinois bonds, and James S. Easley of Virginia, in addition to large land investments in the Northwest, instructed his agent to invest collections in the stock of the La Crosse and Milwaukee Railroad (Bayley to Corcoran and Riggs, Nov. 4, 1852; Winslow and Lanier and Company to *idem*, Nov. 25, 26, 28, Dec. 19, 1851, Corcoran MSS., Division of Manuscripts, Library of Congress; James S. Easley to Peters, Campbell and Company, Oct. 6, 1857, Easley Letter Books, Easley MSS., University of Virginia Library.)

funds owned by its residents. The new cotton, rice, and sugar producing areas, the railroad [3] and canal companies, banking, commerce, and manufacturing all called for additional capital and promised, perhaps, as much security and as good returns as investments in land in the Northwest. Despite such local needs many residents of the older southern states and, indeed, of some of the newer slave states turned their backs upon their section and invested their surplus funds in the rapidly growing commonwealths north of the Ohio.

There were three major periods during which the fever of land speculation swept over the country: 1816–1819, 1834–1837, and 1854–1857. In the first period it was Alabama and Ohio that chiefly attracted speculators; in the second period, Michigan, Mississippi, Illinois, and Indiana; and in the third, Iowa, Illinois, Wisconsin, and Missouri. Although there was a large investment of Virginia and Kentucky capital in the Virginia Military Tract of Ohio before 1820,[4] southern investments in northern lands were made chiefly in the two later periods. The following indictment of the speculative craze of the thirties was penned by William J. Grayson of South Carolina, who, in 1836, participated in the mad rush for land in Indiana:

The restless spirit which had threatened to overthrow the republic took a new direction, and displayed itself in another form. A rage for speculating in land sprang up and extended over the whole country. Men, women, and children, clergy and laity, plunged into the current flowing with promises of universal wealth. The mania raged for a year or two, until the recurrence of a commercial crisis, with

---

[3] Thomas P. Kettell pointed out in 1860 that capital was accumulating in the South and that the railroads in that area, unlike those in the West, had been constructed with local funds (*Southern Wealth and Northern Profits* . . . [New York, 1860], 50, 88, 98, 137–138). It appears that this was not true of the Charleston and Hamburg Railroad, for which a loan of $2,000,000 was negotiated in England in 1838 (Cincinnati *Chronicle;* quoted in *Indiana Farmer* [Indianapolis, 1837–1841], II [1838], 68).

[4] William T. Hutchison, "The Bounty Lands of the American Revolution in Ohio," Ph.D. dissertation, University of Chicago, 1927.

its customary thunders and lightnings, purified the atmosphere, and left all parties astonished, dismayed and ruined.[5]

Outstanding among the intersectional investments were those made by three large planters of Virginia, South Carolina, and Louisiana. The Cabell family possessed wide estates in the Old Dominion, and one of its members—Landon Rose Cabell [6]—invested a large sum in Indiana lands in 1835. In association with Henry L. Brooke, a distinguished member of the Richmond bar, and Philip M. Tabb,[7] Cabell bought 22,500 acres [8] at the auction sale at La Porte where the lands of northwestern Indiana were for the first time made available for purchase. To this sale came Indiana bankers prepared to snap up likely sections or to lend their funds to squatters at the usual frontier interest rates of 24 to 48 percent. Henry L. Ellsworth,[9] federal commissioner of patents and Indiana's principal land baron, Henry King,[10] Pennsylvania capitalist, and that most denounced of frontier characters, the "loan shark," in the person of Lyne Starling,[11] formerly of Kentucky, were also in attendance. The rush for land and

[5] William J. Grayson, *James Louis Petigru* (New York, 1866), 135–136. While a member of Congress, Grayson invested $10,000 in Indiana lands through Henry L. Ellsworth, one of the largest individual owners of prairie lands in the Northwest. Some 7,000 acres in northern Indiana, most of which was in Benton County, were bought. Sales were slow and in 1850, despairing of a better bargain, Grayson sold his interest to Ellsworth for $13,312 (Benton County, Indiana, Deed Records, II).

[6] Alexander Brown, *The Cabells and Their Kin* (Boston, 1895), 397.

[7] "First real estate commission contract, dated September 26, 1836, recorded November 23, 1836, Stark County Records" (William H. Mathew Notes, Indiana State Library).

[8] All details of land entries in this chapter, unless otherwise noted, are compiled from the entry books, too numerous to list here, of the old General Land Office, but now in the National Archives. The principal types of entry books are the cash, warrant, and scrip abstracts.

[9] Claribel R. Barnett, "Henry Leavitt Ellsworth," in *Dictionary of American Biography* (20 vols. and index; New York, 1928–1937), VI, 110–111.

[10] *The Biographical Encyclopedia of Pennsylvania of the Nineteenth Century* (Philadelphia, 1874), 17.

[11] Henry Howe, *Historical Collections of Ohio* (2 vols.; Norwalk, Ohio, 1896–1898), I, 649.

the presence of so many competing capitalists aroused keen excitement and raised the selling price well above normal. The three Virginia associates had to pay as high as $9.05 per acre for some tracts although the average was about $1.75.[12] Their investment was a pure speculation and none of the three apparently intended to settle upon the lands. They made a contract with Jesse Roberts in St. Joseph, Michigan, for the management of their property. Roberts undertook to prevent trespass and pillage and to effect sales, in return for which he would receive one-fourth of all proceeds, after deducting costs and interest. The lands selected by Cabell and his associates were doubtless representative of the area, but they probably needed draining before they could be farmed or sold, and the price paid for them was not justified, as subsequent events were to show. Ten years later much of the land was tax delinquent and advertised for sale.[13]

In the same year that Cabell and his associates plunged so heavily in Indiana land, Wade Hampton (1791–1858),[14] owner of cotton plantations in both the tidewater and piedmont sections of his native state as well as sugar plantations in Louisiana, made a modest investment in Wisconsin. In October and November, he attended the sales at Green Bay and entered 2,080 acres.

The newer South also provided the funds for a large intersectional investment made by a Louisiana planter, E. E. Malhiot. An exile from Canada because of his participation in the Rebellion of 1837, he established himself in the Parish of Assumption on Bayou Lafourche, where he acquired and developed an extensive sugar plantation. Malhiot won the confi-

12 The Indianapolis *Indiana Democrat*, October 14, 1835, spoke of the "immense crowd" which attended the sale and added, "the settlers generally got their homes at or near congress price." On February 15, 1837, it observed that much of the 474,000 acres sold in the district in the previous year went into the hands of speculators.

13 Supplement to the *St. Joseph Valley Register*, undated, Indiana State Library.

14 J. Harold Easterby, "Wade Hampton," in *Dictionary of American Biography*, VIII, 213–215.

dence and respect of the "Cajuns" among whom he settled and was elected by them in 1856 to the Louisiana Senate.[15] Not content with his sugar plantation, he undertook in the same year to establish a modified form of a Canadian seigniory in central Illinois. From the Illinois Central Railroad he bought 22,000 acres of land upon which he colonized a hundred or more families of French Canadians. The settlement was a success but Malhiot's trials with his tenants and with his railroad creditor were many and lengthy. Until his death he continued to manage his varied interests in Louisiana and Illinois.[16] The Civil War did not prevent him from operating his estates both in the Union and in the Confederacy,[17] and his property in neither camp was threatened with confiscation as were the northern possessions of many southerners.

Although much of the domestic and foreign trade of the ante-bellum South was in the hands of outsiders, there were numerous southern fortunes made in commerce. In Baltimore,[18] in the early part of the nineteenth century, the firm of William Wilson and Sons owned a fleet of ships engaged in trade with China, India, Europe, and South America. "This eminent shipping firm," [19] experiencing the same decline in profits which affected the New England-China trade, gradually withdrew from commerce and invested its funds in banking, local real estate, and western lands. In 1836 it bought 3,776 acres in the Springfield, Illinois district. James B. Danforth, who had a

[15] Ivanhoe Caron, "Edouard-Elisee Malhiot," in Royal Society of Canada, *Proceedings and Transactions* (Ottowa, Montreal, 1882–), 3d Ser., XXII (1928), sec. 1, pp. 155–166.

[16] Paul W. Gates, *The Illinois Central Railroad and Its Colonization Work* (Cambridge, 1934), 131, 236–238, 296.

[17] W. H. Osborn to General W. K. Strong, March 29, 1862, and to J. M. Douglass, "Presidents' Letters," Sixty-third Street Archives, Illinois Central Railroad, Chicago.

[18] Another Baltimore resident not elsewhere mentioned in this chapter who bought land in the Northwest was John M. Gordon, who entered 6,764 acres in Michigan in 1836.

[19] George W. Howard, *The Monumental City: Its Past History and Present Resources* (Baltimore, 1873–1880), 470–471.

wholesale and merchandising business in Louisville, Kentucky, also made a speculation in Illinois. Instead of buying land, Danforth subscribed $10,000 to the capital stock of the New York and Boston Illinois Land Company [20] which was organized in 1835 to buy and sell lands in the Military Tract of Illinois. This company, of which Danforth was a trustee, claimed to own 900,000 acres.

Before 1850 there was perhaps no state in which so much absentee-owned capital had been invested as in Illinois, and certainly in no part of that state except the Military Tract was there a greater concentration of "alien" ownership than in the Springfield land district. Between 1833 and 1837 over 7,000,000 acres were sold in this district, a large proportion of which was bought by nonresidents. Many southerners in addition to the firm of William Wilson and Sons were attracted to the Springfield district. Some of the purchases made by southerners are listed below.[21]

Name	Residence	Year	Acres
Brown, William	Harrison Co., Ky.	1833	4,000
Field, Drury J.	Fayette Co., Tenn.	1836	8,414
Field and Holloway	Richmond Co., Ky.	1836	1,611
Goggin, Robert	Madison Co., Ky.	1836	1,566
Hall, Henry H.	Accomac Co., Va.	1833–34	5,080
Hamilton, M. P. R., and E. A.	Bath Co., Ky.	1835	2,479
Huey, Daniel	Mississippi	1835	4,220
Mayer and Harwood	Baltimore, Md.	1836	1,293
Price, Daniel B.	Jessamine Co., Ky.	1835	1,280
Ross, James	Montgomery Co., Tenn.	1835	1,360
Ware, Nathaniel A.[22]	Natchez, Miss.	1833	21,400
Williams, Isaac	Huntsville, Ala.	1835	1,480
Zeller, David	Washington Co., Md.	1835	2,169

[20] *Articles of Association of the New York and Boston Illinois Land Company: Amendments* . . . (Philadelphia, 1839); J. Stoddard Johnston, *Memorial History of Louisville* (2 vols.; Chicago, [1896?]), I, 383, 397.

[21] Compiled from abstracts of the Springfield land office.

[22] Ware is at times listed in the Sangamon County Deed Records as from St. Louis, Natchez, and Hinds County, Mississippi.

Perhaps the most fortunate southern investment in this district was made in 1836 for the estate of A. Hamilton, formerly of Bath County, Kentucky. John and Joseph Berry and other members of the Berry family, likewise of Bath County, entered 11,553 acres in the Springfield district of which 4,161 acres in Sangamon County were entered for the Hamilton estate. The title to the 4,161 acres was in dispute between the Hamilton and Berry heirs until 1876 when George H. and James C. Hamilton were awarded the entire tract with reasonable expenses to the Berrys for their management.[23] The following year the tract was sold to William Scully, the greatest landlord in Illinois, for $215,297.[24] The Berrys kept a part of their other entries as late as 1894 at which time they held at least 1,783 acres in Sangamon County.[25]

The extent of early North Carolina commerce, we are told, has been underestimated by historians.[26] Certainly one North Carolinian, Miles White,[27] who moved to Elizabeth City in 1830, built up a "large coasting and West India trade" from which he made a comfortable fortune. In 1849 he retired from shipping and moved to Baltimore where he engaged in the land business. White and his son Elias purchased extensive Baltimore property, but more interesting for our purposes are their western land ventures. From 1849 to 1860 they spent a good deal of their time in Iowa and other northwestern states looking over lands for investments, lending money to desperate squatters who stood to lose their homes at the approaching sales unless they could borrow sufficient to buy their claims, and making

---

[23] 43 Mortgage Record, Sangamon County, Register of Deeds Office, 563; J. A. Richards, *History of Bath County, Kentucky* (Yuma, Ariz., 1961), 421–424, 514.

[24] 61 Deed Record, *loc. cit.*, 11.

[25] *The Plat Book of Sangamon County, Illinois* (Chicago, 1894), shows Joseph A. Berry owning 1,491 acres, John S. Berry 193 acres, and J. H. Berry 199 acres.

[26] Charles C. Crittenden, *The Commerce of North Carolina, 1763–1789* (New Haven, 1936), 72 and *passim*.

[27] Howard, *Monumental City*, 628–630; Henry Hall, *America's Successful Men of Affairs* (2 vols.; New York, 1895–1896), II, 861.

agreements with local agents to look after their lands, pay the taxes, collect payments, and reinvest receipts. Their total entries made for themselves and others approximated 175,000 acres and literally dot the abstract books of the land offices of Iowa, where the largest proportion was made. The risks were great and the profits high, in good times, but the panic of 1857 and the resulting depression made it difficult for the claim holders to meet their payments, and in many cases they not only defaulted on their contracts but abandoned their claims. However, Iowa lands have generally been a good investment, and the Whites did not have to wait long before their holdings were again in demand. Like so many other absentee speculators, the Whites fared badly in Wisconsin, where they entered some 12,000 acres.[28] Their agent proved untrustworthy, neglected their lands, and permitted them to go to tax sale.[29]

The largest land business in the South and one of the most significant in the entire country was operated by Easley and Willingham of Halifax Court House, Virginia, a few miles from the North Carolina line. James S. Easley, the more active partner in the land business, was a member of the merchandising and importing firm of Easley and Holt, the funds and credit of which were used by Easley and Willingham to deal extensively in lands. It was not the sample act of buying lands in advance of settlement and holding them for a profitable sale that attracted them, although they did speculate in this manner. They also purchased military land warrants in the East and resold them through their western agents for a quick profit. The

[28] There is considerable correspondence concerning White's ventures in Wisconsin lands in the Woodman MSS., Wisconsin State Historical Society Library.

[29] The Whites long remained in the western land business. The business passed from Miles and Elias White to Francis White and from him to Miles White, Jr., who still managed the "few scattered lots" remaining in 1937 (Miles White, Jr., to the author, Baltimore, Md., Sept. 21, 1937). White has an extensive collection of documents dealing with the family land business. Included therein are the sales books, tax books, tax receipts, and a large amount of miscellaneous material concerned with the land affairs. Toward the latter part of the century, the sale of city lots in numerous western cities seemed to be almost as important to the Whites as was the disposal of their farm lands.

largest and most lucrative part of their business was the entering of lands for squatters who had made some improvements upon their claims. Either through their numerous western agents, or personally on their frequent trips through the western states, Easley and Willingham contracted with some 2,000 squatters to enter their lands for them on what they called the "time entry" business. The title was taken in the firm's name and the contract provided for the payment at the end of one year of $140 for 80 acres, $210 for 120 acres, and $280 for 160 acres. The squatter also had to pay the land office fees. Where the partners contracted directly with the squatters for their entries, and payments were made promptly at the end of the year, the profit might run as high as 75 percent,[30] where the business was conducted through an agent $10 might be allowed as compensation, but some agents insisted on an equal division of the profits after the firm had charged 10 percent interest on the warrant, thereby reducing the latter's profit to a mere 42 percent. It may have been of Easley and Willingham that a local historian wrote:

Many of the early settlers were not men of great financial standing . . . and to procure their homes they would permit Mr. Shylock to enter the land in his own name, and . . . the settler would repurchase it . . . [from] the money lender, allowing and promising him forty per cent per annum on the $200 until paid. . . . The money-lender who had come west with a pocket full of land warrants, which had cost him ninety cents an acre, if the squatter paid at the end of two and a half years was getting $400 for an outlay of $144. That these entries would be eaten up by usury and tax was most evident, unless the location was of such character and worth as to command an immediate sale, which in the fewer instances happened, but in the most cases, the land remained in the name of the party furnishing the warrants for entry.[31]

[30] The claims were entered with military warrants, the market price of which ranged from $.90 to $1.15 for most of the period.

[31] Joe H. Smith, *History of Harrison County, Iowa* (Des Moines, 1888), 100.

During the years 1852 to 1857, Easley and Willingham's western land business prospered and their profits were reinvested in additional lands. They also invested substantial sums for or in cooperation with other Virginians, notably Daniel B. Easley, brother of James, John D. Holt, Thomas Leigh, Thomas E. Owens, Evan Raglund, and George Carrington. Altogether this group entered upwards of 400,000 acres in Iowa, Missouri, Wisconsin, Minnesota, Kansas, and Nebraska, a volume of entries probably exceeding that made by any similar group before the Civil War. The panic of 1857 slowed up their operations: squatters defaulted, payments became delinquent, credit extensions had to be made, and in many cases the lands were abandoned by their tenants. This Virginia group thus became one of the largest landholders in the above mentioned states, excluding of course the land grant railroads, and the land business absorbed its attention throughout the century.[32]

In the mid-nineteenth century the loose banking laws which prevailed made it easy for people with some influence but little capital to establish banks of deposit, the funds of which were available for investment in speculative enterprises. It is not surprising, therefore, that numerous southern bankers, attracted by the high interest rates and profits in land speculation, invested no small portion of their funds in northern lands. The investments of the banking firm of Pairo and Nourse of Washington illustrate this tendency. In the early fifties, Charles Pairo entered either personally or through agents 40,000 acres of land in sixteen districts in the states of Ohio, Indiana, Illinois, Wisconsin, Iowa, and in the territories of Kansas and Nebraska. Such far-flung activities made supervision difficult. But worse still, Pairo overextended his investments, and when payments and sales declined in 1857, the firm was forced to suspend. Its balance sheet showed liabilities of $200,000 and assets of

[32] This account is based on a large collection of manuscripts of James Stone Easley and of the firm of Easley and Willingham in the Library of the University of Virginia.

$413,000 of which $218,000 was in western lands.[33] The failure of this firm led the *National Intelligencer* to reflect upon the evils of speculation and to warn other institutions against "a further indulgence in Western lands." [34]

The suspension of Pairo and Nourse led to runs on other Washington banks, especially that of Sweeny, Rittenhouse, and Fant, which dealt in land warrants and lent money for land investments in Kansas. Hamilton G. Fant of this firm had not only lent money on Kansas land at 50 percent interest but also had purchased Leavenworth lots through his western agent, Thomas Ewing, Jr.[35] The firm also cooperated with E. L. Fant and Company of Lecompton, Kansas.[36] The banking house of William T. Smithson of Washington was likewise dealing in land warrants and Western lands. In 1856 it advertised to buy "150,000 acres of land warrants for which . . . [it would] pay the highest market price." [37] The following year it advertised for sale "several thousand acres of fine lands" in Iowa and thirty or forty lots in Chicago.[38] Although forced to curtail operations by the panic of 1857, these firms remained solvent during the ensuing depression.[39]

The most influential Washington banker and the most in-

[33] Washington *National Intelligencer*, Sept. 15–19, 1857.

[34] *Ibid.*, Sept. 19, 1857.

[35] Thomas Ewing, Jr., to H. B. Denman, Leavenworth, Kansas, July 21, 1857, and to Fant, Ewing Letter Books, in possession of Thomas Ewing, Jr. This collection contains considerable correspondence on the investments of Hamilton G. Fant in and around the growing city of Leaveworth.

[36] Advertisement of E. L. Fant, Jr., and Company, Washington *National Intelligencer*, March 18, 1857.

[37] *Ibid.*, Dec. 24, 1856.   [38] *Ibid.*, March 16, 1857.

[39] John Underwood of Washington, like Fant and Smithson, dealt extensively in land warrants which he was prepared to sell or locate on Wisconsin lands. In 1850 he sent thirty 160-acre warrants to Albert W. Parris, his Wisconsin agent, for location or sale (John Underwood to Moses M. Strong, Washington, Dec. 28, 1850, Strong MSS., Wisconsin State Historical Society Library). Underwood also made an investment in lands in Indiana with H. L. Ellsworth.

veterate land speculator was William W. Corcoran.[40] Through his intimate relations with prominent Democratic politicians, among them Robert J. Walker, Jesse Bright, Stephen A. Douglas, R. M. T. Hunter, and John Forney, Corcoran received from the Polk, Pierce, and Buchanan administrations many favors, the greatest of which was the financing of the government's Mexican War loans. Corcoran invested a portion of the profits from these banking and brokerage plums in numerous land speculations. Over a period of years the treasury department had accumulated undeveloped lands, town lots, and other miscellaneous property through forfeiture by defaulting federal officers, such as Samuel Swartwout, and their bondsmen. Many of these defalcations came to light during the panic of 1837, but it was not until 1847 that business conditions justified the government in offering the property for sale. Press advertisements gave descriptions of the land and invited bids for them.[41] Corcoran, who was a large creditor of Secretary of the Treasury Walker, submitted bids ranging from 2 cents per acre for 45,000 acres of Texas lands to 38 cents per acre for 15,800 acres in Mississippi, 22,000 in Illinois, 2,240 in Michigan, and 41 cents for 2,800 in Indiana, and was generally successful against competitors who might bid higher for small portions of individual lots.[42] In addition to getting title of 103,000 acres of land, he secured lots in eight cities, among them New York. Most valuable were the lands in Illinois [43] which within a few years were

[40] The sketch of Corcoran by William B. King, in *Dictionary of American Biography*, IV, 440–441, is conventional and trite. The author did not even list, to say nothing of using, the great collection of Corcoran MSS., Division of Manuscripts, Library of Congress.

[41] Washington *National Intelligencer*, Aug. 24, 1847.

[42] All bids are found in the "Bid Book," archives, Solicitor's Office, Treasury Department, Washington.

[43] Corcoran had earlier engaged in a land venture in Illinois with Amos Kendall which, by 1853, was producing considerable income in the form of rents. With money furnished by Corcoran, 1,580 acres were purchased privately in 1839 in Sangamon, Logan, and Menard counties. The lands were

selling for $5 and $10 per acre. Unfortunately for Corcoran, the quitclaim title which the government gave him was defective, since the dower rights of the wives of the defaulted officers or their bondsmen had not been conveyed, and this defect created serious difficulties in the management of the lands. So many title controversies arose that he feared in 1857 he would never recover "cost and interest." [44] Notwithstanding his early fears, his agent valued the remaining unsold lands, acquired at a cost of less than $25,000, at $578,033, of which title to lands valued at $159,145 was clear.[45]

Corcoran's other land speculations, though smaller, looked at the outset exceedingly promising. He had the largest share in the promotion of the city of Superior, Wisconsin, which was projected as the eastern terminus of the northern transcontinental railroad and he financed the shares of such Southerners as Senator R. M. T. Hunter of Virginia, John C. Breckinridge of Kentucky, and Robert J. Walker, formerly of Mississippi, then of Washington, as well as those of Stephen A. Douglas, Jesse D. Bright, John W. Forney, and W. A. Richardson.[46] Two South Carolina congressmen, William W. Boyce and William Aiken, also had small investments in Superior.[47] This city was subse-

---

subsequently divided, Corcoran keeping his and renting them and Kendall selling his share in the fifties and sixties for as high as $13 per acre (Amos Kendall to Corcoran, May 18, 1841, Jan. 16, 1844, Jan. 16, 1848, and Corcoran to Kendall, Jan. 31, 1848, Nov. 17, 1852, Jan. 1, 1853, Corcoran MSS.; also numerous conveyances in the Sangamon and Logan County Deed Records between Corcoran and Kendall and others).

[44] Corcoran to Captain J. B. Russell of Chicago, Ill., Nov. 16, 1857, Letter Book, Corcoran MSS.

[45] Letter Book No. 26, p. 61, Corcoran MSS. These figures include some lands which were acquired subsequent to 1847 but they may not be greater than the value of those of the original purchase which had been sold.

[46] Corcoran to Robert J. Walker, Nov. 21, 1854; A. Hyde to S. Bright, May 11, 1858, Letter Book, Corcoran MSS. Forney tells how he was drawn into this venture by Stephen A. Douglas, in *Anecdotes of Public Men* (2 vols.; New York, 1873), I, 19–20.

[47] "Statement of Taxes for 1855 on Property Superior paid by Wm. H. Newton," Letter Book No. 9, Corcoran MSS. Aiken visited Kansas and

quently displaced by Duluth as the chief port on the lake, not so much because of the better natural advantages of the latter as because Jay Cooke had supplanted Corcoran after 1860 as the favorite banker of the national administration, and Cooke was a promoter of Duluth. Corcoran also made purchases of land in Illinois with Representative Orlando B. Ficklin, in Indiana with Bright, in Kansas with Major George Deas, and in Arkansas with Bright and Dr. C. B. Mitchell.[48]

Corcoran's Washington partner, George W. Riggs,[49] also made investments in western lands. In 1858 he entered in St. Croix and Dunn counties, Wisconsin, 9,240 acres. Previously he had aided other members of his family in speculations in Illinois.

Another southern banker whose land investments are worthy of notice is Joseph B. Loose of Hagerstown, Maryland. In 1834 Loose went to Michigan, where he invested his capital and that of his family in public lands, acquiring thereby over 4,000 acres. He then went on to Springfield, Illinois, where he took up his residence, established a bank, and with its funds invested largely in Illinois lands and Springfield and Chicago real estate. Loose was fortunate enough to make excellent selections of prairie land from which he could shortly derive a substantial income in the form of rents or could sell at rapidly increasing prices. In 1856 he made another venture in Iowa land, buying 7,380 acres. He returned to Hagerstown to spend his last years, having accumulated a comfortable fortune in the course of his various speculations. In 1879 he was reported to own lots in Springfield and Chicago and farming land in Illinois, Iowa, Kansas, and Nebraska, in addition to extensive property in Virginia and Maryland.[50]

Nebraska in 1857, apparently on a land investment tour and was reported to be "highly pleased" with Nebraska (Omaha *Nebraskian*, June 17, 1857).

[48] The Corcoran MSS. contain many letters concerning these transactions.

[49] Katharine E. Crane, "George Washington Riggs," in *Dictionary of American Biography*, XV, 603–604.

[50] *Biographical Cyclopedia of Representative Men of Maryland and District of Columbia* (Baltimore, 1879), 479.

Another fortunate series of investments was made by the family of Matthew T. Scott, who was president of the Northern Bank of Kentucky at Lexington. He and his two sons, Matthew T. and Isaac W., together with Samuel P. Humphrey of Woodford County, Courtney Pickett of Fayette County, Richard and Joel Higgins, John McFarland, and others of Kentucky, made a series of large investments in Illinois and Iowa. Isaac Scott began these investments at Springfield, Illinois, where he entered 2,340 acres in 1836. His brother entered 18,300 acres at the Danville office in 1854 and in the following year 3,450 acres in western Iowa. The Scotts did not entrust the management of this large estate to local agents but sent Matthew T., Jr., to Illinois to develop the property. He undertook large improvements upon the lands in McLean and Livingston counties, laid out the town of Chenoa, broke up great tracts of land which he cultivated by hired labor and tenants, and soon developed one of the most important real estate and farming businesses in the prairie section. Scott developed a peculiar type of farm lease under which the tenant was encouraged to make improvements which were credited toward the purchase of the land. Many improvements were made but few tenants at the time seemed to be able to complete their contracts and acquire the coveted title. Meantime, the land was rapidly rising in value and the Scotts and their associates became possessed of a valuable estate.[51]

A number of southern railroad promoters found capital to invest in northern lands. Abram Blanding [52] of Richland District, South Carolina, who was closely identified with the movement for internal improvements and the beginnings of the

---

[51] *History of McLean County, Illinois* (Chicago, 1879), 499 ff.; *Atlas of McLean Co. and the State of Illinois* (Chicago, 1874). The deed records of McLean County for the fifties and sixties contain numerous conveyances, mortgages, and leases of Matthew T. Scott, Jr., and other associates.

[52] J. Franklin Jameson, ed., *The Correspondence of John C. Calhoun*, American Historical Association, *Annual Report*, 1899, II, 365, 419, 431; Ulrich B. Phillips, *History of Transportation in the Eastern Cotton Belt to 1860* (New York, 1908), *passim;* Theodore D. Jervey, *Robert Y. Hayne and His Times* (New York, 1909), 419 ff.

Louisville, Cincinnati, and Charleston Railroad, united with James K. Douglas of the same district in the purchase of 4,500 acres in southern Indiana in 1836. Charles Edmonston,[53] a director of the same railroad and a member of the South Carolina House, was one of six Charleston residents who each, in 1835 and 1836, made entries of one to three thousand acres in the Green Bay area of Wisconsin. There was also Thomas Swann,[54] a native of Virginia who moved to Baltimore and there became president of the Baltimore and Ohio Railroad. He united with John H. Brent and Alexander Hunter in the purchase of 2,600 acres in southeastern Iowa in 1839.

Southern politicians as well as commercial, banking, and railroad men were attracted by land speculation in the Northwest. Indeed, the speculative craze of 1835 and 1836 had gone to such extremes and had caused so many persons in influential financial and political positions to make wild ventures that great alarm was felt. Jackson's specie circular of July 11, 1836, had been anticipated by a resolution of the House of June 21, providing for an investigation of the amount of borrowing by members of Congress and other government officials from deposit banks for speculation in public lands.[55] The select committee, after a superficial investigation, reported that it had been unable to secure information from the banks concerning their loans for land investments.[56] The committee had called

[53] Jervey, *Robert Y. Hayne*, 419.

[54] Swann was also president of the First National Bank of Baltimore, mayor of the city, United States senator and representative. For his participation in the Baltimore and Ohio Railroad, see William P. Smith, *The Book of the Great Railway Celebrations of 1857* (New York, 1858), 45, 71, and *passim*.

[55] *Congressional Globe*, 24 Cong., 1 Sess., 456 (June 21, 1836). The Washington *United States Telegraph*, quoted in the Indianapolis *Indiana Journal*, July 23, 1836, fulminated against politician-speculators, especially Amos Kendall and Benjamin F. Butler, who were accused of using public funds for their land activities. Kendall made an investment in Illinois lands which is described elsewhere in this chapter; Butler had an interest in the American Land Company which had large investments in the Northwest.

[56] *Cong. Globe*, 24 Cong., 1 Sess., 482 (July 2, 1836); *Niles' Register* (Baltimore, Philadelphia, 1811–1849), L (1836), 403 ff.

before it Preston S. Loughborough who, though obviously possessed of information about land companies, refused to divulge anything of interest and apparently for good reason.[57] A resident of Franklin County, Kentucky, and in 1836 chief clerk of the post office department in Washington, Loughborough himself was speculating in Illinois lands of which he bought 9,925 acres.

Loughborough may have had information about the land deals in which Senator Arnold Naudain of Delaware was engaged. With Edward Tatnall and Merritt Canby, likewise of Delaware, Naudain entered 11,365 acres in Indiana in 1836 and 1837. The following year the group entered 12,000 acres in Illinois and 2,840 acres in Iowa. Naudain resigned his seat in the Senate on June 16, 1836,[58] whether as a result of the growing opposition to members of Congress speculating in land or whether it was owing to his desire to devote his full time to the business is not clear. In 1837 he was so enamored of the West that he considered making his home in Illinois.[59] By 1849, however, he had failed to advance his fortune through land speculation and he then sought a federal position from his old friend, Thomas Ewing, Secretary of the Interior.[60]

A more tragic case is that of Thomas Ludwell Lee Brent, a Virginia planter who served for a time in the diplomatic service. Like some other gentlemen farmers of the South and East, Brent had a grand dream of establishing a vast estate in the West, operated by tenants, on which he might reside in baronial splendor. In 1836 he went to Michigan where he bought 21,687 acres of public lands. Unfortunately, he exhausted his funds in purchasing land and had nothing to expend on the development of his estate. He was land poor and upon his death a

[57] *House Reports*, 24 Cong., 1 Sess., Vol. III, serial 295, No. 846, pp. 1–6.

[58] *Cong. Globe*, 24 Cong., 1 Sess., 451 (June 17, 1836); Indianapolis *Indiana Democrat*, June 29, 1836.

[59] Dubuque *Iowa News*, July 15, 1837.

[60] A. Naudain to T. Ewing, Philadelphia, May 11, 1849, Ewing MSS., Division of Manuscripts, Library of Congress.

large part of his holdings passed out of the family's possession.[61]

The western land speculations of Charles W. Short [62] are interesting. He established himself at Transylvania University, Lexington, Kentucky, and later at the University of Louisville, as a national authority on medicine and botany. Perhaps it was a field trip which took him to Illinois in 1836 where at the Springfield office he entered 720 acres of land. In 1845 appeared his *Observations on the Botany of Illinois*. That his interest in Illinois was sustained is evident from the fact that he entered 4,960 acres at the Danville office in 1853. A relative, William Short, also of Louisville, entered 2,260 acres in the same district in 1853 and 1854.

In the light of the approaching "irrepressible conflict," the land investments made by some southern politicians in the fifties are surprising. William B. Stokes, who represented a central Tennessee constituency in Congress from 1859 to 1861 and 1865 to 1871, entered 7,000 acres in the pineries of Kanabec and Isanti counties, Minnesota, in 1856 and 1857. Stokes was a staunch unionist, and in the critical days of 1860 and 1861 when the southern states were being urged to secede, he fought valiantly to preserve the Union and to keep his state a part of it.[63] The secession of Tennessee did not change his attitude; his state was wrong and the Union must be preserved at all hazards. During the war he was in command of a Union regiment and in the postwar period was a radical Republican.[64]

---

[61] Judge Albert Miller estimated Brent's fortune at $90,000 to $100,000. He also says that Brent bought 70,000 acres of land in Michigan. If the latter statement is correct, the larger part of the land was probably entered at the government sale by others than Brent. Miller's account of "Thomas L. L. Brent," in the Michigan Pioneer and Historical Society, *Collections* (Lansing, 1877–1929), IX (1886), 192–196, is interesting.

[62] Johnston, *Memorial History of Louisville*, II, 455–456; Filson Club Publications (Louisville, 1884–), XX (195), George H. Genzmer, "Charles Wilkins Short," *Dictionary of American Biography*, XVII, 127–28.

[63] *Cong. Globe*, 36 Cong., 1 Sess., 365–368 (Jan. 7, 1860).

[64] Oliver P. Temple, *East Tennessee and the Civil War* (Cincinnati, 1899), 203, 219.

A Kentuckian whose economic interests and national sympathies coincided was Jeremiah T. Boyle of Danville. According to a local historian, Boyle was a slaveholder who was averse to slavery and favored gradual emancipation. He built up a large law practice and became interested in various railroad schemes and land speculations. Among the latter was the Iowa Land Company which was organized to promote the towns of Clinton, Elvira, and Dewitt, and otherwise to speculate in Iowa and Illinois lands. It is not clear what part Boyle played in its affairs but he is listed with L. M. Flournoy of Paducah, Kentucky, and others as "promoters" of the company. Boyle was a Unionist in 1860 and took up arms in support of the North.[65]

On the other side was John C. Breckinridge, Kentucky politician who, while vice-president of the United States, entered with Francis K. Hunt 2,813 acres in Winnebago County, Iowa. Breckinridge had once resided in Iowa where he had learned something of the state and its resources and he was attempting to capitalize upon that experience. It has also been seen that he had a share in the promotion of Superior, Wisconsin. Hunt has been described as "one of the first lawyers in Kentucky." [66] When secession came, Breckinridge wavered for a time but eventually went with the South; his associate remained a unionist.

An uncompromising member of the Southern Rights wing of the Democratic party was Eli S. Shorter of Eufaula, Alabama, who was a planter , lawyer, politician, and railroad official. He advocated disunion in 1850 and again in 1858 if Kansas were not admitted under the Lecompton constitution, and declared that should Alabama withdraw from the Union "her sons will be prepared to defend it in the forum or in the field." [67] Despite

[65] *First Annual Report of the Transactions of the Iowa Land Company. June 2, 1856* (Chicago, 1856); Johnston, *Memorial History of Louisville*, I, 388–390.

[66] Ranck, *History of Lexington*, 54; *War of the Rebellion: A Compilation of the Official Records of the Union and Confederate Armies* (Washington, 1880–1901), Ser. I, Vol. XVI, Part I, 457.

[67] *Cong. Globe*, 35 Cong., 1 Sess., 770 (Feb. 18, 1858). See also *ibid.*, 34 Cong., 1 Sess., 399 (April 9, 1856).

his uncompromising attitude upon the territorial question and his open support of disunion, Shorter did not hesitate to invest in northern lands. In 1855, 1856, and 1857, and again in 1859, he toured Iowa and Nebraska, buying 3,320 acres in the former and 9,625 acres in the latter state. Two years later he was a colonel in the Confederate infantry.[68]

Eufaula furnished two other persons who invested in western lands. Between 1849 and 1859 Selden S. Walkley entered 8,280 acres in Iowa.[69] Jefferson Buford, aroused by the activities of the New England Emigrant Aid Company to "save Kansas for freedom," issued in 1855 a stirring appeal for personal aid and financial support for an expedition to colonize Kansas with slavery defenders.[70] Shortly afterwards he proceeded to Kansas with a band of supporters, dubbed by their northern opponents "Border Ruffians," and took an active part in the Kansas conflict. In common with most pro- and antislavery leaders in the territory, Buford seemed as much interested in his land activities as in the slavery question. With Rush Elmore, a former Alabaman who had become a territorial judge of Kansas and who was himself something of a speculator, Buford organized and laid out the town of Virginia.[71] He also bought 1,760 acres of Delaware

[68] Omaha *Nebraskian*, Sept. 16, 1857; W. Brewer, *Alabama: Her History, Resources, War Record and Public Men* (Montgomery, 1872), 126–127; William Garrett, *Reminiscences of Public Men in Alabama for Thirty Years* (Atlanta, 1872), 617.

[69] Mention might be made of Horace Everett of Sumter County, Alabama, who in 1855 entered 35,000 acres in western Iowa. At that time Everett's residence was given as above but a year later, when he was engaged in entering 20,000 acres in the Plattsburg, Missouri, district, it was given as Iowa. Everett formed a partnership with Abiel Leonard and opened an office in Council Bluffs. See the advertisement in Council Bluffs *Bugle*, September 4, 1855. In 1863 Everett was collector of internal revenue in Iowa (*Official Records*, Ser. III, Vol. III, 84).

[70] The story of Buford's expedition is told in Walter L. Fleming, "The Buford Expedition to Kansas," *American Historical Review*, VI (1900), 38–48; and Elmer LeRoy Craik, "Southern Interest in Territorial Kansas, 1854–1858," in Kansas State Historical Society, *Collections* (Topeka, 1881–1928), XV (1923), 334–488, especially 397.

[71] Act of February 19, 1857, incorporating Virginia Town Association. Kansas Territory, *Session Laws* (1857), 313.

Trust lands for $4,672 and 160 acres at the Iowa Point sale for $448. In addition, he purchased a squatter's claim on the Delaware Trust lands for which he paid $1,000. This he stood to lose because of a technicality and he besought the government to protect his right to the claim.[72]

Another Alabama politician who made investments in northern lands was Williamson R. W. Cobb of Jackson. Cobb was a Democratic member of the national House of Representatives from 1847 to 1861. Like Buford, he was present at the Delaware Trust sale at Leavenworth where he bought fifteen city lots. His later investments are very devious and difficult to follow but it seems that he arranged with John F. Kinney to enter jointly 7,680 acres in Nebraska. Cobb was a director and stockholder in the Nebraska Real Estate and Exchange Company[73] and entered personally 1,120 acres in the eastern part of Nebraska. When the Civil War came, his lands were deeded to his son-in-law to avoid confiscation.[74]

No less prominent than Breckinridge, Buford, Shorter, and Cobb among the southern politicians who invested in northern lands was John Slidell, Democratic representative and later senator from Louisiana. Elected to Congress in 1842, Slidell soon became a power in the Democratic party, through his own shrewdness and wit and the fact that he was related by marriage to August Belmont, the New York banker. He became the political boss in Louisiana and the power behind the throne in the Buchanan administration. Having acquired an interest in the huge Houmas land claim in Louisiana, which was grossly inflated by later interpretation of loosely stated boundaries to include over 100,000 acres of the richest cotton and sugar producing land in the South, Slidell, through a subterfuge, won senatorial action confirming the inflated claim. Fortunately, other

[72] Jefferson Buford to Hon. B. Fitzpatrick, Westport, Missouri, accompanying letter of Fitzpatrick to Jacob Thompson, Secretary of the Interior, April 16, 1857, Indian Office.

[73] Nebraska City *Nebraska News*, Oct. 10, 24, 1857.

[74] Omaha *Nebraska Advertiser*, Sept. 27, Oct. 4, 1862.

small claimants who had patents for their possessions learned in time of the action and persuaded Congress to rush through a measure repealing the act. Slidell, meantime, had purchased 80,000 acres of swampland in Louisiana on which little down payment was required, making him one of the largest landowners in the South. That his large, undeveloped investment in Louisiana did not absorb his resources is astonishing.

Belmont was devoted to the welfare of the Democratic party, as were also William W. Corcoran and Elisha Riggs, Washington bankers and former partners. Belmont employed Corcoran's often used device to reward politicians for valuable favors received: enter public land in their joint names in the West with the understanding that a portion of the profits were to go to the politician whose name would appear in the records as a partner in the business. Riggs and Slidell entered 9,000 acres in northeastern Wisconsin in 1857,[75] and the following year they entered 16,000 acres in western Iowa. Belmont and Slidell jointly entered 20,000 acres in western Iowa in November, 1858. Belmont and Slidell broke off relations in 1859, apparently because the former had lost confidence in Buchanan and had transferred his support to Douglas. "Essentially a moderate" in 1860, argues Louis Sears of Slidell, he "found himself supporting the most extreme wing," and when Louisiana seceded, Slidell went with his state.[76] After the attack upon Fort Sumter, he became alarmed for his investments in the North and urged his friend

[75] Paul W. Gates, "Private Land Claims in the South," *Journal of Southern History*, XXII (May, 1956), 198–201. A. Hyde to L. Riggs, Baltimore, June 27, 1870, Corcoran MSS., mentions 30,000 acres in Wisconsin which were purchased by Slidell and Riggs. If the figure is correct, it is probable that much of the land was entered by agents, perhaps in their own names and assigned to Slidell and Riggs. This would make a total of 66,000 acres in which Slidell had an interest in Iowa and Wisconsin.

[76] Louis M. Sears, *John Slidell* (Durham, N.C., 1925), 159–160. Belmont's pique at not gaining the post of minister at Madrid may also have alienated him from Buchanan (draft, letter of James Buchanan to John Slidell, Washington, June 24, 1859; Slidell to Buchanan, July 3, 1859, Buchanan MSS., Historical Society of Pennsylvania Library.

Corcoran to arrange a sale. On May 14, 1861, Corcoran nego-
tiated a sale to a Mr. Fay, the payment to be made in New
Orleans city bonds.[77]

A southern politician who engaged in a variety of speculations was Robert J. Walker. Financial agent of the Illinois Central Railroad,[78] promoter of the city of Superior and of the St.
Croix and Lake Superior Railroad and the Texas and Pacific
Railroad,[79] shareholder in the Chicago Land Company, and
land speculator in Wisconsin, Mississippi, and Louisiana, Walker
was as active in business as in politics. The year 1856 found him
enjoying financial success almost beyond his dreams as witnessed
by the following quotation from a letter of April 28 to James
Buchanan:

I have sold most of my Mississippi & Louisiana lands without war-
ranty for very large cash prices & am selling the remainder from time
to time. Besides my Wisconsin property has increased nearly a hundred fold in value & where I bought as farms, by the *acre*, are now
flourishing cities. To crown all, my quicksilver property in Cali. has
turned out of enormous value.[80]

A land speculation different from those mentioned above was
promoted by Dr. Alexander Graham of Lexington, Virginia. He
formed a syndicate which purchased the much sought after
military reservation at Fort Snelling, Minnesota. Like the lands
of defaulting officers and their bondsmen which were sold to
Corcoran for a song, numerous Indian [81] and military reservations
were disposed of to faithful supporters of the parties in power

[77] Hyde to Slidell, Washington, May 14, 1861, Corcoran Letter Book, Corcoran MSS.

[78] Gates, *Illinois Central Railroad*, 69–71.

[79] Corcoran to Walker, Aug. 25, 1856, and Hyde to Walker, Nov. 24,
1856, Corcoran Letter Book, Corcoran MSS. Walker was operating at least in
part on borrowed capital, his debt to Corcoran being $11,426 on January 15,
1855. This debt remained unpaid as late as 1867 (Corcoran to Walker, Jan.
15, 1855, and memo of May 24, 1867, *ibid.*).

[80] Letter in Historical Socciety of Pennsylvania Library.

[81] For the story of a small but valuable Indian reservation in Kansas, see
Paul Wallace Gates, "A Fragment of Kansas Land History: The Disposal of

during the years 1850 to 1870 at what might be called bargain prices, and the sale of Fort Snelling is more or less typical of the others. Graham, while visiting his friend, John B. Floyd, secretary of war, learned that the Fort Snelling reservation was for sale. Here was the opportunity of a lifetime and Graham did not neglect it. He informed Franklin Steele, a prominent Minnesota speculator, who decided to have a share in the purchase of the tract. To secure capital, Graham and Steele approached two influential New Yorkers, Richard Schell,[82] a broker and "speculator" who was a heavy contributor to Democratic campaign funds, and John Mather, a member of the New York legislature. These four men formed a syndicate and purchased the 8,000 acres for $90,000, a price well below the estimated value of the land and one which did not reflect the competitive demand for the tract.[83] Henry M. Rice, Democratic "boss" of Minnesota, was interested in the sale and it was noted that Douglas ostentatiously denied that he had had any share in the transaction.[84]

After 1854 Illinois lands, previously so popular with Southerners, were in private hands and it was Iowa, Kansas, and Nebraska which attracted the most attention. The following tabulation of land sales shows the wide distribution of such investments in the South.[85]

---

the Christian Indian Tract," *Kansas Historical Quarterly*, VI (1937), 227 and *passim*.

[82] "The Covode Investigation," *House Reports*, 36 Cong., 1 Sess., Vol. V, no. 648, serial 1071, pp. 511–512.

[83] "Fort Snelling Investigation," *House Reports*, 35 Cong., 1 Sess., Vol. II, no. 351, serial 965, *passim*.

[84] Letter of Stephen A. Douglas, Aug. 29, 1857, in Chicago *Times*, copied in Washington *National Intelligencer*, Sept. 4, 1857. Douglas' denial of interest in the Fort Snelling sale may have been correct, but the letter is a shifty effort to skirt the truth as closely as possible. For the later history of this scandalous sale see Theodore C. Blegen, *Minnesota: A History of the State* (Minneapolis, 1963), 178–180.

[85] Compiled from abstracts in the National Archives. Unless otherwise indicated the districts are in Iowa.

Name	Residence	Land district	Acres
Boulden, Jesse H.	Bourbon Co., Ala.	Ft. Dodge	1,148
Branner, John	Jefferson Co., Tenn.	Des Moines	11,752
Burson, Zachariah L.	Washington, Tenn.	Des Moines, Sioux City	1,904
Clark, Thomas	Orleans Parish, La.	Osage	4,382
Curry, George W.	Monroe Co., Va.	Council Bluffs, Sioux City	1,480
Drexel, Frederick	Taylor Co., Va.	Council Bluffs	1,120
Fain, Samuel N.	Jefferson Co., Tenn.	Fairfield	9,916
Ford, John R.	Danville, Ky.	Ft. Dodge, Des Moines	3,400
Fowler, Samuel	New Orleans, La.	Chariton	20,661
Irwin, G., & T.	Baltimore, Md.	Ft. Dodge	4,564
Lash, Israel G., Jr.	Forsyth Co., N.C.	Des Moines	4,564
Lowd, William W.	Orleans Parish, La.	Council Bluffs	1,690
Lungren, Samuel S.	Washington Co., Md.	Des Moines	2,680
Lushbaugh, Benjamin F.	Washington Co., Md.	Osage	5,143
McCown, Andrew R.	Hancock Co., Va.	Council Bluffs	1,460
Maxwell, Harvey G.	Tuscaloosa, Ala.	Ft. Dodge	1,440
Merrill, Harvey G.	Orleans Parish, La.	Council Bluffs	8,120
Orr, Charles C.	Orleans Parish, La.	Sioux City & Dakota City, Neb. Terr.	5,134
Pace, Jerman	Pittsylvania Co., Va.	Council Bluffs	2,531
Peters, Stephen F.	Campbell Co., Va.	Council Bluffs	6,600
Pratt, William H.	Mobile, Ala.	Council Bluffs	4,890
Rawson, William A.	Stewart Co., Ga.	Sioux City	2,744
Rieman, A., & J.	Baltimore, Md.	Ft. Dodge	4,120
Walton, Simon H.	Mason Co., Ky.	Des Moines	3,320
Watkins, Isaac R.	Charlotte, Va.	Ft. Dodge	9,665
Wilkinson, James W.	Charleston, S.C.	Ft. Dodge	3,518
Wolfinger, Michael	Washington Co., Md.	Des Moines	2,000
Wormald, James	Mason Co., Ky.	Chariton	2,880

The panic of 1857 and the sharp fall of agricultural prices caused scarcity of money in the West, and squatters, faced with auction sales of their claims if they did not pre-empt them, were forced to seek outside assistance at frontier interest rates. The squatters and newspapers friendly to them clamored for the postponement of the land sales.[86] Unfortunately, the

[86] Strongly divergent views were invariably expressed by westerners when the government was preparing to bring public lands into market. Generally opposed to sales were the squatters, frontier newspapers, and local politicians

depression produced a government deficit, and the Buchanan administration could scarcely afford to relinquish the anticipated revenue from the sale of lands. Perhaps also the Democratic leaders recognized that the cheap land sections of the West, especially Iowa, Kansas, Nebraska, Wisconsin, and Minnesota, were lost to their party, and that they could therefore disregard the piteous appeals for postponement. There was ordered to be sold in the depression years an area equivalent to Missouri and most of this land was located in states or territories already controlled by the Republicans. The "loan sharks" again put in their appearance at these sales, and some of the southerners who entered large tracts in the years 1858–1860 were employing their funds in this way. Perhaps they may have been influential in preventing postponement of the sales in order that they might be able to lend their funds to needy squatters.

This was the period when Shorter, Slidell, Belmont, Taylor, and Walker made most of their purchases. Other southerners of note also made investments in the last years before secession. James Calloway of Wilkes County, North Carolina, entered some 6,880 acres at the bitterly opposed sale at Lecompton, Kansas, in 1859 and 1860. In the spring and summer of 1858,

---

who deplored the advantages which the sales would give to the "loan sharks"; favorable were the more ardent of the "booster" element (except in a depression as the years following 1857), the local capitalists and land speculators as well as those influential easterners who were seeking opportunities for lucrative investments. The government was betwixt the devil and the deep blue sea, since it needed the revenue from the sales but feared the resentment of the squatters. When the opposition became too strong, sales were sometimes postponed. After 1854 there was an added incentive to have the lands brought on the market as under the Graduation Act their price automatically declined after they had been subject to sale ten years. A careful study is needed of the question of holding or postponing land sales as it was of vital importance to the squatters and others interested. Jacob Thompson, secretary of the interior, gives some attention to the problem in his *Annual Report* for 1860, p. 4. For further detail on efforts to secure postponement of land sales see Paul W. Gates, *Fifty Million Acres: Conflicts over Kansas Land Policy, 1854–1890* (Ithaca, N.Y., 1954), 72–105, and *History of Public Land Law Development* (Washington, 1968), 145–148.

four Virginians, William Hurley of Henrico County, Michael Hurley of Norfolk County, Jerman W. Pace of Pittsylvania County, and Edwin G. Halsey of Campbell County, entered in western Iowa 11,500, 5,760, 2,500, and 1,760 acres respectively. One other most elusive person Solomn Tifft of Jackson, Mississippi, listed in the Mississippi census of 1852 as an attorney having property valued at $500,[87] entered between October, 1859 and September, 1860 a total of 27,480 acres in eastern Nebraska. So much southern capital was invested in Kansas in the short period from 1854 to 1861 that Senator James H. Lane was moved to lament in 1862, "We have in Kansas a larger proportion of rebel property than any other state in this Union." [88]

It thus appears than many southern planters, bankers, shippers, lawyers, politicians, and others invested in lands in the northwestern states in the ante-bellum years. Every slave state east of the Mississippi was represented as was also Texas. So popular did northern land investments become in the South that land agents in Minnesota and elsewhere advertised in southern papers, "Land investments made for Southern and Eastern capitalists that will net forty and sixty percent per annum." [89] The author's tabulation, by no means complete, of the southern purchases of government land of 1,000 acres or more in the northwestern states shows a total in excess of 1,500,000 acres.[90]

[87] Census data furnished by Miss Mary E. Cameron.

[88] *Cong. Globe*, 37 Cong., 2 Sess., 3379 (July 16, 1862).

[89] Advertisement of Tracy and Farnham, in Washington *National Intelligencer*, Sept. 19, 1854.

[90] The entry books of all the states of the Old Northwest, Minnesota, Iowa, Kansas, and Nebraska were examined. An effort was made to take account of all land entries of more than one thousand acres but where the entries of individuals were widely scattered it was difficult to compile them. Examples are the entries of Miles and Elias White. They are scattered over many dozen huge folio volumes and are not massed together as are those of Cabell, Slidell, and Belmont. The first examination missed the White entries and only after the name was encountered in practically every Iowa abstract volume for the years 1850 to 1860 was it found desirable to go over the ground again and collect their entries. It is certain that other southerners whose entries were encountered

There is also evidence that other southerners were purchasing lands in the North, not from the federal government but from other sources. For example, Dr. Stephen Duncan of Natchez, "a 4,000 bale planter and the owner of 500 negroes," was accused, with other large planters of investing "great amounts" in land and securities in the North or "elsewhere out of the South." [91] Joshua B. Leavens of Mobile, Alabama, claimed ownership of 28,000 acres in the Military Tract of Illinois in 1838.[92] The famous Kentucky divine, Robert J. Breckinridge of Danville, owned in Iowa in 1857 a full section of 640 acres assessed at $3,840; in 1858 he bought in Illinois in partnership with a nephew 320 acres for $4,000.[93] A very substantial purchase, the facts of which were found in the deed records of Champaign County, Illinois, was made by a group of wealthy residents of Shelby County, Kentucky. William M. King, the Harbisons— William, William Scott, John, Baxter D., and George L.— Francis J. Peters, and others bought 12,755 acres in Champaign and Piatt counties, Illinois, for a total of $76,535. Baxter Har-

---

less frequently but were equally scattered would be missed in such a study. The very volume of the material precluded a more complete analysis. Another cause of understatement of the amount of southern entries in the Northwest is the fact that the names of persons who located lands with military warrants as found in the warrant abstracts are not accompanied by the addresses of the locators. If there was excess payment upon the tract occasioned by its acreage being larger than the amount of the warrant, the warrantee's or the assignee's name would appear in the cash abstract which always gives the address. In as much as a large part of the speculative entries after 1847 were made with warrants, it will be appreciated how much this factor may have minimized the figure of southern entries.

[91] Percy L. Rainwater, *Mississippi: Storm Center of Secession, 1856–1861* (Baton Rouge, 1938), 140–141; Dunbar Rowland, *Encyclopedia of Mississippi History* (2 vols.; Madison, Wis., 1907), I, 666.

[92] Advertisement in Quincy (Illinois) *Argus*, Dec. 1, 1838, mentioning 28,000 acres of military bounty lands owned by Joshua B. Leavens of Mobile, Alabama, and cautioning people against buying them because of estate difficulties.

[93] Oliver Cock to Rev. R. J. Breckinridge, Burlington, Iowa, Dec. 17, 1857; S. M. Breckinridge to *idem*, St. Louis, April 5, 1858, Breckinridge MSS.

bison moved to Champaign County where he managed the sale of a part of this large holding for the others who remained in their native state.[94] A careful examination of the deed records of other counties in the northwestern states would doubtless show the investment of additional southern capital.

City property in the northwestern states also attracted a substantial amount of southern capital. Outstanding among such investments are those of John C. Breckinridge, Hunter, Corcoran, Boyce, and Aiken in Superior; Breckinridge in Prairie du Chien and Burlington;[95] Buford, Fant, and Corcoran in Leavenworth; Smithson and Easley in Elwood and White Cloud, Kansas; Walker, Smithson, and Loose in Chicago; J. B. Danforth and Charles H. Lewis of Jefferson County, Kentucky, in Springfield; Breckinridge and Graham in St. Paul; Easley in Council Bluffs; and Francis L. and Robert W. Smith[96] of Alexandria, Virginia, in Sioux City. Mention might also be made of the Baltimore Western Land Company which advertised city lots in Bloomington, Iowa, in 1843, and of the part played by William Stokes of Louisville and H. W. Varnton of Georgetown, in the promotion of Mound City, Illinois, in 1860.[97]

The rekindling of the old fires of sectional hatred did not end but, instead, seemed to accelerate the flow of southern capital into the North. After the adoption of the Kansas-Nebraska Act, 800,000 acres of land in the states of the Upper Mississippi Valley were bought by southerners. Even the financial crash of

[94] In the deed records of Champaign County there are numerous conveyances between the various members of this group which show the division of the land and its subsequent resale. Baxter Harbison who with George received 3,320 acres, sold land to the amount of $134,492 between 1858 and 1902.

[95] The Breckinridge MSS. contain frequent allusions to investments in Superior, Prairie du Chien, Burlington, St. Paul, and elsewhere.

[96] Francis L. Smith to George W. Jones, Alexandria, Va., May 2, 1866, Jones MSS., Library of the Historical, Memorial and Art Department of Iowa, Des Moines.

[97] *Report of Jesse E. Peyton, Esq., to the Eastern Stockholders of the Emporium Real Estate and Manufacturing Company of Mound City* (Philadelphia, 1860).

1857 did not end the capital migration, for 170,000 acres were bought between 1858 and 1860 and some land was purchased by southerners just as the secession movement got under way. The quantity and comparative lateness of these purchases lends weight to the accusation brought against Dr. Duncan that he and other conservative unionists were investing their funds in the North where they would be remote from any possible danger zone.

Some of the land purchased by southerners was sold advantageously within a few months, but a much larger amount had to be carried for years, sometimes for a generation, before a satisfactory price could be secured. Meantime, interest, agents' fees, and the rapidly rising tax burden increased the original investment. It is impossible to estimate with any degree of accuracy the amount of southern capital which was invested in northern farming lands and city lots in the ante-bellum years, but one may give a minimum figure about which there should be little quibbling. An examination of the deed records of such prairie counties as Benton and White, Indiana, and Vermilion, McLean, Logan, Sangamon, and Christian, Illinois, reveals that large amounts of land owned by absentee speculators were being sold in the fifties for prices ranging from $5 to $15.50 per acre. Values of undeveloped land in Wisconsin, Iowa, and Nebraska would certainly be lower, but improved land before the panic would doubtless be considered worth $5 per acre. Most of the lands of the Whites, Easley and Willingham, and some other southerners were entered for squatters and therefore would have a higher valuation than raw land possessing no improvements. A conservative estimate of the value of the property owned by southerners in the Upper Mississippi Valley would be between $4,000,000 and $8,000,000. The probability is that the total amount would be greater, considering the city lot business and the small holdings which do not appear in the present estimates.

Absentee ownership of land, though found everywhere in the West, was not regarded favorably by the local residents, and these southern investments were destined to produce ill will and friction. The outbreak of the Civil War gave westerners an opportunity to fulminate against the southern speculators and to demand the confiscation of their lands. It irked many, as Mrs. Jane Gray Swisshelm reveals,[98] that Breckinridge and Slidell could participate in the rebellion without the government taking action to confiscate their Wisconsin and Minnesota property. An examination of the Congressional debates upon the confiscation bills in 1861 and 1862 shows that the investments of these two men were more generally known than those of any other Confederate or southern speculator and that several members of Congress were seeking to frame a bill which would enable the government to confiscate their possessions. Senator Lyman Trumbull was especially anxious to have the holdings of Slidell confiscated, and again and again he referred to them. On April 7, 1862, he said that he was "unwilling that rebel chiefs like Slidell and Mason who are said to be large landholders in the loyal States . . . should be permitted to enjoy the fruits of their estates situated within our jurisdiction." [99] Again on April 24 he expressed his fear that the bill under consideration would not strike at Slidell's property.[100] On May 6 he quoted from a constituent who mentioned additional northern lands owned by Slidell:

Five or six years ago, when attending the land sales at Danville in this State, I met an agent of John Slidell . . . who entered for him some forty thousand acres of land, and I learned that the next year he entered some thirty thousand acres in Iowa. Last week, when in

[98] Mrs. Swisshelm considered the Confiscation Act of 1862 deplorably weak, resenting especially the fact that confiscated property of persons participating in the rebellion might be recovered by their heirs. She writes feelingly of such Confederate leaders as Breckinridge who "holds" property in her adopted state of Minnesota and John Slidell whose "twenty-five thousand acres of Minnesota land is to be secured to him and heirs" (Arthur J. Larson, ed., *Crusader and Feminist: Letters of Jane Gray Swisshelm, 1858–1865* [St. Paul, 1934], 134 and *passim*). She apparently confused their Wisconsin property mentioned above.

[99] *Cong. Globe*, 37 Cong., 2 Sess., 1560 (April 7, 1862).

[100] *Ibid.*, 1813 (April 24, 1862).

St. Louis, I met this agent and he informed me that Slidell still owned these lands.[101]

Trumbull added, "there are a great many such instances all over the State of Illinois and all over the western States where these rebels hold real estate, for they have been making investments for years in our lands. Are we not to touch them?" Finally, on June 27 he complained that the Senate bill would not permit the government to touch the $100,000 worth of property which Slidell owned in Illinois.[102]

Similarly, Representative William Windom of Minnesota inveighed against "Breckinridge, Toombs, Slidell, and many others of the same class in the South, [who] own large tracts of land in my own State." He asked:

Do you think the people there will contentedly bear the burdens we impose on them when they see this property untouched by the government? When I return to my constituents, and they ask me why these lands were not confiscated, will they be quite satisfied with the answer, "I was afraid it would irritate and offend Messrs. Breckinridge, Toombs, & Co., and therefore I rolled the whole burden on you.[103]

Senator James R. Doolittle was also anxious to find a means of confiscating the "large amount of real estate" which Slidell owned "both in Illinois and in Wisconsin, as well as in Louisiana." [104] Representative Thomas D. Eliot of Massachusetts approved a bill to confiscate the "large estates owned by enemies in Michigan, Wisconsin, Illinois, Iowa and Missouri, the proceeds of which are made to support the leading rebels in the armies and government of the South." [105]

Professor Randall has shown how ineffectively the North enforced the confiscation laws during the Civil War.[106] He esti-

[101] *Ibid.*, 1959 (May 6, 1862).   [102] *Ibid.*, 2972 (June 27, 1862).
[103] *Ibid.*, 2244 (May 20, 1862).   [104] *Ibid.*, Part IV, Appendix, 140.
[105] *Ibid.*, 37 Cong., 2 Sess., 2357 (May 26, 1862).
[106] James G. Randall, *Constitutional Problems under Lincoln* (New York, 1926), 289–291. For further examination of the difficulties of applying con-

mates that the total returns from the sale of confiscated property under the acts of 1861 and 1862 were approximately $300,000, none of which came from the states of Wisconsin, Iowa, Minnesota, or Illinois. Confiscation proceedings could be avoided by transferring property to loyal citizens and by this means Slidell saved his investments in the North. Despite the bitter resentment against him, John C. Breckinridge did not suffer confiscation of his extensive investments, perhaps because they were held jointly with others whose loyalty was not in question. Some of his lands were sold for taxes, however.[107] Stokes, being a Unionist, was in no danger of losing his lands, and Walker, for the same reason, had nothing to fear for his northern possessions. He may, however, have suffered the loss of his southern property.

Easley and Willingham were Union supporters in 1860 and 1861 and opposed the action of their state in seceding. In May, 1861, they continued to hope that "the difficulties and disturbances now existing between the two sections of our glorious country may soon be settled without bloodshed; and the prosperity of our country may again be restored." [108] As late as May 20, 1861, they contemplated a trip to Iowa and Illinois but the outbreak of war forced its postponement.[109] Neither of the partners entered the Confederate service and both were pardoned by President Johnson on June 26, 1865.[110] Meantime,

---

fiscation to property of Confederates in the North see Henry D. Shapiro, *Confiscation of Confederate Property in the North*, Cornell Studies in American History, Literature, and Folklore, no. 7 (Ithaca, N.Y., 1962).

[107] E. A. C. Hatch to John C. Breckinridge, St. Paul, June 20, 1869; M. D. Browning to *idem*, Burlington, June 24, 1869; J. Landler to *idem*, Prairie du Chien, Sept. 15, 1869; S. T. Hillis to *idem*, Watson, Illinois, Sept. 27, 1870, Breckinridge MSS.

[108] Easley and Willingham to J. P. Casady, May 9, 1861, Letter Book, Easley MSS.

[109] James S. Easley to E. B. Stiles, May 20, 1861, *ibid.*

[110] Southerners possessing property worth over $20,000 were exempted from President Johnson's amnesty proclamation of May 29, 1865. See J. T. Dorris, "Pardon Seekers and Brokers: A Sequel to Appomattox," *Journal of Southern History*, I (1935), 276 ff. Easley and Willingham wrote of their pardon in a letter of October 26, 1865, to Col. John Scott, Letter Book, Easley MSS.

their land business in the northwestern states was neglected, collections ceased, taxes were unpaid, many tracts were sold for taxes, and federal attorneys took steps to confiscate their holdings. The Wisconsin lands were seized by the District Attorney and confiscation proceedings were pending in the Milwaukee court when the war ended.[111] The titles to many tracts had thus become deeply involved and it was years before they were cleared.

Unlike Easley and Willingham, Malhiot had no difficulty in continuing the management of his estates in Illinois and Louisiana, but it should be pointed out that his Louisiana plantation was within the Confederate lines for only a short period. Dr. Hamilton Griffith of Louisville, Kentucky, on the other hand, who had made a speculation in Kansas lands, was informed in 1867 that his property had been condemned by the federal court, but as no sale had been made, the condemnation might be set aside upon presentation of his pardon.[112] Meantime, taxes and penalties which were "pretty heavy" had accumulated against the property.[113] Other southerners who had difficulty in straightening out their land affairs were Francis and Robert Smith of Alexandria, Virginia, who, in 1866, wrote former Senator George W. Jones[114] of their "quite large" investment in Sioux City about which they were anxious, and William Hurley of Henrico County, who, in 1866, was in Iowa "trying to straighten up my affairs" concerning 12,000 acres of land bought in 1858.[115]

Of all the southern investors in northern lands, Corcoran was

[111] Joseph Harris to Easley and Willingham, Treasurers Office, Door County, Sturgeon Bay, Wis., Sept. 25, 1865; Easley and Willingham to Waldo Ody and Company, Dec. 6, 1865, Easley MSS.

[112] Professor Randall says, "There were many forfeitures in Kansas but no proceeds turned in" (*Constitutional Problems*, 290).

[113] Van Doren and Havens to Dr. Hamilton Griffith, Feb. 1, 1867, Letter Book of Van Doren and Havens, Kansas State Historical Society Library.

[114] Francis L. Smith to George W. Jones, Alexandria, Va., May 2, 1866, Jones MSS.

[115] William Hurley to James S. Easley, Sidney, Iowa, Nov. 3, 1868, Easley MSS.

in the most trying position at the outbreak of the war. He had been intimate with most of the officials in Washington for a generation before and had done many favors for Whigs, Democrats, Americans, and even Republicans. Nevertheless, he was closely identified with the southern Democrats and his sympathies were definitely with the South. But Corcoran's extensive property, then estimated at $3,000,000 to $4,000,000, was largely in Washington lots and in farming lands in the Northwest. Furthermore, many of his banking and business associates as well as political friends were northerners. At the outbreak of the war he was in a serious dilemma, not knowing what steps to take. He opposed the breakup of the Union and was deeply shocked at the fratricidal war. His position in Washington soon became intolerable because of the suspicion to which he was subject. He was accused of being a secessionist,[116] of contributing $30,000 to the Democratic campaign fund of 1862,[117] and of contributing to the cost of constructing cruiser *No. 290*, later the *Alabama*.[118] Despairing of fair treatment at the hands of the new forces in control in Washington and wearied by the constant clamor against him, Corcoran withdrew to Paris in 1862 where he remained for the duration of the war. Meantime, his art gallery was taken over by the government, which needed additional office space, his other Washington property was damaged by an outraged public or rabble, easily influenced by the clamor against him, and confiscation proceedings were brought against his lands in the North. Although not pressed to conclusion, these proceedings further confused titles to much of Corcoran's property and created great difficulties for him on his return to America after the conclusion of the war.

Despite their unfortunate experiences in the management of their lands during the Civil War, at least three prominent

---

[116] George Morey to Governor John A. Andrew, Nov. 21, 1861, *Official Records*, Ser. II, Vol. II, 165.

[117] New York *Herald*, Oct. 24, 1862; New York *Times*, Oct. 24, 1862.

[118] Hyde to Corcoran, Oct. 13, 1863, Corcoran MSS.

southern investors in northern lands expanded their investments in the North after 1865. Corcoran made a substantial investment in Oregon in 1870; Easley and Willingham invested many thousands of dollars in tax titles in Iowa in the postwar years,[119] and Miles and Elias White entered lands in Nebraska in 1868. Some of these investments were made to recoup earlier losses but in general they seemed to indicate a feeling that land values were more certain to rise in the North and that the investments would be more remunerative than in the South.

Robert P. Swierenga, in *Pioneers and Profits: Land Speculation on the Iowa Frontier* (Ames, Iowa, 1968), has a chapter on the most extensive investment by southerners (Easley and Willingham) in northern lands. Henry Cohen traces the investments of W. W. Corcoran for himself and some political cronies in northern land and town lots, in *Business and Politics in America from the Age of Jackson to the Civil War: The Career Biography of W. W. Corcoran* (Westport, Connecticut, 1971). Paul W. Gates examines the southern investments in Kansas, in "Land and Credit Problems in Underdeveloped Kansas," *Kansas Historical Quarterly*, XXXI (Spring, 1965), 41–61.

[119] It is interesting to note that James S. Easley did not concentrate his investments in northern lands so completely after the war as he had in the fifties. In 1870 he invested $17,000 in the Richmond and Danville Railroad.

4. *Land Policy and Tenancy in the Prairie Counties of Indiana*

The great prairie section of Indiana stretching from the Wabash to the Kankakee long challenged the attention of agricultural economists and social planners because of the high rate of farm tenancy, the large average size of farms, the declining population of the rural areas, the poor tenant homes that did not harmonize with the richness of the surrounding soil, and a type of farming which for two generations depleted the soil and reduced its fertility.

This section, a continuation of the Grand Prairie of Illinois, has had an agricultural history sharply different from that of southern Indiana. In three prairie counties, Benton, Newton, and White, more than half of the farms were operated by tenants in 1930, and in three others, Jasper, Warren, and Tippecanoe, over 40 percent were tenant operated. On the Illinois side of the Grand Prairie the rate of tenancy was even higher. Contrast this with the sixteen counties in southern Indiana which had less than 20 percent of their farms operated by tenants. The largest farms in Indiana were also to be found in the prairie counties. Two farms totalling over 17,000 acres were reported from Newton County, and Jasper and Newton each contained eleven other farms over 1,000 acres in size. In Benton and Newton Counties, the average size of farms was well over 200 acres, and, in White, Warren, and Jasper, it was over 160 acres. In few southern counties did the average size of farms exceed 125 acres. Furthermore, the tendency was toward larger farms in the prairie counties, while in the rest of the state it was in the other direction. Counties having the highest land values per acre had the largest farm units, and counties with low land values had on the average small farms. One may not be surprised, therefore, to note that the rural population of the richest counties in Indiana was declining more, in some cases, than the rural population of less wealthy counties.

Another striking fact concerns Benton County, the richest of the agricultural counties in proportion to its size. Despite its great agricultural wealth, the farmers of Benton County were not as well housed as were the farmers of eleven other Indiana counties which reported higher valuations of farm dwellings. One reason for the disparity is that these other counties have lower tenancy ratings than Benton, and the value of dwellings on owner-operated farms was generally higher than on tenant farms. Perhaps the residents of few areas of Indiana felt satisfied that their past farming policies had been based on proper soil conservation practices, but it was in the prairie counties that the greatest concern was felt. Here the soil had been depleted to an alarming degree, particularly on tenant operated farms, here the land had been tilled more consistently to grain production, and here, in the twentieth century, livestock had been somewhat neglected.[1]

A study of the early settlement of the prairie counties reveals that responsibility for the high degree of tenancy, the large farms, the declining population, the poor tenant homes, and the soil depletion is to be attributed in part to the operation of the land system in the nineteenth century.

Solon Robinson, writing in February, 1835, from his home in Lake County, Indiana, expressed the view that if the public lands of northwestern Indiana were not offered for public sale until 1836 and if pre-emption rights were granted by Congress, the area would be well taken up by settlers who would be able

[1] The statistics in this and the preceding paragraph are taken from the *Fifteenth Census of the United States* (1930), I–III.

to acquire ownership of their claims. This, said Robinson, "will prevent non-residents from obtaining large bodies of land; a circumstance which always injures the rapid growth of a country." [2] Robinson was over-optimistic as to the number of settlers who would be dwelling in that part of the state in 1836, but he was correct in calling attention to that feature of the national land policy to which many of the later land and agricultural problems owe their existence—the cash sale system.

The Land Ordinance of 1785 and subsequent laws had placed no restrictions upon the amount of public land that individuals or groups could acquire at the government offices, and it was not until after 1862 that any serious attempts were made to restrict land entries. The policy of unlimited sales and unrestricted transfer of titles made possible "land monopolization" by speculators, who acquired much of the choice lands in certain areas, notably in the Military Tract of Illinois, the prairie sections of Indiana and Illinois, and the timber areas of Michigan, Wisconsin and Minnesota. [3] This contributed to the early disappearance of cheap or free land and the emergence of tenancy. In Indiana the dead hand of the speculator created many problems which were to stunt the growth and waste the resources of some sections of the state. It is interesting to note that Robinson criticized nonresident owners, but did not raise his voice against resident speculators, with one of the largest of whom in Northern Indiana he had close business relations.

Unimproved lands and town lots were the chief items of speculation in the United States before the era of wide scale stock distribution. [4] In the nineteenth century, New England, the

[2] Herbert Anthony Kellar, ed., *Solon Robinson, Pioneer and Agriculturist*, Indiana Historical Collections, XXI–XXII (2 vols.; Indianapolis, 1936), I, 62.

[3] There is considerable detail on early land entries in Illinois, Michigan, Wisconsin, Minnesota, and Iowa, as well as Indiana, in Chapter 3, above, and in Paul Wallace Gates, "Disposal of the Public Domain in Illinois," *Journal of Economic and Business History*, III (Feb., 1931), 216–240; and *The Illinois Central Railroad and Its Colonization Work* (Cambridge, 1934).

[4] A. M. Sakolski, *The Great American Land Bubble* (New York, 1932), reveals the propensity of the American people to speculate in lands.

middle states, and the older southern states poured great sums of money into land investments in the new territories and states as they were opened to settlement. In the boom years 1835 to 1837 and again in 1847 to 1857 whole townships were swept into the control of absentee proprietors, and holdings of 5,000 and 10,000 acres were widely established while holdings of 50,000 to 100,000 acres were not unknown. The fertile state of Indiana naturally attracted the attention of nonresident capitalists and hundreds of thousands of acres of its lands were bought by people who had no intention of either settling upon or improving them.

It was in southern Indiana that the lands were first opened to entry and here they were generally taken up before the speculative boom of the middle eighteen-thirties got under way. This section was early overrun by squatters who settled promiscuously over the land before it was offered for sale, made improvements, and organized claim associations to provide a quasi-legal land and title registration system in the absence of government action. The claim association was also a mutual protective organization to assist its members against claim-jumpers or speculators who might try to seize or buy their homes.[5] Having settled, the squatters petitioned Congress to grant them pre-emption rights, and Congress, responsive to appeals from pioneer farmers, granted the coveted pre-emption privilege in a series of special acts. When squatters' appeals did not bring congressional action, the pioneers had another means of safeguarding their homes against outsiders who might attend the auction sale to buy the choice claims. This was to appear *en masse* at the sale and by intimidation or force prevent competitive bidding. Of course, the squatters had to purchase their lands at the minimum price of $1.25 per acre, and when they lacked the

[5] An early constitution of a claim association in Lake and Porter counties is that found in Kellar, *Solon Robinson*, I, 69–76. William Clark, presiding officer of the first meeting of this association and one of the three "arbitrators," was scarcely a typical impecunious frontiersman. He entered 11,039 acres, paying for some as high as three dollars an acre. He later became a county judge.

cash they had, perforce, to borrow from "loan sharks" at extortionate rates of interest—twenty-four and forty-eight percent—but they preserved their equity, at least temporarily. Thus squatters got title to their lands in southern Indiana, even though they took the law into their own hands to protect their "rights," and they made the land system more democratic in its operation than its framers intended.

True, there was some speculative purchasing of lands in southern Indiana. Among the larger purchases were those made by Josiah Lawrence, Lucius Barber and their associates who entered 22,000 acres,[6] Omer and George Tousey of Dearborn County who bought 16,000 acres, and Charles Butler, representing the American Land Company, one of the largest aggregations of capital in the eastern states, who purchased 9,000 acres.[7] New England capitalists were represented in this section by the Boston and Indiana Land Company whose local agent was Judge John Law of Vincennes.[8] Law and his New England associates bought 29,000 acres of land located near the canal connecting Evansville and Terre Haute. In addition Judge Law sold to

[6] The details of land entries were compiled from the original cash and warrant entry books formerly in the General Land Office, Department of the Interior, but now in the National Archives, and from plat books and deed records of the counties concerned.

[7] It was this Charles Butler who was later to induce the state of Indiana to compromise with the bondholders of the Wabash and Lake Erie Canal. His associate, Frederick Bronson, likewise a member of the American Land Company, bought a large tract of land in northern Indiana, as will be seen below (G. L. Prentice, *The Union Theological Seminary in the City of New York: Its Design . . . with a Sketch of the Life and Public Services of Charles Butler, LL.D.* [Asbury Park, N.J., 1899], 427–531).

[8] Judge Law believed the Wabash Valley to be the "richest country on the face of the globe" and maintained, in 1835, that Toledo, at the northern end of the Wabash Canal and not Chicago, was destined to be the "great outlet from the lakes to the Ohio and Mississippi Rivers." The other major points in Indiana and Illinois for which he predicted rapid growth were Lafayette, Evansville and Alton (fragment of letter of John Law to his brother William, Vincennes, Aug. 19, 1835, in *Indiana Magazine of History* [March, 1928], XXIV, 52–54; William Wesley Woollen, *Biographical and Historical Sketches of Early Indiana* [Indianapolis, 1883], 332–334).

the Company his interest in the town of Lamasco which he and
Judge W. Call and Lucius M. Scott had laid out on the Ohio
River. For years thereafter the Boston and Indiana Land Company was engaged in advertising its lands for sale through newspapers and by pamphlets distributed in the East.[9] Other large
land purchases made in southern Indiana were:

Name	Entered	Acres
Blanding, Abram, & Douglas, James J.	1836	4,500
Borden, John	1848	5,120
Breed, Rufus	1849	7,680
Dunn, George H.	1836	1,520
Hobart, James T.	1837	2,600
Hutchins, Eusebius	1847	3,200
Johnston, William K.; Springer, David; & Fate, William	1848	2,400
Leland, A. W.	1836	3,580

Despite these sales, the total amount of speculative purchases in
southern Indiana was small when compared with that in northern Indiana. It was neither large enough to retard seriously the
development of the area nor to produce in the same degree the
agricultural problems which characterize the northern section.

In central Indiana there was even less large-scale speculative
purchasing than in the south. Here most of the land passed
directly from the government to actual settlers.

The land system worked the least satisfactorily in northern
Indiana, especially in the prairie counties. Here the speculators,

[9] The lands were entered in the names of William Sullivan, George Pratt,
and George W. Thatcher, all of Boston. James W. Seaver, also of Boston, was
one of the leaders of the enterprise. Seaver was also interested in the Boston
and Western Land Company whose investments were in central and northern
Illinois and southern Wisconsin, and he bought lands with Henry L. Ellsworth
in the upper Wabash Valley (James W. Seaver to William S. Russell, Boston,
Aug. 25, 1838, Boston and Western Land Company, letter book I, Woodman
MSS. (Wisconsin Historical Society). The Boston and Indiana Land Company
published an advertising folder of its lands, dated August 14, 1843, *Boston
and Indiana Land Company*, a copy of which is in the Indiana State Library.
For a newspaper advertisement of the lands see the Washington *National
Intelligencer*, March 19, 1844.

both absentee and resident, acquired enormous tracts of land before the actual settlers appeared and when the immigrants began to come into the country they found that the lands had long since passed into private hands and could only be acquired at high prices. An area which from the outset had labored under numerous handicaps to its settlement had now added to them the retarding effect of large speculators' holdings.

From the first appearance of the white men in Indiana the prairies were regarded with disfavor and were slow to attract settlers. Their streams were sluggish, meandering and difficult of navigation; their soil was suspected of being infertile; their lack of forest cover gave them no protection against the wintry blasts and greatly increased the costs of building, fencing and fuel; their low relief and poor drainage made parts of them difficult to cultivate until they were drained, and the constant existence of surface water that was used for drinking purposes produced fevers, chills and other bodily disturbances which were attributed to the unhealthy nature of the prairies. The unfavorable character given to this section by some early writers likewise proved a handicap to the settlement of the region. As Richard Power has well shown,[10] immigrants preferred to go farther west in their search for land rather than to settle in an area in such disrepute. Central Illinois and even far off Iowa and Minnesota drew settlers while such prairie counties as Benton, Newton, Jasper and parts of White, Tippecanoe, and Warren were almost completely avoided. But if actual settlers disdained the prairies, one man from Connecticut had an almost sublime faith in them from his first visit—Henry L. Ellsworth.[11]

[10] Richard Power, "Wet Lands and the Hoosier Stereotype," *Mississippi Valley Historical Review* (June, 1935), XXII, 33–48.

[11] Although outstanding in American agricultural history Ellsworth has not received the attention that his importance would seem to warrant. There are good short sketches in the following: *National Intelligencer*, January 1, 1859; Elmore Barce *et al.*, *History of Benton County, Indiana* (2 vols.; Fowler, Ind., 1930–1932), II, 116 ff.; Elmore Barce, *Annals of Benton County* (Fowler, 1925), *passim*; *Dictionary of American Biography*, VI, 110–111.

The Ellsworths of Connecticut rank with the Adamses of Massachusetts in the number of statesmen, governors, senators, diplomats and jurists they have produced. After graduating from Yale, Henry L. Ellsworth became a lawyer, an insurance company executive, a farmer, secretary of the Hartford County Agricultural Society, and mayor of Hartford. In 1832 he came to the attention of Andrew Jackson who appointed him a member of a commission to visit the Indian country to pacify the warring tribes. In the next two years he travelled extensively in present Oklahoma, Kansas, and Nebraska, closely observing the soil and farming possibilities of different areas, and keeping comprehensive notes of his observations.[12] His journal [13] reveals him to be a critical and highly interested observer. It is true his opinion of the Kansas country seems strange to us now. He noted with disfavor the "scarcity of timber for fences, firewood and buildings," and concluded that on this account much of the land would never be suitable for farming.[14] One is the more surprised, therefore, to find him selecting the treeless prairie section of Indiana for a field for investment and permanent location. It is probable that on one of his trips to or from the Indian country, Ellsworth first viewed the Wabash Valley. He was enormously impressed with the rich prairie lands of Benton, Tippecanoe, Warren, and White Counties and decided to invest his own capital there and to persuade his friends to do likewise.

[12] Washington Irving and Charles J. Latrobe accompanied Ellsworth on his first trip to the Indian country and both wrote their accounts of the expedition, as follows: Irving, *A Tour on the Prairie*, in the *Crayon Miscellany*, Holly edition (New York, 1895); Latrobe, *The Rambler in North America* (New York, 1835).

[13] Stanley T. Williams and Barbara D. Simison, eds., *Washington Irving on the Prairie, or a Narrative of a Tour of the Southwest in the Year 1832 by Henry Leavitt Ellsworth* (New York, 1937). See also the Report of the Commissioners, M. Stokes, Henry L. Ellsworth, and J. T. Schermerhorn, Fort Gibson, Feb. 10, 1834, *House Reports*, 23 Cong., 1 Sess., Vol. IV, serial 263, no. 474, pp. 78–131.

[14] Letter of Henry L. Ellsworth to Lewis Cass, Washington, May 13, 1834, *loc. cit.*, 76.

In 1835 Ellsworth became commissioner of patents, an attractive position which enabled him to witness all the important mechanical progress that was being made in the country. He was especially interested in farm machinery such as ditching machines, steam plows, and fencing devices. But more than anything else he wished to make this bureau an agency which would aid the farmers as well as industry. He felt, perhaps rightly:

> For commerce and manufactures, much has been done; for agriculture . . . much remains to be done. Husbandry seems to be viewed as a natural blessing, that needs no aid from legislation. Like the air we breathe, and the element of water, which sustain life, the productions of the soil are regarded by too many as common bounties of Providence, to be gratefully enjoyed, but without further thought or reflection.[15]

Ellsworth urged Congress to establish an agricultural museum, recommended that a part of the Smithson bequest be used for vocational education for farmers, and requested that funds be provided for the collection and dissemination of information on agricultural practices at home and abroad.[16] The beginning of an annual publication on agriculture by the Patent Office and the free distribution of seeds resulted from his efforts and entitle him to be called the "father of the United States Department of Agriculture." [17]

Ellsworth was no swivel-chair farmer, nor did he undertake a mere speculation in lands. He was confident that the prairies of Indiana and Illinois would be dotted with prosperous settlements in a few years time and he became the great advocate of prairie farming. The prestige of his official position as commissioner of patents and the *entrée* he had to farm journals enabled him to give wide publicity to his ideas. Ellsworth's tremendous enthusiasm for the prairie induced him to abandon his ancestral

---

[15] Commissioner of Patents, *Annual Report*, 1837, *House Documents*, 25 Cong., 2 Sess., Vol. V, serial 325, no. 112, pp. 4–5.

[16] See the *Annual Reports* of the Commissioner of Patents for 1837 to 1844.

[17] *Dictionary of American Biography*, VI, 110–111.

home in Connecticut and to throw in his lot with the Hoosiers.
During the thirties when credit was easy and land speculation
was at its height, numerous eastern and southern capitalists
bought large tracts of land in the western states which they tried
to develop into great estates operated by numerous tenants paying rent to the landlord. Daniel Webster,[18] the Wadsworths of
New York,[19] Thomas Ludwell Lee Brent of Virginia,[20] and
Romulus Riggs of Philadelphia [21] are among those who bought
large tracts for such a purpose. Ellsworth had a similar plan in
mind but, unlike some of the others, he moved into the area
which he proposed to develop and gave it his personal attention.

It was the Grand Prairie of Indiana and Illinois that most
attracted Ellsworth as a field for investment, and he centered

[18] Webster and Thomas H. Perkins of Boston bought large tracts in Ohio,
Michigan, Wisconsin and northern Indiana but it was in the valley of the
Illinois River near Peru, Illinois, that the former planned his estate. Here on
a tract of 1,000 acres he proposed to erect substantial buildings for his son,
Fletcher, and his manager, N. Ray Thomas, and to build fences, and stock the
farm with the best blooded cattle available. Large sums were spent on the
farm between 1836 and 1840 but the venture was not a financial success and
was abandoned. For correspondence concerning the farming operations see the
letters of N. Ray Thomas and Fletcher Webster to Daniel Webster, 1836–
1840, in the Webster MSS., New Hampshire Historical Society.

[19] James and William Wadsworth of Livingston County, New York, entered
46,000 acres in Ohio and Michigan. Henry Greenleaf Pearson, *James S.
Wadsworth of Geneseo* (New York, 1913), has little on the western land
venture.

[20] Brent was a clerk in the State Department in 1811 and in the diplomatic
service from 1814 to 1834. In 1836 he is reported to have purchased 70,000
acres of land in Genesee and Saginaw Counties, Michigan. Here he cleared a
large tract for improvements but died before he could accomplish his objectives. For an account of "Thomas L. L. Brent," by Judge Albert Miller,
see the Michigan Pioneer and Historical Society, *Collections*, IX (Lansing,
1886), 192–196.

[21] Romulus Riggs, brother of Elisha Riggs, the New York banker, acquired
title to 40,000 acres in the Military Tract of Illinois. He planned to sell
16,000 acres as their value rose, and to retain the other 24,000 acres for his
children. The reserved lands were to be leased for five years at low rents and
the latter were to be doubled at the end of that time and again in ten years.
See letter of Romulus Riggs to Elisha Riggs, June 19, 1845, Riggs MSS.,
Library of Congress.

his attention on that portion embracing Benton and Tippecanoe Counties, Indiana, and Vermilion and Iroquois Counties, Illinois. This area, he believed, had "the best soil and the most favorable climate." [22] He began buying land in June, 1835, when he visited the Danville, Fort Wayne, and Crawfordsville land offices and entered 18,000 acres, 10,000 of which were in Tippecanoe County. He chose the city of Lafayette for his home and made a substantial investment in lots and improvements there.[23]

Ellsworth began to farm his extensive holdings in Tippecanoe in 1836.[24] Laborers were employed to make improvements and they, in turn, were encouraged to become tenants upon the improved sections. There was a ready demand in the southern states for hay, which became Ellsworth's first commercial crop. Like most prairie residents, he plunged into the cattle and hog business in a large way, but prairie cultivation interested him more than livestock production. Here he found exercise for his ingenious and fertile Yankee mind. Before part of the prairie could be cultivated it had to be drained, and Ellsworth tinkered with various ditching devices, one of which combined ditching and fencing. This machine was designed to provide cheaply for two of the most expensive requirements of prairie farming. He was also fascinated by the new improvements which were being made in the plow in an effort to adapt it to prairies. The first plowing of the tough prairie sod was an expensive operation as

[22] Letter of H. L. Ellsworth, Jan. 1, 1837, to Henry William Ellsworth, in the latter's *Valley of the Upper Wabash, Indiana* (New York, 1838), 163.

[23] Indianapolis *Indiana Democrat*, June 29, 1835, quoting the Lafayette *Wabash Mercury;* Lafayette *Journal,* Nov. 13, 1854.

[24] His son Edward, was placed in charge of the work since Henry L. Ellsworth, despite his unbounded enthusiasm for the prairie, was not prepared as yet to give up his position in the Patent Office where he believed he could do much to advertise the prairies. Ellsworth resigned as commissioner of patents in 1845 and settled in Lafayette where he undertook the personal supervision of his vast estate (letter of Ellsworth to his successor, Edmund Burke, Jan. 1, 1836, Commissioner of Patents, *Annual Report* [1845], 380; Barce, *Annals,* 55).

it took a special kind of plow which had to be drawn by three or four yoke of oxen. Only a few pioneer farmers could afford to buy or hire such equipment, but on a large farm the cost per acre of breaking the sod was of course considerably reduced, and Ellsworth found his cost of prairie breaking much less than he had anticipated. When the steam plow was introduced in the fifties he was as delighted as a child with a new toy, and he was a firm believer in its future importance. Large scale operations and the use of machinery for seeding, cultivating, and harvesting further reduced Ellsworth's costs of production and convinced him for a time that the prairie could be inexpensively cultivated and at large profits, but better in large farms units than in small ones.[25]

Ellsworth wavered in his judgment as to the relative advantages of prairie cultivation and cattle raising. In 1837 he advised absentee proprietors to cultivate their lands through tenants and hired labor and held out to them hopes of high returns on their investments.[26] Four years later, he discovered that prairie cultivation required too large an investment of capital for fencing, plowing, and labor and he urged the nonresident owners to graze cattle on their holdings. They could get $1 to $2 per acre for pasturing cattle; at this rate, he estimated their land would be worth from $16 to $50 per acre.[27] In 1846, Ellsworth's faith in grain-raising in the Wabash Valley was revived and he wrote a glowing description of it which appeared in the *Annual Report* of the Commissioner of Patents.[28] A year later, however, after a bad grain season, he wrote:

[25] Barce *et al.*, *History of Benton County*, II, 131–135, prints some exceedingly optimistic descriptions of Ellsworth's farming operations which are taken from Ellsworth's circulars and letters.

[26] Letter of H. L. Ellsworth, Jan. 1837, in H. W. Ellsworth, *Valley of the Upper Wabash*, 166.

[27] Henry L. Ellsworth, *Letter to Elizur Goodrich, Hartford, Conn.* (Washington, 1841). This was intended as Appendix II to H. W. Ellsworth, *Valley of the Upper Wabash*.

[28] Commissioner of Patents, *Annual Report*, 1845, 380–389.

I am satisfied that stock raising at the west is much more profitable than growing small grain. . . . The profits of wheat appear well in expectation on papers, but this prospect is blasted by a severe winter, appearance of insects, a want of harvesting, bad weather in harvesting, in threshing . . . and lastly, a fluctuation of the market itself.

That Ellsworth had a foreboding of evils to come is seen by the following quotation: "Constant cropping of corn and small grain carried from the field will . . . diminish gradually, at least, the fertility, and the farm is at length worn out. On the contrary, by feeding the crop on the land, the farm *every year grows better.*" [29] Had Ellsworth's advice been followed, the soil qualities of the prairie section might have been less seriously depleted in later years.

The panic of 1837 forced the contraction of Ellsworth's plans for a time, but by the middle forties, when business conditions were improving, he began to plunge more deeply into the purchase of land. At the Crawfordsville land office between 1847 and 1852 he entered 73,500 acres largely with military land warrants which he could buy from $.65 to $$1.10 per acre.

Ellsworth wished to attract both capital and settlers to the prairies. He reasoned that each additional investment, whether by absentee proprietors or by settlers, would make the prairies better known and further their development. To call attention to the prairie country he prepared a booklet with the title *Valley of the Upper Wabash, Indiana, with hints on its agricultural advantages: Plan of a dwelling, estimates of cultivation and notices of labor saving machines,* which was published in 1838. Restrained in tone in comparison with some of the contemporary guide books, the work cannot be considered too optimistic in its description of the prairies. True, the cost of fencing is understated and the probable profits from prairie farming are equally overestimated. Also, too much space is devoted to discussions of

[29] Commissioner of Patents, *Annual Report,* 1847, 538.

the cultivation of flax, sugar beets, tobacco, and hemp and not enough to problems of pioneer life on the prairies. Nor is the description of the Wabash Valley as well done and as valuable for the historian as are Peck's and Mitchell's guides to Illinois.[30] One is also troubled by the numerous references to large-scale farming and the inadequate attention given to the needs and problems of the average settler.[31] But, after all, the book was written not so much for them as for men of capital. It is obviously the work of Henry L. Ellsworth, whose hand is seen on practically every page, although Henry William Ellsworth, his son, appears as the author on the title page.[32] Included in the book is a letter of the former, written on January 1, 1837, and apparently first published in the Sangamo *Journal* of Illinois. It was also published in S. A. Mitchell, *Illinois in 1837,* and in A. D. Jones, *Illinois and the West.* The following quotation from this letter shows Ellsworth's unbounded enthusiasm for the prairies:

If it be asked, what are the profits of cultivation? I answer, if the land is rented for five years, the profits accruing during this period will repay the capital advanced in the commencement, with 25 per cent. interest per annum, and leave the farm worth $20 per acre at the expiration of the lease. Probably the profit would be much greater.[33]

[30] J. M. Peck, *A Gazetteer of Illinois* . . . (Jacksonville, 1834); [S. A. Mitchell], *Illinois in 1837* . . . (Philadelphia, 1837).

[31] The *Genesee Farmer,* of Rochester, New York, which might be expected to be unfriendly to such a book, wrote about it as follows: "Mr. Ellsworth has drawn his picture of that section [Northern Indiana] . . . in strong and bright colors, but perhaps not stronger than facts would fully justify. . . . We cordially recommend it to the notice of emigrants to the Mississippi Valley" (VIII [Dec., 1838], 394). For a local puff see Lafayette *Indiana Eagle,* January 16, 1839. The editor of the Logansport *Telegraph,* October 20, 1838, while admitting that he had not seen the book said: "It has been suggested that there are some grounds for doubting its impartiality."

[32] Henry L. Ellsworth was commissioner of patents at the time the book appeared and it would have been inexpedient, to say the least, to permit his name to appear as the author.

[33] Ellsworth, *Valley of the Upper Wabash,* 167.

The book announced the formation of a partnership between John Curtis and Henry W. Ellsworth and advertised the purpose of the new firm as follows:

They propose to purchase of Government and individuals, lands in Indiana and Illinois, for such persons as are desirous to make investments, and to take charge of the same, or of *other lands* already purchased; pay taxes, and, when requested, to put lands into cultivation, and generally to promote, in the best possible manner, the interests of their employers.

The undersigned will take capital to invest in new lands, and allow the capitalist the legal title and a deduction of 8 or 10 per cent. interest, and divide the extra profits, which, it is confidently believed, will not be less than 25 per cent more.[34]

One of the first persons whom Ellsworth induced to make an investment in the Wabash Valley was William J. Grayson of Charleston, South Carolina. Grayson was an eminent literary figure and a successful politician. He served in Congress for two terms and while in Washington he met Ellsworth. In 1836 Grayson entered into a partnership with Ellsworth for an investment in Indiana lands. Grayson was to furnish $10,000 for the purchase of lands, was to pay taxes and to pay for such improvements as were jointly deemed advisable; Ellsworth was to manage the lands and to share equally in the profits after deduction of all costs plus 6 percent interest on the investment.[35] This type of contract was used by Ellsworth with some variations in his land deals with dozens of eastern and southern people who were persuaded to invest their savings in prairie lands.

Southerners from Maryland, Washington and even from Texas invested with Ellsworth in Indiana and Illinois lands. Two Baltimore capitalists, Ramsay McHenry and James McHenry Boyd, furnished $20,000,[36] and the Washington banking

[34] *Ibid.*, 173–175.

[35] The agreement is registered in the White County Deed Records, E, 23; and in the Benton County Records, 2.

[36] Benton County Deed Records, 2.

firm of Pairo and Nourse, which had large land holdings in seven western states and territories, bought 11,000 acres through Ellsworth, in Benton County.[37]

Most interesting of the absentee investors who were attracted to Indiana lands were the members of the "Yale Crowd," so-called by the local abstractors and attorneys of Benton County. Ellsworth, a faithful alumnus of Yale, had intermarried with the Goodrich family and had close relations with the Chauncey family, both almost as well known in Connecticut as the Ellsworths, and likewise loyal sons of Yale. Six of the members of these families with associates bought 95,000 acres in Indiana and Illinois, of which 45,000 were in the Wabash Valley. Elizur and Chauncey Goodrich bought 5,340 and 3,960 acres respectively in the Crawfordsville, Fort Wayne and Danville districts. Elihu and Nathaniel Chauncey invested $40,000 with Ellsworth in lands, acquiring thereby 16,500 acres in Indiana and 5,720 in Illinois, together with a valuable farm near Lafayette which was intended as an addition to the city.[38] Isaac Chauncey and Peter Schermerhorn of New York entered 5,800 acres at Crawfordsville and 7,000 acres at Danville. Other Connecticut Yankees who invested in prairie lands through Ellsworth were Robert and David Watkinson, who bought 9,500 acres. Noah Webster, and dozens of others, who entered from 40 to 2,000 acres.[39]

[37] Compiled from abstracts of land entries, Crawfordsville Land Office, National Archives, Washington, and the Benton County Deed Records.

[38] White County Deed Records, F, 573. Elihu, Nathaniel and Isaac Chauncey are given considerable attention in William Chauncey Fowler, *Memorials of the Chaunceys, including President Chauncey, His Ancestors and Descendants* (Boston, 1858), *passim; The Dictionary of American Biography*, IV, 40–41, has a sketch of Isaac Chauncey. For a sketch of Chauncey Allen Goodrich, see William L. Kingsley, *Yale College: A Sketch of Its History* (New York, 1879), 47–50.

[39] The Deed Records of White and Benton Counties, Indiana, and Vermilion County, Illinois, contain innumerable conveyances to and from the members of the "Yale Crowd." The conveyances, as above noted, frequently contain the details of the agreements made with Ellsworth.

To the Benton County lawyers, all Yankees who invested in lands through Ellsworth were members of the "Yale Crowd." Thus Joseph S. Cabot and James W. Seaver, of Boston, more properly associated with Harvard, who bought 7,600 and 3,300 acres respectively, are included. Another purchase made with Ellsworth was by Jeremiah Fowler, a downeaster from Lubec, Maine, who provided money for the purchase of 1996 acres. Mention should also be made of John Thompson of New York who entered 26,000 acres at Crawfordsville and Winamac. All the lands that were entered in combination with Ellsworth were managed by him until his death.

In 1857 Ellsworth, now an old man beset by family troubles, by his own lack of capital which prevented him from developing his vast estate as he had dreamed of doing, and by his inability to secure the profits which he had promised his eastern associates, removed to New Haven. There he spent the last two years of his life, dying in 1858.[40] The great champion of prairie farming had passed on, his dream of prairie development unshattered but still unfulfilled. The settlement of Ellsworth's estate was not easy because of complications arising from a late will which left most of the property to Yale and cut off his children and Wabash College, earlier intended for substantial inheritances,[41] with small portions. The will was contested[42] and Yale was induced to accept a compromise according to which the share to Wabash College was partially restored and the shares of Ellsworth's children and grandchildren were enlarged. Wabash College received 960 acres in Warren and 2,280 acres in Benton County and $1,000 in cash.[43] Yale received 10,895 acres of which 6,043 were

[40] Barce *et al., History of Benton County,* II, 126.

[41] The Ellsworth children's share of the estate was reduced from one-fifth each to the use of property valued at $25,000 for each for life.

[42] The story of the contest is well treated by Judge Barce *et al., History of Benton County,* II, 136–140. The authors used the White County Circuit Court, Complete Record No. 3, in the court house in Monticello.

[43] Conveyance of Sept. 24, 1860, recorded in Benton County Deed Records, Nov. 22, 1860; James Insley Osborne and Theodore Gregory Gronert, *Wabash*

in Benton County, and the rest scattered among nine other Indiana counties, three Illinois counties and two Missouri counties. Yale also received numerous lots in Fort Wayne, Williamsport, Lafayette, and other cities.[44] There remained to the Ellsworth family 110,328 acres, which were located as follows:

In Illinois counties

Vermilion	7,953
Iroquois	7,123
Macon	240
	15,316

In Indiana counties

Allen	1,955
Benton	74,779
Jasper	267
White	440
Newton	2,014
Montgomery	40
Warren	2,420
Tippecanoe	5,053
Lake	8,044
	95,012

College: The First Hundred Years, 1832–1932 . . . (Crawfordsville, 1932), 62. This is perhaps the best of the histories of small colleges in the United States. In 1862 Wabash was leasing a part of its Benton County land but in 1866 to 1879 it was selling its holdings at prices ranging from $6 to $22.50 per acre. See the Deed Records of Benton County for these years.

[44] White County Circuit Court, Complete Record No. 3. The Treasurer of Yale University and the Librarian of the University Library were kind enough to permit the author to use the manuscripts dealing with the settlement of the Ellsworth estate but the records are disappointingly meagre. One manuscript contains an analysis of the Ellsworth estate, June 1, 1868, which indicates that Yale paid $28,342.26 for obtaining the estate. A part of this was used, no doubt, to buy the interests of those who had a share in the lands, and the rest was for legal expenses and other costs in connection with the trial. By 1869 Yale estimated its share of the estate to be approximately $100,000 of which $60,000 was in unpaid contracts for lands sold, together with the valuation of land remaining unsold. Of the latter there were 2,076 acres averaging in value $9 per acre. As late as 1888, Yale still held mortgages on land in Benton County (copies of mortgages and analyses of the estate, Ellsworth MSS., Yale University Library).

Eastern interests probably had an equity in a substantial amount of this land but the firm of Peckham and Smith [45] of Lafayette, which acted as the agent of the family, advertised the entire 110,328 acres for sale. The Ellsworth heirs, Wabash College, and Yale were engaged for the rest of the century in selling and renting these lands, making collections, building some improvements and otherwise trying to capitalize upon their inheritances. But the death of Henry L. Ellsworth, the court battle, and the continued absentee proprietorship left the estate with little personal attention.

It would be equally interesting to study the land operations of Solomon Sturges [46] and his associates in the same detail as those of Ellsworth but space permits only a brief mention of them. Sturges was a resident of Zanesville, Ohio, where he had large interests in farm lands, banks, and railroads. In 1836 he began to purchase extensively in the prairie section of Indiana and Illinois and elsewhere until he and other members of his family had accumulated 173,000 acres of which 32,000 were in White County, Indiana. These lands were classified as "swamp" but were merely prairie lands which were wet for part of the year. They were considered especially valuable for stock or dairy farms, and, to attract purchasers to them, Sturges advertised them in farm journals and by broadsides.[47] His unique advertising method is indicated by the following quotation:

Now, as I hold in abhorrence all speculators, none such need apply. I wish to sell to actual settlers. . . . I have preached that Congress should only sell lands to actual settlers. Congress never would do right (everybody knows that), so I have tried to take care of the "dear People," as far as I could myself.[48]

[45] Peckham and Smith, *To the Public,* a nineteen-page pamphlet with no date, in the New York Public Library.

[46] Sturges was President of the Central Ohio Railroad in 1857 (William Prescott Smith, *The Book of the Great Railway Celebrations of 1857 . . .* [New York, 1858], Part II, 17).

[47] Broadside of Dec. 26, 1854, Pratt MSS., Indiana State Library.

[48] *Prairie Farmer,* May 20, 1858.

Associated with Sturges was Alvah Buckingham, also of Zanesville. Buckingham was president of the Bank of Muskingum in 1839, and was the principal promoter of the Wabash Valley Bank of Logansport.[49] It was doubtless the funds of these banks which made possible his extensive investments in lands and railroads. The Buckingham family entered 103,000 acres of land of which 13,000 were in northern Indiana. Across the state line in Illinois, the Sturgeses and Buckinghams owned 80,000 acres of prairie land. No one except Ellsworth had a larger interest in the Wabash Valley than these land dealers and they directed their efforts to settling their lands with persons who could buy at prices profitable to themselves. Their advertising gives no hint, however, that it was their intention to withhold their vast acreage from sale and to settle it with tenants, as Ellsworth originally intended doing.

Numerous other persons of capital were attracted to the Wabash lands in the boom period of the thirties and fifties, as the following tabulation shows.[50]

Name	Residence	Acres
Allen, H.	St. Lawrence Co., N.Y.	3,511
Aspinwall & Howland	New York	2,560
Baker & Harvey	Otsego Co., N.Y.	10,873
Barnett, A.	Jefferson Co., Ky.	7,296
Bates, H.	Marion Co., Ind.	2,400
Beers & Sullivan	Jefferson Co., Ohio	6,360
Bell, W. H.	Washington, D.C.	5,540
Boggs & Evans	Pickaway Co., Ohio	8,173
Bordon, J.		5,120

[49] Warren Jenkins, *Ohio Gazetteer and Traveller's Guide* (Columbus, 1839), 525; A. Buckingham to D. D. Pratt, Chicago, June 14, 1860, Pratt MSS., Indiana State Library.

[50] The data for this table were compiled from the records in the General Land Office, National Archives, Washington, the plat books and Deed Records of Benton and White Counties, and the Ewing, Hamilton, Tipton and Pratt collections, Indiana State Library. It is not a complete table of all the large land entries. Data on the swamp, canal, Michigan Road, and other state lands were obtained only in Benton and White Counties.

Name	Residence	Acres
Breed, R.		8,080
Bronson, F.	New York	7,730
Brooks, J.		19,480
Canby, I. T.	Montgomery Co., Ind.	2,070
Carey, J. E., & J.	Otsego & Albany cos., N.Y.	4,270
Case & Wolcott	New York	3,340
Collins, S. L., & M.	Lucas Co., Ohio	2,555
Cowles, H. B.	Tippecanoe Co., Ind.	2,846
Cutler, L.	La Porte Co., Ind.	3,494
Delafield, J.	New York	6,392
Denny, T.	New York	4,050
DeWolfe, C. E.		3,600
Ensminger, H.		5,060
Fletcher & McCarty	Marion Co., Ind.	3,846
Fulkerson, A.	Licking Co., Ohio	2,014
Gilchrist, D.	Otsego Co., N.Y.	2,640
Gilpin, J. F., & V.	New Castle Co., Del.	2,947
Grinnell, J., M. H., & H.	New Bedford, Mass.	2,188
Haas, I.		5,200
Hord, R.	Caroline Co., Va.	3,300
Horner, J.	Albany, N.Y.	2,600
Hurd, O.	St. Joseph Co., Ind.	13,850
Jenks, N.	Ontario Co., N.Y.	12,952
Jessup, E.	Fairfield Co., Conn.	9,306
Kent & Willard	Floyd & Newton cos., Ind.	11,570
Lanier, J. F. D.	Jefferson Co., Ind.	2,596
Latimer, P.	Huron Co., Ohio	2,927
Leech, J. A.	Union Co., Ind.	3,420
Luck, J. A.	Union Co., Ind.	3,500
Martin, W.	Jefferson Co., N.Y.	4,460
Mendenhall, J. R.	Union Co., Ind.	2,950
Millington, A.	Washtenaw Co., Mich.	15,654
Minturn, R. B.	New York	4,880
Morison, R. S.	La Porte, Ind.	3,840
Morse & Beardsley,	Otsego Co., N.Y.	13,675
Polke, W.	Fulton Co., Ind.	9,204
Pomeroy, B.	Stonington, Conn.	2,160
Rockwell, C., & J.	Norwich, Conn.	2,209
Rood, W.	Montgomery Co., N.Y.	2,484
Ryder, J., & A. L.	Westchester Co., N.Y.	4,597

Name	Residence	Acres
Schenck, J. N. C.	Warren Co., Ohio	2,342
Smith, O. H.	Fayette Co., Ind.	5,664
Sumner & Clark	Washington, D.C.	3,264
Switzer, W. N.	La Porte Co., Ind.	6,117
Starling, L.	Franklin Co., Ohio	4,091
Steenberger & Allen	Shenandoah Co., Va.	4,028
Thompson, J.	New York	26,000
Van Rensselaer, J.	Oneida Co., N.Y.	3,000
Walker, J.	Bucks Co., Pa.	6,253
West, N.	Essex Co., Mass.	2,471
Williams, J.	Utica N.Y.	2,316
Williams, J., & W. B.	Dutchess Co., N.Y.	3,560
Williams, T. W.	New London, Conn.	2,740
Willis & Henry	New York	3,473
Wright, J.	Huron Co., Ohio	2,897

These large speculative purchases in northern Indiana must not be regarded as unique. Investments on an equally large scale were made in Michigan, Wisconsin, Illinois, and Iowa at the same time. But nowhere was there a greater concentration of absentee and speculator ownership than in the prairie counties of Indiana, and in few other sections did the dead hand of the speculator have such a far reaching influence.

By 1855 all the public land in Indiana had been disposed of and yet vast stretches of the state were totally unimproved. Absentee proprietorship and high land prices were to a large extent responsible for the tardy development of such areas, especially the Grand Prairie. By the eighteen-fifties, when the agricultural pattern of central and southern Indiana was already well established, Benton, Newton, and Jasper counties remained almost untouched by settlers, and White, Warren, and Tippecanoe still contained a large proportion of undeveloped land. As late as 1860, scarcely 6 percent of the land in Benton County was improved and only 13 percent was improved in Jasper and Newton.[51] Only two other counties had a smaller pop-

[51] Computed from Eighth Census of the United States, 1860, *Agriculture*, 38, 42. The percentage of improved land for the state in 1860 was 35.

ulation than Benton in 1860. It was not until well into the 1860s
that these counties began to develop and much of their land was
not improved until after 1880. The words of Solon Robinson,
written in 1841, in which he deplored the unfortunate effects
of land speculation were proving only too true:

It is evident that no man can cultivate such large tracts as many have
been anxious to possess, of such a soil as ours. It were better by far
that our uncultivated lands were occupied by hardy and industrious
laborers, whose every stroke of plough, hoe, or spade, would add in-
trinsic value to it, than to lie dormant, waiting some hoped for rise
in value. It is a subject well worthy of our careful inquiry, whether
our greediness has not driven many good citizens to look further,
without faring better, while we have fared worse. Our settlements
are too sparse, and we ought to use all honorable means to invite
immigrants to fill up our waste lands. To do this we must be more
liberal.[52]

Many of the absentee proprietors bought their tracts as simple speculations. It was their intention to hold the land until
rising prices, which they could reasonably expect within a generation, should enable them to sell at a profit. They had no intention of improving their land or in any other way aiding in the
development of the prairies. When taxes were assessed against
their property for local improvements, many of them delayed
payment as long as possible. The Ellsworth lands and those of
other easterners were delinquent in tax payments in Benton
County in 1860 as much as eight years. Thus the speculators
not only kept the land out of the hands of actual settlers but
prevented the collection of taxes which were needed for road
improvements, school expenses, and other local government
costs. Where actual residents insisted upon public expenditures
for schools and roads they were forced to tax their own property
more heavily to compensate for the unimproved lands of the
nonresidents who paid little or nothing into the treasury.

52 Kellar, *Solon Robinson*, I, 217–218.

Farm tenancy early appeared in the prairie counties of Indiana and developed rapidly there in contrast to the southern counties where its growth was slow. From the outset Ellsworth had planned to improve his possessions by placing tenants upon them who would continue to break up and cultivate new land, construct fences and buildings, and otherwise increase the value of the property. Meantime, they would be paying rent amounting to one-third of the crops they raised. Ellsworth's *Valley of the Upper Wabash*, describing his plan of placing tenants upon the land, was set forth as an inducement to attract capitalists to prairie investments.[53] It is remarkable that Ellsworth was criticized neither by the press of Indiana, including the farm journals, nor by politicians for proposing to introduce into pioneer Indiana an institution which all agreed was un-American. Indeed, until well after 1860 one finds politicians praising the American land system because it was, according to them, building up a nation of farm owners, and was not permitting such an alien institution as tenancy to develop. Yet here was Ellsworth publicly inviting capitalists to invest funds through him in Indiana where tenants could be attracted to the lands.

Ellsworth was not solely responsible for the introduction of tenancy into Indiana. As early as 1823, Lazarus Noble of Lawrenceburg advertised his farm for rent,[54] and, after 1835, one finds scattered advertisements in the Indiana papers of farms for rent.[55] The Potawatomi and Miami reserved sections, lying

[53] In his letter of January 1, 1837, he said: "It is customary to rent land (once broke and fenced) for one-third of the crops, delivered in the crib or barn. At this rent the tenant finds all." He advised the employment of young men "to take the farm on shares" (*Valley of the Upper Wabash*, 166). In his subsequent circulars and letters he frequently mentions his tenants and his success in employing them.

[54] Lawrenceburg *Indiana Oracle and Dearborn Gazette*, Oct. 4, 1823.

[55] Lafayette *Free Press and Commercial Advertiser*, May 27, 1836; Logansport *Canal Telegraph*, March 18, 1837; Logansport *Herald*, Jan. 29, 1840; Lafayette *Tippecanoe Journal*, Feb. 2, 1843, July 31, 1845. The Monticello *Prairie Chieftain*, December 23, 1852, contains an advertisement of R. Bury of Lafayette, who wanted to purchase or rent a farm of 40 to 160 acres.

adjacent to the Wabash River and the route of the Wabash and
Erie Canal, were regarded as choice lands and were much in
demand by the early settlers. The Ewings of Fort Wayne who,
with Cyrus Taber, Allen Hamilton, and Senator John Tipton
had succeeded in wresting most of these lands from their untu-
tored owners, rented them to incoming settlers who preferred
to settle upon them, temporarily, rather than to take up more
remote locations back from the river.[56] Elsewhere in Indiana,
lands were being rented by local proprietors to new arrivals,
some of whom, after a short period of tenancy, were able to
purchase farms of their own.[57]

Nor were Ellsworth and the "Yale Crowd" the only nonresident capitalists who intended to develop their estates through
tenants. In fact, in practically all the western states easterners
bought tracts of land as permanent investments to be developed
by tenants. When such easterners appeared in a community where
the land office was located, they were welcomed by the local
press, feted by the "prominent citizens," and encouraged to
invest in the area provided they did not attempt to encroach
upon the rights of squatters who had claims on public lands.
Thus as early as 1825 the *Michigan Sentinel* of Monroe, Michigan, exulted over the fact that a number of "robust capitalists"
from western New York had arrived to purchase lands.[58]

Ellsworth secured tenants for some of his land by advertising
them enticingly in the local papers. In 1854 he announced for
sale 50,000 acres of "farm lands" near the Wabash in Tippecanoe, Warren, Vermillion, Montgomery, White, Cass, Miami,
Wabash, Allen, Whitley, and other Indiana counties. If immi-

[56] The Ewing, Hamilton and Tipton manuscripts in the Indiana State
Library contain frequent allusions to rents received by W. G. and G. W.
Ewing, Allen Hamilton, and John Tipton from these Indian sections in the
years following 1837.

[57] It was not customary to record leases in the deed records but one finds
numerous leases in the Deed Records of Benton and White Counties for the
forties and fifties and of course later.

[58] Monroe *Michigan Sentinel*, Sept. 23, Dec. 1, 1825.

grants could not buy they might lease the lands for two or three years for one half the crops and at the end of the period receive a deed for the land without further payments. Stock and labor were acceptable in place of cash.[59] In 1848, Ellsworth advertised 30,000 acres of land for sale and ten houses in Lafayette for rent.[60] His tenants found their lot by no means an easy one and not many remained on the land. In addition to plowing, fencing, and building homes there was need for draining part of the land. Few sections could be drained satisfactorily without securing the coöperation of owners of adjacent lands, but where the owner was a nonresident, or Ellsworth himself, the chances of assistance were slight. Immigrants were unwilling to put themselves to much expense of time or labor to ditch lands, the benefit of which would largely go to the landlord in increased land values. The alternative to farming was the cattle industry, but capital was necessary for this and the ordinary immigrant lacked it. The prairie possessions of absentee proprietors, therefore, had little to offer impoverished immigrants who were seeking cheap land.

The more substantial immigrants who brought with them to the West considerable sums of money were likewise not attracted to the prairie counties. Ellsworth, Sturges, and other proprietors were holding their lands for $5.00 and $10.00 an acre, which, added to the cost of bringing the prairie under cultivation, made them high in price, even taking into consideration their great fertility. From 1840 to 1855, there yet remained equally fertile public land in Illinois and Iowa which could be bought for $1.25 an acre. Later, lands in Michigan, Wisconsin, Kansas, and Minnesota were thrown open to entry. After 1862 land could be acquired free under the Homestead Act. Some of this land was

---

[59] Lafayette *Wabash Standard*, July 18, 1845; Lafayette *Tippecanoe Journal*, July 31, 1835.

[60] Lafayette *Courier*, Dec. 29, 1848. Included in the advertisement is a statement that persons returning from Lafayette may get freight to Benton County.

as close to railroads as was the Benton County land which, until
the late sixties, remained quite distant from transportation lines.
Immigrants with capital, unless they were attracted to a particular area because of the earlier settlement there of friends or
other members of their own nationality, frequently preferred
to move to undeveloped areas where the land was still open to
entry or where they could acquire it cheaply. By so doing they
could profit from the rising value which subsequent settlement
would give to their claims and they, like the absentee speculators, generally bought more than they could carry.

It may be argued that it was not the speculators but the wet
lands which deterred immigrants from settling in the prairie
counties. It is true that the extremely wet lands could not be
cultivated until they were drained and that their drainage would
call for heavy financial expenditures. Unfortunately, the absentee proprietors were either unable or unwilling to invest more
capital in lands which still brought them no revenue, and the
tenants, as has been seen, could scarcely afford to invest their
money or very much of their labor in improvements of which
they might be dispossessed at any time. Had the lands been
democratically owned by farmers operating quarter-section tracts,
cooperative ditching systems might have been arranged, the
reduced costs would not have been insurmountable, and the wet
lands would doubtless have been brought under cultivation
much sooner.

Absentee ownership not only kept both the impoverished
immigrants and those supplied with capital away from the prairie
counties but it also delayed the construction of railroads. Many
Indiana counties aided materially in their own development by
liberally subsidizing the construction of railroads through grants
or loans. But absentee proprietors were loath to make contributions for this purpose, even though they might be benefited
greatly by the transportation lines. Furthermore, the virtually
nontaxable lands of the absentee proprietors so reduced the tax
base of the area that the counties could not sell bonds to finance

railroad subsidies. Railroad lines which did not need to depend upon local aid for their construction, such as the Wabash, the Monon, and the Logansport and Peoria, were built through the prairie country in the fifties,[61] but there yet remained vast stretches of land so far from railroads that transportation costs were prohibitive. Other railroad schemes were proposed but they had to wait until the 'seventies and 'eighties when prairie development had progressed sufficiently to make possible their financing. Before 1870 Benton County could not boast a single mile of railroad. Settlers who would have worked hard to secure them by voting county subsidies and by exchanging mortgages on their own lands for bonds of the railroads were not encouraged to settle in Benton or other prairie counties, despite the publication of the colorful advertisements of Ellsworth and Sturges.

In the late fifties most of the prairie land still owned by the original speculators was sold to another group of capitalists who took their places as great landlords.[62] Ellsworth's eastern associates had grown tired of waiting for their promised $10 and $20 per acre and were glad to sell for much less rather than continue to suffer tax penalties and especially further loss of income from their capital. This second stage of large land ownership was not characteristically speculative in its nature but was more constructive. The new owners were generally Hoosiers who lived in the prairie counties where they had already built up considerable fortunes from the cattle trade, railroad construction, banking, and the sale of town lots. They were a part of the community, had grown up with it, and were now showing their confidence in it by investing their surplus at home. They were an aggressive group of men who had the capital and the driving force to make the prairies productive.

[61] Frederic L. Paxson, "The Railroads of the 'Old Northwest' before the Civil War," Wisconsin Academy of Sciences, Arts, and Letters, *Transactions* (Oct., 1912), XVII, Part I, 243–274.

[62] These sales can be traced through the deed records of the prairie counties.

One of the most able of this later class of landlords was Moses Fowler, Lafayette banker, cattleman, partner in a large meat-packing firm, and railroad contractor. With Adams Earl and others he bought 20,000 acres in Benton County, and in White and Warren Counties he acquired 25,000 acres.[63] Fowler became a power in Benton County. He pastured great herds of cattle and raised with the aid of his numerous tenants tens of thousands of bushels of corn. His sales of grain and stock from his Benton County farms were said to amount to as much as $150,000 per annum.[64] He moved the county seat from Oxford, where Henry L. Ellsworth and David Watkinson had been influential in locating it, to Fowler, which town he laid out.[65] He aided in financing and constructing the Big Four Railroad which runs diagonally through Benton County to Chicago. The completion in the seventies of this railroad running through the Fowler lands made possible their more intensive development.

Edward C. Sumner, another of the great cattle kings of Indiana, bought 30,000 acres in Benton County, the greater part of which was acquired from Ellsworth and other members of the "Yale Crowd." For most of the land he paid $5 per acre but for a part he was forced to give as much as $30 per acre. Judge Elmore Barce has described the extensive cattle trade in which Sumner was engaged during the seventies and eighties on his Benton County lands, and he has noted the sale of 1100 head of cattle in 1882 for a price of nearly $100,000.[66]

Lemuel Milk and his associates operated on an even larger

[63] Information as to the acreage of the Fowler, Sumner, Boswell, Raub, Atkinson, Milk, Gaff and Goodwin estates is from the following sources: Benton County Deed Records; *Counties of Warren, Benton, Jasper and Newton, Indiana: Historical and Biographical* (Chicago, 1883); Barce *et al.*, *History of Benton County;* George Ade, "Prairie Kings of Yesterday," *Saturday Evening Post* (July 4, 1931), CCIV, 14 ff.

[64] *Biographical History of Eminent and Self Made Men of the State of Indiana* (2 vols.; Cincinnati, 1880), II, 9th District, 13–14.

[65] Barce *et al.*, *History of Benton County*, II, 147; *Counties of Warren, Benton, Jasper and Newton, Indiana*, 233 ff.

[66] *History of Benton County*, III, 64 ff.

scale than Fowler or Sumner. They are said to have owned 65,000 acres of land in Indiana and Illinois of which 40,000 were in the Beaver Lake region of Newton County, Indiana. Here, after a part of the tract was drained, there were pastured 10,000 sheep, 2,500 cattle, and 300 horses. One field of corn contained 2,000 acres.[67]

Other large holdings in Benton County, most of which were established in the fifties were: those of Parnham Boswell, 12,000 acres; of Cephas Atkinson, 12,000 acres; and of Adams Danforth Raub, 6,000 acres.[68] In Newton County James M. Gaff of Cincinnati bought 11,000 acres and Alexander J. Kent acquired 25,000 acres. In Warren County perhaps the largest landholder was James Goodwin who built up an estate of 10,000 acres. In White County John Kious owned an estate of 4,000 acres and Miller Kenton one of 5,000 acres.[69]

These men did not make the mistake of sinking all their money in land but had funds left with which to develop their holdings. Under them began the real improvements upon tracts which had been in private ownership for a generation. They grazed great herds of cattle upon their lands and gradually fenced their tracts. But grain feeding was necessary for part of the year and these prairie kings, so picturesquely described by George Ade, turned to raising corn.

Increasing land values and taxes made necessary more intensive use of the land than the great proprietors were able to

[67] George Ade, *loc. cit.*, 77, Cf. Illinois Central Railroad, *Sectional Maps . . . 850,000 Acres yet for Sale* (Chicago, 1867), 66.

[68] In 1876 Raub advertised 6,000 acres of pasture for rent (*Benton Democrat*, March 24, 1876). The following year Parnham Boswell advertised 1,550 acres of grazing or grain land for sale for $30 per acre. The property included a large residence of eleven rooms, tenant houses, orchard, and 150–200 acres of timber (*ibid.*, May 25, 1877).

[69] Monticello *Prairie Chieftain*, Oct. 2, 1850. Large ownership of land in Jasper and Newton Counties was revealed in the twentieth century with the publication of the *Standard Atlas of Jasper County, Indiana* (Chicago, 1916). It reports B. J. Gifford as the owner of 24,000 acres in Jasper County and John J. Lawler as the owner of 18,000 acres in Jasper and Newton Counties.

introduce. Cattle and hog raising with grain production as a side line had to be reversed and grain raising became the principal method of farming the prairies. The large estates were gradually broken up into small tenant farms and a system of crop sharing was introduced. The tenants were frequently drawn from the laborers previously employed by the proprietors.

When the estates were divided into tenant farms, the owner-manager was no longer needed. Thereafter, the generation of cattle kings slowly faded from the picture and their heirs moved to Lafayette, Indianapolis, Florida, and California. The second generation, being out of touch with the land, became more concerned with the income to be derived from it than with such problems as erosion, soil exhaustion, and declining fertility. They wanted immediate returns, and forgot that land is not inexhaustible. Grain was the principal and safest cash crop from the point of view of the absentee proprietors, and tenants, in some cases, were actually discouraged from keeping cattle. A local historian wrote as early as 1883, "Jasper County is still too new, its soil too little exhausted, to encourage or feel the necessity of a regular system of agriculture," [70] but conditions became progressively worse as time passed. The soil was gradually depleted and of course production per acre declined.

The land system which had worked fairly satisfactorily from the settlers' point of view in southern Indiana in the early part of the nineteenth century failed in its objectives in northern Indiana, where great landlords first acquired titles to the land and democratic ownership was subsequently impossible. The pre-emption law of 1841 was a gesture to actual settlers (squatters) but it did not check speculation, and the Homestead Act of 1862 came too late. By then all the public lands in Indiana had passed into private hands. There yet remained a large acreage of undeveloped land which, however, was withheld from impoverished immigrants by its high price. Indiana could no longer be a refuge

[70] *Counties of Warren, Benton, Jasper and Newton*, 419.

for the poorer class of immigrants who were seeking free or cheap land.

The first generation of speculators contributed nothing to the development of the prairie country. Even Ellsworth, less a speculator than a promoter, did more harm than good by helping to bring about a speculators' monopoly in the prairie country. When these speculators sold their land it went to a second, more dynamic group of promoters who could partially develop their holdings but who still prevented democratic ownership. When the second series of owners divided their estates into tenant holdings, it was too late for tenants or other small farmers with little capital to buy the land. Rising land prices, $50 per acre and more for improved sections, fastened tenancy and absentee ownership upon the prairie counties. The much vaunted land system had failed of its objective in the Wabash Valley and the prairie farther west. It had not established democratic farm ownership but had produced a system at variance with American democratic ideals.

Stephen F. Strausberg's "The Administration and Sale of Public Land in Indiana, 1800–1860," Ph.D. dissertation, Cornell University, 1970, examines the functioning of public land policies in the Hoosier State. The Introduction, by Paul W. Gates, to the three-volume *John Tipton Papers*, edited by Dorothy Riker and Nellie Robertson (Indianapolis, 1942), gives attention to the methods by which speculator-traders and government officials secured the allotments given to chiefs and headmen of the Miami and Potawatomi Indians in Indiana. Allan Bogue, in "The Iowa Claim Clubs: Symbol and Substance," *Mississippi Valley Historical Review*, XLV September, 1958), 231–253, is critical of the claim associations for the part they played in protecting the speculative activities of their members.

5. Land Policy and Tenancy in the Prairie States

Thomas Jefferson believed that political democracy could be maintained in the United States only if it were made to rest on the firm foundation of economic democracy. "The small landholders are the most precious part of a state," he said, contrasting this ideal economy with a congested population in urban centers which would, he feared, threaten democracy because it would be subject to control by agitators and demagogues. He urged the adoption of a policy of cheap land that would attract laborers from abroad and from the eastern cities to the newly developing areas of the West and the South. Thus he proposed to create a nation of farm owners who would be the very warp and woof of democracy.[1]

Jefferson's faith in democracy was not widely shared by his contemporaries, and the national land system that was devised made difficult, though not impossible, his agrarian ideal. That land system was based on the assumption that the public lands were a national treasure to be drawn upon for revenue purposes and hence must be sold, not given away or transferred in small tracts to actual settlers. As only men of capital could buy land at the relatively high price for which it was held and in the

---

[1] Julian P. Boyd, *The Papers of Thomas Jefferson* (Princeton, N.J., 1950——), VIII, 682. The essay by Henry George on "Jefferson and the Land Question," in Andrew A. Lipscomb, ed., *The Writings of Thomas Jefferson* (Washington, 1903), XVI, i–xiv, is valuable, as is also Joseph Dorfman, "The Economic Philosophy of Thomas Jefferson," *Political Science Quarterly*, LV (March, 1940), 98–121.

amounts at which it was offered for sale, land-hungry settlers were practically denied the right of ownership.[2]

The march of democracy was accompanied by a series of attacks upon the conservative land policy. The unit of sale was gradually brought within reach of actual settlers; moreover, squatters were protected against speculators who were seeking to buy the squatters' claims and oust them from their improved lands. The various pre-emption acts, especially the prospective pre-emption act of 1841 and its subsequent amendments, weakened the revenue principle of public land policy, since they permitted settlers to squat upon public lands not officially opened for sale, and subsequently to buy land on which their improvements were located for the minimum price of $1.25 per acre without having to bid for it against competitors.[3] The next attack upon the revenue principle came in 1847 when Congress, seeking to recruit soldiers for the Mexican War, offered a bounty of 160 acres of public land to each man who served twelve months in the army. Subsequent acts in 1850, 1852, and 1855 granted land bounties to veterans of all Indian wars and to soldiers of the Mexican War who served less than twelve months. Altogether 61,225,430 acres were donated as military bounties in this short period.[4] The records indicate that few soldiers actually settled on the lands they were entitled to receive but instead sold their rights or warrants to brokers for prices mostly ranging from 60 to 90 cents an acre. The warrants

[2] The early land system is described in Payson J. Treat, *The National Land System, 1785–1820* (New York, 1910); Benjamin H. Hibbard, *History of the Public Land Policies* (New York, 1924); and Malcolm J. Rohrbough, *The Land Office Business: The Settlement and Administration of American Public Lands* (New York, 1968).

[3] Roy M. Robbins, "Preemption: A Frontier Triumph," *Mississippi Valley Historical Review*, XVIII (Dec., 1931), 331–349, and "Horace Greeley: Land Reform and Unemployment, 1837–1862," *Agricultural History*, VII (Jan., 1933), 18–41.

[4] Thomas Donaldson, *The Public Domain* (Washington, 1884), 237; Paul W. Gates, *History of Public Land Law Development* (Washington, 1968), 276.

were thus made available to speculators and settlers in the western states who henceforth used them instead of cash in buying land.[5] By indirection, the Government had, in effect, reduced the price of offered land after the auction sale.

Another step in reducing land prices came in 1854 when those lands which had long been open to entry and which settlers had spurned were reduced in price in proportion to the length of time they had been on the market, the lowest price being 12½ cents an acre. Newly opened lands, however, could only be purchased for $1.25 an acre or with land warrants. Finally, in 1862, when the Homestead Law was passed, Jefferson's philosophy seemed to have triumphed over that of his revenue-minded opponents.

Such was the interpretation of the changes in the American land policy generally given by politicians during the nineteenth century. This was the view, for example, of Thomas E. Ewing, Secretary of the Interior, who stated in 1849 that "our admirable" land system prevented "large monopolies of land, and speculations injurious to those who purchase for cultivation. The capitalist cannot purchase up the national domain. . . . Hence, land is now seldom purchased on speculation." [6] Twenty years later, Joseph S. Wilson, commissioner of the General Land Office, said that the federal land system, by "withholding from public sale all surveyed land for a time sufficient to give the actual settlers the choice of the best localities," had saved them "from the monopoly of speculation. . . . The results of this beneficent policy are seen in numerous States and Territories occupied by multitudes of small tract owners where otherwise might now be found great land proprietors. . . . It has developed as the ruling class of the population a self-reliant yeo-

---

[5] The abstracts of military land warrant entries show that little land was located by the warrantees.

[6] Commissioner of the General Land Office, *Annual Report*, 1849, 6–7. In five years Ewing's two sons were to demonstrate in Kansas how far from the truth was his characterization of the land system.

manry, the true popular element of a democratic republic." [7]
Wilson was a good bureaucratic administrator but not one to
admit major faults in the system.

In 1876, Senator Lewis V. Bogy of Missouri, in a speech upholding the speedy destruction of the forest cover and exhibit-
ing profound misunderstanding of the effect of past land policies,
declared:

There is no speculation in acquiring large tracts of public lands. It
is a mistake to suppose so. The fact is, in the valley of the Mississippi,
where the lands are rich and you might suppose it would have been
a speculation to purchase lands, there has been no speculation in the
acquisition of lands, and the few that tried it lost money by it. What
an idea, that of speculating in lands in this country. . . . Why, sir,
there is no speculation, and there never will be in our day or in many,
many generations to come.

Then to confound his California opponent against whose views
he was arguing, Bogy maintained: "The sooner the speculator
gets to California and Oregon and Washington, the better. I believe there are a great many speculators there already. The
sooner the wild lands of any country are bought by individuals,
the better for that country." [8] When such wisdom was expressed
by a senator from a public land state, one may well understand
why so many serious blunders were incorporated in land legislation.

Statements of this kind were frequently made, but along the
frontier and among the social reformers of the day there was
notable dissent. They were aware that the land system had been
liberalized, but contrary to the statements of the three officers
who were closely identified with the affairs of the General Land
Office (Bogy had served as Commissioner of Indian Affairs in
the Department of the Interior) the Jeffersonian ideal was not
being altogether attained. Most responsible for this failure were

[7] Commissioner of the General Land Office, *Annual Report,* 1869, 20–21.
[8] *Congressional Record,* 44 Cong., 1 Sess., Feb. 17, 1876, p. 1144.

two features of the land system that were permitted to continue too long to allow for remedy. These features were the revenue principle and the right of unrestricted entry.

The land system functioned most democratically in the timbered section of southern Indiana and Illinois. Here settlers came in the generation preceding the panic of 1837, squatted upon lands, improved them slowly, and ultimately secured title to them under the pre-emption laws. Relatively little large-scale purchasing occurred in this area and consequently from the outset there developed a pattern of ownership which was democratic.[9] Small farms operated by owners were the common type; tenancy came in slowly and even today has not made much headway.

True, the settlers in southern Indiana and Illinois, like those of central Illinois and Iowa of a slightly later date, had great difficulty in raising the necessary funds to buy their claims when the government auction was announced. The pre-emption laws protected them to the day of the sale but, if by then the settlers had failed to pre-empt their claims and make their payments, the lands would be thrown open to any purchaser.[10] Impoverished settlers who were unable to buy their claims could either wait in the hope that no one else would do so or they could throw themselves into the hands of the "loan sharks" who were prepared to lend them the land office money at usurious rates. Settlers were greatly excited when a public land auction was announced, and they made desperate efforts to negotiate loans.

In such a period of turmoil, money lenders appeared in the land office towns well in advance of the sale and announced that they were prepared either to enter the squatters' claims and deed them one half of the land, or to enter the claims for the squatters and sell the land to them for an advance of 40, 50, or 60 percent of the purchase price plus the maximum interest al-

[9] See Chapter 4.
[10] Section 14, Act of Sept. 4, 1841, 5 *United States Statutes-at-Large*, 457.

lowed by law.[11] Such usurious practices drove the squatters to political action and led them to send numerous petitions to the federal government in which they urged the postponement of sales until some more favorable occasion.[12] A Wisconsin petition insisted that unless the sales were postponed, four-fifths of the settlers on public lands in that state would be "thrown upon the tender mercies of money lenders from the east whose iron grasp will long be felt." [13] Hard pressed as it was for funds after 1838, yet at the same time anxious not to flout western sentiment, the General Land Office sometimes postponed sales for a year or two. This only delayed the inevitable; faced with the alternatives of losing their land or borrowing from a "loan shark" or "pelf gatherer," as the money lenders were called,[14] the squatters chose the latter as the lesser of two evils.

In the flush years of the thirties and again in the fifties capitalists from the East and the old South took great quantities of money with them to the western land offices, employing it there to make loans to desperate squatters. The largest of these money lenders were James S. Easley and William W. Willingham of Halifax County, Virginia, who together loaned $500,000, and Miles and Elias White of Baltimore, who loaned $200,000 to

[11] Announcement of E. S. & J. Wadsworth & Co., Chicago, Ill., in the Milwaukee *Advertiser*, Dec. 22, 1838; circular of Anderson R. Murray, Wisconsin Land Agency, Madison, Wis., Jan. 10, 1850, Riggs MSS., Library of Congress; announcement of Richard F. Barrett in the Burlington *Iowa Territorial Gazette and Burlington Advertiser*, Sept. 15, 1838, and the *Iowa News*, Sept. 29, 1838.

[12] Numerous letters and petitions from residents in the western states poured into the General Land Office in the thirties, forties, and fifties, urging that sales be postponed because of the poverty of the settlers, widespread sickness, poor crops, low prices, and fear of the loan shark.

[13] Letter of Charles Durkee, R. H. Deming, F. S. Lovell, of South Port, Racine County, Wis., to John Norvell, Detroit, Mich., General Land Office correspondence in Treasury Annex, Washington, D.C. See also the *Iowa Territorial Gazette and Burlington Advertiser*, Sept. 21, 1839, quoting the Chicago *Democrat;* and James Stuart, *Three Years in North America* (Edinburgh, 1833), II, 398.

[14] *Iowa Territorial Gazette and Burlington Advertiser*, Sept. 21, 1839, quoting the Chicago *Democrat*.

hard-pressed squatters.[15] Numerous other wealthy capitalists or their agents invested large sums in land entries for squatters.[16]

The intervention of these money lenders between the Government and the settler had, by 1860, "cost the settlers and improvers of these lands Five or Six Hundred Millions, in the shape of usury, extra price, Sheriff's fees, cost of foreclosing mortgages, etc.," said Horace Greeley, one of the most astute observers of public-land policies. "Tens of thousands," Greeley continued, "have thus paid the Government price of their quarter section twice or thrice over before they could call them their own. Hundreds of thousands are thus paying enormous interest for them to-day, and hoping to pay up the principal some time—as perhaps they will." [17] The most serious effect of the intrusion of the loan shark was the emergence of a class of farmers whose property was heavily mortgaged. Settlers favored with good crops and fair prices were frequently able to meet the interest and pay off the principal, but thousands of others, overtaken by disaster in the way of drought, grasshoppers, crop failures, low prices, and high costs of marketing goods were prevented from fulfilling their contracts. In such cases, the contracts might be extended for a time at the same high rate of interest, but sooner or later they would be foreclosed. Other settlers, discouraged by their ill luck, did not wait for foreclosure; they abandoned their improvements, even though they had obviously raised the value of the land, and moved on to another frontier, still seeking the elusive "cheap" or free land. It was reported in

---

[15] The land business of Easley & Willingham and Miles White is discussed in Chapter 3, above. Also see Robert P. Swierenga, *Pioneers and Profits: Land Speculation on the Iowa Frontier* (Ames, Iowa, 1968), 158–185.

[16] After the Homestead Act was adopted and free lands were available, settlers still depended on loan sharks for loans with which they might commute their homestead claims into pre-emption entries. The five-year clause of the Homestead Act deterred many from taking advantage of the bounty of the Government.

[17] New York *Tribune*, Jan. 26, 1860.

1860 that Le Grand Byington, prominent Iowa money lender, had inserted in an Iowa newspaper 109 separate notices warning as many parties that he was going to foreclose mortgages on their land.[18] The money lender, contrary to his intentions, thus found himself in possession of large quantities of partly improved western land. As taxes, interest, and agents' fees increased his investment, the price for which he held the land was raised to five and ten dollars an acre in the fifties and sixties, to twenty dollars in the seventies, and to even higher prices in later decades.[19]

With these resale prices in prospect, it was still seemingly worth while for settlers possessing some capital and willing to risk it in prairie lands to try to complete their payments over a long period of years. They could if they managed well and had good luck. The task was becoming harder, however, as land values rose, and more and more new settlers found the opportunities of becoming farm owners in the prairie states distinctly limited. Cheap lands, and in fact free lands of a kind, still beckoned them on to the setting sun. But the hazards of farming on the high plains were so much greater and the advantages of settling in well-established communities with schools, roads, churches, marketing facilities, medical attention, and the companionship of neighbors so marked as to induce many to remain in the more favored prairie section, even if that meant becoming tenants instead of land owners. The early establishment of tenancy was the inevitable but unexpected result of the money lenders' activities in the West. To prevent western settlers from falling into the clutches of money lenders, Greeley favored a free homestead policy.[20]

The absence of restrictions upon the amount of land one could

[18] *Ibid.*, Feb. 7, 1860.

[19] A study of the deed records of a dozen prairie counties in Indiana and Illinois indicates that these prices were common.

[20] New York *Tribune*, Jan. 26, 1860.

acquire from the federal government not only made it possible for money lenders to enter quantities of land for squatters but also permitted capitalists to buy large amounts of wild lands as investments. After 1862 the bulk of the land newly surveyed was reserved for "pre-emptors" and "homesteaders," although speculative purchasing was still permitted in the offered land in the Lake States, Iowa, parts of Kansas, Nebraska, Colorado, Missouri, Oregon, Washington, and California. In the South all public lands were reserved for actual settlers between 1866 and 1876, but after that date southern lands were restored to unrestricted cash entry. It was not until 1888 and 1889 that the old system of permitting unlimited purchasing of public lands was everywhere abolished, and this reform was not achieved until the best arable lands had passed into private hands.[21] Favored by such a friendly land system, capitalists by the hundreds were induced to invest their surplus funds in western lands. Through agents or in person they attended the widely scattered public-land offices, selected what appeared to be the choicest land on which squatters had not as yet established their claims, and then sat back to wait for the expected rush of immigrants and purchasers.[22]

Early travelers rarely failed to record their impressions upon first seeing the great prairies of Indiana, Illinois, and Iowa. Stretching for miles and miles until the earth and sky seemed to meet, carpeted with a rank growth of tall, thick grass and prairie flowers, and abounding in game birds and animals, the prairies were something new. Pioneer settlers from forested areas suspected them of being infertile; others feared them because in the swampy areas malarial diseases were prevalent; still others disliked them on account of their remoteness from navigable streams. The first settlers, therefore, avoided the prairies and

[21] Paul Wallace Gates, "The Homestead Law in an Incongruous Land System," *American Historical Review*, XLI (July, 1936), 660 ff.

[22] Capitalists rarely clashed with squatters over the selection of lands. They early acquired a respect for the law of the claim associations.

chose for their new homes the timbered lands of southern Indiana and Illinois, or the narrow fringes of woodland along the streams in the middle portions of these states.[23]

The settlers' loss was the speculators' gain, for when the boom years of 1835 to 1837 set in, the speculators made a mass attack upon the prairie lands. Why the speculators foresaw so much better than early settlers the future value of prairie land is difficult to explain; but the fact is clear. Eastern capitalists and their agents by the hundreds flocked to the Crawfordsville and La Porte land offices in Indiana and the Springfield, Danville, Vandalia, Chicago, and Galena offices in Illinois, looking for prairie land. In the vanguard of this movement, as we have seen, was Henry L. Ellsworth, federal commissioner of patents and member of Connecticut's most illustrious family.

John Grigg, prominent publisher of Philadelphia, was equally impressed with the prairies as a field for investment. Between 1836 and 1837 he bought 124,000 acres in central Illinois, the funds for which were in part supplied by E. B. Bishop of Connecticut, C. P. Smith of Brooklyn, New York, I. V. Williamson and Samuel A. Mitchell of Philadelphia, and John B. August of Illinois. Next to Ellsworth and his associates, this group controlled more prairie land than any other group of investors in America until the fifties. To aid in the sale of the lands Mitchell, like Ellsworth, compiled an emigrant guide, *Illinois in 1837*, which was said to be "full of exaggerated statements, and high-wrought and false-colored descriptions," and not to be relied upon.[24]

[23] Descriptions of the geography and early settlement of the prairies of Illinois may be found in the following: Harlan H. Barrows, *Geography of the Middle Illinois Valley*, Division of the State Geological Survey, *Bulletin*, No. 15 (Urbana, 1915); E. M. Poggi, *The Prairie Province of Illinois*, University of Illinois, *Bulletin*, XXXI (1934); Arthur Clinton Boggess, *The Settlement of Illinois, 1778–1830*, Chicago Historical Society's Collection, V (Chicago, 1908); William Vipond Pooley, *The Settlement of Illinois from 1830 to 1850*, University of Wisconsin, *Bulletin*, History Series, I (Madison, 1908).

[24] A. D. Jones, *Illinois and the West* (Boston, 1838), 147–148. Another writer of travel guides contended that nearly three fourths of Mitchell's book

A third group of eastern capitalists who bought prairie land on an extensive scale consisted of Frederick, Arthur, and Isaac Bronson of New York with whom were associated Benjamin F. Butler of Albany Regency fame, Charles Butler, later known for his success in inducing Indiana and Michigan to resume payments on their defaulted debts, and William B. Ogden, subsequently mayor of Chicago and prominent in railroad and lumbering circles. This group, organized as the American Land Company, entered over 350,000 acres in the states of the old Northwest and the new South between 1833 and 1837. Of this amount nearly 50,000 acres were in Indiana and Illinois.[25]

Hundreds of other capitalists invested in prairie lands in Illinois in the thirties, the larger acquisitions of which are seen in the following table.[26] Illinois residents like Barrett, Duncan, Blankenship *et al.,* Houghan, and Wadsworth & Dyer were using funds of banks they controlled to enter land for settlers; others like Hayward and Russell represented groups of eastern capitalists whose funds they were investing; Ferris & West, Kilbourne & Buell, Picquet, Sprague, and Waschefort represented colonizing groups planning to settle on the land their representatives purchased.

---

was "unwarrantably and illegally taken" from his writings (J. M. Peck, *The Traveller's Directory for Illinois* [New York, 1839–1840], 10). The writing of emigrant guides and travel accounts, which already had assumed large proportions, was, in no small degree, a matter of borrowing copious extracts from previous guides and serving them up as new and original material. The wonder is not that contemporaries were taken in by these compilers and plagiarists but that historians have so frequently used the literature of land promoters as reliable sources.

[25] *First Annual Report of the Trustees of the American Land Company* (New York, 1836); *Catalogue of 96,046 acres of land belonging to the American Land Co.* (New York, 1844); *Catalogue of lands in the Northwestern States belonging to the American Land Company* (New York, 1847); abstracts of land entries, General Land Office.

[26] Wadsworth & Dyer and Richard F. Barrett of Springfield, Illinois, made most, if not all, their entries for settlers, as did Lyle Benedict, of Albany, New York, who made entries for settlers in Iowa.

Name	Residence	Acreage
Barrett, R. F.	Springfield, Ill.	45,600
Biddle, E. R. & T.	Philadelphia	46,000
Bolles, P.	New York	13,800
Chauncey, Elihu	Philadelphia	30,625
Chauncey & Biddle	Philadelphia	13,320
Dorsey, B. L. & E.	Jefferson Co., Ky.	19,400
Duncan, Blankenship, *et al.*	Springfield, Ill.	10,678
Edwards, B. F.	Springfield, Ill.	19,800
Ferris & West	New York State	15,200
Goodrich & Blish	Hartford, Conn.	15,254
Green, H. R.	Providence, R.I.	18,460
Hale, P.	Washington, D.C.	15,650
Harris, J. H., *et al.*	Tazewell Co., Ill.	40,000
Hayward, J. S., *et al.*	Hillsboro, Ill.	26,600
Houghan, T.	Springfield, Ill.	31,900
Kilbourne & Buell	Berkshire Co., Mass.	10,342
King, H., *et al.*	Lehigh Co., Pa.	17,940
Lawrence, G.	Syracuse, N.Y.	15,400
Mercer & Symington	St. Louis	10,360
Munn, S. B.	New York	10,200
Murray, J. B.	New York	12,300
Newkirk, M.	Philadelphia	15,000
Oakley & Wilcox	Tazewell Co., Ill.	16,064
Pettit, H. N.	Morgan Co., Ill.	14,440
Picquet, Joseph	Alsace, France	11,353
Russell, W. S.	Boston	15,700
Sprague, N. B.	Providence, R.I.	14,540
Taylor, W.	St. Louis	22,000
Taylor & Bussing	New York	23,400
Wadsworth & Dyer,	Chicago	16,000
Ware, N.	St. Louis	21,400
Waschefort	Cincinnati	10,840
Wright, S. G.	Monmouth, N.J.	10,000

In her *Patterns from the Sod*, Margaret Beattie Bogue brings out that in the eastern Illinois (Danville) land district sixteen individuals or groups entered in the thirties from one to three thousand acres, nine entered from three to ten thousand acres, and four entered from ten thousand to fifty-eight thousand acres. For the years from 1846 to 1856, when the public lands were gone, thirty-seven individuals or groups entered from one to three thousand acres, thirty entered from three to ten thousand acres, and thirteen entered from ten thousand to fifty-eight thousand acres.[27]

Meantime, as parts of Wisconsin and Iowa territories were opened to settlement, land speculators promptly appeared there as they had in Indiana and Illinois, acquiring large tracts of land. The following list shows the larger entries made in these territories in the thirties:

Name	Residence	Location of entries	Years	Acreage
Barrett, R. F.	Springfield, Ill.	Iowa	1836	29,046
Benedict, L.	Albany, N.Y.	Iowa	1838–39	20,400
Carroll, C. H. & W. T.	Livingston Co., N.Y.	Wisconsin	1836	11,230
Comstock & Merle	Jo Daviess Co., Ill.	Wisconsin	1836	14,000
Healey & Kercheval	Detroit	Wisconsin	1836	21,000
Jones, D.	Detroit	Wisconsin	1835–36	16,200
Lyon, L.	Kalamazoo Co., Mich.	Wisconsin	1835	23,400
Murray, C. A.	England	Wisconsin	1836	20,000
Russell, W. S.	Boston	Wisconsin	1835–39	26,800
Smith, G.	Chicago	Wisconsin	1839	18,400
Starling, L.	Franklin Co., O.	Iowa	1839	27,000
Walker, M. C.	Rensselaer Co., N.Y.	Wisconsin	1839	12,600
Watson, J. T.	New York	Wisconsin	1839	10,200

Nowhere in the West were land titles in greater confusion than in the Military Tract of Illinois, located in the triangle between the Illinois and the Mississippi Rivers. This area had been set aside to satisfy the numerous 160-acre military land bounties promised to veterans of the War of 1812. The warrants were located in the Tract by lot, the patents being issued to the soldier or to his heirs. Few soldiers were prepared to

---

[27] Illinois State Historical Library Collections, XXXIV (Springfield, Ill., 1959), 20.

move so far afield as western Illinois in 1818, and consequently they sold out to speculators who came to control the major part of the Military Tract. Holdings ranged in size from a single quarter-section to the 40,000 acres owned by Romulus Riggs of Philadelphia,[28] 42,000 and 85,000 acres owned respectively by Samuel and Richard Berrian of New York, and to the 128,000 acres owned by Colonel Joseph Watson of New York.[29] Many of these speculators were disappointed in not being able to dispose of their holdings in the Tract promptly and, if they were unable to pay their taxes, they lost their land at the tax sales. Tax titles were of dubious value, but they complicated the situation; in the resulting confusion, the squatters found it easy to settle upon the absentee-owned land, because the titles were beclouded. Squatters' claims were thus added to patent titles and to the tax titles of successive years; confusion was thus worse confounded.[30] In 1836, the New York and Boston Illinois Land Company was formed by some forty holders of property in the Tract who together held 200,000 acres by patent title and 800,000 acres under tax titles.[31]

In the years following the panic of 1837 there was a lull in speculative purchasing of prairie lands, but when the turn came after the middle forties, eastern capitalists began to seek the

[28] The papers of Romulus Riggs in the Library of Congress contain frequent discussions of sales and leases of these lands.

[29] *House Executive Documents,* 26 Cong., 1 Sess., Vol. VII, serial 365, no. 262.

[30] The sale of tax-delinquent land in the Military Tract and the issuance of tax titles produced a sharp clash between the holders of patent titles and the purchasers of tax titles. The former organized the Patent Title Association to defend their interests (Peoria *Register and North-Western Gazetteer,* Sept. 3, 1841, March 11, May 6, 13, Aug. 26, Sept. 30, Oct. 7, 1842).

[31] New York and Boston Illinois Land Company, *Annual Report,* 1837; *For Sale the Following Lands, Situate in the Military Tract and Belonging to the New York and Boston Illinois Land Company* (n.d. n.p.); *Proceedings of the Illinois Land Company* (New York, 1839); *An Act to incorporate the Quincy House Company, Passed March 1, 1839* (New York, 1839); General John Tillson, *History of the City of Quincy, Illinois* (Chicago, n.d.); *Remarks on the Affairs of the Illinois Land Company* (New York, 1840).

western land offices once more. They soon entered the balance of the prairie lands and brought to an early close the era of the public domain in Indiana, Illinois, eastern and central Iowa, southern Wisconsin and southern Minnesota, and the eastern parts of Kansas and Nebraska. Princely domains were acquired by individuals and groups who thereby forestalled and subsequently took tribute from actual settlers. The families of Ebenezer and Alvah Buckingham and Solomon Sturges of Zanesville, Ohio, and Chicago together bought 276,000 acres in the prairie states from Indiana to Kansas; Thaddeus H. Walker of Washington County, New York, acquired 100,000 acres in Kansas, John and Charles Dement of Dixon, Illinois, made entries to the amount of 142,000 acres, and Robert Ives of Providence, Rhode Island, brought his holdings of Illinois land to 82,000 acres. But it was in Iowa that speculation took place on the largest scale.

Iowa had escaped the earlier orgy of large-scale purchasing by nonresidents, and until the opening of the fifties the amount of land entered there was small. The situation changed quickly, however, for during the next few years land buyers swarmed into the state at a rate unparalleled elsewhere in the country, before or since. In less than ten years, over 20,000,000 acres were entered, the larger part of which went into the hands of speculators and loan sharks. In this period the firm of Cook, Sargent and Downey of Davenport, Iowa, aided by Boston capital, entered 180,000 acres; William J. Barney, Dubuque loan shark and speculator, entered 191,000 acres and Horatio W. Sanford, likewise of Dubuque, 250,000 acres. The following table which lists entries of more than 20,000 acres made in the fifties reveals the extent to which Iowa lands were acquired by speculators and absentee owners.

Senator William M. Stewart of Nevada is quoted by Henry George in 1871 as saying that, of the 447,000,000 acres of government land disposed of, not 100,000,000 had passed directly

Name	Address	Acres
Allen, B. F.	Polk Co., Iowa	35,000
Brown & Ives	Providence, R.I.	78,000
Byington, L.	Johnson Co., Iowa	29,500
Cochran, A.	Loudon Co., Va.	20,000
Coffin, W. B.	Boston	22,200
Cooke, P., *et al.*	Erie Co., Ohio	32,000
Culbertson & Reno	Iowa City, Iowa	82,000
Daniels, F.	Windsor, Vt.	28,000
Dennison, J. M.	Rock Island, Ill.	23,000
Easley & Willingham	Halifax Co., Va.	328,000
Everett, H.	Pottawattamie Co., Iowa	36,000
Fowler, S.	Fairfield, Iowa	21,200
Goss & Bissell	St. Croix, Wis.	31,000
Gower, J. H.	Johnson Co., Iowa	34,500
Henn, Williams & Co.	Fairfield, Iowa	84,500
Higginson, J. C.	Dubuque, Iowa	33,500
Lamson, Ward	Fairfield, Iowa	34,000
Langworthy, S. M.	Dubuque, Iowa	61,600
Officer & Pusey	Springfield, Ill., etc.	48,000
Richards, B. B.	Dubuque, Iowa	59,000
Roebling, J. A.	Trenton, N.J.	20,000
Sherman, J., H., & C.	Ohio and Iowa	33,000
Slidell, Riggs & Belmont	Louisiana and New York	35,000
Temple, E.	Lucas Co., Iowa	90,000
Tousey, O.	Dearborn Co., Ind.	23,500
Williams, Jesse	Fairfield, Iowa	39,000
Wilson, R. K.	Webster Co., Iowa	29,200

into the hands of farmers.[32] If this is an overstatement, the estimate of the commissioner of the General Land Office in 1868 that only 30,000,000 acres were then held by speculators in the public land states is certainly an understatement.[33] In three prairie states alone, 20,500,000 acres of land were held by speculators of which 10,000,000 were in Iowa, 5,500,000 were

[32] Henry George, *Our Land and Land Policy, National and State* (San Francisco, 1871), 4.

[33] George W. Julian quoted this figure in a speech of March 7, 1868, *Congressional Globe*, 40 Cong., 2 Sess., 1867–1878, p. 1713.

in Illinois, and 5,000,000 in Indiana. This growing concentration of land ownership in the hands of nonresidents aroused alarm in the West and among thoughtful men in the East. Representative Henry D. Moore of Pennsylvania, who had taken part in suppressing the anti-rent war in New York, called attention to the fact that one New Yorker owned an entire county in Illinois upon which he might ultimately settle between 100 and 200 tenants. Senator Jim Lane of Kansas observed: "I ask the Senate to remember that no greater damage can be inflicted upon a State than to have its lands held in large quantities by non-residents. I have travelled days over . . . Iowa without seeing a house, and on asking the reason, the answer was it was because the land belonged to non-residents." [34] Agitation in Congress, among labor organizations, and in the western press produced a series of changes in land policy after 1860 which were designed to end speculation in public lands; but they came too late. The bulk of the arable lands in the prairies had already gone into private ownership.

Tenancy is in no small part a product of the so-called democratic land system of the nineteenth century. This relation is clearest in the prairie states. Here the largest amount of speculative purchasing occurred, so far as Federal lands were concerned, and here may be seen some of the more serious effects of the resulting large-scale ownership. In the newspapers of this section there appeared as early as the thirties ominous advertisements announcing lands and farms for rent. [35]

[34] *Cong. Globe*, 31 Cong., 2 Sess., 1251–1253 (June 10, 1850), and 37 Cong., 2 Sess., 2249 (May 21, 1862).

[35] Lafayette (Ind.) *Free Press and Commercial Advertiser*, May 27, 1836; Logansport (Ind.) *Canal Telegraph*, March 18, 1837; Logansport *Herald*, Jan. 29, 1840; Lafayette *Tippecanoe Journal*, Feb. 2, 1843; July 31, 1845; Burlington *Iowa Territorial Gazette and Burlington Advertiser*, April 18, 1840; Bloomington *Iowa Standard*, April 29, 1841, Sept. 24, 1841, May 16, 1844; Baraboo (Wis.) *Sauk County Standard*, Sept. 25, Dec. 12, 1850, Jan. 16, 1851; Monticello (Ind.) *Prairie Chieftain*, Dec. 23, 1852; Des Moines

Land speculators, as distinguished from money lenders, bought western lands for various purposes. Many of them expected to be able to dispose of their land at an early date; others, more experienced, were prepared to wait as much as a generation for their profits. The less experienced speculators sank their funds in unproductive land and, while waiting for purchasers, frequently went bankrupt. Their lands became tax delinquent, and soon were sold for the amount due on them; thereafter tax titles clouded the speculator's equity. In numerous instances, the money for these unprofitable speculations had been borrowed from eastern banks and the latter were forced to foreclose. In this way large holdings passed into the hands of banks, which were thus drawn into the land business on an extensive scale. Speculators who had funds to carry their investments found it desirable to get some return from the land until such times as they could sell it at a good profit. They, therefore, rented their lands to tenants. This not only assured some financial return over and above the amount due for taxes but protected the land against depredations and resulted in some permanent improvements.

Another class of investors in western lands began their operations at the outset with the intention of establishing for themselves a permanent investment from which they and their descendants might draw rents as the landed aristocracy of England had done for centuries. These investors were not concerned with the social philosophy of Jefferson, George Henry Evans, and Horace Greeley concerning lands, nor with the fact that most leaders of American democracy professed to believe that the land system was devised to assure settlers easy access to land ownership and to prevent the establishment of an aristocratic system of tenure. There were no safeguards in the land laws to prevent them from engrossing the land; in buying their

Iowa Star, Feb. 3, 1853; Paris (Ill.) *Wabash Weekly Republican*, Aug. 18, 1854.

large holdings they violated neither the spirit nor the letter of the law. At the very time the politicians were boasting that the American land system did not permit such alien institutions as tenancy and absentee landlordism, both were being established in the prairie states.

There was nothing new in capitalists buying large tracts of land from which they might derive a substantial entrepreneurial income in the future. In colonial times numerous prominent men had attempted to do this, many of them successfully, and tenancy and absentee landlordism had thus been established. In the period of rapid inflation and easy banking from 1834 to 1837, and again in the fifties, easterners by the hundreds borrowed large sums to buy estates in the West. Such notable persons as Henry L. Ellsworth, Daniel Webster, James W. Wadsworth of Geneseo, New York, Romulus Riggs, William W. Corcoran of Washington, William Scully of Ireland, and Matthew T. Scott of Lexington, Kentucky, are among those who brought tenancy to the prairie states in the mid-nineteenth century.

Romulus Riggs, Elisha Riggs, and William W. Corcoran were attracted to the prairies of Illinois, where they accumulated large tracts of land as permanent investments. Their agents were not always reliable, and tax titles soon made their operations difficult. Squatters persisted in occupying some of their lands, in stealing their timber, and at times in intimidating prospective purchasers. During the Civil War the title to Corcoran's holdings was further beclouded by confiscation proceedings. Despite these difficulties, the owners found it possible to require the squatters to pay taxes, perhaps for a year or two. Then, if threatened with ouster proceedings, the luckless squatter who had made substantial improvements upon the land had to agree to pay rent or lose the value of his years of toil. The correspondence of Romulus Riggs reveals that as early as 1844 and 1845 he was able to rent a part of his land to tenants for one-third the crop or else for $.50 an acre.[36] Corcoran's 22,000 acres of

[36] Mankin Champion, McDonough County, Ill., March 31, Aug. 2, 1844,

Illinois land came into demand in the fifties and he likewise arranged with squatters or other settlers for the leasing of numerous tracts. He first required that his tenants protect existing improvements and add to them, pay taxes and a small rent. Soon he was able to charge $.75 to $1.00 an acre and even higher rents in the sixties and seventies. Corcoran put much of his income from the lands into further improvements and, of course, his rents rapidly increased. By the nineties, despite substantial sales of land, his rent roll averaged between $8,000 and $9,000 a year.[37]

Henry L. Ellsworth who, it has been seen, entered for himself and his associates some 220,000 acres in Indiana and Illinois, most of it in the Wabash Valley, said in his publicity material in 1838 that capitalists could enter virgin lands and draw large profits from tenants who would settle upon them. Here, in the Wabash Valley, he made extensive improvements, began a series of spectacular farming operations, and invited tenants to settle upon his tracts. Unfortunately, he began on too large a scale and soon found that he had insufficient funds with which to drain the wet lands and to push operations on the large scale that he had planned. After his death in 1858 his estate was divided, but a large part of it passed into the hands of other landlords who succeeded in making of the Wabash Valley an area where large farm units, a high rate of tenancy, and a great deal of absentee ownership prevails.[38]

The Scott family, Isaac W., Joseph, Matthew T., Senior and Junior, and William S., of Lexington, Kentucky, was also among the successful landlords in Illinois and Iowa, entering 34,700 acres, of which 22,000 acres were in Livingston, McLean, and Piatt Counties, central Illinois. Speaking of the area in which

---

July 21, 1845, June 6, 1846, to Romulus Riggs; Daniel Bush, Pittsfield, Pike County Ill., May 1, 1845, to same, Riggs MSS.

[37] The Corcoran MSS., Library of Congress, contain many letters concerning rents, improvements, tenants, and taxes. Corcoran's land investments are discussed in more detail in Chapter 3, above.

[38] See Chapter 4, above.

the Scott lands were located in Illinois, a local historian observed: "Very little of the land passed from the government direct to the real tillers. When the pioneers began turning the sod, already nearly all . . . was owned by those who were 'holding for a rise.' " [39] The Scott holdings were exceedingly rich and fertile, and once railroads reached the area, these lands were certain to be in demand. In the mid-nineteenth century Matthew T. Scott, Jr., came to Illinois to manage the family holdings. Over a twenty-year period he sold part of the estate for more than $208,000 in order to pay taxes and finance improvements. He attracted tenants to the rest of the land by promising to give them title to small tracts if they would make substantial improvements. His object was, of course, to increase the value of his adjacent land. Houses, barns, and fences were constructed, and the prairie was made to bloom, but few of the tenants seemed able to fulfill their contracts and get title. A portion of Scott's estate, diminished to some 4,300 acres, passed to a daughter, Julia S. Vrooman, wife of Carl Vrooman, a former U.S. assistant secretary of agriculture, who "scientifically farmed" it.[40]

The rise of tenancy in the prairie states cannot be adequately studied without mention of the holdings of William Scully. A large landowner in Ireland, Scully came to Illinois in the fifties, where he acquired 47,000 acres of carefully selected land in Logan, Grundy, Livingston, Tazewell, and Sangamon Counties. Like Scott, Scully settled numerous tenants upon his lands by agreeing to convey tracts to them if they would make certain prescribed improvements. The lands were thus brought under cultivation and some were conveyed to tenants, but many of the contracts were never fulfilled and the rights reverted to Scully. To a considerable extent his profits were reinvested in additional property, some farm land being acquired in the seventies at $50 per acre. In Kansas and Nebraska, Scully purchased

[39] *History of McLean County, Illinois* (Chicago, 1879), 499.
[40] *Who's Who in America*, XVI (Chicago, 1930), 2259.

160,000 acres which he also rented to tenants. Scully's method of leasing was a sore trial to property owners in the neighborhood of his lands. He refused to make improvements upon his land himself and permitted his tenants, when their leases expired and they wished to leave, to take with them such movables as they had put on the land, including houses and fences. The result, of course, was that the buildings and fences were wretchedly poor and the Scully lands came to be considered the "most forlorn-looking estate in Illinois." [41] The dwelling houses, it was said, were "mere sheds," unpainted and with few windows. The "miserable tenants" attracted to the land were generally Scandinavians, Bohemians, and Poles who were ignorant of everything but how to raise corn and fatten hogs. The Chicago *Tribune* held that there was not a "more impoverished set of farmers in Illinois than the Logan County tenants of Scully" and that the "land is so impoverished that it breeds burs and weeds, the seeds of which are carried to surrounding farms." [42] The tenants, required to pay the taxes on the land, naturally opposed high levies. Consequently, roads and schools were deplorable in "Scullyland." Worst of all, perhaps, was the constant cropping to corn which led to soil exhaustion. Scully's leasing policy became the object of attack by western papers, and efforts were made in Illinois to force the sale of his lands by discriminatory taxation and by legislation forbidding aliens to own land. [43]

Many speculators and money lenders who in the thirties and fifties had invested in lands with the expectation of turning them over quickly at a profit, were unable to carry their lands until profitable sales could be made. They were forced to disgorge,

[41] Chicago *Tribune*, clipped in the Bloomington (Ill.) *Pantagraph*, March 21, 1887.

[42] Chicago *Tribune*, clipped in Lincoln (Ill.) *Herald*, March 29, 1887. See also the *History of Logan County, Illinois* (Chicago, 1886), 367–369.

[43] See the Bloomington *Pantagraph* and the Lincoln *Herald* for 1887.

and in the sixties and seventies their holdings passed into the hands of more successful land dealers. Some of these new owners rented to tenants, but others attempted to carry on large-scale farming operations through the use of farm machinery, armies of laborers, and herds of mules and horses.

The era of large-scale farming operations began in the prairies with the fifties and lasted for a generation. The region comprising Jasper, Newton, Benton, and Warren counties, Indiana, through Vermilion, Ford, Champaign, McLean, and other central Illinois counties, and thence into Iowa is the heart of the prairie region where the bulk of the land was owned by large holders. Here were 1,200 farms ranging in size from 1,000 to 45,000 acres. Between the Kankakee and the Wabash Rivers in Indiana were established 74 farms in excess of 1,000 acres owned and operated by "cattle kings," such as Moses Fowler, Adams Earl, Edward C. Sumner, and Lemuel Milk. The estate of Fowler and Earl in Benton, White, and Warren counties contained 45,000 acres, that of Sumner in Benton County held 30,000 acres and Milk's in Newton County was 12,000 acres. In addition to large herds of cattle, sheep, and hogs, these farms produced huge quantities of corn cultivated by a large array of farm machinery. Across the Indiana-Illinois line were the 40,000-acre Burr Oaks Farm of Michael Sullivant in Ford County, the 26,000-acre farm of John T. Alexander in Champaign County, the 25,000-acre estate of Isaac Funk in McLean County, and the 10,000-acre farm of Milk in Iroquois and Kankakee counties.[44] Numerous other farms, like the 7,160-acre farm of Samuel Allerton in Piatt County, the 9,000-acre farm of John D. Gillett in Logan County, the 7,000-acre farm of John Sidell and the 4,480-acre farm of William A. Rankin in Vermilion County, and hundreds of others ranging from 1,000 to 5,000 acres reveal the extent of large-scale farming in Illinois in 1880. Farming operations on these estates were conducted

[44] Paul W. Gates, "Large Scale Farming in Illinois," *Agricultural History*, VI (Jan., 1932), 14–25.

on a scale commensurate with their size and were the wonder of the world. Descriptions of them found their way into numerous farm journals where they received not unfriendly notice. In 1871 a reporter for *Harper's Weekly* visited Burr Oaks, the largest of these farms, where he was amazed to find 40,000 acres owned and managed by Michael Sullivant. The "vast oceans of growing grain," the quantities of farm machinery, the great herds of cattle and draft horses, and the 250 men employed on the farm impressed him strongly.[45]

Large-scale farming in Iowa was somewhat slower in getting under way and was never as prevalent as in the prairie counties or Illinois and Indiana. In practically every Iowa county there were some farms in excess of 1,000 acres, but the large number of such farms was in the western tier of counties where, in 1890, the census revealed 103 large farms. In the northwestern corner of the state the Close Brothers in 1878 began farming operations on a scale only equaled on the Bonanza Farms of the Red River Valley of the North. They acquired over 100,000 acres of which 14,000 acres were in cultivation within two years.[46] Unlike Oliver Dalrymple of the Red River Valley,[47] the Close Brothers favored breaking up their huge estate into small farms to be rented to tenants. By 1882 they had leased 280 farms and had thirty more ready for occupancy. For some years the Close Brothers were engaged in constructing tenant houses, building fences, breaking the prairie land and seeding it to wheat, attracting tenants to their land and supervising closely their farm practices. Their spectacular operations, which were widely pub-

[45] *Harper's Weekly*, Sept. 23, 1871, 897.

[46] Jacob Van Der Zee, *The British in Iowa* (Iowa City, Iowa, 1922), 59 ff.

[47] Harold E. Briggs, "Early Bonanza Farming in the Red River Valley of the North," *Agricultural History*, VI (Jan., 1932), 26–37, and "The Development of Agriculture in Territorial Dakota," *Culver Stockton Quarterly*, VII, No. 1 (Jan., 1931), 21. Most recent work on the bonanza farms of North Dakota is Hiram M. Drache, *The Day of the Bonanza: A History of Bonanza Farming in the Red River Valley of the North* (Fargo, 1964).

licized in England, attracted a good deal of capital to the area, increased the number of large-scale farms, and contributed greatly to the development of tenancy.[48]

Large-scale farming in the prairie states had its heyday in the latter third of the nineteenth century, though some of the large farms survived as single units into the twentieth century. The following tabulation shows the appearance of farms in excess of 1,000 acres, the increase in their numbers, and the subsequent decline: [49]

State	1860	1870	1880	1890	1900	1910	1920	1930
Illinois	194	649	649	383	282	203	184	190
Indiana	74	76	275	241	224	142	130	114
Iowa	10	38	274	428	340	214	137	134

The era of large-scale farming was of relatively short duration. Starting as great cattle ranches on which stock was grazed, these large estates soon became fattening grounds for western cattle. The profits from the cattle business were reinvested in draining, fencing, and breaking the prairie; also in farm build-

---

[48] Numerous other large farms in Iowa attracted attention. Thus the 2,100-acre farm of the Day Brothers in Winneshiek County, of which 1,800 acres were under plow, is described in the *Iowa Homestead*, Aug. 20, 1870; the 3,000-acre farm of R. A. Babbage, in Butler County, in *ibid.*, March 10, 1871; the Timothy Day farm of 3,500 acres in Van Buren County is given attention in the *Iowa Farmer and Horticulturist*, IV (Sept., 1856), 121–122; the 1,400-acre farm of Alfred Churchill in Clinton County is described in the *Lyons Mirror*, clipped in the *Iowa Farmer and Horticulturist*, IV (July, 1856), Peter Melendy's farm of 1,100 acres wins attention in *ibid.*, (July, 1856), 56 and IV (Oct., 1856), 135–136, and in A. T. Andreas, *Historical Atlas of Iowa* (Chicago, 1875), 277; the 1,500-acre farm of J. A. Carpenter, in Lyon County, is discussed in the Des Moines *Republican* of June 18, 1872, clipped in the Sioux City *Journal*, June 22, 1872; the George M. Schmidt farm of 4,000–5,000 acres is mentioned in *ibid.*, Jan. 12, 1872; the 3,200-acre farm of L. W. Tubbs, the 2,000-acre farm of H. W. Summers, the 2,000-acre farm of S. D. Davis, the 1,500-acre farm of W. G. Summers, and the 1,200-acre farm of Valentine Plumb are all mentioned in the *History of Mills County, Iowa* (Des Moines, 1881).

[49] The statistics of large-scale farms and tenancy have been compiled from the *United States Census Reports*, 1860–1930.

ings. Each year more land was brought under the cultivation of corn. Toward the end of the century land values rose so rapidly that grain economy gradually displaced the earlier cattle operations. The change occurred when the older generation of cattle kings was disappearing from the scene; their children, lacking the forceful characteristics of their fathers, were content to play a less notable role in prairie farming. They were also troubled by the rising costs of labor and the difficulty of maintaining an adequate supply of workers in competition with industrial employment. More intensive use of the land was necessary and it was advisable to give the workers an interest in the land to keep them attached to it. Tenancy was the answer and large estates were divided into small tenant-operated farms. Some of the large farms continued to operate as units until the grain economy had been well established, but more of them were divided before the change had been carried far. Sullivant and Alexander, who tried to make the necessary improvements on borrowed capital, lost their farms. Fowler and Sumner kept control and personally managed their princely estates throughout their lifetimes, whereas their heirs were content to surrender their land to tenants who were subject to the supervision of farm managers and, more important, to the inexorable demand for constantly increasing rents.

Another factor leading to the breakup of the large farms was the necessity of selling off a portion to provide for improvements on the remainder. Thus Matthew T. Scott disposed of much of his land but kept as a residue some of the choicest. Some large farmer owners wished to take advantage of the high land values that prevailed in the latter part of the nineteenth century and sold their property to a number of buyers. Rarely was it possible to find a buyer for a 5,000- or 10,000-acre farm, so great was the capital involved; hence division was the only solution. Finally, it should be said that many of these farms had been built up on borrowed funds, the source of which was stopped in the panic of 1873. When creditors would not be put off, division resulted.

It was apparent before 1880 that tenancy had already became fastened upon the prairie states and was rapidly spreading. The loan sharks and speculators who were forced to rent their possessions to tenants in order to meet taxes and other costs, the persons seeking to establish great landed estates for themselves and their families, and the large-scale farmers all had a share in introducing a system which at that very time was being widely condemned as both un-American and undemocratic. The censuses of 1860 and 1870 revealed the existence of many large farms in the prairies, but the statistics of tenancy were not gathered until 1880, at which time an astonishingly high percentage of farms in a relatively new part of the country was shown to be operated by tenants. States like Kansas and Nebraska, only recently opened to settlement and still in the pioneering stage, were shown to have 16 and 18 percent of their farms in the hands of tenants. Illinois had the highest rate of tenancy in the North—31 percent—with Indiana and Iowa coming next, each with a rate of 24 percent. These percentages do not tell the whole story, however. In the southern counties of Illinois and Indiana, where settlers had penetrated before the speculators and where the pre-emption system had enabled them to acquire small farms fairly easily, the amount of tenancy was relatively small, and of course this pulled down the average for these states. It was in the "Grand Prairie" of central Illinois and Indiana that tenancy was most common. In Benton County, Indiana, for example, where Henry L. Ellsworth had purchased large quantities of land in the thirties and fifties, and on which some tenants had been established soon after the land was entered, 45 percent of the farms were rented on shares or for cash. In Ford and Champaign Counties, where were located Burr Oaks and Broadlands, the tenancy rates were 45 and 40 percent respectively. In Christian County, Illinois, where E. E. Malhiot had settled a colony of French Canadians on his 22,000-acre estate, 48 percent of the farms were rented. Scullyland, as

Logan County, Illinois, was sometimes called, could boast the highest rate of tenancy, 50 percent. Numerous other counties in central Indiana and Illinois had between 30 and 45 percent of their farms operated by tenants.

In Iowa democratic ownership of land nowhere existed as markedly as it did in southern Indiana and Illinois and tenancy was common everywhere. In some eastern and central counties high rates prevailed, but it was in the northwestern counties, where the Close Brothers and others associated with them were operating, that the rates were highest. The percentage of tenant farmers in Iowa increased consistently from 1880, when it was 24, to 28 in 1890, 35 in 1900, 37 in 1910, 41 in 1920, 47 in 1930, and 49 in 1935, the highest point. Since then it has somewhat declined. Counties having the smallest percentage of tenants bordered on the Mississippi River (Dubuque and Lee, each with 33 percent in 1930); those with the largest percentage were in the northwestern corner of the state (Ida, 61 percent, and Lyon, 63).

The early statistics of tenancy do not fully reflect the extent to which large-scale ownership of land existed. Numerous large farms, remnants of the Mesozoic age of prairie agriculture, were still managed as units, but were soon to be divided into small tenant-operated farms. There were also large estates, as yet undeveloped, which soon were to be carved into small tenant units. Finally, it should be pointed out that many, if not most, of the small farmers who had succeeded in acquiring ownership of their land through entry at the government land offices, had bought more land than they needed. Entries of 320, 480, and 640 acres were common in the prairies, despite the fact that few farmers had the funds or physical capacity to farm such large quantities of land. Eventually, the numerous farmer-speculators gave a part of their land to their children, leased one or two quarter sections or sold and took a mortgage for a large part of the price agreed upon. The purchasers, like those who had earlier contracted with loan sharks for the entry of their lands, might, with luck, meet their payments and eventually acquire title. Many did not. They lost their equity and became tenants.

This is not to say that small family farms did not flourish in the prairies, but on the better lands there was at least one tenant farm for every owner-operated farm. The land system had not achieved its must talked-about goal, but neither had it completely failed. Shrewd observers of the rural scene were aware that speculation in land and the high prices the states, land grant railroads, and speculators asked for their holdings greatly increased the difficulties of pioneer settlers in creating farms where much capital was necessary for successful development. Too many people refused to recognize the evidence of malfunctioning of the land system, abundant as it was, until it was too late.

Historians have been quite uninterested in the emergence of tenancy and its relationship to land speculation. Indeed, Robert P. Swierenga denies that the land speculator contributed to the emergence of tenancy, in *Pioneers and Profits: Land Speculation on the Iowa Frontier* (Ames, Iowa, 1968). Richard C. Overton, in *Burlington West: A Colonization History of the Burlington Railroad* (Cambridge, Massachusetts, 1941), questions any relationship between railroad land grants and tenancy, despite the fact that the Burlington railroad was renting a portion of its grant to tenants in southwestern Iowa in the 1870s and 1880s, as shown in the archives of the Burlington Railroad. Allan G. Bogue touches upon tenancy in *From Prairie to Corn Belt: Farming on the Illinois and Iowa Prairies in the Nineteenth Century* (Chicago, 1967), and more directly in "Foreclosure Tenancy on the Northern Plains," *Agricultural History*, XXXIX (January, 1965), 3–16. Margaret Beattie Bogue, *Patterns from the Sod: Land Use and Tenure in the Grand Prairie, 1850–1900*, Illinois State Historical Library Collections, XXXIV (Springfield, Ill., 1959), has chapters on "Farm Tenancy in a Changing Economy" and "Critics and Criticism of Farm Tenancy." Theodore L. Carlson, *The Illinois Military Tract: A*

Study in Land Occupation, Utilization and Tenure (Urbana, Illinois, 1951), is also useful. Some of the best articles on public land policies are brought together by Vernon Carstensen, editor, in *The Public Lands: Studies in the History of the Public Domain* (Madison, Wisconsin, 1963).

Important for their insight into the machinery of public land administration are George Anderson, "The Administration of Federal Land Laws in Western Kansas, 1880–1890," *Kansas Historical Quarterly,* XX (November, 1952), and "The Board of Equitable Adjudication, 1846–1930," *Agricultural History,* XXIX (April, 1955), 65–72.

Research in early land values has established Thomas LeDuc as the leading exponent of high land values on the frontier. His scattered writings are stimulating and provocative and deserve careful consideration: "The Disposal of the Public Domain on the Trans-Mississippi Plains: Some Opportunities for Investigation," *Agricultural History,* XXIV (October, 1950), 199–204; "Public Policy, Private Investment and Land Use in American Agriculture, 1825–1875," *Agricultural History,* XXXVII (January, 1963), 3–9; and "History and Appraisal of the United States Land Policy to 1862," in *Land Use Policy and Problems in the United States,* edited by Howard W. Ottoson (Lincoln, Nebraska, 1963), 3–27. For LeDuc's part in establishing the high land value concept in the determination of values to be paid Indians for improper compensation for lands they ceded in the nineteenth century, see Berlin B. Chapman, *The Otoes and Missourias: A Study of Indian Removal and the Aftermath* (Oklahoma City, 1965). To keep their feet on the ground historians need to be familiar with the views of that towering reformer and critic of public land policies, Henry George. A well-balanced treatment is Charles A. Barker, *Henry George* (New York, 1955).

6. *Hoosier Cattle Kings*

Corn-belt landlords have never had their glorious days writ large in the annals of American history. Nor have their fads and follies, their wealth and their culture, their political influence, and their economic power been intimately pictured in any *Gone with the Wind*. Yet these country grandees of the corn belt, whose landed possessions outrivaled in size and productiveness anything of which the planter aristocrats could boast in the antebellum period, had much of the same flamboyant quality, the haughty pride, the lust for life and possessions, the love of display and political power that characterized the slaveowners of the South.

Nowhere is their influence as far reaching in shaping the early growth of settlement and the land use and ownership patterns of the West as in the Kankakee and Wabash valleys of Indiana. Here in the mid-nineteenth century were established estates ranging from a few thousand acres to great baronial holdings that spread over four or five government townships. Here in the pioneer period which we are accustomed to equate with equality and democracy there developed an aristocracy that "wore beaver hats . . . and broadcloth . . . the high stock collar and the encircling cravat" and maintained "the manners and highly civilized traditions of the East." [1] Their homes were great rococo mansions set down in lonely splendor in the prairie or in the neighboring cities. The gulf between these aristocratic

[1] George Ade, "Prairie Kings of Yesterday," *Saturday Evening Post*, CCIV (July 4, 1931), 14.

landlords and the cow hands, the hired laborers, and the tenants living in their crude shacks was as great as that which existed between the eastern industrialist and the low-paid workers who operated his factories.

The landed aristocracy of the prairies had its origin in two notable groups which started with different objectives but ended with much the same results. The first of these coming somewhat earlier to the prairies consciously planned to establish themselves in the new country as the landed gentry. The second started as cattle feeders and drovers who, finding it necessary to assure adequate pasture for their livestock, bought many thousands of acres of land for cattle ranges.

When land was cheap, the titles easy to acquire, and money flush, numerous men of capital bought great tracts in the Wabash and Kankakee valleys which, unlike other speculating groups, they planned to improve. Their model was not the southern planter with his army of slaves but rather the rich and cultured families of the Genesee, the Wadsworths, the Carrolls, the Churches, and the Fitzhughs, whose broad acres were cultivated by battalions of tenants.[2] Some of these ambitious and proud capitalists planned to entail their holdings in order to assure their continuation in the family for future generations. Ponderous Daniel Webster, democratic Henry L. Ellsworth, and aristocratic Nathaniel West are but three among many who acquired large holdings in Indiana and Illinois on which they undertook to erect baronies tenanted by scores of farm operatives.

Webster, whose twelve thousand acres extended over a number of states, concentrated his attention upon a tract in central Illinois to which he sent a Massachusetts farmer to assume charge at a compensation of two thousand dollars per year.

[2] Neil A. McNall, "The Landed Gentry of the Genesee," *New York History*, XXVI (1945), 162–176. It is worthy of note that both Wadsworth and the Carroll families invested heavily in western land in 1835 and 1836. James S. and William W. Wadsworth bought fifty-five thousand acres in Ohio and Michigan, and Charles H. and William T. Carroll bought ninety thousand acres in Michigan and Wisconsin.

"My wish," he said, "is to have a very large farm, as large as one active man can well superintend the management of— If this estate be not large enough at present, find out what adjoining lands may be bought and at what prices. . . . The farm must be well stocked—you will employ your own labourers. . . ."[3] Ill luck in the death of his agent, combined with extravagant management, over-optimistic planning, and heavy debts, resulted in failure and the property passed out of the hands of the family. West, like Webster and Ellsworth of New England ancestry, bought some thirty-two hundred acres in Indiana which were managed by the family for many years.

Henry L. Ellsworth, a democratic offshoot of a fine old Federalist family of Connecticut, became the principal propagandist of, and leader in, the movement to bring settlers to the prairies. Inspired by his eloquent defense of the prairies and his own large investments in them, and the slowly developing awareness that they might after all be the coming area for livestock and grain farming, numerous friends and associates and readers of the Ellsworth brochure rushed to buy through him, his son, or other land agents lands that seemed to promise so much.[4] In Chapter 4, above, are shown many nonresidents of Indiana who seemed to have been convinced that land in the Wabash and Kankakee valleys, would soon, indeed almost overnight, be in demand by settlers to whom they could retail their lands. That they were risking their funds in property which Americans had as yet experimented with but little for farming and had no realization of the large expenses that would have to be incurred before the prairies could be made productive was only to become

[3] Daniel Webster to N. Ray Thomas, Washington, March 5, 1838, in C. H. Van Tyne, ed., *The Letters of Daniel Webster* (New York, 1902), 666–667.

[4] The story of Ellsworth's western-land business is told in Chapter 4, above. I do not intend to imply that all these acquisitions were made for the same purpose as those of Webster, West, and Ellsworth. Some were definitely planned as speculations. Levi Beardsley has described in his *Reminiscences* (New York, 1852) his own extensive investments in land in Ohio and Indiana and his efforts to improve his property.

known years later. The Ellsworths and a host of real estate promotors have contributed to developing various areas, but the costs in premature starts, financial losses, and defeat of those who were induced to commence without adequate resources have been large.

Ellsworth's connections with Indiana began in 1835 when his first purchases were made and improvements upon the land were instituted. A decade later, he took up residence in Lafayette and thereafter devoted his full energies to attracting settlers to the area. Experimenting with farm machinery, crop rotation and methods of feeding livestock, breaking plows, ditching and corn-cutting machines, fencing materials, and the feeding of ground corn-cob meal to cattle and hogs all fascinated him. In 1849, he was reported to have twelve hundred acres in corn that averaged sixty bushels to the acre, but his one hundred acres in wheat were ruined by the rust. Instead of driving his livestock overland as was commonly done at the time, Ellsworth transported them on his own boat by way of the Wabash Canal to Toledo where they were reshipped by lake vessel. On the return trip, he brought in lumber for construction of tenant houses and twenty-eight miles of fencing.[5] With hired help and tenants who were settled upon small farms rented on a share basis, Ellsworth brought considerable land into use, but he had overextended himself. His plans for the larger development of his great estate were not completed, and after his death in 1858, much of the land Ellsworth had held passed into the hands of another and equally bold adventurer in prairie development.

Despite Ellsworth's persistent plugging for prairie farming and his extensive improvements, the settlement of the flat, wet land of northwestern Indiana proceeded slowly, owning to its poor drainage, the numerous sloughs filled with a rank growth of reeds and cattails, and the toughness of its sod that resisted the crude cast-iron plow then in use. To drain the land and bring it into cultivation required more capital than the ordinary

[5] *American Agriculturist*, VIII (Nov., 1849), 348.

frontiersman could raise, and the region—the last frontier of
Indiana—was long neglected by immigrants and left undeveloped by the scattered few who settled there. George Ade, whose
father was a contemporary of the cattle barons who will be discussed, and who himself came to own twenty-four hundred acres
in Newton County, has ascribed this lack of progress to the
"backwoodsmen . . . [who] preferred to loaf," and consume
whiskey. Here Ade was expressing the prejudice of the person of
eastern or foreign ancestry against the Hoosier type. Loafing and
whiskey drinking, however, were not responsible for the slow
progress in settling the prairies.

Actually this was not Ade's best judgment, for none knew
better than he the physical characteristics of the area which long
impeded settlement and development. His description of the
Grand Prairie and the features that made difficult its improvement is almost classic.

Our part of the commonwealth was far away from railroads and
so shaggy and waterlogged that it was commonly regarded as a hope-
less proposition.

The untouched prairie which was not wholly or partly submerged
was a crazy quilt of high-stemmed and gorgeously colored flowers
from late spring until the killing frosts of autumn. To break through
the ribbed soil, bury this wild growth and convert a tangy and fibrous
flower garden into a corn field was a whale of a job. Every low spot
on the prairie was a slough rank with reeds and cattails, and breeding ferocious gallinippers by the millions. Also a large kind of horse-
fly, called the "green head," which was so warlike and blood-hungry
that when it attacked a horse, in swarm formation, it would either
kill him or weaken him so much that he had no value as a work
animal. Oxen were used in breaking the raw prairie, and even these
tough and thick-skinned animals suffered tortures when attacked by
armies of green heads.

The first ditches . . . . were deep furrows made with a thirty-
inch plow. As many as thirty yoke of oxen would be used in one
ditching outfit. On level ground the big plow could be pulled along,

ripping and tearing through the tough roots of the bull grass and needle grass and the ironweeds and all the other knotty growth, by fifteen yoke of oxen. In mushy ground and bad going the whole thirty yoke had to be used, some of them to move a capstan ahead of the gang and also to supply power when the pull had to be made by capstan. . . . You will understand that reclaiming the prairie was no job for a weakling, a lazybones or anyone not prepared to meet a pay roll.[6]

Here in a land possessing little natural drainage [7] and no timber, there was an abundance of government land for sale as late as the mid-nineteenth century, when elsewhere in Indiana it had long since been sold. At the same time the Ellsworth estate was being subdivided, the lands of the Wabash Canal were open for purchase, and the counties were disposing of hundreds of thousands of acres they had received as swamp land. Passed over by immigrants who, lacking capital to develop the flat land, were going to more remote but better drained areas in Iowa and even Kansas and Minnesota, these prairies were later bought by a group of robust capitalists, most of whom had cleared small fortunes for themselves in other enterprises. These were the "driving and untiring Vikings" who "refused to accept anything less than despotic control of widespread domains. They were simply Napoleonic in their aspirations. They owned land by townships instead of sections. They were sometimes friendly with their henchmen and dependents, but never intimate. They

[6] Ade, "Prairie Kings of Yesterday," *Saturday Evening Post*, CCIV (July 4, 1931), 14, 76. The ditching plow must have been a remarkable machine to be hauled by such heavy traction power and "cutting a V shaped ditch from two to three feet deep, from two to three feet wide on the bottom and from four to six feet in width at the top" (Elmore Barce, *Annals of Benton County* [Fowler, Ind., 1925], 92). A cut of the plow is shown in *ibid.*, opposite page 50.

[7] Indiana—mostly northern Indiana—has more artificially drained farm land than most other states. For a drainage map see "Land Available for Agriculture through Reclamation," Part IV of National Resources Board, *Report on Land Planning* (Washington, 1936), 36.

were dynamic in energy, forceful of speech, and more than a few of them were picturesquely profane." [8]

These "high geared financiers who came and saw and took possession" were neither sterile speculators whose dead hand would prevent settlement nor ambitious landlords hoping to bring to success Ellsworth's long-range plan of a society of wealthy and cultured aristocrats maintained by the fruits of the labor of numerous tenants. Without exception they bought their land for the immediate purpose of assuring adequate pasture for the herds of cattle they were fattening for market.

The rapid growth of the cattle-feeder industry in the prairies of Indiana and Illinois after 1850 was made possible by a supply of cheap corn, a growing demand for beef in Eastern cities, and a large supply of rich grassland that was in the early period an open-grazing common and was free and accessible to any live-stock. Native stock perhaps not in the best of shape could be purchased from isolated farmers at little cost, turned loose on the prairie blue stem from April to December, provided with salt once or twice a week, and occasionally looked after by a herdsman to see that they did not wander too far from the proper range, meantime putting on valuable weight. After the prairie grass was killed, the calves were put in covered enclosures and fed on stacked prairie hay with perhaps a small ration of corn or meal, or even corn fodder. Two summers of pasture feeding with some grain put them in shape for slaughter, and they would then be driven to market.[9] All this before the day of fencing, tiling, and ditching, and land values ranging from fifty to two hundred dollars an acre, made for low costs in cattle feeding and high profits from the sale of livestock.

When settlers, speculators, and land companies began to en-croach upon the grazing commons of the squatting cattlemen and to engross their pastures, the latter were forced to buy the

[8] Ade, "Prairie Kings of Yesterday," *Saturday Evening Post*, CCIV (July 4, 1931), 75.

[9] Rensselaer (Ind.) *Gazette*, May 25, 1859.

land they had been using to keep control of it. Swiftly they pushed their purchases until they had acquired much of the prairie in a strip of territory sixty miles wide and one hundred and fifty miles long on both sides of the Indiana-Illinois border extending northward from the line of the Big Four Railroad.

Perhaps the most influential of this group of cattlemen was Moses Fowler of Lafayette who had a large part in shaping the land and social pattern of the region. Fowler was a vigorous, hard-driving, and ruthless man who "wanted property, wanted wealth; had a consuming ambition to be rich, and . . . permitted no maudlin sentimentality to stand between him and his cherished object." [10] In 1839, he moved to Lafayette where he soon became one of the leading businessmen. Here, on a grand scale and in a spectacular manner, he carried out his numerous operations, always with substantial material benefits to himself. Drygoods, wholesale grocery, a fleet of steamboats running between Lafayette and New Orleans, banking, meat packing, financing and building the Big Four Railroad, real estate, and livestock were the businesses in which he amassed a fortune for himself. It was said that the Chicago meat-packing firm in which he was a partner was the second largest in the West during the Civil War.[11] Fat, war-time profits permitted Fowler in partnership with his brother-in-law, Adams Earl, to buy huge tracts of land amounting to forty-five thousand acres in Benton, Warren, and White counties. When the property was divided, Fowler had twenty-five thousand acres.

On his Benton County tract of twenty thousand acres, Fowler fattened as many as two thousand cattle. At first native grade cattle were bought. In 1868, he was feeding Texas cattle, but the increasing demand for better quality beef induced him to develop his own herd of Herefords of which he had as many as five hundred. In partnership with William S. VanNatta, an

[10] Boswell (Ind.) *Argus*, quoted in Lafayette (Ind.) *Weekly Journal*, Sept. 6, 1889.

[11] Lafayette *Daily Courier*, Aug. 20, 1889.

owner of eleven hundred acres in Benton County, Fowler imported from England purebred Herefords in the eighties as a foundation for his herd. Within a short time he had become a cattle fancier who was able to exhibit choice stock at state and county fairs and to advertise for sale fifty "thoroughbred Hereford bulls, 50 thoroughbred Hereford cows and Heifers and 300 grade and cross bred Herefords one and two years old." [12]

Fattening native or Texas cattle or even purebred Herefords on the Indiana prairies was enormously profitable for a time, but increasing land values and taxes made the cattle kings consider more intensive use of their holdings. Fortunately, there was at hand a ready supply of immigrants who, in the absence of farms they could buy, were willing to become tenants on the estates of the cattle kings. In this way and without any definite plan, the pastures were slowly divided into quarter- half- or full-section tracts, which were fenced, perhaps tiled or ditched, and planted to corn. The older generation of cattlemen resisted this change at times and to hold their own turned to better grades of stock or even purebreds. But when the sons of the cattle kings inherited their estates the change to tenant farms with emphasis on grain farming came rapidly. In this way, responsibility was largely shifted to the tenant, and when farm managers were employed to safeguard the interest of the landlord, the latter was completely freed of responsibility. He could thereafter concentrate his attention on banking in Lafayette, he could take up residence at Indianapolis, or remove to remote areas where the winter storms and freezing temperatures were left behind. Absentee landlordism had now arrived, for good or for ill. This history of the Fowler estate well illustrates this evolution.

Slowly a part of the Fowler land was broken up and planted

[12] *Breeders' Gazette*, VII (March 5, 1885), 372; Sherman N. Geary, "The Cattle Industry of Benton County," *Indiana Magazine of History*, XXI (1925), 27–32.

to corn under the charge of a superintendent with the aid of hired laborers or tenants. For example, in 1877, arrangements were made with a tenant to break six or seven hundred acres and to farm it for five years in corn, the compensation to be twenty-five cents per bushel for all corn produced.[13] About the same time, ditching was being done on some of the wetter land, sixty miles being dug in 1879. Cattle feeding remained, however, the principal activity, and the sales of livestock comprised the bulk of the gross returns of $150,000 a year from the operations of the Fowler land.[14] A decade later more of the land was being divided into tenant farms of a section each, and a considerable amount of tiling was being done. In 1888, it was reported that "a very large force of laborers have been put to work to ditch and tile several sections" of land belonging to Moses Fowler. At the time of his death in 1889, less than half of the land was being farmed by some fifty tenants who kept it in corn and oats, with a small amount of clover.[15] The tenant holdings were relatively large farm units and did not support a population sufficient to satisfy the business interests of the community.

Little criticism seems to have been directed at Fowler prior to his death on account of the slowness with which his land was developed and the few farmers for whom it provided a livelihood. True, elsewhere in the prairies the large estates of the cattle kings were being developed more rapidly first as bonanza farms and then as small tenant farms which supported a sub-

[13] This tenant maintained he could produce corn at fifteen cents per bushel (Lafayette *Courier*, quoted in Fowler [Ind.] *Benton Review*, June 11, 1885).

[14] *Biographical History of Eminent and Self-made men of the State of Indiana* (2 vols.; Cincinnati, 1880), II, 9th District, 13–14.

[15] In 1890, Fowler's executors sold his two-fifths share of the growing corn on 5,495 acres for $7,121. They also sold 76,000 bushels of corn, 40,000 bushels of oats, 660 tons of hay, and 171 head of cattle that he owned. Most of the livestock was held in partnership with William S. VanNatta (Final Record, Tippecanoe County Probate Records, LXV, 95; Fowler *Benton Review*, Dec. 22, 1887, and April 12, 1888).

stantial population, while the Fowler land as late as 1887 had few families living on it. The West respected men of wealth and little criticism of them was permitted in the newspapers, save those of Greenback faith, or in the county histories and biographical volumes that appeared everywhere in the eighties.

Despite their respect for large property owners, the people of Benton and Tippecanoe counties were shocked at the size of Fowler's personal estate on which he had followed the prevalent custom of evading taxes by failing to make complete declarations. The estimated value of the personal property and real estate was between three and four million dollars, much of which was in securities, deposits, and notes on which no personal property taxes had been paid for years. The size of the estate was breath-taking; it had made Fowler one of the three richest men in Indiana, the other two being William H. English and Clement Studebaker.[16] The heirs had to settle for delinquencies in taxes covering nine years with heavy penalties.[17]

While no provision was made for charity or education, Fowler's widow and descendents were later to make generous donations to Purdue University.[18]

More disturbing to the residents of Benton were the sections of Fowler's will which stipulated that "No part of the real estate in Benton County . . . shall be sold or alienated . . . for the period of twenty-five years" after his death.[19] Such restrictions on alienation are, of course, not uncommon, but this provision seemed to doom Fowler, the county seat of Benton, where most of the lots were owned by the family, and it would prevent the development of the large property west of the town, then in

[16] Fowler *Benton Review*, Aug. 22, 1889.

[17] Final Record, Tippecanoe County Probate Records, LXV, 549.

[18] Fowler apparently had some plan to endow a "female college" for which a square mile of choice land had been designated as the location (Fowler *Review*, quoted in Lafayette *Daily Courier*, Aug. 23, 1889; DeWitt C. Goodrich and Charles R. Tuttle, *Illustrated History of the State of Indiana* [Indianapolis, 1875], 642).

[19] Lafayette *Daily Courier*, Aug. 27, 1889.

pasture. The *Benton Review* said the will embodies "some very grave mistakes."

The result is to establish a system of tenantry in this region for twenty years [twenty-five] and to perpetuate a condition of things which has done more than all things to make all classes of business in Fowler and Earl Park unprofitable since they were first laid out as towns. This very fact has kept away from us a class of enterprising men who did not dare to hazard their capital in towns surrounded by what they term a "floating population." They had read of the misery, the want, and utter degradation of the people in some portions of Ireland where landlordism prevails and could not do otherwise than associate this condition in Benton County with afflicted Ireland.

We were talking with a gentleman of sound judgment . . . who expressed it as his opinion that in twenty years from now these Fowler lands would be so worn out as to be practically worthless and would fail to yield their increase, whereas if they could now be sold the purchasers would see to it that their improvement would be gradual from year to year and at the end of a score of years their value would be much greater than today.

If sold in small tracts instead of divided into tenant-operated farms of a section each, the land would provide for nearly three hundred families who would be a desirable class of citizens with deep interests in the community.[20]

These murmurings against the Fowler will and the blighting effect it was expected to continue to have upon the county were "loud, deep and prolonged," the local paper reported.[21] Later, in commenting upon the move to the West of five tenant families from the county and the larger emigration that was to

[20] Fowler *Benton Review*, Sept. 5, 1889. The same point of view has been expressed in more recent times by Elmore Barce and Robert A. Swan, *History of Benton County, Indiana* (3 vols.; Fowler, Ind., 1930–1932), I, 111–112, who say: "With a soil of matchless fertility and a favorable climate, we could easily support a population of ten times" the present population. "If the day ever comes in Benton County when the tenant system may be dispensed with and the farm lands divided into freeholds of 40 and 80 acres each, the whole community will at once advance, both in population and in material wealth."

[21] Fowler *Benton Review*, Sept. 19, 1889.

occur in the spring, the *Benton Review* placed the responsibility on the large landowners who "are working the greatest injury to our prospects" by the "excessive" and "oppressive" rents they charge. Fowler, Sumner, Earl, and other large owners were a "curse to the community." [22] The Boswell *Argus* joined in the attack upon Fowler, who was pilloried as a "financial monster, born and made possible by bad laws and unjust social conditions," a speculator, a beneficiary of "unearned increment," who "neither planted . . . or pruned . . . neither sowed, harvested or garnered . . . never made a brick, carried a hod or shoved a plane, yet he lived in a palace . . . was clothed in purple and fine linen, and fared sumptuously every day." [23] Even the sedate Lafayette *Daily Courier* spoke of Fowler's "critics [who] were numerous and severe." [24]

Dispute among the children and widow of Moses Fowler led to a part of the will being set aside and the restrictions on alienation of the land were nullified. The heirs did, however, agree with Moses Fowler that "real estate . . . is the best investment" and for many years the hope that the lands would be placed on the market was not fulfilled.[25] Despite the long continued intrafamily litigation over the control of one-third of the estate inherited by a legally incompetent grandson,[26] foreclosure of a part of the property inherited by a daughter, and donations to Purdue University, the third- and fourth-generation descendants of Moses Fowler continued to own well into the twentieth century approximately 13,000 acres in Benton County. Of this amount 7,259 was held in trust for Moses Fowler Chase. James Moses Fowler, a grandson, who died without issue in Miami Beach, Florida, in 1944, left in trust his 2,400 acres for the benefit of his seven nephews and nieces, the trust

[22] *Ibid.*, Oct. 31, 1889.
[23] Quoted in the Lafayette *Weekly Journal*, Sept. 6, 1889.
[24] Lafayette *Daily Courier*, Aug. 20, 1889; see also Lafayette *Weekly Journal*, Aug. 23, 1889.
[25] Fowler *Benton Review*, June 12, 1890.
[26] Indianapolis *News*, April 20, 1903.

to continue for twenty-one years after the death of the last of them.[27]

While the pessimistic prophecies rendered at the time of Fowler's death have not been entirely fulfilled, it was common knowledge that absent ownership had not been good for the land. In 1938, it was said that improvements were poor and backward, very little livestock was fed on the farms, the land had been cropped too closely to corn, little fertilizer had been applied, and the soil had been seriously depleted.

Adams Earl, after whom Earl Park was named, was closely associated with Moses Fowler for many years in shipping grain and livestock on flatboats down the Wabash, Ohio, and Mississippi rivers to New Orleans, operating a wholesale grocery, meat packing, banking in Lafayette, and in the land and cattle business. He also had an ice business and a distillery, the slops and refuse of which were fed to livestock. On his large tract in Benton County, in the management of which his nephew, Adams Raub, had a share, he pastured from two to four thousand native-grade or Texas cattle.[28]

Like other cattlemen whose costs were increasing, Earl and Raub found that feeding grade cattle was proving less profitable than it had earlier. They turned, therefore, to purebred stock, and in the early eighties began importing Herefords from England. In 1882, they imported 132 breeding animals, most of which were of the "noblest blood lines" in the British Isles.[29] The best of this stock was taken to a sixteen-hundred-acre "model" farm in Tippecanoe County, called Shadeland, where Earl and his son-in-law, Charles B. Stuart, developed one of the largest and best-known Hereford herds in the United States. A glance at the *Annual Catalogue of the Shadeland Farm Herd of Hereford Cattle* of 1896 shows why Shadeland was called "the

[27] Benton County Probate Order Book, XXXVII, 415.

[28] In 1876, Raub offered to rent his six-thousand-acre pasture in Benton County or to take in cattle in lots of fifty or more for summer pasture.

[29] *Breeders' Gazette*, II (June 22, July 13, Aug. 3, 1882), 10, 92, 176.

great American Hereford show place of its time." [30] Here are described over one hundred purebred Herefords including Sir Bartle Frere, Lady Wilton 77th, Shadeland Climax, and the Earl of Shadeland 22d, of whom it was said: "His Hereford character was so magnificent, his early maturity so complete, his levelness so perfect, his flesh covering so uniform, his general appearance so taking, and his substance and finish so remarkable, that the Championship could not be denied him." The claims may sound exaggerated but an examination of the advertisements of the leading Hereford breeders in 1899 indicates that the foundation of many of their herds was Shadeland bulls. In that year Earl and Stuart sold Shadeland stock to breeders in Pennsylvania, Michigan, Iowa, Missouri, Kansas, Texas, and California as well as in Ohio, Indiana, and Illinois.[31] The large importations of Herefords by Fowler and VanNatta and Earl and Stuart, the large scope of their operations, and their vigorous promotion of the Hereford strain brought them into active participation in the American Hereford Cattle Breeders Association, of which VanNatta was president and Stuart was director.

In the meantime, Earl and Raub introduced Herefords on their ranch in Benton County which rapidly thereafter displaced the grade stock. A principal market for their young bulls was the cattle companies of the Great Plains which were making efforts to improve their stock.[32] Fewer cattle were now maintained and a part of the land was divided into small tracts that were fenced, modest dwellings and corncribs were constructed, and fifty-five tenants were settled upon the farms. The death of Adams Earl in 1898 brought to an end the large-scale operations in purebred stock both on the Benton County land and on Shadeland. Ultimately, 4,719 acres of the Earl estate were acquired by

[30] Alvin H. Sanders, *The Story of the Herefords* (Chicago, 1914), 442.

[31] *Breeders' Gazette*, XVI (Dec. 18, 1889), 589.

[32] In 1884, Raub and Hixson, with whom Adams Earl was associated, sold a carload of grade Hereford bull calves of twelve to fourteen months to C. A. Elliott & Co., Del Norte, Colorado, for $120 per head (*Breeders' Gazette*, V [Feb. 14, 1884], 234).

the children of Thomas J. Watson, President of the International Business Machines. To this amount the Watsons added a section of Fowler land making at that time their total possessions in Benton and Tippecanoe counties 5,359 acres.[33]

George Ade has significantly limned Edward C. Sumner, one of the ablest of the Hoosier cattle kings.

He was a Green Mountain boy with a Calvin Coolidge training in thrift and acquisitiveness, and when they turned him loose in Indiana, where his New England gift for absorbing assets could have full play, he tried to annex all grazing land between the rising and setting sun . . . Like other benevolent despots of his generation, he lived in a mansion, and his manner of living was regal as compared with that of his dependents . . . [He] now reposes beside a monument which would be a suitable reminder of any European monarch, which is proper, because the kingdom ruled by Old Ed was larger than some of the kingdoms of the Old World and a good deal more active.[34]

Sumner commenced buying land in 1846 in Benton County, Indiana, and in 1849 in the adjacent Iroquois County, Illinois. Within a few years, he had built up holdings that exceeded thirty thousand acres. Of this amount, the seventy-seven hundred acres in Iroquois County cost him no more than a dollar an acre.

Sumner's energies were largely devoted to the fattening of cattle upon his land and the production of grain. Four herds of five hundred each ranged over his property. Sumner took pride in his cattle, which he loved, and, as he became prosperous and more aloof from the common man, he continued to lavish attention upon them.

In the fifties, Sumner drove his cattle overland to market in New York, the herdsmen starting one hundred cattle every two weeks in the growing season. This was no longer necessary or feasible, however, after the completion of the Big Four Rail-

[33] Another absentee landlord who was well known in other fields was James W. Gerard, owner of 884 acres in Benton County.

[34] Ade, "Prairie Kings of Yesterday," *Saturday Evening Post*, CCIV (July 4, 1931), 77–78.

road through Benton County. Thereafter, the reputation of his herds for size and quality attracted buyers who vigorously bid for them to a point that assured him high returns. After all, the land had been acquired at low prices, labor charges certainly were not high, and other costs never became heavy. A granddaughter later recalled two large sales made by Sumner, one in 1880 when six hundred steer averaging fourteen hundred pounds brought $42,600, and the other, two years later, when eleven hundred cattle were bought for the export trade for $100,000.[35]

As the advance of settlers forced Sumner to confine his herds, he "built mile after mile of heavy plank fencing, hauling the material with horses and oxen from the nearest stations." To drain the low areas, twelve yoke of oxen were kept to haul the heavy ditching plow that was said to cut a drain eighteen inches deep and five feet wide. Caring for such large herds and performing the work of fencing, draining, and tiling the land called for large numbers of laborers. To supply them, Sumner made frequent trips to Chicago to bring back "a carload of farm hands," mostly German immigrants.[36]

Like the other cattle barons of the prairie, Sumner found laborers increasingly undependable, and he slowly turned to tenants to whom he rented a part of his land on a share basis. At first two-fifths, later one-half, of the grain went to the landlord as his share, and the remainder was sold to him at the market price for feeding to his cattle. By 1876, he had fifteen tenants, mostly on the Illinois side in Iroquois County, who were raising nothing but corn on their farms year after year. Not only was the grain regularly taken off the land and fed to cattle on the Indiana land, but the cornstalks were cut off at the roots and fed elsewhere, leaving nothing to put back into the soil. No rotation was practiced. The tenant houses which were little more

---

[35] Barce and Swan, *History of Benton County, Indiana*, III (1932), 66.

[36] Ade, "Prairie Kings of Yesterday," *Saturday Evening Post*, CCIV, (July 4, 1931), 77.

than shacks did not serve to attract the best type of farmers to
the land, and the township in which the Sumner farms were
located, despite the high quality of the soil, was regarded as
backward.[37]

Sumner's large possessions made him especially vulnerable
when farmers began to display unfriendliness toward "mo-
nopolistic" landowners. He looked with jaundiced eye upon all
assessments and used his influence to beat them down through
intimidation, legal action, and failure to pay taxes. For this he
was charged with being a "tax shirker" by the local Greenback
paper. He was also accused of driving his herds of cattle on to
his Illinois land the first of April when property was being
assessed in Indiana and of reversing the procedure when the
Illinois assessors were at work in May.[38]

The size of Sumner's operations is indicated to some extent
by the inventory prepared at the time of his death in 1882. It
showed him in possession of 600 beef cattle, 11 yoke of oxen,
40 mules, 61 horses and colts, and 19,000 bushels of corn in
cribs. His landed possessions had shrunk to twenty thousand
acres.[39]

In the absence of a will, Sumner's estate was divided among
his children, two daughters receiving the Indiana land and a son
the Illinois land. In the third generation one granddaughter, an
only child, received a third of the Sumner lands while three
other grandchildren inherited each a ninth and five inherited
each a fifteenth. Such a division was unsatisfactory to those with
a small share. When Jennie E. Caldwell, the more fortunate
granddaughter and a childless widow, died in 1912, she was in
possession of sixty-three hundred acres valued at $900,000, but
on which there was a mortgage of $116,000. Her will provided

[37] H. H. Beckwith, *History of Iroquois County* (Chicago, 1880), 487.

[38] Watseka (Ill.) *Iroquois County Times*, March 9, 23, April 6, 13, and
July 20, 1878.

[39] Inventory of the estate of Edward C. Sumner, Sept. 1, 1882, Probate File
357, Benton County.

an unpleasant surprise to the other grandchildren, for none of them were major beneficiaries. After some bequests to other relatives, the will provided that the remaining fifty-four hundred acres should be placed in trust for the benefit of the Jennie E. Fowler Home for "honest, virtuous, sick and financially helpless mothers and their babes." [40] At this turn of events, the other grandchildren of Edward Sumner began an almost endless litigation to break the will and divide the property among themselves. [41] Eventually, a compromise was reached whereby the latter were to receive $250,000 in lieu of all claims against the property, but not all the litigants accepted this action, and the fight was resumed. When all the contestants were exhausted, there remained to the Home but a fourth of the original tract it was bequeathed. Ill luck dogged the Home: it was destroyed by fire shortly after it was opened; and again, fourteen years after it was reconstructed, it had to close because of diminishing revenue from the landed endowment. [42]

Despite the losses sustained through litigation and mortgage foreclosure, three grandchildren of Edward C. Sumner owned 1,611 acres, and the Home owned 1,358 acres in Benton County. Of the Illinois land, the heirs held 6,800 acres.

Jesse Sumner, who inherited the Illinois land, passed it on to his three sons. When one of these sons, William Reynolds Sumner, died in 1936, leaving no children, his two brothers, the only heirs, presented a statement to the court for inheritance-tax purposes that provides an interesting commentary on one type of estate management. The property consisting of 1,628 acres on the Illinois side and 547 acres on the Indiana side was divided into six tenant farms. Never since the land was first farmed in the sixties had anything but corn and oats been raised on it. No livestock was kept on the land, the corn and stalks were fed elsewhere, and no manure or fertilizer was applied.

[40] Benton County Deeds, IV, 81.

[41] Fowler *Benton Review*, Feb. 22, 1912.

[42] Petition of Lee Dinwiddie, Trustee of the Jennie E. Caldwell Home, Nov. 15, 1932, in 741 Probate Records, Benton County.

The owners had "always been opposed to the spending of any money for improving or conserving the soil, the logical consequence having been . . . that the soil has been robbed of most of its available fertility." Tests showed that the soil would require ten years for rehabilitation because it was acid and poor in available plant food. The tenant improvements were of the simplest and cheapest type, only one of the houses had a cellar, and all were the subject of constant complaint. The fences were in bad repair and required replacement, drainage was inadequate and called for the expenditure of $30,000 to prevent further erosion and drowning of crops, and finally, morning glories, bull nettles, and cockleburs infested the land. The brothers concluded their indictment of the farm management of their father and brother by saying that the farm had a reputation of being "worn-out land." [43]

Alexander Kent, of whom it was said that "he was . . . a rearing, tearing, compacted bundle of energy," played a large part in the development of Newton and Jasper counties in Indiana. With his brother Phineas, he bought 30,000 acres, much of which, although classed as swampland, was suitable for grazing. Extensive feeding of livestock raised by Kent and of feeders imported from the plains marked the first use of the land. But no matter how sentimental the cattle barons were concerning their livestock, they had to adapt themselves to changing conditions, the result of rising land values. Kent invested in improving the land, constructing miles of fences, digging ditches in low areas, and erecting homes for workers. His cattle ranch became a bonanza farm with great fields in corn. Continued labor difficulties induced him to sell a part of his holdings to workers on long-term credit and to rent small tracts on a grainshare basis. It was said that "half the local population" was "on his pay roll as herdsmen or field hands." [44] In 1860, fifty-four settlers had

[43] Inventory of property, estate of W. R. Sumner, by Aaron T. and Edward C. Sumner, Iroquois County Probate Records.

[44] Ade, "Prairie Kings of Yesterday," *Saturday Evening Post*, CCIV (July 4, 1931), 76.

either bought small tracts of him on which they were making payments or had borrowed of him to finance improvements, the amount of the debts ranging from $50 to $480. In 1877, Kent seemed anxious to dispose of much of his property, for he offered for sale 20,000 acres. Much of this was only slightly improved, though it was fenced, but a 5,000-acre tract was advertised as being well-drained and in cultivation with twelve houses on it.[45] Another tract of 5,000 acres had 260 acres in cultivation, three houses, and two orchards.[46]

Perhaps the most extensive estate in the Kankakee Valley was that of Lemuel Milk and his partners. Their holdings in Kankakee and Iroquois counties, Illinois, and Newton County, Indiana, were estimated at 65,000 acres. Milk experimented with sheep raising, having at one time a flock of ten thousand, but cattle, which were better adapted to the area, constituted the major part of his business. He bought young stock, instead of raising them, fed them until they were three years old and then drove them to market. From fifteen hundred to twenty-five hundred head were kept on his farms in addition to fifteen hundred hogs and three hundred horses that were used for farming purposes. Ditching and draining were undertaken on a large scale. One field of 2,000 acres was put in corn, and in another year ten thousand bushels of flaxseed were harvested. The bonanza-farm period lasted for a short while, but it was not long before Milk was carving up a part of his estate into farms that ranged from 80 acres to a full section, which were rented to tenants. At one time Milk had fifty-six tenant farms. Apparently, Milk learned early that first-rate housing attracted a superior class of tenants, for the improvements were stated to be "better than we usually find on rented farms." [47] In 1886, thirty of Milk's Illinois farms,

[45] Kentland (Ind.) *People's Press*, Aug. 24, 1877.   [46] *Ibid.*, Oct. 2, 1884.
[47] Kankakee (Ill.) *Gazette*, quoted in Watseka (Ill.) *Iroquois County Times*, Nov. 18, 1875; *Sectional Maps showing the Location of over 2,500,000 Acres, Selected Farming and Woodlands in the State of Illinois. 850,000 Acres yet for Sale by the Illinois Central Railroad* (Chicago, 1867), 66; Beckwith, *History of Iroquois County*, 370 ff.

ranging in size from 80 to 640 acres, were offered for sale at prices from thirty to fifty dollars an acre according to location and improvement.[48] Several thousand acres of the Indiana land remained in the possession of the family into the twentieth century.

Few residents of Warren County, Indiana, or Vermilion County, Illinois, could have been ignorant of the affairs of the Goodwine family whose large cattle operations, extensive estates, and numerous children kept them in the public eye. James B. and John W. Goodwine were among the early pioneers of these two counties. Both entered largely into the business of buying, fattening, and driving cattle to market, and both used their profits to buy and improve estates. James acquired 10,250 acres in Warren County on which he pastured from twelve hundred to fifteen hundred cattle. John purchased 5,400 acres in Vermilion County, Illinois, where he maintained somewhat smaller herds. The most recent ownership maps of these counties show a number of thousand acres still in the hands of the family.[49]

From the brewing and distilling business, James W. Gaff, of Aurora, Indiana, and Cincinnati, Ohio, accumulated a fortune, part of which was invested in a cattle ranch of 11,000 acres in Newton County. As many as one thousand cattle were fattened on the ranch which was completely fenced. Homes for laborers and tenants were constructed, and a considerable amount of

[48] Watseka, *Republican*, Jan. 6, 1886.

[49] *Portrait and Biographical Album of Vermilion and Edgar Counties* (Chicago, 1889), 207; Battey & Co., *Counties of Warren, Benton, Jasper, and Newton, Indiana* (Chicago, 1883), 171. Farther south in Vermillion County, Indiana, and Vermilion County, Illinois, the Collett family acquired five thousand acres which, after a period of feeding livestock, were divided into small farms. In 1879, two British visitors reported that John Collett had in the past as many as forty tenants on his land who rented farms for three dollars an acre. The cost to Collett was no more than twenty-five cents an acre, leaving him a satisfactory return. On other land, Collett paid tenants twelve and one-half cents for every bushel of corn they raised (notebook of Clare Reed and Albert Pell, Nov. 12, 1879, in Appendix, Agricultural Interests Commission, "Report of the Assistant Commissioners," in *Parliamentary Papers, 1880*, XVIII [London, 1880], 17-18).

ditching was done.[50] Much of the Gaff land was later taken over by William Raff and J. Lawler as part of their 22,000-acre holding in Newton and Jasper counties.

No account of Hoosier cattle kings would do justice without at least mentioning Henry T. Sample (4,000 acres), Robert W. Sample (3,800 acres), Cephas Atkinson (12,000 acres), Joseph Heath (4,000 acres), Parnham Boswell (12,000 acres), Hugh Scott (4,500 acres), LeRoy Templeton (7,000 acres), Orlando Bush (4,000 acres), John Kious (4,000 acres), and Miller Kenton (5,000 acres).[51] The prairie counties are dotted with little villages that were either named after or by the prairie landlords, such as Atkinson, Boswell, Chase, Conrad, Earl Park, Fowler, Gifford, Kentland, Raub, Rensselaer, Reynolds, Templeton, and Wolcott.

The cattle kings reigned from the outbreak of the Civil War to the eighties, by which time most of the principal figures had passed beyond the great divide. Fowler, Sumner, Earl, Milk, Kent, and the others were important men whose achievements rank them with titans in industry and commerce. They had a major share in improving and developing the prairie to its present state of productiveness. The wealth that came to them from the cattle industry, rents, and sales of their holdings permitted them to live in regal grandeur on their estates, in Lafayette or in one of the smaller towns of the region.

They built huge "mansions" with "Brussels carpet on the floors and decanters of port on the walnut sideboards." [52] The "two story brick mansion" of Edward Sumner has been described by Judge Elmore Barce:

[50] Battey & Co., *Counties of Warren, Benton, Jasper and Newton, Indiana,* 793.

[51] The Daniel Sigler farm of 2,604 acres in Jasper County was sold in 1888 to Hamilton Brown of Fort Dodge, Iowa (Rensselaer [Ind.] *Republican;* quoted in Kentland [Ind.] *Gazette,* July 5, 1888).

[52] Ade, "Prairie Kings of Yesterday," *Saturday Evening Post,* CCIV (July 4, 1931), 14.

There were great drives and porches at the front—a large hall at the entrance, and on the lower floor seven large rooms with frescoed ceilings fourteen feet in height. The upper story comprised eight large rooms. In all rooms, above and below, were fireplaces and grates. To the rear of the mansion were two large pantries, and quarters for the servants.[53]

Another mansion, the third home built by Jacob Cassel, was "both mammoth and imposing. The stair casing and the panels are of oak and walnut. There are six large rooms above, five below, and two halls." [54] The former home of Abraham Mann, an extensive cattle feeder with a farm of four thousand acres, was described in 1879 as having "twenty spacious rooms, including dairy and laundry, and exclusive of the large halls, closets and garret. It was built at a cost of . . . $30,000. The adjoining grounds are laid out with taste and planted with flowers and evergreens. A greenhouse is attached to the premises." [55] When 1,310 acres of the old Mann place, together with the house, were sold to A. G. Belt, owner of the Steak 'n Shake restaurants, the "palatial" three-story house was described as having thirteen rooms, five bathrooms, and a ballroom on the third floor.[56]

The Fowler and Earl homes in Lafayette, built respectively in 1852 and 1859, were superb illustrations of the lavish splendor with which the cattle barons surrounded themselves.[57] Fowler's English gothic type house was adapted from the plans of a "country villa" outlined and described by Andrew Jackson Downing, the distinguished architect and landscape gardener, in his *The Architecture of Country Houses; Including Designs*

[53] Barce and Swan, *History of Benton County, Indiana*, III, 67.
[54] *Ibid.*, 102.
[55] H. W. Beckwith, *History of Vermilion County* (Chicago, 1879), 676.
[56] Bloomington (Ill.) *Pantagraph*, Oct. 18, 1945.
[57] These homes were not "lavish" in comparison with the turreted castles and baronial halls then being constructed by millionaires in New York and Newport, but for a town and area scarcely out of the frontier stage they were indeed splendid.

for Cottages, Farm Houses and Villas.[58] Red brick, later covered with stucco, was substituted for the recommended New Jersey sandstone. Downing had urged that the house "should have no common-place, contracted or mean site. It should stand on a commanding locality . . . overlooking a fine reach of picturesque but cultivated landscape." This was provided by placing it in the center of a lot comprising an entire city block and the "picturesque" was shortly furnished by the construction of the present Wabash Railroad which cut across a corner of the estate. The grace and charm of the structure was matched by the interior finish in oak and black walnut that was elaborately handcarved, the intricate scroll-work, the frescoes, the marble fireplaces, and the gold leaf in the ceiling, since removed. Extensive changes were later made by a grandson of Moses Fowler, and still later the home became the headquarters of the Tippecanoe County Historical Society.

Adams Earl built his house on a high knoll in the midst of a ten-acre plot, a part of which was kept for a deer park. No means were spared in making the home fit for the entertainment of the most aristocratic people. High ceilinged rooms with eight beautifully constructed marble fireplaces, some in alabaster white and others in black carrara marble, heavy draperies, carpets covering the floor from wall to wall, exotic vases, exquisite china from the best potteries of England, and massive walnut and mahogany furniture all combined tastefully to give distinction to the home.

With these mansions and the lavish decorations, oil paintings, European and oriental bric-a-brac, and furniture that filled them from main floor to garret, went a social life that was scarcely harmonious with frontier existence. High society, an aristocracy, had come to the prairies. Essentially a rural aristocracy at the outset, though some of its best-known members always dwelt in towns and cities, there was a tendency to move to neighboring

[58] New York, 1850. Visits to the Fowler and Earl homes at the invitation of Miss Alameda McCollough and Mrs. A. C. Clouser were most helpful.

urban centers either in the first or second generation. Rising corn-belt cities like Springfield, Decatur, Bloomington, Champaign, and Danville, Illinois, and Lafayette, Crawfordsville, Logansport, and Indianapolis, Indiana, attracted the sons of the cattle kings, where they entered into banking, real estate, the law, and politics. The income from their estates, divided into numerous and on the whole highly profitable farms, assured them independence and a comfortable living. It also made possible donations to local universities and colleges and other philanthropic institutions.[59]

The heritage of the cattle kings is shown in the plat books and ownership maps of the prairie counties, which reveal large blocks of land held by their families in the 1930s. But memories of the cattle kings, their buoyant optimism, their driving energy, their great herds of cattle, the speed with which they brought the prairie into cultivation, their rapid accumulation of wealth, their lavish mansions, and their conspicuous consumption are fast fading. Their share in converting the wild prairie of yesterday into the rich corn belt of today was as vital and in its way as romantic as that of the lonely pioneer in coonskin, or the cowboy with his six-shooter, but it has been much less known.

George Ade has been called a gentle humorist, a benign observer, and a wry philosopher. Though his writings receive little attention today, he wrote one minor classic that historians need to know: "Prairie Kings of Yesterday" (*Saturday Evening Post*, CCIV [July 4, 1931], 14 ff.). Here he described in his inimitable fashion the way the cattle kings of the Kankakee Valley accumulated their huge holdings and the frontier society that was based on this aristocratic pattern of ownership.

[59] The donations of the Ellsworth, the Fowler, and the Earl families to Purdue University and Wabash College are illustrations.

7. Cattle Kings
in the Prairies

During the controversies over the meat shortage and the price control policies of the Office of Price Administration's post–World War II years, attention was directed to the mechanics of the contemporary cattle industry. Many Americans learned for the first time that large numbers of the cattle from the Great Plains were brought into the prairie states for a period of fattening before they were shipped to market. Herds of white-faced cattle were shipped to the great farms of John W. Sudduth, the Funks, the Mecherles, the Sibleys, and many others in the prairie states, where they were fed a considerable share of the huge corn crop raised in the area. When the movement was at its height, whole trainloads of cattle were moved to the feed lots. In prosperous years nearly two million feeder cattle were brought into the prairie states for fattening.[1]

John W. Sudduth is an interesting example of the large prairie farmers who specialized in fattening cattle. On his 2,200-acre farm south of Springfield, Illinois, Sudduth fed from 600 to 1,000 cattle. He bought Herefords averaging 900 pounds, fed them three months, and then shipped them to Chicago for butchering. All the corn raised on his three farms, which totaled 3,000 acres, was used, and much more was bought from other farmers. Cottonseed meal was also purchased for feed. Such

[1] In 1945, between July and October, 1,786,533 feeder cattle were shipped from stockyards to farms for fattening (*Breeders' Gazette*, XCI [Jan., 1946], 12).

feeding practices served to put into the soil rich manure which kept it in a high state of productivity.[2]

Similarly, Walter Meers, who operated the large Mecherle farm as well as land of his own in McLean County, Illinois, fed 600 cattle. Both he and his landlord, George Mecherle, took pride in the success they enjoyed in their cattle business and the increased value it gave to their land. To the Funk farms in McLean County and the Sibley farms in Ford County, where cattle feeding was a basic feature of farm management, 1,400 and 650 feeders respectively were imported annually from the ranges. Throughout the Corn Belt wise farmers, whether large or small operators, included feeding of hogs or plains-reared cattle as part of their business.[3]

This feeder industry in the Corn Belt was a modern adaptation of the earlier business of cattle breeding, grazing, fattening, and driving that flourished after 1835. In that period, when the prairies were the cattleman's frontier, conditions were ripe for the emergence of "cattle kings"—extensive dealers in livestock who acquired and subsequently developed great estates running into many thousands of acres. These cattle kings lived the life of the ranch owner of the Great Plains in their eighties; they had "the same problems to face, and developed the same technique in the ranging and marketing of cattle." Each of these cattle kings recorded with the county clerk earmarks and brands for identifying his stock. There was also the typical ranchers' trouble with estrays and with rustlers, to suppress which societies and vigilante committees were organized.[4]

Frontier cattle were a hardy type possessing few of the fine qualities that characterize the modern beef animal. Wild, raw-boned, their meat stringy and their color—dun, black, brindle,

[2] Personal interview with John W. Sudduth, Springfield, Ill., Sept. 22, 1945.

[3] Bloomington *Pantagraph*, Nov. 1, 24, 1946; Jan. 22, Feb. 8, July 25, 1947. Unless otherwise designated, newspapers cited in this article were published in Illinois.

[4] C. A. Harper, "The Railroad and the Prairie," *Transactions of the Illinois State Historical Society for the Year 1923* (Springfield, 1923), 105.

and yellow—denoting their mongrel character, they were an inferior lot. But they did provide milk and they could be broken to the plow or wagon where horses and mules were unobtainable. On the other hand, they required slight attention, lived on the prairie grasses, and consumed little grain. Furthermore, if enclosed on bluegrass pasture and given grain they could gain enough weight to make a presentable appearance to the meat packer.

The abundance of tall sweet grass made the prairies a natural area for the cattle industry. Unwanted by settlers who preferred the timbered tracts, they were mostly uninhabited for years after the first coming of the whites. They did provide excellent pasture, however, which attracted the cattle of the timbered farms to them. Cattle buyers who roamed the farm country searching for stock that could be acquired at low prices found it possible to pasture herds on the public lands at little or no costs. In the thirties Indiana, Illinois, and Missouri were a breeding and herding ground for Ohio, whose cattle had acquired a favorable reputation and brought good market prices. Cattle were driven to Ohio, sometimes farther east, for fattening and then were marketed as Ohio stock.[5]

The coming of the railroad to the prairies accelerated the westward movement of the cattle industry. Cattle could now be fattened anywhere on the prairies and shipped by rail to Chicago, St. Louis, Indianapolis, Cincinnati, or even New York and Boston in as many days as it had previously taken weeks to drive them to market and without suffering the same serious losses in weight. Rising land values in older, more settled areas and the resulting more intensive land use impelled the westward migration of the cattle industry, while the availability of cheap prairie land made accessible by railroads attracted it. By 1860

[5] Cattle driving from Ohio is described by Rev. I. F. King, "The Coming and Going of Ohio Droving," *Ohio Archaeological and Historical Publications*, XVII (Columbus, 1908), 247–253. King mentions Michael Sullivant and Isaac Funk as successful Ohio drovers, though his information about the latter is inaccurate.

Illinois was gridironed by railroads, and the center of the cattle industry had moved from Ohio to the Prairie State.[6] Until the eighties the Corn Belt continued to maintain more cattle than the Great Plains. With the westward movement of the cattle industry went increasing specialization in grain farming, improvements in pasture, breeds, and feeding practices, and the flowering of large cattle ranches.

Railroad extension into Kansas, Nebraska, and the Dakotas made possible the Long Drive of Texas cattle northward and their widespread distribution over the plains. This area then became the breeding ground for feeders that were shipped into the Corn Belt for the finishing process. Feeder cattle had been brought into Illinois from Missouri and Texas before 1860 but not on a large scale. Thereafer their introduction into the Corn Belt in ever-increasing amounts forced major changes in the livestock business. No longer was it profitable to breed and raise cattle on the high-priced prairie land in competition with cattle raised on the cheaper land in the plains states; instead, feeder cattle from Texas and Kansas were imported and fattened for periods of one month to ten or more and then were marketed. Prairie farms thus became way stations on the cattle route from source to consumption. This is not to say that cattle raising on the prairie ceased; it adapted itself to new conditions.

[6] In 1863, New York City received from Illinois 118,692 beeves of the total of 264,091. Of course the Chicago packing houses drew largely from Illinois, and "government contractors and commissaries, in the west at least, have found here their main dependence." Despite the large drains on Illinois cattle during the war years, the number of neat cattle in the state increased rapidly as is shown by the following table, compiled from the Illinois State Agricultural Society, *Transactions*, V (Springfield, 1865), 23:

Year	Number of neat cattle in Illinois listed for tax purposes
1859	1,337,565
1860	1,425,978
1861	1,428,362
1862	1,603,949
1863	1,684,892

Purebred stock was replacing the native breeds so common in the frontier period. Stock improvement associations were organized by progressive farmers to import purebred Shorthorns from England. The farm journals devoted quantities of space to the Shorthorns, and it was not long before most influential and successful farmers could boast of their thoroughbred stock. By 1878 it was possible for a local historian to boast that the introduction of the Shorthorns had almost completely changed the color and form of Illinois cattle.[7] In the eighties the Herefords, then challenging the predominance of the Shorthorns, produced further change. At the same time, livestock received better care, such as earlier grain feeding, construction of shelters, protection against disease, and even veterinary aid. For a generation longer some of the cattle kings continued to raise their own thoroughbreds, but an ever-increasing proportion of feeder and stocker cattle from the plains were substituted for home-raised cattle. Indeed, it was possible to say: "The plow drove out the cow until in the heart of the corn country but few females of the beef type remained. For thirty years or more in some such sections, it has been a proverb that 'it does not pay to keep a cow a year for the chance of a calf.' "[8]

Cattle buyers and drovers were important links in the livestock business. Their risks were great, their losses numerous, and their profits high. Many of the prairie cattle kings started as buyers or drovers and invested their profits in land for grazing. Experiments with prairie cultivation showed them that corn was the ideal crop for the prairies, and as laborers, later tenants, became available, they began to plow their pastures and to plant them in corn. The bonanza farm developed on the prairies when cattle ranches were fenced and fields of thousands of acres were

---

[7] *History of Livingston County, Illinois* (Chicago, 1878), 279.

[8] Herbert W. Mumford and Louis D. Hall, "Economic Factors in Cattle Feeding," Part IV of "Cattle Feeding Conditions in the Corn Belt," University of Illinois Agricultural Experiment Station, *Circular*, No. 175 (Urbana, 1914), 7.

plowed and planted in corn by hired hands using batteries of newly developed farm machinery.[9]

The cattle kings now became great landlords who employed armies of workers to perform the tasks of grain and livestock farming. Their greatest triumph came in the period from 1862 to 1873 when high prices, expanding demand for their products, and slower increase in costs left them with net returns that put them into the millionaire class. The panic of 1873, with its swift decline in agricultural prices, brought disaster to some of these landlords who were operating on borrowed capital. Others who survived, and most of them did, were learning the advantages of permitting tenants, substituted for farm laborers, to share the responsibilities and risks as well as the advantages of farming the large estates. Division of farms into small operating units solved the labor problem, for there were numerous applicants for tenant holdings who would make more intensive use of the land and probably produce greater returns to the landlord. So the bonanza farm followed the earlier cattle ranch into limbo and the present farm pattern was established.

Two of the earliest of the Illinois cattle kings who left notable marks on prairie development were Isaac Funk and Jacob Strawn. Funk settled in Funks Grove, southwest of Bloomington, in 1824; seven years later Strawn took up residence near Jacksonville. Buying, fattening, and driving cattle to market absorbed their attention, not farming or raising cattle. They scoured their neighborhoods for young stock which they bought and drove to their locality for grazing and a final period of corn feeding. Keener competition for beef cattle extended Funk's and Strawn's buying trips into Missouri, the Indian country, and Texas.[10] Experience soon taught them how to judge cattle, what

[9] Paul W. Gates, "Large-Scale Farming in Illinois, 1850–1870," *Agricultural History* VI (Jan., 1932), 14–25. Also see Chapter 5, above.

[10] Springfield *Illinois Journal*, clipped in Springfield *Illinois State Register*, Nov. 15, 1855. Isaac Funk and James Nichols were reported to have paid $27,000 for 1,200 head of cattle they bought in Texas and drove to Illinois in 1855.

prices to pay, and how to bargain with the isolated prairie farmers who had no knowledge of market conditions or means of transporting livestock to slaughterhouses. When the cattle were ready for market, Funk and Strawn set out with motley crews to drive the grazing herds overland. Funk marketed his cattle in Galena, Peoria, Chicago, and Ohio cities, while Strawn generally drove to St. Louis.[11] Before the telegraph there was no way of knowing whether markets were glutted or the extent of demand, and the element of chance was greater than today. Possessed of a shrewd business sense, both men always seemed able to surmount any obstacles and rarely failed to make a profit on their transactions.[12]

Although cattle were the major interest of Funk and Strawn, they found it desirable to fatten hogs which salvaged the corn that cattle wasted. Also, hogs reached marketable age more quickly than cattle, an advantage if a decline in price threatened or if quick returns were essential.

Costs of cattle feeding on the prairies were low. Hired hands were employed at small wages from the floating population then flooding Illinois in search of land; cheap or free grass was available; little fencing was necessary until settlers began to push into the prairie; and taxes were few and light.

Profits were invested in timbered land at first, but later Funk and Strawn bought prairie tracts. The following tabulation indicates their early purchases: [13]

[11] Eugene D. Funk, "Crops since 1824," *Prairie Farmer*, CXIII (Jan. 11, 1941), 108. A New York reporter who visited the Jacob Strawn farm and talked with the owner spoke of his judgment of cattle being "nigh infallible": "He will ride into a drove of cattle, glance over it with incredible quickness counting the numbers, singling out the average ox, computing from him the whole drove, and offering a price for the whole more promptly than many would for a single ox" (New York *Tribune*, June 15, 1855).

[12] For a contemporary description of cattle driving in Illinois, see William Oliver, *Eight Months in Illinois with Information for Emigrants* (Newcastle upon Tyne, Eng., 1843; reprinted Chicago, 1924), 104 ff.

[13] Compiled from abstracts of entry books of Illinois land offices, National Archives, Washington; the land sales books of the Illinois Central Railroad,

Year	Funk	Strawn
1829	1,040	
1830	400	
1831		1,190
1832	400	
1834	560	
1835		1,220
1836	760	
1837	1,360	
1838	720	
1839		1,670

Both men successfully weathered the panic of 1837, although their operations were temporarily reduced. The prosperity of the fifties and sixties affected them favorably, their incomes rising to five and six figures in the best years. Visitors to the Funk farm during the Civil War were astonished to see fields of 2,000 to 3,000 acres in grain, and 1,600 cattle, 500 sheep, 500 hogs, and 300 horses and mules in the pastures. Funk's annual drives of livestock to the Chicago market totaled as high as 1,500 cattle and 6,000 hogs in some years.[14] The value of his livestock in 1863 was estimated at a million dollars.[15]

Strawn's operations were on an equally large scale and elicited as much favorable comment. On his 10,000-acre farm he had a field of 3,000 acres in corn. His "vast" herds of cattle necessitated fencing for which he spent in one year $10,000.[16] A force

---

Central Station, Chicago; and the county deed records of Morgan and McLean counties (Jacksonville and Bloomington, Ill.).

[14] James Caird, *Prairie Farming in America* (New York, 1859), 55–56; "The Prairie State," *Atlantic Monthly*, VII (May, 1861), 590; New York *Tribune*, July 30, 1861; *American Agriculturist* (New York), XXII (Sept., 1863), 263; James Shaw, *Twelve Years in America* (Dublin, 1867), 194–195; Leonidas H. Kerrick, "Life and Character of Hon. Isaac Funk," McLean County Historical Society, *Transactions*, II (Bloomington, 1903), 503.

[15] *Michigan Farmer* (Detroit), II (Aug., 1863), 63.

[16] New York *Tribune*, June 15, 1855; Chicago *Democratic Press*, in Springfield *Illinois State Register*, March 2, 1854; *Prairie Farmer*, XIV (Nov., 1854), 428.

of two or three hundred laborers was employed to do the work necessary for such a large business.[17]

Throughout their lives Funk and Strawn continued to deal in cattle on a large scale, but their increasing landed possessions gradually absorbed more of their time. With settlers moving into the prairie, the groves they both owned came into demand and brought high prices. Funks Grove proved to be a gold mine to its owner, so keen was the demand for its timber. It was estimated that more than a million dollars worth of building materials, fencing, ties, and fuel wood were taken from it by 1903. Funds from the sale of their timber and the high profits they enjoyed from the cattle business in the boom years of the Crimean War made possible larger purchases of land than in any previous year. A son-in-law said of Funk: "The stock business now, instead of being the end or ultimate object of their ambition, became the means or instrument for accomplishing another object—the purchase of land. The stock business was to become the machine with which the money might be made to pay for the land." [18]

The boom years of the fifties brought to Illinois hundreds of thousands of immigrants with little resources and hundreds of speculators with large purses, all looking for land. To protect their interests, Funk, Strawn, and other cattle kings joined in the scramble for the remaining public lands. At this point Funk plunged heavily into land purchases, buying 4,836 acres from the Illinois Central Railroad and 8,000 from the government. Strawn's purchases were only slightly less. In one deal he acquired 3,590 acres from John Grigg, a wealthy Philadelphia speculator who had tired of his Illinois investment amounting to more than 100,000 acres.[19] By 1856, when the public lands

---

[17] Cincinnati *Cist's Weekly Advertiser*, Dec. 13, 1848; *Country Gentleman* (Philadelphia), IV (Sept. 21, 1854), 184; Delphi (Ind.) *Journal*, April 6, 1859.

[18] Kerrick, "Isaac Funk," McLean County Historical Society, *Transactions*, II (1903), 506, 509.

[19] EE Deed Record, Sangamon County (Springfield, Ill.), 334.

were gone, Funk and Strawn had acquired respectively 26,000 and 20,000 acres.

Meantime, their farming operations were changing. Heavier cattle of improved breed were being produced, and increasing amounts of corn were necessary to provide for concentrated feeding. As farming became more intensive there was more labor to be performed. Miles of fences and ditches had to be constructed, new land had to be broken, and corn had to be planted in ever larger amounts. Improvements in the plow and the use of the harrow, the cultivator, the seeder, and the drill took care of some of this work, but human labor was indispensable even though it was becoming less available. The high wages paid on railroad construction, industrial and building jobs in western cities, and the cheapness of land farther west absorbed much of the available labor or impelled it to move to the next frontier where government land was still to be had. When the Civil War came, the army drained the West of its remaining manpower. In 1861, Funk was quoted as saying: "No man can afford to hire men to grow and market grain at present prices. Men do not half work; few earn the money they exact; at present prices of grain, none do." He observed that if men received less pay they would save more money.[20] The sour note is understandable, for high wages and the scarcity of labor were forcing Funk and Strawn to modify their farm practices.

The shortage of labor induced Funk and Strawn to divide a part of their estates into 160-acre units on which former employees or incoming immigrants were established as tenants. The landlord built small homes for the new occupants, provided them with a team, farm implements, and credit until their first crop came in, and either paid them a stipulated sum for every bushel of corn they produced or allowed them one-third of the grain. Tenants who provided their own team and farm implements and boarded themselves were permitted by Funk to retain three-fifths of the grain. Strawn preferred to pay a fixed sum for

[20] New York *Tribune*, July 30, 1861.

every bushel the tenant produced for him and to employ the tenant to feed the grain to his cattle. It was not difficult to secure tenants on such terms and the problem of labor was thereby met. True, there was a fairly high turnover among the tenants, who grew restless and left when they learned there was no chance to buy the farms on which they were settled. But from the continuing stream of immigration that was flowing into the prairies it was always possible to secure replacements.[21]

Funk continued to raise corn with the aid of hired hands and fed his crop and his share of the tenants' crops to his cattle. He also bought much of the tenants' share for feeding, and when this did not assure adequate supplies he "put cattle out with other farmers to have them fed, paying so much a pound for the gain."[22]

By 1865 the estates of the cattle kings like Funk and Strawn were no longer ranches for the pasturing of cattle but were congeries of small farms operated by tenants whose principal and too often only crop was corn. The livestock was being crowded into small enclosures or into the broken land along the streams. Tenants not only freed the landlord of responsibility for and supervision of the management of much of the land, but provided him with grain rent that sooner or later was to make him independent of the cattle business. At this point the landlord no longer needed to live on or in the vicinity of his land.

Strawn and Funk both died in 1865, leaving estates estimated to be worth one and two millions respectively. Like most Illinois landlords, they "believed passionately in land as the only stable form of investment" and hoped that their estates would be re-

[21] Watseka *Iroquois County Times*, October 21, 1875, reported a correspondent in Wellington as saying: "A number of parties with us, are riding the country over in quest of farms to rent, offering to pay one-third, two-fifths, $3.00 and $3.25 an acre, according to convenience and nearness to market." In 1876 it was said that the scarcity of jobs in cities was driving workers to the country in search of farms to rent (*Indiana Farmer* [Indianapolis], XI [June 3, 1876], 5).

[22] Kerick, "Isaac Funk," McLean County Historical Society, *Transactions*, II (1903), 503.

tained in family ownership.[23] Some of the heirs remained on the land or in its vicinity and turned to raising purebred stock on a smaller scale.[24] Others moved to Bloomington, Jacksonville, and elsewhere to engage in business and politics. The third generation went even farther away, thereby contributing to the development of absentee landlordism. Both estates shrank, especially the Strawn estate, although more than 2,700 acres still remained to the family in 1920. Eugene Funk, a grandson of Isaac, could boast in 1941 that 22,000 acres of Funk land were still intact. Though somewhat of an exaggeration, more than half of the Funk land was then owned by the descendants of Isaac in the third and fourth generations,[25] who have taken a leading part in the great hybrid seed industry, banking, city improvement, and other economic activities, in addition to their management of thousands of acres of farm land.

Three brothers of Jacob Strawn settled early in LaSalle, Marshall, and Livingston counties where they entered largely in the cattle business for which they acquired 12,000 acres. From his La Salle County land Abner Strawn—a nephew of

[23] Eugene D. Funk, "Crops since 1824," *Prairie Farmer*, CXIII (Jan. 11, 1941), 108.

[24] In 1875, James G. Strawn, son of Jacob Strawn, and A. C. Funk, grandson of Isaac Funk, were advertising for sale thoroughbred Shorthorn cattle and Berkshire swine, which was quite a change from the day when nothing but natives or Texans interested their father and grandfather (*National Live-Stock Journal* [Chicago], VI [Sept., 1875], 373).

[25] *The Atlas of McLean County and The State of Illinois* (Chicago, 1874), shows thirty-three individual or partnership ownerships in excess of 1,240 acres; of these, nine were heirs of Isaac Funk. The largest of the McLean County holdings was the 5,836 acres owned by David Davis. Then came the 4,800-acre holding of the Henline Brothers that was used for cattle raising. The total acreage of members of the Henline family was 6,000 (Bloomington *Pantagraph*, March 9, 1877). The location and extent of prairie land holdings in the twentieth century may be obtained from the plat books compiled and published by W. W. Hixson & Co., of Rockford, Illinois (now the Rockford Map Publishers). These plat books have taken the place of the county atlases of the nineteenth century, which are listed and described in Solon J. Buck, *Travel and Description, 1765–1865*, Illinois State Historical Library Collections, IX (Springfield, 1914), 255 ff.

Jacob—shipped to eastern markets from 3,000 to 6,000 steers annually. By the seventies he was replacing Texan and native grades with Shorthorns.[26] He settled numerous tenants upon a part of his land that was cut into small farms and induced some of his tenants and workers, perhaps the younger generation, to move to Newton County, Indiana, where he was improving tracts.[27]

David Strawn kept on his 7,000-acre ranch a herd of 2,500 to 3,000 cattle, most of which were bought as feeders. In the fall of 1859 he marketed 2,500 cattle weighing an average of 600 pounds for which he received $31 per head. It was his practice to start feeding corn, of which he raised 30,000 bushels that year, as soon as it hardened. His success in building up an estate from the cattle business led him to advise farmers to feed their grain to livestock rather than to sell it for others to feed.[28] At the time of his death in 1875 Strawn had twelve tenants on his land.[29] Christopher Strawn, a nephew of David, managed large farm and cattle interests for his family, ran for Congress on the Greenback ticket in 1878, and later became attorney for the Santa Fe Railroad. The Strawn family long retained considerable holdings in Livingston and LaSalle counties.

The land and cattle business of Titus Sudduth was almost as large as that of the Funks and the Strawns. Sudduth was less of a dealer in livestock and more of a feeder, as his son John later became. On his 12,000 acres in Sangamon, Menard, Christian, Ford, and McLean counties, seven tenants were paid eight cents a bushel for all the corn they could raise, Sudduth providing everything but the labor. The modern livestock share lease was

[26] *National Live-Stock Journal,* VI (June, 1875), 219.

[27] *Counties of Warren, Benton, Jasper and Newton, Indiana* (Chicago, 1883), 706.

[28] Rensselaer (Ind.) *Gazette,* Dec. 21, 1859.

[29] Ottawa *Free Trader,* Sept. 27, 1873; File No. 6, Box 110, Probate Records, LaSalle County (Ottawa, Ill.).

not used but the tenant was hired to feed and care for the cattle and hogs which were kept on most of the farms. The inventory of property made after Sudduth's death in 1899 revealed that 680 cattle, 162 hogs, and 64 horses and mules were on the farms.

Sudduth's estate was divided among his four children and two grandchildren, who retained the property in close family ownership. While some of the second generation were absentee owners, notably Laura Sudduth, owner of seven farms until her death in 1932, and Florence Hooper, who received the Christian County land, others, like John Sudduth, continued to manage the land and expanded upon the cattle business of their father.[30] Although some transfers of land were made, the descendants of Titus in the second and third generations still owned 11,000 acres.

Two cattle kings whose operations attracted attention because of the heavy weight and high quality of their livestock were Benjamin F. Harris and John Dean Gillett. Both became well-known figures in the livestock industry in Illinois; both loved the attention their 2,000-pound steers received at fairs, at the slaughterhouses, and in the trade journals; both left estates which were held and even increased by their descendants.

In 1834 Harris started buying Ohio cattle which he drove eastward to markets in Pennsylvania. Success in these drives permitted him to expand his operations until he was scouring Ohio, Indiana, and Illinois in search of cattle that could be bought cheaply and yet would bring good prices in the East. Harris described in his autobiography drives from Ohio and Illinois to Lancaster, Pennsylvania. Herds of 100 to 430 cattle were swum across the Wabash at Attica and driven through Muncie, Indiana, Springfield and Columbus, Ohio, and over the mountains to Cumberland and Hagerstown, Maryland, and to

[30] Material for the Sudduth business came from the probate records in Sangamon County and an interview with John W. Sudduth, September 22, 1945.

Gettysburg, Harrisburg, and Lancaster, Pennsylvania. It was on a buying trip through Illinois that he became acquainted with the prairies in Champaign and Piatt counties where he determined to establish a cattle farm. In 1842 he moved to this area and began purchasing land until he accumulated 5,000 acres. For a time he continued to buy cattle in Illinois, Missouri, and later Kansas and to fatten and drive them to market, but the increasing value of his land and the greater profits to be made from improved stock induced him to withdraw from the business of droving and to concentrate on developing his estate and raising heavy stock.

A part of Harris' land was used for grain and hay and the remainder was kept in pasture for the herds of cattle that were raised by him or bought from others. By 1855 he had 700 acres in corn and small grain from which he harvested 48,000 bushels. He pastured as many as 950 cattle and 200 hogs and bought as high as 63,000 bushels of corn for feed, in addition to using all he raised. In a day when huge fat bullocks were in demand, he fed his stock until they averaged close to a ton each. Tenants were established on his land in the fifties; shortly afterward he moved to Champaign to engage in banking while the business of raising, buying, and fattening cattle was managed first by a brother, later by his son.[31] At his death in 1905 the 4,071 acres he still owned were appraised at $306,389, and the value of his entire estate exceeded a half million dollars. Doubtless the land would have been appraised at a higher figure had it been tiled, but Harris was not one to spend much on improvements. Through intermarriage with the Burnham family, whose holdings were among the largest in Champaign County, the Harris possessions were augmented to 8,500 acres. They exhibited

[31] *Prairie Farmer*, X (Dec., 1852), 353; XV (July, 1855), 207; Springfield *Illinois State Journal*, March 20, 1856; Albany (N.Y.) *Knickerbocker*, in Freeport *Bulletin*, May 29, 1856; William Ferguson, *America by River and Rail* (London, 1856), 376, 377; Mary Vose Harris, ed., "Autobiography of Benjamin Franklin Harris," *Transactions of the Illinois State Historical Society for the Year 1923*, 72–101.

unusual persistence in being held together in the twentieth century.[32]

John Dean Gillett's far-flung operations in land and cattle made his name almost a byword for prairie landlordism and superior quality beef in America and England. Where William Scully, a close neighbor of Gillett's in Logan County and an even larger landowner, was subjected to a bitter political attack for his accumulation of land and his Old World tenant policies,[33] Gillett was the American most responsible for a series of public and private investigations and for British discrimination against the importation of American cattle.

A scion of substantial Yankee stock, Gillett migrated to central Illinois in 1838 at the age of nineteen. With his partner, Robert Latham, he bought considerable Logan County land for speculation, entered land for settlers on "frontier" terms, laid out and promoted towns, improved farm lands ,and by the middle fifties was selling a part of his extensive holdings. Railroads, banking, and other features of the economic life of Lincoln, the county seat with which they were intimately associated, attracted their attention and brought high returns in increasing town lot sales. It was in the development of his own prairie lands, however, that Gillett was most absorbed.

Gillett was ambitious to own a great estate on which he could dwell in lordly splendor surrounded by his laborers who cared for his herds of cattle. In the late forties and fifties he bought from the government the greater part of his 16,000 acres, which made him owner of one of the largest prairie estates. Cattle attracted him as much as did land and he built his property into a ranch on which he could raise his own breeds and fatten other cattle bought from neighbors. No dilettante cattle fancier, he wasted no time or money in importing expensive bulls and

[32] The appraisal of the Harris estate is in the probate records, Champaign County (Urbana, Illinois). Margaret Beattie Bogue has described the farm operations of the Harris family in her *Patterns from the Sod: Land Use and Tenure in the Grand Prairie, 1850–1900* (Springfield, Ill., 1959), 78–83.

[33] See Chapter 8, below.

cows and in building up a herd of purebred Shorthorns as did some of his neighbors. Yearling cattle bought locally, combined with his own strain of Shorthorn grades, and fattened for market on the prairie blue stem grass and the corn he raised constituted his business. He specialized not in purebred but in fat stock.

Gradually improvements were made on Gillett's ranch that transformed it into a modern agricultural estate. One hundred and forty-four miles of fencing were constructed, tenant houses were erected, extensive tile drainage was undertaken, and 6,500 acres were broken and put in corn. When Gillett began improving his land the pressure of incoming immigrants was such that it was easy for him to secure hired hands to do most of the work. As late as 1877 he employed 100 hands during the growing season.[34] Before this, however, tenants were being substituted for the less dependable farm laborers. A stake in the business would make tenants more dependable, would induce them to use their best talents and energy in improving the land, and would shift to them a part of the risk involved in grain growing and livestock feeding. A portion of the estate was cut into tenant holdings on which homes were constructed—in 1877 there were nineteen tenant improvements—and funds were provided to enable the tenants to buy and fatten steers. When the cattle were ready for market they were to be sold to Gillett provided he offered a "price as good as any other." [35] On the cultivated land tenants were paid fifteen cents a bushel for corn they raised if they furnished everything except the land and ten cents a bushel if Gillett furnished teams and implements.[36] All corn produced on the estate was fed to cattle and additional quantities were bought. Gillett experienced the usual frontier landlord's troubles with tenants and was forced to levy upon tenant prop-

[34] Watseka *Republican*, March 8, 1877.

[35] See the five agreements between tenants and John Dean Gillett, I Miscellaneous Deeds, Logan County (Lincoln, Illinois).

[36] *National Live-Stock Journal*, VIII (Aug., 1877), 347; Bloomington *Bulletin*, March 4, 1887.

erty to protect his equity. There is no evidence, however, that he was harsh in his treatment, while there is plenty of local newspaper evidence that shows him to be more indulgent, more forbearing, than was his neighbor William Scully.

Gillett's livestock business was on a scale that would do credit to anything short of the cattle companies of the western plains. From 2,400 to 3,000 cattle were grazed on the estate—though never housed—and more than a thousand hogs salvaged the corn not utilized by the cattle. As many as 1,200 steers were marketed annually.[37] The stock was pastured for three years before grain feeding began. To bring them to the best condition for market as much as 130 to 235 bushels of corn were fed each steer. It was estimated that for every steer thus fed some 500 pounds of pork was produced.[38]

While most of his contemporaries were content to market their stock with less grain feeding, Gillett, having his own abundant supply to feed and not lacking capital, could carry the cattle to a higher state of fattening. Steers pushed to an immense size by heavy grain feeding became his special pride and were exhibited at the Chicago Fat Stock Show and elsewhere. At the 1878 show Gillett "carried off more prizes than any other exhibitor," despite the fact that he "pays no attention whatever to pedigree." His choicest steer was selected as the best three-year-old grade, the best three-year-old of any breed, and the best beef animal of any age. This was the third year that this steer, sheltered only at exhibitions, won distinction.[39]

Select groups of Gillett's fat cattle were shipped to Chicago and some went on to Buffalo, Albany, New York, and Montreal

[37] Lincoln *Herald*, Aug. 21, 1873; Watseka *Republican*, March 8, 1877; Chicago *Times*, in Bloomington *Pantagraph*, Nov. 17, 1878.

[38] Mumford and Hall, "Economic Factors in Cattle Feeding," University of Illinois Agricultural Experiment Station, *Circular*, No. 175, 6.

[39] *National Live-Stock Journal*, X (Jan., 1879), 17–19; Lincoln *Herald*, Nov. 30, Dec. 21, 1882; Feb. 8, 1883; *Prairie Farmer*, LII (Nov. 12, 19, 1881) 364, 389.

where they attracted excited bidding among butchers and meat packers and favorable publicity in the city papers and farm and livestock journals.[40]

In 1875 Gillett and a New York exporter shipped some of his choicest cattle to England that took the country "by storm." The appearance of his two-thousand-pound steers—1,400 of them in three years—fattened to a high state of perfection won favorable notice from cattle dealers, quality breeders, and butchers. Among British farmers already threatened by the competition of cheap although inferior American refrigerated beef, they created consternation.[41] Import restrictions—among them the requirement that all cattle from the United States be slaughtered within five days after landing and that none should be permitted in the interior of the country—were clamped on American cattle on the ground that they were diseased.[42] British experts were dispatched to investigate the threatened cattle invasion that might have results as significant for England's rural economy as the earlier flood of American wheat.[43] Gillett's farming and cattle business was studied in detail by one of the experts, James MacDonald, who came to this country to inquire into costs of raising beef. Although he was critical of Gillett's feeding practices, MacDonald was impressed with the size and efficiency of

[40] Chicago *Drovers' Journal,* in Lincoln *Herald,* Dec. 23, 1875; Oct. 13, 1881. For an interesting description of Gillett's operations, see James Mac-Donald, *Food From the Far West or American Agriculture With Special Reference To The Beef Production and Importation of Dead Meat From America To Great Britain* (London, 1878), 142–148.

[41] For comments upon British reaction see *National Live-Stock Journal,* VI (Oct., 1875), 389; VIII (Feb., 1877), 68; *Prairie Farmer,* XLVIII (Nov. 24, 1877), 373; Edinburgh *Scotsman,* in Toronto *Weekly Globe,* July 18, 1879; John P. Shelton, "Report on the American and Canadian Meat Trade," *Journal of the Royal Agricultural Society of England* (London), Ser. II, XIII (1877), 295–355. See also Alvin H. Sanders, *The Story of the Herefords* (Chicago, 1914), 372 ff.

[42] *National Live-Stock Journal,* IX (April, May, 1878), 160, 209.

[43] "Correspondence connected with the Detection of Pleuro-Pneumonia Among Cattle landed in Great Britain from the United States of America," *British Parliamentary Papers,* Session of 1878–1879 (London), LVIII.

operations on the Gillett farm, the excellent quality of its cattle, and the low cost of producing beef.[44] He assured his anxious countrymen, however, that the importation of American chilled beef or of beef on the hoof was no serious threat to British agriculture because of its generally inferior quality and the high cost of transportation.[45]

Gillett continued to ship his best cattle to eastern cities and to England for some years after the original excitement created by his first venture in 1875. In 1883 the *North British Agriculturist* commented upon a "splendid consignment" of 180 Shorthorn bullocks by Gillett and Son who were called the "most extensive and successful feeders of cattle in America." The cattle, despite the long voyage, were held to be in prime condition, "admirably finished, never to have tasted a turnip." They were fattened on grass, hay, and grain, and "for wealth of meat, grandeur of scale, similarity of type, and extraordinary numbers [they] made a favorable impression upon Scottish breeders and feeders." [46]

Despite the praise his cattle received, it became apparent to Gillett that 2,000-pound three- and four-year-olds were in less demand than lighter two-year-old steers, the feeding of which had been more carefully managed. He turned to breeding his own stock, which he could bring up to 1,700 pounds in two years. In 1886 he had a thousand calves of his own breed and no longer bought feeders. At the same time he stopped shipments to England as discriminatory regulations and cattle losses made them less profitable.[47]

Gillett found a ready market in the eighties for his yearling bulls on the western plains. Efforts by plains cattlemen to im-

---

[44] MacDonald, *Food from the Far West*, 143–148, 279–283. "The Report of the Agricultural Interests Commission" on agriculture of the United States and Canada, *British Parliamentary Papers*, Session of 1880, XVIII, contains much of value to the student of agricultural history.

[45] MacDonald was disputed in this matter by the *National Live-Stock Journal*, VIII (Feb., Aug, Dec., 1877), 68, 347, 528.

[46] *Agricultural Gazette* (London), XVII (Jan. 15, 1883), 62.

[47] Lincoln *Herald*, Sept. 16, 1886.

prove the size and quality of their herds led to large purchases of bulls from his Shorthorn mixtures. In 1880 Colonel Couch of Texas bought 75 bulls at $100 each and other cattlemen in Colorado, Wyoming, Kansas, Nebraska, and Texas bought "many hundreds of young bulls and heifers" of Gillett.[48] In 1882 Gillett sold two carloads of bulls to "Congressman" Richard H. Whiting to stock his Kansas ranch.[49]

From his land and cattle business Gillett accumulated an estate estimated at one and a half million dollars at the time of his death in 1883. A life interest in the land was devised to his wife and the seven surviving daughters and one son, and the fee to the third generation. Gillett's love for his land is apparent in his efforts to entail the estate as far as the law would allow and also in the admonition to his descendants that they follow his example in retaining ownership of the land and restricting the right of alienation. This respectful attitude toward landownership in the prairies and the desire to rivet the property in family hands for succeeding generations is typical of midwestern landlords.[50]

A glance at the ownership map of Logan County for 1920 shows how seriously the children and grandchildren of old John Dean took his advice. Not only were the original holdings retained but considerable additions were made to them. The second and third generation descendants including Jessie D. Gillett, a daughter of John Dean, whose holdings exceeded 4,000 acres, William and John Dean Gillett Barns, Logan and

---

[48] Chicago *Daily Record*, in Lincoln *Times*, Sept. 16, 1880.

[49] Chicago *Tribune*, in Lincoln *Times*, June 8, 1882.

[50] John Cassedy of McLean County, who had been active in land leads for a generation, stipulated in his will in which he left to his four daughters his 742 acres of land valued at $70 an acre that "no portion of the land . . . shall be sold until the youngest of my daughters . . . shall have arrived at the age of twenty-one (21) years, and it is my desire that no Judge or Court will permit any foolish heir who may be talked up by pretended friends or greedy lawyers to have any portion of said land sold before the time named in this item." Any heir who might try to dispose of the land was to be cut off with one dollar (will of Nov. 27, 1873, in probate file 5524, McLean County).

John Dean Gillett Hill, John Dean Gillett Oglesby, and others owned 21,000 acres in Logan County and several thousand acres in surrounding counties. The influence of Logan County's great land baron and cattle king was still felt throughout the region.

Logan County had more than its share of cattle kings and other large landowners who brought it an unfavorable notoriety in the late nineteenth century. The chief reason for this was the presence of the 29,000-acre holding of William A. Scully, on which Old World landlord practices were being instituted. Other than Gillett the principals in the cattle industry were Elisha Crane and the Buckles and Scroggin families. Crane fed between 400 to 800 cattle regularly on his 2,600-acre farm.[51] John Buckles and Leonard K. Scroggin on their 4,500- and 3,500-acre farms engaged in "breeding, buying, rearing and trafficking" in cattle. Numerous other holdings of 1,500 to 3,000 acres are shown on the ownership plats in the *Atlas of Logan County, Illinois* for 1873. So productive and profitable was the Logan County land that owners were reluctant to sell, and many of the estates were retained in family possession for several generations. Close ownership of land and unwillingness to sell made it almost impossible for tenants to buy in Logan County; consequently, there was a continuous movement of dissatisfied tenants out of the county and a high turnover among them with immigrants from abroad tending to displace the older Americans. No other rural county in Illinois had such a discontented and unstable population in the latter part of the nineteenth century.[52]

Two influential cattle kings who early concentrated on breeding rather than size were James N. Brown on his 2,250-farm in Sangamon County and "Long" John Wentworth on his 2,500-

[51] In 1867, Elisha Crane advertised 1,000 acres to rent which he wanted broken and put in corn. He was prepared to rent for three years. In this case, as in many others, the large owner obviously hoped to have the heavy labor and cost of breaking the prairie sod borne by the tenant in return for little or no charge for rent for a number of years (Lincoln *Herald*, Oct. 31, 1867).

[52] Lincoln *Herald*, May 1, 1873; Feb. 3, 17, Sept. 21, 1876; March 8, 1877; April 20, 1882; June 28, 1883.

acre farm in Cook County. Brown was a more typical cattle king with his 500 to 600 cattle, 200 to 400 hogs, and smaller amounts of other livestock which were fed the grain produced on 600 acres. Wentworth had fewer animals but kept only purebreds, which he sold for breeding purposes to other farmers.[53] Brown related how, in 1834, he brought "several head of the best Durham cattle of Kentucky" to his Illinois farm from which he built up through proper crossing a "herd of cattle that will compare favorably with any . . . on the continent." [54] Both Wentworth and Brown were active in importing expensive sires from England. At the annual fairs their cattle won more blue ribbons year after year than those of any other fancier in the state.[55] Upon Brown's death his sons carried on the purebred livestock business, selling their surplus at annual auctions.[56] Later they turned to fattening Texas cattle while at the same time carrying their purebred strain. In 1871 the Brown farm, now containing 3,400 acres, maintained a thousand grade steers in additon to the purebred Shorthorns. It was said that the annual income from beef cattle was about $75,000; sales of Shorthorn breeders

[53] John Wentworth's sales of livestock were frequently reported in the *Prairie Farmer* and the *National Live-Stock Journal* in the seventies and eighties.

[54] James N. Brown, "Grain, Grass and Stock Growing in Central Illinois," Illinois State Agricultural Society, *Transactions* I, (Springfield, 1855), 429 ff.

[55] Letter of James N. Brown, Island Grove, Oct. 29, 1855, Bloomington *Pantagraph*, Dec. 19, 1855; Caird, *Prairie Farming in America*, 59–61; Illinois State Agricultural Society, *Transactions*, III (1859), 301–304; *Boston Cultivator*, clipped in *Country Gentleman*, XXII (Aug. 6, 1863), 92–93. At the "Proceedings Attending the Admission of the Name of James Nicholas Brown to the Illinois Farmers' Hall of Fame, Wednesday, January 25, 1911," considerable information about Brown's contributions to the development of better grade cattle was included in the oratorical proceedings. See *Tranactions of the Illinois State Historical Society for the Year 1912* (Springfield, 1912), 163–192.

[56] See advertisement of "Large Sale of Prize Short-Horn Cattle . . . forty (40) head," *National Live-Stock Journal*, I (July, 1871), 388; and "Third biennial sale of forty short-horn cattle" by James N. Brown's Sons, *Prairie Farmer*, XLIV (May, 1873), 175. See also *National Live-Stock Journal*, VII (May, 1876), 207.

grossed $28,000 in 1871.[57] Three years later the Brown brothers were feeding 1,400 Texas cattle on the 6,000 acres then under their management. They bought six-year-old Texans in October and November, fed them for ten months, and received for their feed during that time more than the previous owners were paid for caring for the stock for six years.[58]

In neighboring Piatt County another large estate was being developed by Samuel W. Allerton, a highly successful cattle buyer. After some initial experience in buying and driving cattle to market, Allerton established himself in Chicago in 1860 where he centered his extensive operations. Here were brought the herds of cattle and hogs he raised on his ranches in Ohio, Illinois, Iowa, Nebraska, and Wyoming. As the volume of his cattle business increased he expanded the acreage of pasture and grazing land he controlled. Most of the 11,655-acre estate in Piatt County was used for feeding cattle, 800 or 900 steers being regularly fattened on it. Emphasis upon livestock, however, soon passed, and the property was tiled and divided into tenant farms on which the usual grain share lease was used.[59] The following tabulation shows purchases by Allerton in Piatt County.

Year	Seller of land	Acres	Price per acre	Amount paid
1863	William Martin	1,280	$10.00	$12,800
1865	Williams & Henderson	160	18.75	3,000
1866	Ainsworth and Ater	80	10.00	800
1866	H. C. McComas	6½	20.00	130
1867	Illinois Central R.R.	314	10.00	3,140
1871	John Matsler	80	46.87	3,750
1873	Watts and Bodwell	600	20.00	12,000
1874	D. Williams	40	37.50	1,500
1879	B. F. F. Yoakum	240	31.66	7,600

[57] *National Live-Stock Journal,* II (Sept. 1871), 444.

[58] *Ibid.,* V (April, 1874), 123. See also MacDonald, *Food from the Far West,* 140–142; *Prairie Farmer,* LII (Oct. 15, 1881), 337.

[59] Monticello *Piatt Standard,* Dec. 10, 1873; Champaign-Urbana *News-Gazette,* June 30, 1936; Emma C. Piatt, *History of Piatt County* (Chicago, 1883), 253.

Year	Seller of land	Acres	Price per acre	Amount paid
1880	W. Voorhies	2,000	30.00	60,000
1880	E. J. Clark	240	20.83	5,000
1880	Williams and Dempsey	1,797	35.19	63,241
1881	James Clark	120	30.00	3,600
1882	W. O. Dooley	120	33.33	4,000
1885	James F. Vent	40	35.00	1,400
1885	Horace R. Calif	480	35.00	16,800
1885	Reid and Wilson	479	57.03	27,320
1891		40	112.50	4,500
1892	W. F. Stevenson	1,187	58.97	70,000
1893		162	72.22	11,700
1894		100	70.00	7,000
1899		48	70.00	3,360
1901	Asler C. Thomson	1,080	50.00	54,000
1901		70	80.00	5,600
1902–18	11 small purchases	892		130,227

With Hiram Sibley of Western Union Telegraph fame, Allerton shared in the division of the Sullivant estate, the largest farm property in Illinois, which failed in the late seventies. The greater proportion of this property went to Sibley, the chief creditor, but Allerton acquired the 3,800-acre Twin Groves farm in southern Vermilion County. Joseph Sullivant had used this land for fattening annually 800 Texas steers, but Allerton converted it into a grain farm. Twenty-five men and sixty to seventy teams were used to produce the corn that was fed on the Piatt County farm.[60] In addition to these holdings Allerton acquired 4,212 acres in Henry County, 7,000 acres in Nebraska, 2,500 acres in Ohio, 17,500 in Iowa, and a ranch in Wyoming.

A true son of the soil, Allerton was never reconciled to absence from it. Despite the growing complexity of his meat-

[60] H. W. Beckwith, *History of Vermilion County* (Chicago, 1879), 1024–1026; *Portrait and Biographical Album of Vermilion and Edgar Counties, Illinois* (Chicago, 1889), 286. Sullivant became agent for the 7,600-acre Buckingham ranch in Morris County, Kansas, on which in the eighties feeder cattle —at first Texas grades and later a mixture of grades and purebreds—were fattened for market (Council Grove [Kan.] *Republican*, Feb. 10, 1882; March 23, 1883).

packing banking, and streetcar operations, he gave much thought to the development and use of his lands. Landownership he regarded as an obligation as well as a valuable and remunerative right. Like any natural resource, the land was exhaustible; its resources could easily be depleted and its output diminished unless it was properly farmed. Crop rotation with clover once in four or five years, tiling, weed controls, feeding at least a part of the grain to steers with hogs to follow them were his rules for profitable farming. Good seed corn he felt to be as important as a good breed of cattle, and he suggested the basic techniques which were subsequently used to produce modern hybrid seed. In the hope of weaning farmers from their wasteful methods, Allerton published a brochure *On Systematic Farming: A Short Treatise on Present Farming Conditions and How to Improve Them.*

In the division of the Allerton estate, Robert Allerton, a son, came into possession of the Piatt County land. Robert Allerton, unlike his father, disapproved of absentee landlordism and decided to build a home for himself in the midst of his 11,655-acre tract. Consequently, near Monticello, he built an elaborate manor house which is one of the show places in Illinois. Robert Allerton was a modernist with regard to farm practices and soil conservation and through his farm manager was to prescribe carefully the operations of the seventeen tenants on the estate. He and his father rented their land on the share basis; the improvements were owned by the Allertons, and the tenants were encouraged to make stock raising an important feature of their operations. In the twentieth century a large part of the estate was conveyed, or was promised to state and county governments for an old folks' home, a tuberculosis sanitarium, a model farm on which soil conserving practices could be taught, and for a forestry project. In 1956, Robert Allerton gave to the University of Illinois the great Georgian mansion he had built in the center of a 1600-acre landscaped tract with long avenues of stately Norway spruces, copies of famous statuary, and vast gardens surrounded by privet hedges. To provide for the maintenance of the park as an "educational and research center," eight commerical farms containing 3,775 acres were also given for endowment.[61]

Land being the favorite investment that it is in Illinois, no self-respecting banker, lawyer, or newspaper proprietor in the small towns and cities of the downstate counties can hold, it would seem, a proper position among his fellow men unless he owns a few farms and can talk intelligently about hybrid corn, the chinch bug, yields per acre, crop rotation schemes, farm machinery, and tenant problems. One has only to spend a short time in such flourishing communities as Pontiac, Paxton, Dwight, Morris, Lincoln, Monticello or larger cities like Bloomington, Springfield, Decatur, and Champaign-Urbana to realize how intimately the fortunes of many city people are tied to the soil through farm ownership. Samuel Allerton had hundreds of imitators, large and small, who as their fortunes grew, invested them in the purchase of farm after farm. Thus the Oughton and the McWilliams estates were being acquired in the eighties and nineties, farm by farm, and in the same way were numerous, other larger or smaller estates being erected in what has generally been regarded as one of the surest and safest types of investment the country offered.

Of the rest of the Illinois farm land of Samuel Allerton, the Henry County tract went to his wife, who subsequently disposed of it, and the Vermilion County Twin Groves Farm was devised to Vanderburg and Allerton Johnston, grandsons of the founder of the estate. The latter tract, constituting 3,695 acres, later owned by Vanderburg Johnston, a resident of Arizona, was divided into seven tenant-operated farms ranging in size from 241 to 652 acres which were managed by the First National Bank of Chicago.[62]

Adjacent to Twin Groves Farm was the 6,000-acre farm of

[61] Jessie Borrer Morgan, *The Good Life in Piatt County* (Moline, Ill., 1968), 243–249.

[62] Champaign-Urbana *News-Gazette*, June 30, 1946.

John Sidell on which 1,500 cattle and 1,000 hogs were regularly fattened. In 1873 Sidell employed fifty men to work his property, but he was already beginning to divide it into tenant farms, doubtless through necessity. In some cases tenancy made possible continued ownership of large estates, but Sidell received only temporary relief by its introduction. Sale of a part of the farm was resorted to in the hope of saving the rest; later more had to be sold.[63] A like fate befell the 5,000-acre cattle farm of Zopher Tuttle in Livingston County. Declining returns from the livestock business and rising labor costs led Tuttle to rent his land to tenants who raised mostly corn. Soon the entire property had passed out of possession of the family. The 37,000-acre ranch of Franklin Oliver in Livingston County, on which 1,500 cattle were once grazed, likewise was divided and sold.[64]

In neighboring Grundy County, which included a high percentage of flat level prairie land, four large estates were early established of which three were based on the cattle business. In the eighteen thirties and forties William Hoge, Abraham Holderman, and Philip Collins came to Grundy County with more capital than the average frontiersman then moving to prairie country brought with him. Hoge's purchases and those of the family totaled 5,000 acres, Holderman's purchases amounted to 6,770 acres, and the Collins family bought 3,000 acres. Extensive operations in cattle yielded substantial revenue even before tenants could be induced to cultivate the holdings. Additional land was acquired, and the *Atlas of Grundy County*, published in 1874, showed the various Holdermans owning 11,265 acres, the Hoges 9,540 acres, and the Collinses 8,734 acres. Fencing, draining, and then breaking part of the land followed and, with the influx of people looking for farms to rent, these families di-

---

[63] Pontiac *Sentinel*, Aug. 7, 1873; Hoopeston *Chronicle*, Aug. 14, 1873; Danville *Commercial*, Sept. 4, 1873.

[64] *History of Livingston County, Illinois* (Chicago, 1878), 789. *The Plat Book of Livingston County, Illinois, 1893* (Chicago, 1893), shows that Zopher Tuttle still owned 3,176 acres. See also Watseka *Iroquois County Times*, July 9, 1875.

vided their land into quarter-section farms. Although there were divisions of the estates in the century since they were first established, much of the land continued in the possession of descendants. In the twentieth century the Collins family were renting thirty-one farms, the Holderman family sixteen, and the Hoge family a few less. In 1910 it was stated that the farms of the Collins family had not been adequately managed: the fences and buildings were in poor condition, the soil was exhausted, and morning glories infested the fields; consequently the best tenants were not interested in farming the land. The Hoge farms, on the other hand, were said to have been well maintained. The Scully estate in Grundy County constitutes the other large holding that was early established. This 8,600-acre holding—divided into sixty-six farms—like the even larger Scully holding in Logan County, was not used for cattle feeding as were most of the other large estates in the period before tenant farmers could be profitably used on the land.[65]

Like Logan, McLean, Livingston, and Iroquois counties, Vermilion County had more than its share of cattle kings and large landed estates. Besides Sidell's "model farm" and Sullivant's Twin Groves, there were the 4,000-acre livestock farm of Abraham Mann,[66] the 4,480-acre tenant-farmed estate of William A. Rankin,[67] the 4,500-acre farm of John W. Goodwine, and others as follows:

[65] Jeremiah Collins, who died in 1910, left 3,747 acres appraised at $325,081 and other property appraised at $162,044. For testimony concerning the value of the land and its run-down character, see File 3024, Probate Court, Grundy County (Morris, Illinois).

[66] In 1945, A. G. Belt bought 1,310 acres of the old Mann property together with the palatial thirteen-room house with its five bathrooms for $200,000, one of the largest sales in years. Belt planned to fatten a thousand cattle to provide a part of the beef for his Steak 'n Shake restaurants (Bloomington *Pantagraph*, Oct. 18, 1945).

[67] The Rankin farm is described in the Hoopeston *Chronicle*, May 14, 1874. For the others, see the ownership maps in *An Illustrated and Historical Atlas Map of Vermilion County, Ill.* (Philadelphia, 1875).

James S. Sconce	2,093	James Mix	1,520
William M. Fithian	2,810	John C. Smith	2,480
Thomas Armstrong	2,237	William Fowler	3,113
Thomas Hoopes	1,715	Thomas Smith	1,120
Nelson Sumner	2,200		

In Edgar County, just south of Vermilion, were two extensive livestock farms owned by James Gaines and Terrence Clark. In 1875, Gaines had on his 4,400-acre farm 380 cattle, 65 of which were "thorough-bred" Shorthorns; in the previous year he pastured 1,000 cattle. Some of his fat stock weighed 2,800 to 3,000 pounds.[68] Clark also used his estate of 3,400 acres for fattening livestock.[69]

The names of John T. Alexander and Michael L. Sullivant are closely woven into the agricultural history of Illinois and the development of its land-use pattern. Altogether a hundred thousand acres of Illinois land were owned and to some extent improved by them with the aid of small armies of workers.

After considerable experience in driving cattle for others from Ohio and St. Louis to Philadelphia, Baltimore, New York, and Boston, Alexander started his own business of buying, fattening, and driving to market. His skill in judging cattle and his willingness to take risks brought him high profits, interspersed in bad years with heavy losses. The profits he used partly to expand his business and partly to buy land for a stock farm in Morgan County that ultimately reached 7,200 acres. Annually the size of his drives increased until in 1859 he marketed 15,000 cattle though at a loss to himself that year. The Civil War gave him his big opportunity. He sent buyers into that part of Mis-

[68] James Gaines acquired his large acreage by inheritance, marriage, and purchase with profits from his cattle business. A letter of his and the editor's comment upon it provide interesting material for the history of the cattle trade in Illinois (*National Live-Stock Journal*, III [Jan. 1871], 71; VI [May, 1875], 184).

[69] Mention might also be made of a 2,100-acre livestock farm of Jacob Augustus.

souri where the tumult of war had upset the market with in-
structions to purchase every steer and mule they could get at
low prices. Fattened and restored to prime condition on his
ranch, the stock brought him inflated war prices and large net
returns. The war left him owning his well-developed Morgan
County ranch, worth, says Joseph McCoy, who featured Alexander in his classic account of the cattle trade, $540,000; cash in
the bank of $100,000; his pastures full of cattle; and everything
clear of debt.[70]

In 1866, Alexander bought Broadlands, the 22,000-acre farm
of Michael Sullivant in Champaign County, on which the latter
had kept 5,000 cattle and 4,000 broken-down government
horses.[71] For five years Alexander used Broadlands as a "sort
of hotel ground for the grazing and rest of immense herds of
freshly arrived Texans." In one year of this period, 4,000 Texans besides some native stock were pastured on the land and
6,000 acres were put in grain to provide for the livestock feeding program.[72] At the same time Alexander was buying cattle
from other feeders and shipping direct to eastern markets. His
shipments in 1867 and again in 1868 were 40,000; in 1870 they
reached the unprecedented total of 70,000.[73] By 1873 Alexander
was the most influential man in the American cattle trade and
was elected president of the newly-organized Live Stock Men's
National Association.[74]

Operating on such a large scale, Alexander was more subject
to the market fluctuations than were smaller operators. His net
was enormous in good years but his losses were huge when

[70] Joseph G. McCoy, *Historic Sketches of the Cattle Trade of the West and
Southwest* (Kansas City, 1874), 163–178.

[71] *Moore's Rural New Yorker* (New York), XIV (July 18, 25, 1863),
229, 237.

[72] United States Commissioner of Agriculture, *Report,* 1870 (Washington,
1871), 135–136; "Report of the New York State Cattle Commissioners,
1868," New York *Senate Document,* No. 9 (1869), 94–95.

[73] *Prairie Farmer,* XL (Aug. 7, 1869), 249; McCoy, *Historic Sketches
of the Cattle Trade,* 176.

[74] McCoy, *Historic Sketches of the Cattle Trade,* 253.

prices fell. Some years he had to carry over large herds that suffered numerous winter casualties. The Spanish fever brought in by the ticks on the Texas longhorns wrought terrific havoc among Illinois cattle that were not immune to it. In addition to his own casualties, Alexander had to meet claims of neighboring farmers for losses attributed to his importations. Opposition to the transportation of Texas cattle and his own losses therefrom induced Alexander in 1869 to concentrate on home-grown cattle. His calamities continued, however, and combined with the heavy interest charges on a debt of nearly a half-million dollars forced him in 1871 to assign Broadlands. For some time thereafter he continued to deal in livestock but in a smaller way.[75]

Meantime, Sullivant turned to his Burr Oaks farm of 40,000 acres in Ford and Livingston counties which he developed in much the same way as Broadlands. Less emphasis was placed on livestock, for only a thousand hogs and a few hundred cattle were pastured. Most of the grain was sold off the farm. A highly-organized army of 250 hands was employed to do the work.[76] Sullivant prospered for a time on the bonanza farm but declining prices after 1873, a series of wet seasons and poor crops, and heavy interest obligations proved difficult to bear.[77] In 1879 Burr Oaks was lost to his creditors.

Neighbors and business interests in Champaign and Ford counties looked upon the Alexander and Sullivant farms as something to boast about because of their mammoth size, but also as something to deplore because of their harmful effects upon the community. The area about Broadlands was said to be "without roads, but few dwellings, cultivated by hirelings, who have no interest in the work, no schools and no enterprises, save what is carried in the person of one individual." If, on the

[75] Illinois State Agricultural Society, *Transactions,* VII (1870), 135–136; 24 Champaign County Deeds, 350.

[76] Pontiac *Sentinel,* July 28, 1870; *Harper's Weekly* (New York), XV (Sept. 23, 1871), 897–898; New York *Post,* in Blomington *Weekly Leader,* Oct. 2, 1872; Paxton *Record,* Feb. 6, 1879.

[77] *National Live-Stock Journal,* X (March, 1879), 99.

other hand, the tract were divided into small farms the area would have "331 residences, 331 men, all owners, all interested, no hirelings, no necessary waste, schools, roads, enterprise, thrift and prosperity." [78] Both Alexander and Sullivant were respected for their energy and business capacity but the people had a feeling of relief when they failed and their land was divided into smaller farms. [79]

The greatest concentration of prairie landownership by cattle kings was in the Kankakee and Wabash valleys on both sides of the Illinois-Indiana line. For example in Benton, Newton, and Jasper counties, Indiana, and Iroquois and Kankakee counties, Illinois, Moses Fowler's 25,000 acres, Adams Earl's 20,000 acres, Edward Sumner's 30,000 acres, Alexander Kent's 30,000 acres, and Lemuel Milk's 65,000 acres were used for the fattening of herds of thousands of cattle. These and a dozen others almost as large and still others of a few thousand acres dominated the scene in nine prairie counties. The early concentration on cattle feeding was slowly replaced by corn production, division of the farms, and the introduction of tenancy. In some instances family bickering over the division of estates and extended litigation reduced original holdings. Nevertheless, landlordism and absentee ownership were pronounced in this region, and with them came a close approximation of a one-crop system with soil depletion, exhaustion, and diminishing values. Here may be

[78] J. S. Lothrop, *Champaign County Directory, 1870–1871, With History of the Same* (Chicago, 1871), 419.

[79] Gibson *Courier*, in Pontiac *Sentinel*, Nov. 6, 1878; and in Bloomington *Pantagraph*, Nov. 6, 1878. Close to Sullivant's Burr Oaks farm were the 3,800 acres acquired and developed by Gustavus and William Foos of Clark County, Ohio. After an initial period in which a large herd of cattle was fattened on the land, it was divided into thirteen tenant farms and a considerable part was put in grain. Cattle and hogs continued, however, to be raised to a large extent. The property, reduced to some 2,900 acres, was owned in the third generation by three granddaughters of William Foos who were residents of New York State (Gibson *Courier*, in *Champaign County Gazette*, June 13, 1877; Paxton *Record*, Jan. 13, 1887; Champaign *Times*, quoted in John R. Stewart, ed., *Standard History of Champaign County, Illinois* [Chicago, 1918], 478).

seen some of the worst results of the concentration of landownership for which the cattle kings were responsible.[80]

Some cattle kings pushed into Iowa, Missouri, Kansas, and
Nebraska where they acquired even larger ranches for the feeding of cattle. Nelson Morris, prominent Chicago meat packer,
had a 30,000-acre cattle ranch in Lake County, Indiana, another
30,000-acre ranch in Nebraska, and a 300,000-acre ranch in
Texas.[81] William and David Rankin had 5,000-acre cattle farms
in Vermilion and Henderson counties, Illinois, and holdings of
nearly 30,000 acres in northwestern Missouri on which cattle
feeding and farming operations were conducted on a scale as
large as and certainly with more success than those of Michael
Sullivant. John S. Bilby, "the largest individual land owner in
America," began cattle feeding in McDonough County, Illinois.
He next spread his acquisitions and feeding business over three
counties in northwestern Missouri where he held 26,000 acres.
He acquired a total of 650,000 acres in ranches in Kansas, Nebraska, Texas, Oklahoma, and Mexico.[82] John Evans, Jr., commenced his cattle business in Henderson County, Illinois, where
he had a 1,100-acre farm. In the seventies he bought 7,500 acres
in Mills and Pottawattomie counties, Iowa, on which he pastured some 1,400 cattle and as many hogs. Much of the Rankin,
Bilby, and Evans land was long held by their families.

The day of the cattle king in the prairies lasted roughly from
1850 to 1885, though the forces that were impelling a shift from
cattle feeding to tenancy and grain farming were under way earlier.[83] Every prairie county and in some places almost every

---

[80] See the description of the establishment of these large estates in the
Wabash and Kankakee valleys in Chapter 6, above.

[81] Rudolph A. Clemen, *The American Livestock and Meat Industry* (New
York, 1923), 158.

[82] *Past and Present of Nodaway County, Missouri* (Indianapolis, 1910),
601–604.

[83] Lincoln *Herald*, Sept. 5, 1860; Danville *Republican*, Jan. 26, 1860;
Western Farmers' Annual and Rural Companion for 1860 (Indianapolis,
1860), 24; Kentland (Ind.) *Gazette*, Oct. 31, 1872; Monticello *Piatt County*

township could boast, albeit rather sourly, of its big cattle farm.[84]

Wealth amassed locally won for these cattle kings prestige and a respectful following among rural neighbors who measured success in terms of the accumulation of land and livestock. This permitted the cattle kings and other large landlords to exercise political power out of all proportion to their numbers. They were found in the inner circles of the Republican and Democratic parties in which they exerted a conservative and not altogether enlightened influence. Some, affected by the respectful attention paid them by the small farmer element, wrapped themselves in the mantle of statesmanship and were elected to the state legislature, to Congress, and to the governor's chair, not always, however, to the advantage of their state or section. Among the cattle kings who served in the Illinois legislature were Isaac Funk and three of his sons, George, Lafayette, and Duncan, James N. Brown, Robert Latham, partner of John Dean Gillett, David T. Littler, son-in-law of Gillett, who was elected to the state Senate, John Wentworth, and David A. Rankin.[85] Wentworth also served three terms in the national House of Representatives; Benjamin F. Funk, son of Isaac Funk, served one term; Jessie Sumner represented her eastern Illinois district four terms in the twentieth century; Richard J. Oglesby, another son-in-law of Gillett, was governor and subsequently a member of the United States Senate. Among the largest landowners to serve in Congress were David Davis, in the United States Senate and later on the Supreme Court, and Representative Vespasian Warner, son-in-law of Clifton H. Moore, owner of Clinton County's richest estate and himself owner of numerous farms.

Herald, Sept. 13, 1876; Pontiac *Sentinel*, Jan. 9, 1878, June 9, 1880; Pontiac *Free Trader and Observer*, Sept. 7, 1883.

[84] George Ade, "Prairie Kings of Yesterday," *Saturday Evening Post* CCIV (July 4, 1931), 14, 75; H. W. Beckwith, *History of Iroquois County* (Chicago, 1880), Part II, 369–376.

[85] Springfield *Illinois State Journal*, Jan. 30, 1865; Bloomington *Bulletin*, Jan. 4, 1887; McLean County Historical Society, *Transactions*, II (1903), 634.

Even the Grange and other farmer movements were kept in hand by the cattle kings to such a degree that their attention was fastened upon the abuses of the railroads and currency problems rather than upon such issues as taxation, credit, landlord-tenant relations, and methods of entailing estates. It is interesting to note that of the fifteen delegates sent by Logan County—where one half of the farms were tenant operated—to the Farmers Convention in Springfield in 1872, thirteen were proved farm owners. Among these thirteen were Elisha Crane, whose large land and cattle business has already been mentioned, John A. Hoblit, Atlanta banker and member of a family whose holdings were in excess of 1,800 acres, and Thomas Edes, owner of 478 acres of farm land. The other two delegates may possibly have been tenants; certain it is that they were either not sufficiently affluent to pay for biographical sketches in the county histories or were not interested in presenting to posterity their claims to fame. LaSalle County also sent as delegates to the Farmers Convention three of its extensive landowners and cattle feeders, Robert and Abner Strawn and Elias Trumbo. John Cassedy, a member of the Illinois legislature from McLean County, and John D. Murdock of Douglas County, Illinois, owners respectively of 742 and 850 acres of farm land, were also active in the Grange.[86]

Alexander J. Kent, despite his extensive holdings in land and cattle in Indiana, went even farther on the road toward agrarianism. In a series of articles in the Kentland *Newton County Democrat* in which he called himself a Democrat and antimonopolist, he deplored the concentration of landownership as well as of corporate wealth.[87]

The combination of cattle kings and other large landlords

---

[86] Ottawa *Free Trader*, May 24, 1873; *Illustrated History Atlas Map of Douglas County, Illinois* (Philadelphia, 1875), 32; *History of McLean County, Illinois* (Chicago, 1879), 1044.

[87] Kentland (Ind.) *Newton County Democrat*, Nov. 28, 1872; Jan. 2, 1873.

sought to minimize assessments upon unimproved land or land used for grazing. To that end they fought increased taxes and assessments designed to make possible improvements in roads, schools, and local government.[88] They continually harassed local tax authorities by suits to set aside assessments, refusals to pay taxes, and efforts to compromise delinquent taxes, to evade the payment of penalties, and to recover tax titles.[89] When they had tenants on their land, they shifted the tax burden to them and thereby secured additional support for their views on expenditures by local governments.[90] They refused to declare their intangibles in the form of gold and silver, stocks, bond, notes, and bank deposits for the personal property tax, thereby evading payment of many thousands of dollars and increasing the burden on real property.[91]

[88] The low assesments that prevailed in the prairie counties of Illinois are not, of course, to be attributed to large owners only, for undoubtedly small owners have their share of responsibility. For the 1947 assessments issue, see Bloomington *Pantagraph,* June 21, 1947.

[89] James A. Mix, A. Honneywell, George H. White, and Snell, Taylor and Company, holders of large tracts in Iroquois County, were denounced as "notorious taxfighters" who opposed homestead exemption laws and took advantage of the faulty publication of the delinquent tax list to avoid paying taxes (Watseka *Iroquois County Times,* Jan. 20, 1876, March 9, 23, April 13, 1878; *History of McLean County, Illinois,* 503). Mix was a well-known land agent and speculator who in 1856 advertised for sale 35,000 acres which he had acquired from the government, much of which was in Iroquois County. In 1875 he advertised a 921- and a 495-acre farm with three farm houses, stables, cattle sheds, and granaries; also 2,500 acres of unimproved prairie and 1,540 acres partly in bluegrass (Chicago *Daily Democratic Press,* Oct. 18, 1856; *Indiana Farmer,* X [April 10, 1875], 7). The Bloomington *Leader,* Oct. 18, 1872, in a political attack upon Clifton H. Moore, DeWitt County's greatest landlord, mentioned his protests against taxes for the support of free public schools.

[90] A writer in the Clinton *Register,* March 16, 1888, said that tenants were opposed to the propsal for a new county courthouse on the ground that three-fourths of its cost would be charged to them in the form of higher rents.

[91] Edward C. Sumner, one of the wealthiest of the Illinois-Indiana cattle kings, was accused of evasion of the personal property tax in the sum of $8,000 (Watseka *Iroquois County Times,* April 6, May 4, 1878, quoting

The slowness with which all-weather roads have been extended in rural areas of the prairie counties and the backwardness of their educational system, the low salaries of their teachers, and the retention of the one-room school are twentieth-century indications of the reluctance of the controlling interests to tax themselves for modern improvements.[92]

In every pioneer community where livestock interests and small farmers were struggling to get established, friction soon appeared over the problem of fencing. The cattlemen early took advantage of the open prairies on which their cattle grazed and had no reason to advocate fencing. On the other hand, the settlers could make little progress in raising grain—their chief livelihood—until their cultivated land was protected from the depredations of livestock. Furthermore, farmers specializing in thoroughbred stock were troubled because unfenced grade bulls might mix with their animals.[93] Since farmers were generally later comers and they were the ones needing the fences, it was easy for the cattlemen to argue that they should build them. But to fence a quarter-section farm cost $500 or more, an expense that few pioneers could afford.[94]

Fencing, therefore, became a major issue with each side trying

---

from the Indianapolis *News* and the Lafayette [Ind.] *Courier*). The estate of Moses Fowler was assessed a heavy penalty for many years of evasion of the personal property tax by the leading cattle king of Benton County, Indiana (Tippecanoe County Probate Records [Lafayette, Ind.], Final Record, LXV, 549). It should be remembered that violations of the personal property tax have been common among all classes.

[92] *Prairie Farmer*, XLIII (Aug. 10, 1872), 249. Harry R. O'Brien, in an illuminating article in the *Country Gentleman*, LXXXIV (Sept. 20, 1919), 10–11, entitled "More about Retired Farmers," describes the opposition of retired farmers to improved roads.

[93] *National Live-Stock Journal* (April, 1871), 261.

[94] "The Fence Question," Illinois State Agricultural Society, *Transactions*, V (1865), 690–695; "Statistics of Fences in the United States," United States Commissioner of Agriculture, *Report*, 1871 (Washington, 1872), 497–512. Both articles express concern at the heavy cost to which settlers had to go to protect their land from cattle. One writer estimated the cost of fencing to be $12 an acre (*National Live-Stock Journal*, I [April, 1871], 277).

to place the obligation on the other. Legislature after legislature in the prairie states struggled with the issue, vacillating and procrastinating and finally adopting ineffective measures that still left the obligation in the hands of farmers. In Illinois the livestock men delayed the adoption of a herd law until 1867 and it was passed then only because the cattle kings were beginning to turn their land into grain cultivation and were adopting the farmers' point of view. James N. Brown, whose large farm in Sangamon County has been noticed, took an active part in the movement in 1865 for a herd law.[95] Here as elsewhere no great victory was won, for the act of 1867 proved ineffective and the problem of fencing continued to annoy the farmer.

In the handling of the drainage question friction also developed between the cattle kings and the small farmers. Farmers favored the organization of drainage districts in which taxes could be levied for ditching and drainage, while cattlemen opposed such action on the ground that it would increase their obligations without bringing in commensurate returns. Many bitter fights emerged over the issue of drainage.[96]

After the Civil War the importation of Texas longhorns into the Corn Belt by the tens of thousands precipitated an issue that divided the cattlemen into two factions, one favoring the exclusion of Texas cattle because of the Spanish fever and the other opposing exclusion. So serious was the loss of cattle from the Spanish fever that farmers "became perfectly enraged at Texas cattle, and would have mobbed a man to death who would have dared to talk in favor of Texas cattle, much less shipped a carload of them," says Joseph G. McCoy.[97] The heaviest importer

[95] Springfield *Illinois State Journal,* Jan. 7, 23, 1865.

[96] A hint at this opposition appears in the *National Live-Stock Journal,* X (May, 1879), 195.

[97] McCoy, *Historic Sketches of the Cattle Trade,* 149. To Tolono, at the junction of the Wabash and Illinois Central Railroads in Champaign County, were brought 12,000 Texas steers in the summer of 1868. By September the ravages of the Texas fever had brought death to 726 native cattle in the immediate area. Small wonder that the farmers threatened dire action to those

of Texas cattle suffered losses of $75,000 from the depredations of the Spanish fever upon his Shorthorn cattle and from claims of farmers in his neighborhood. The enraged prairie farmers demanded legislation prohibiting further shipments of Texas cattle and swarmed to the capitals and to public meetings to support the movement. Possibly the farmers were fearful that the vast numbers of Texas cattle descending upon them might tend to break prices. Cattlemen like the Brown brothers, Harris, and Gillett, who at this time disdained Texas cattle, joined the movement for prohibition, but others like Alexander who dealt largely in them naturally opposed it.

McCoy, a former Illinois cattleman who was now developing Abilene as the principal cow town of Kansas, foresaw disaster for the cattle trade if such exclusion laws were enacted. He has described how he marshaled the opponents of exclusion and after a prolonged fight secured an amendment which virtually nullified the measure.[98] Indignant farmers continued for years to press for exclusion. As late as 1881 a measure to ban the shipment of diseased Texas cattle to Illinois was introduced in the state legislature.[99]

Cattle kings and other large landlords were the principal beneficiaries of a land system that made easy the creation of estates of many thousands of acres. They first developed their properties into ranches for the feeding of livestock, then into bonanza farms, and finally into the modern pattern of tenant-operated farms. They brought a concentration of ownership and tenancy early to the prairies and sought to perpetuate that concentration by including in their wills all the restrictions on alienation that the law allowed. The passing of a hundred years has not mate-

responsible for bringing in the Texans ("Report of the New York State Cattle Commissioners, 1868, New York," New York *Senate Document*, No. 9, p. 96; clipping attached to letter of William H. Osborn, president of the Illinois Central Railroad, to John M. Douglass, Aug. 17, 1868, Newberry Library, Chicago).

[98] McCoy, *Historic Sketches of the Cattle Trade*, 185 and *passim*.

[99] *Prairie Farmer*, LII (March 12, 1881), 85.

rially affected the ownership of these early cattle kingdoms except that a number of descendants now own parts of the whole earlier owned by the cattle kings. In most instances the later generations have entertained the same profound respect for landownership that induced their ancestors to seek to entail it.

Cattle kings and bonanza farmers retarded the growth of the community first by using their land extensively and later by encouraging and even requiring abusive and careless farm practices. Hired hands and shiftless tenants worked the land which small farm owners might otherwise have acquired. The hired hands were migratory workers who were undependable, drank heavily, sometimes shirked their work, and were frequently in trouble with the law. The tenants, having no hope of acquiring ownership of the land they farmed, had little initiative to make improvements or to farm properly. Their chief concern was to raise the largest possible corn crop—their principal source of cash. Some of the second and third generation heirs of the cattle kings, especially if absentee landlords, showed a tendency to extract as much from the land as possible. Even where the modern farm manager was employed he also had a strong motive to make favorable cash rent returns to his employer. Some great estates developed into rural slums in the nineteenth century and even in the twentieth century exhibited backward social features that would shame poorer sections elsewhere.[100]

Other cattle kings and their heirs took pride in maintaining and further improving their estates. They found that careful attention to farm practices, insistence upon a proper system of rotation including clover or alfalfa on the land one year in four, weed elimination, and the application of manures, lime, and phosphate at appropriate times retained or increased production

[100] Compare the old New York State style of homes in the rural areas of the Finger Lakes counties that are notable for their commodiousness, pillars and porches, style, and landscaping, all well maintained, with the drab, nondescript, unpainted, and poorly maintained tenant houses in central Illinois.

while modern improvements with well-kept and attractive houses assured good tenants.

Helen M. Cavanagh's *Funk of Funk's Grove: Farmer, Legislator, and Cattle King of the Old Northwest* (Bloomington, Illinois, 1952), is a fine treatment of the most successful of the Illinois cattle kings. Margaret Beattie Bogue's *Patterns from the Sod: Land Use and Land Tenure in the Grand Prairie, 1850–1900* (Springfield, Illinois, 1959) describes the cattle kings of eastern Illinois and the development of their estates through tenants. Allan G. Bogue's *From Prairie to Corn Belt: Farming on the Illinois and Iowa Prairies in the Nineteenth Century* (Chicago, 1963) is also useful. Lewis Atherton's *The Cattle Kings* (Bloomington, Indiana, 1967) is satisfactory for the Great Plains but misses the story of the cattle kings of the prairies and the great Miller & Lux story of California and Oregon.

8. Frontier Landlords
and Pioneer Tenants

Not all frontiersmen were pioneer farmers struggling to create homes for themselves in the wilderness or on the prairie, or
lonely cowboys watching over their charges on the boundless
plains, or fur traders and trappers penetrating the most remote
areas in their search for the beaver, the mink, and the otter, or
miners optimistically wrestling with nature for the yellow nug-
gets. There were other frontier residents whose history is not so
romantic but whose influence in shaping the emerging social and
economic pattern was quite out of proportion to their numbers.
The Indian agent with his power to disburse thousands of dollars of annuities, to contract for quantities of supplies, to hasten
or delay Indian removal, to control allotments of land and the
transfer of allotments, was a marked figure wherever he was stationed.[1] The army officers at their lonely posts at Fort Dearborn,
Fort Snelling, Fort Scott, and Fort Riley played their part in
building western America many years before their presence was
made unnecessary by the onrush of settlers and the establishment
of local government. The frontier editors who early appeared in
every ambitious little community and started papers filled with
stale news of European wars and with congressional harangues
lifted bodily from the *National Intelligencer* and the *Congres-*

---

[1] For an analysis of the role of the Indian agent as reflected in the career
of John Tipton see Paul Wallace Gate's introduction to Nellie A. Robertson
and Dorothy Riker, eds., *The John Tipton Papers*, Indiana Historical Collections, XXIV (Indianapolis, 1942), 3–53.

sional Globe are worthy of attention. The territorial officials, the United States land officers, the lawyers whose services were in demand before there was a legal title to a piece of land in the area, the note shaver, the moneylender or banker representing eastern capitalists are types found on every frontier.

Transcending all these non-farmer pioneers in importance were the large landowners. To anticipate the settlers, they moved with, sometimes ahead of, the vanguard of frontiersmen, following closely the footsteps of the surveyor. Great holdings of land, sometimes running to a quarter of a million acres and more, were acquired by them for resale to other speculators or to actual settlers, or to rent to tenants. At every government land sale these men were in attendance; at every land office town they maintained conspicuous offices; their advertisements provided much of the patronage of the struggling frontier newspapers and in not a few instances the newspaper was simply an adjunct of the land business.[2]

These landowners expressed their supreme confidence in the future of the West by sinking many thousands of dollars—in part borrowed capital—in the purchase of wild land, frequently retaining little or nothing for taxes, interest, fees, development costs, and other expenses connected with landownership. If the expected profits did not materialize within a short period, their taxes remained unpaid, tax titles of dubious value issued, and patronage was thereby created for lawyers and the courts, and further financial aid given to the newspapers in the form of the much-fought-over "tax delinquent list." The tales widely bandied about in the West of crippling losses sustained by some of these landowners and the tremendous extent of the tax delinquent list, which at times seemed to indicate that few absentee, or even resident, owners were able to meet their taxes, have led some writers to conclude that no profits were made in the western land business. It is true that most holders of western land at one time or another complained about being land poor but it

[2] See Chapters 2 and 5, above.

is also true that in practically every town, large or small, the local squire, the bank president, the owner of numerous mortgages, the resident of the "big house," the man whose wife was the leader of "society," got his start—and a substantial start—as a result of the upward surge of land values in the nineteenth century.

Having made their plunge, which for the moment gave them nothing but a cold shock and threatened to engulf them entirely, some of these owners of great estates looked for means by which they might make their investments profitable. Thus Romulus Riggs of Philadelphia, who had acquired 256 quarter-sections of land in the Military Tract of Illinois during the thirties, first tried to secure sufficient return from his land to meet his taxes and then to add something for current income. When he discovered the Illinois Suckers' propensity for hooking or stealing timber from nonresident or speculator-owned land he decided that action was necessary or else his investment might become worthless. Legal action, he soon learned, was not the proper step to take as it aroused frontier prejudices and generally proved ineffective. Riggs found it possible to make agreements with squatters upon his land whereby they undertook to prevent unauthorized cutting on a number of sections in return for the right to use the land. A little later he induced squatters to agree to pay the taxes. Then, when their improvements, such as a one-room log house, a little fencing, and a few acres of cultivated land, represented sufficient labor and investment to put them in a receptive mood, Riggs demanded a cash rent in excess of the taxes. Thus was tenancy born on the frontier.[3]

It was in the prairie counties of central Illinois that frontier landlords and pioneer tenants were most numerous, as in these

---

[3] This brief statement about the management of the 40,000-acre estate of Romulus Riggs is based on a study of the extensive collection of Riggs Papers in the Library of Congress.

Isaiah Romulus Dyck

same counties were found a generation later the largest of the estates and the highest proportion of tenancy. Long avoided by settlers and speculators, the prairie counties began to attract attention to some degree in the late thirties but more largely a decade later. One of the first persons to recognize the possibilities in prairie farming on a large scale was Henry L. Ellsworth, who, in 1835, acquired 18,000 acres in Vermilion and Iroquois counties, Illinois, and Benton County, Indiana, which he developed with the aid of laborers and tenants. As federal commissioner of patents he used his influence to interest men of capital in making investments in prairie lands which, he promised, would become highly profitable when tenants were established on them. Ellsworth advertised the prairies and the opportunity for investments in them in government documents, emigrant literature, and newspapers. Tenants, he maintained—and here he is supported by much contemporary evidence [4]—could easily be secured for absentee-owned estates provided some improvements were made; and on a crop-share basis the returns to both tenants and landowners would be large. Ellsworth's own advice on renting land is interesting:

It is customary to rent land (once broke and fenced) for one-third of the crops, delivered in the crib or barn. At this rent the tenant finds all.

I would advise to employ smart, enterprising young men, from the New England States, to take the farm on shares. If the landlord should find a house, a team, cart, and plough, and add some stock, he might then require one-half the profits of the same. I would advise to allow for fencing or ditching a certain sum, and stipulate that the

---

[4] In an article of 1852 derected "To Western Emigrants," Solon Robinson said, "No matter if you have no money, you can rent land very low, and will soon be in a condition to let land instead of hiring it" (*Albany Cultivator*, X [Feb., 1843], 37). James Caird, who toured Illinois in 1858, observed that share renting was "very common in Illinois" (*Prairie Farming in America* [New York, 1859], 93). In reading the prairie newspapers of the forties and fifties one is struck by the number of notices offering farms for rent and, less frequently, advertisements calling for farms to rent.

capital invested should be returned before profits were divided. A farmer could in this way earn for himself from $700 to $1,000 per annum, on a lease for five years. . . .[5]

Ellsworth's faith in the prairies and the alluring descriptions he gave of them induced many eastern capitalists to buy wild land in Indiana and Illinois. Dozens of people invested through him sums ranging from a few hundred to ten and twenty thousand dollars, and the total area that came under his control in this way ran to seven or eight townships. Other persons who were induced by Ellsworth to invest in prairie lands kept the management of their estates in their own hands. Possibly John Grigg, whose large land business is described below, was one of them.

Ellsworth undertook to establish for himself and his family a patriarchal estate which he hoped to have well developed by tenants before advancing age required handing it over to his children. Part of the land was held as speculation, the proceeds to be used to finance improvements on the remainder. Hired laborers and tenants were used to construct fences, dig ditches, cultivate the land, and manage the livestock. As early as 1845 Ellsworth was offering to lease unimproved lands for one half the crops for two or three years, at the end of which period a fee title would be given without further payments. A considerable amount of land was thus brought into cultivation but Ellsworth failed in his attempt to establish a profitable, well-managed, and modern estate like that of the Wadsworths of New York. Inadequate capital, the high cost of drainage and fencing, expensive and impractical experiments, and declining health, together with the crushing effect of the panic of 1857, defeated him. His estate, after some litigation, passed into the hands of more practical and hardheaded frontiersmen like Edward C. Sumner, Adams Earl, and Moses Fowler, who were to achieve the goal that Ellsworth had sought.[6]

[5] Letter of Henry L. Ellsworth of Jan. 1, 1837, in Henry William Ellsworth, *Valley of the Upper Wabash, Indiana* (New York, 1838), 166–167.

[6] Ellsworth's land business is described in Chapter 4, above.

While Riggs, Ellsworth, and other frontier landlords succeeded in establishing tenancy at an early date on their holdings they were not able to obtain much rent until the middle of the century. The panic of 1837 and the resulting period of hard times, the scarcity of money on the frontier, the absence of transportation facilities, and the poor demand for farm products made it difficult to collect rents or to sell land for anything like the prices anticipated, although it was not difficult to secure tenants. In the late forties the tide turned; immigrants by the tens of thousands began coming to the prairies annually, bringing with them some capital; eastern capitalists again bought land by the section and even by the township; agricultural prices recovered and, of course, land values skyrocketed.

In the midst of this land boom which lasted from 1847 to 1857, the federal government adopted several policies which further stimulated land speculation and hastened the end of the public domain in Illinois.

Military bounty land warrants covering 61,205,490 acres were granted to soldiers and officers of the Mexican War and to veterans of previous wars. These warrants were dumped on the market, where they dropped as low as sixty cents an acre, thereby doubling the amount of land which speculators could acquire through the use of these rights. At the same time, the wet, overflowed, or swamp lands were donated to the states in which they were located in the hope that they would be drained. Little was done to drain these swamp lands at the time; instead the lands soon found their way, in huge tracts, into the hands of speculators. Finally, the long discussed project for a central railroad to extend through the heart of Illinois received the blessing of the government, together with a grant of 2,595,000 acres of land to aid in its construction. The completion of this railroad, the longest as yet undertaken, together with the impetus it gave to the building of other prairie railroads, aided in bringing most of the prairie country within easy reach of modern transportation. As a result of these factors the era of the public domain was

Repeating!

brought to an end in Illinois prior to the adoption of the Homestead Act.

Second only to federal land policy in permitting as well as encouraging the establishment of large estates in Illinois was the land policy of the Illinois Central Railroad. As part of its efforts to sell its land grant the railroad invited capitalists to purchase land without limit and assured them, as Ellsworth was doing, that tenants could be secured to farm their land who would bring them high returns in the form of rents. A considerable part of the early sales of the railroad were made to colony promoters and landlords who were planning the creation of huge estates or bonanza farms.[7] The Malhiot estate, subsequently the Vandeveer estate in Christian County, the Sullivant estate in Ford and Champaign counties, the Funk and Gridley estates in McLean County, and the Danforth estate in Kankakee and Iroquois counties, were established in part from purchases of railroad land. The utmost patience was shown these and other large buyers of the railroad land when their payments became delinquent, though later events showed that most contracts for large purchases had to be canceled sooner or later.

Landlordism and tenancy were also encouraged by the high prices the Illinois Central charged for its land. Few settlers were able to pay the $5, $10, or $20 which it charged per acre and if they were tempted by the optimistic descriptions of prairie farming to make a try at it they had to buy on time. Only advance interest was charged the first two years; in 1859 it was made the first four years. The principal payments proved to be hard to meet, few purchasers being able to complete payments on schedule. Lenient treatment by the railroad could not get around the fact that overdue payments resulted in added interest, and an in-

---

[7] Two pamphlets that were in the nature of promotion literature, sponsored by the Illinois Central, invited large investments by capitalists: James Caird, *Prairie Farming in America; With Notes by the Way on Canada and the United States* (New York, 1859); and *A Guide to the Illinois Central Railroad Lands* (Chicago, 1860), 39.

creased debt. After long delays the Illinois Central encouraged settlers to surrender their contracts and take title to a small part of the whole, the payments on which had been completed.[8] Some settlers in this way became owners of tracts too small to farm economically. Others never could complete their payments on the land to which their improvements had given increased value. Some, when pressed by the railroad, borrowed money on the security of their land, took title and mortgaged it to their creditor. From this mortgaged status some were to emerge as full owners, others were to be defeated and to have their farms foreclosed. Tenancy or emigration were open to them.

To the speculators and landlords of the thirties who, like the owners of the Riggs estate, had managed to carry their holdings through the dark days after 1837 was now added a new crop of frontier landlords who were looking for the chance either to rent their land or to sell it at enhanced prices. Over one-third of the area of Illinois was in the wild state, being held by the railroad, which was asking from $5 to $20 an acre for its well-located tracts, or by John Grigg, Solomon Sturges, or the numerous other speculators—all eager to sell at prices which were beyond the means of most immigrants, or to rent at a price equivalent to the government's charge for its land. True, the railroad and many speculators granted long credit but some down payment was required, if only advance interest, and few immigrants could even provide that. Furthermore, it must be remembered that prairie land, which comprised the bulk of the holdings of both the railroad and the speculator landlords, needed artificial drainage, that it was difficult for the man of small means to break up his land without the employment of expensive breaking plows and numerous yoke of oxen, and that fencing and building materials were not easy to obtain without the expenditure of considerable money.[9] It seemed, then, that only

[8] Paul Wallace Gates, *The Illinois Central Railroad and Its Colonization Work* (Cambridge, 1934), *passim*.

[9] Clarence H. Danhof, "Farm-Making Costs and the 'Safety Valve': 1850–60," *Journal of Political Economy*, XLIX (June, 1941), 317–359.

men with some capital could contract for and meet the payments on railroad or speculator-owned land. In fact, the Illinois Central Railroad was careful in its advertising literature to warn the poorer class that they could not begin prairie farming without $1,000 or more for necessary expenditures.[10]

The experience of John Grigg in selling his great 124,000 acre estate in central Illinois is important as showing the rising value of unimproved land.[11] Grigg was not bothered by the lack of capital that so harried many of his contemporaries. His lands became encumbered neither by mortgages nor tax titles and when conditions improved he was in a position to take advantage of rising land values. By the middle forties he was selling land at $3 an acre, a price which was not exceeded, except for scattered forties, until 1851 and 1852 when prices ranging upward to $6 an acre were received, although $4 and even $3 remained more common. In the later fifties he received as high as $9 and $10 an acre, but somewhat lower prices were the usual thing. In the three counties of Sangamon, McLean, and Logan, Grigg's sales, mostly in the forties and fifties, were as follows: [12]

County	Acres	Price received
Logan	3,378	$21,831
McLean	8,639	36,121
Sangamon	26,532	128,727
Christian	16,910	87,370
Total	55,459	$274,049

[10] *A Guide to the Illinois Central Railroad Lands,* 37.

[11] Information on the entries of public lands is complied from the abstracts of entries in the National Archives, Washington. Duplicates of these records for Illinois are on file in the State Auditor's office, Springfield. Most Illinois counties have a volume of abstracts of original entries in the recorders' offices.

[12] Data concerning purchases, sales, and leases of land other than original entries have been compiled from the deed, mortgage and miscellaneous records of the various counties covered by this chapter. Since much of the data here given is collected from many volumes it has not seemed wise to give more than this general reference, except in cases of specific information when the volume and page are cited.

Grigg apparently planned neither to withhold his land for higher prices nor to rent to tenants. His policy was to push the land into buyers' hands as rapidly as possible and he was content with an average price of $5 an acre. Had he been willing to retain his land for a few years longer or had he attempted to secure tenants he might have fared better.

A major beneficiary of the rising land values and the growing demand for farm rents was William W. Corcoran, the well-known Washington banker and patron of the Democratic Party.

Over many years the federal government had come into the possession of a vast quantity of property through defalcations of treasury officials who had speculated in western land and whose investments and those of their bondsmen had been forfeited to the government. Greatest of these defaulters and absconders was Samuel Swartwout, collector of the port of New York, who had misappropriated more than a million dollars for speculations in western lands. In 1847 the time was deemed right for the government to sell these forfeited lands which had not been restored to the public domain and to which the government's title was not entirely clear. Corcoran, through his friend, Robert J. Walker, was sufficiently informed of the matter to be able to bid low but successful prices ranging from thirty-seven to forty-one cents an acre. Choicest of these lands were 22,199 acres in Illinois that were bought for thirty-eight cents an acre. This land was widely scattered, one-half being in Grundy, Macon, Coles, McDonough, Bureau, Fulton, and Will counties.

Corcoran's investments in Illinois being scattered, he was obliged to place them in charge of a number of agents who gave him a good deal of trouble by the lax manner in which they conducted the business, their inability to collect the rents when due and to pay the taxes before penalties and tax titles had encumbered the property. Corcoran was unable to give the business the close supervision that it needed, especially after 1861, when he was forced by circumstances to leave the country on account of his alleged pro-southern sympathies. Despite these difficulties and the fact that confiscation proceedings were brought against some of his lands, the estate developed in a profitable way.

Absentee ownership and nonresident agents seemed to make necessary the cash rent system for the farming land. Corcoran gave leases for as much as five years but reserved the right to sell the land at any time. By means of partial remission of rents or direct financial assistance, he encouraged his tenants to build fences and to erect houses and barns. If the property were sold before the expiration of the lease, improvements put on the land by the tenants might be removed. Rents in the fifties ranged from merely nominal sums plus taxes and stipulated improvements to $1 and $2 an acre for well developed farms. Over his lifetime they totaled $150,000 on an original investment of $8,000. His sales were made at $2 to $10 in the fifties and after the Civil War were made at $30 to $53 an acre. The total income from sales is unobtainable but, the incomplete records reveal notable success in the speculation.[13]

Both Riggs and Corcoran found that they had underestimated the difficulties of managing lands in remote areas. For many years they were subjected to a constant stream of petty annoyances over timber-stealing and squatting, difficulties over tax payments and the collection of rents, and repeated demands by tenants for capital improvements to be made at the expense of the landlord. Their correspondence reflects rank pessimism and thorough disillusionment with the western land business despite the increasing returns it yielded.

Ellsworth was more typical than were Riggs and Corcoran of the great nineteenth-century prairie landlords because he knew intimately the details of farming, gave the land and farming

[13] There is an abundance of detail on this land business in the Corcoran MSS., Library of Congress. Henry Cohen has a valuable treatment of the "Vicissitudes of an Absentee Landlord: A Case Study," in which the Illinois land business of Corcoran is intensively examined, in David M. Ellis, ed., *The Frontier in American Development: Essays in Honor of Paul Wallace Gates* (Ithaca, 1969), 192–216.

business his close personal supervision, and identified himself completely with the development of the prairies. His generation witnessed the emergence of numerous estates ranging from 5,000 to 45,000 acres in central Illinois and northwestern Indiana that were owned, developed, and operated by agricultural Napoleons possessing Ellsworth's vision and optimism plus the energy, shrewd judgment, confidence, and capacity to drive themselves as well as their laborers and tenants to such a degree as to make successful their spectacular enterprises.

These prairie landlords followed a fairly common agricultural pattern based on livestock and grain-raising, with greater or less emphasis upon the one or the other, but varied widely in their rental policies, their financial practices, and their use of hired labor. It was in Sangamon, Logan, DeWitt, Piatt, McLean, Livingston, Grundy, Ford, Champaign, Vermilion Iroquois, and Kankakee counties that these large estates were located. The Vandeveer estate in Christian County, the Gillett estate in Sangamon and Logan counties, the David Davis and Asahel Gridley estates in McLean County, the C. H. Moore estate in DeWitt County, and the Hoge, Holderman, and Collins estates in Grundy County are well worth study but only the more significant historically can be given attention here.

No description of frontier landlords of Illinois would be complete if it did not include Michael Sullivant. The Sullivant family had early settled in central Ohio, where it had acquired 53,000 acres through the location of military warrants given to Virginia veterans of the Revolution.[14] A tract of 5,000 acres near Columbus had been cleared and made into a highly productive farm on which 2,300 acres of corn and 250 acres of wheat were grown and herds of sheep and 200 to 300 mules were pastured. Michael Sullivant with other prominent Ohio livestock farmers and dealers was an organizer of the Ohio Company for

[14] William Thomas Hutchinson, "The Bounty Lands of the American Revolution in Ohio," Ph.D. dissertation, University of Chicago, 1927, 159, 197.

Importing English Cattle, in 1833. He invested $4,500 in the highest priced Durham bull and two Durham cows.[15] Tiring of this venture, Sullivant and his brother Joseph rented their Ohio farm to tenants on a share basis and undertook to carry their large scale farming and ranching operations into Illinois and later into Kansas.

Attracted by the deep rich soil of the Grand Prairie of east-central Illinois at a time when that area was still largely untouched by white settlers, the Sullivants bought from the government, from the Illinois Central, and from speculators who had preceded them at the land office at Danville. 80,000 acres in Champaign, Ford, Livingston, and Vermilion counties, paying for the railroad land $5 and $10 an acre and for the government land $1.25 an acre. A compact tract of 22,000 acres in Champaign County was chosen for the big farm which they proposed to develop. In February, 1855, the Sullivant party left Columbus for Illinois with thirty horses, thirty-five men, and nine heavy wagons designed to serve as tents until suitable buildings could be constructed. The party arrived on the land in time for spring plowing, additional laborers were recruited, and great herds of horses and mules were employed to break the prairie, seed it to corn, and fence the land—now appropriately called Broadlands.[16] From 1855 to 1866 Sullivant conducted operations at Broadlands on a scale that is reminiscent of the great plantations in the South. Between 100 and 200 laborers were employed in the summer, vast fields were planted to corn,

[15] Robert Russell, *North America: Its Agriculture and Climate* (Edinburgh, 1857) 124–125; Commissioner of Patents, *Annual Report*, 1851, Part II. Agriculture, 98–103; *Country Gentleman*, X (Sept. 10, 1857), 173; *The Crisis* (Columbus, Ohio), April 25, 1861; *Michigan Farmer*, new series, II (Aug., 1863), 62–63. When Sullivant left for Illinois in 1855 his home farm near Columbus contained 5,000 acres and the family still had an additional 8,000 acres of the 53,000 it had earlier acquired. *Caldwell's Atlas of Franklin County, Ohio* (Columbus, 1872), 50, shows a 750-acre farm still in the possession of the Sullivant family.

[16] Chicago *Weekly Democrat*, May 13, 1854; Chicago *Daily Democratic Press*, March 6, 1855, quoting the *Ohio Statesman*.

and great herds of cattle were pastured. In one year 1,000 tons of hay were sold.[17] Later, when the estate was better developed, it was said to have 1,800 acres of corn, 340 acres in other grain, and to be pasturing 5,000 cattle and 4,000 worn-down government horses. Two hundred horses and mules and a large herd of oxen provided the motive power for the plowing, harrowing, seeding, and cultivating.[18]

Despite the large number of laborers he employed, Sullivant had mechanized his farm to a degree that surprised a correspondent of the Cincinnati *Enquirer* who wrote:

Almost all of Mr. S's farming is conducted by labor saving machinery, so that it is estimated that, throughout, one man will perform the average labor of four or five as conducted on small farms. He drives his posts by horse-power; breaks his ground with Comstock's "spade"; mows, rakes, loads, unloads and stacks his hay by horse-power; cultivates his corn by improved machinery; ditches any low ground by machinery; sows and plants by machinery, so that all his laborers can ride and perform their tasks as easy as riding in a buggy.[19]

Sullivant's land purchases were financed by loans made by various banks and by the generous credit terms allowed by the Illinois Central, his debt being at the outset $225,000. Heavy interest charges, together with other costs involved in breaking, ditching, fencing, planting, and harvesting his crops, soon raised his total debt to half a million.[20] For a time during the Civil War, Sullivant fared well, his net profit in 1862 being $80,000, which was invested in additional improvements.[21] Less favorable

[17] *Wisconsin Farmer*, XVIII (March, 1866), 93.

[18] *Moore's Rural New Yorker*, XIV (July 18, 25, 1863), 229, 237.

[19] Quoted in the *Cultivator and Country Gentleman*, XXVIII (Aug. 9, 1866), 91.

[20] J. W. Foster, land commissioner, Illinois Central Railroad, Jan. 27, 1861, to William H. Osborn, Archives, Illinois Central Railroad. In 1857 Sullivant gave a trust deed to cover a mortgage of $150,000 on his Ford County land. The debt was owed to banks and individuals in Ohio, Indiana, Kentucky, and Virginia (2 Deed Records, Ford County, 231).

[21] *Michigan Farmer*, new series, II (Aug., 1863), 62–63.

years followed, however, and the high interest charges on his debt obliged him to sell part of his 80,000 acres as he had originally planned to do. Unfortunately, unimproved prairie land in Champaign, Ford, and Livingston counties had not as yet attained the level for which he was holding. Circumstances therefore dictated the selling of Broadlands in 1866—22,551 acres for $270,000.[22] It was stated that the sale of the stock, grain, hay, and farming implements on the estate added nearly $100,000 to the purchase price.[23] Sullivant then turned to a still larger tract of 40,000 acres in Ford and Livingston counties, which was more remote from transportation facilities and in one of the least developed portions of Illinois.

In the next ten years Burr Oaks became the best-known farm in America, so widely published were the stories about its vast operations. Like Broadlands under its new owner, and the great farms of Jacob Strawn, Benjamin F. Harris, John Sidell, and Edward C. Sumner, all on the Illinois prairie, Burr Oaks was a true "bonanza farm" experiment in which individual fields of thousands of acres were plowed, harrowed, seeded, and harvested, by the greatest array of farm machinery as yet assembled. A reporter of *Harper's Weekly*, who visited the farm in quest for pictures and information, was impressed with the size of the farm, the 16,000 acres in grain, the nature of the management, the specialization and division of labor, the meager buildings and few improvements, but especially with the quantity of the labor-saving machinery in use. He wrote:

The machinery in use at Burr Oaks would handsomely stock two or three agricultural implement stores: 150 steel plows, of different styles; 75 breaking-plows; 142 cultivators, of several descriptions; 45 cornplanters; 25 gang harrows, etc. The ditching-plow, a huge affair of eighteen feet in length, with a share of eleven feet by two

[22] 8 Deed Records, Champaign County, 45.

[23] Paxton *Record*, March 3, Sept. 8, 1866; *Prairie Farmer*, XVIII (Sept. 15, 1866), 172.

feet ten inches, is worked by sixty-eight oxen and eight men. These finish from three to three and a half miles of excellent ditch each day of work.[24]

Hauling this equipment required 350 mules, 50 horses, and 50 yoke of oxen. One thousand hogs and probably a larger number of cattle were fed on Burr Oaks. Perhaps the largest crop produced on Burr Oaks with the aid of this great array of farm machinery was that of 1871, when the output of corn amounted to 600,000 bushels.

Tenancy was not introduced on Burr Oaks at first, but unmarried laborers, mostly Swedes and Germans ranging in numbers from 200 to 400, were employed from April through January, being housed in rough barracks. Thus by constructing the fewest and most inexpensive improvements Sullivant was able to make his capital go a long way in buying land and in raising corn from it year after year.[25] Sullivant's second venture in large-scale farming fared well until the panic of 1873 set in motion a downward movement of prices. To compensate for this reduced income the area in cultivation was enlarged until there were 23,000 acres in corn, but this in turn greatly increased the burden of debt the estate was carrying. The panic also knocked the props from under the real estate market and Sullivant was again cheated of the opportunity of selling his surplus and unimproved lands to aid in carrying the remainder. In 1871 Burr Oaks was mortgaged for $478,000, more than half of which was owed to Hiram Sibley, of Rochester, New York. This money was borrowed at 10 percent interest and 5 percent commission, high rates for Illinois at the time and high enough

[24] *Harper's Weekly*, XV (Sept. 23, 1871), 897–898, 900–901. Included among a number of interesting illustrations is a sketch of nine breaking plows, each hauled by four yoke of oxen, cutting a 20-inch furrow but only 2½ to 3 inches deep. Plowing was done in the spring, and corn was planted in the turned-over furrow.

[25] Paxton *Record*, Aug. 10, 1871.

to make the enterprise hazardous without a combination of good crops and satisfactory prices.[26]

Sullivant found it increasingly difficult to keep all the details of the farming business in his own hands and divided the estate into large units over which overseers were appointed. Division of authority was not a panacea; other and more fundamental difficulties had to be surmounted. Drainage of the prairies was essential but it was costly, and Sullivant proceeded slowly, too slowly for his own good. In 1870 it was reported that nothing as yet had been done to drain the tract.[27] Dependence upon his corn crop put the "patroon," as Sullivant was called, in a dangerous position when that crop was light, but little was done to diversify save to pasture considerable numbers of cattle and hogs.

Continued financial worries and inability to sell surplus land forced a change in plans. Laborers on the estate and farmers in the vicinity were invited to become tenants of Sullivant, who was still reluctant to give up his well-earned title of "Corn King of America." In 1874 Sullivant advertised several thousands of acres to rent on shares in tracts of eighty acres or larger. He also wanted several "good farm bosses" to take charge of gangs of fifteen to twenty men with teams, the compensation to be according to ability.[28] This policy of establishing tenants on the land, which brought satisfactory returns to other large landowners in the sixties and seventies, was adopted too late to save Sullivant's estate. A series of poor harvests and an ever-mounting interest burden, together with continued management difficulties, forced an assignment in 1877 and foreclosure two years later.[29]

[26] 11 Mortgage Records, Ford County, 321 ff.; Paxton *Record*, Feb. 6, 1879.

[27] Pontiac *Sentinel and Press*, July 28, 1870.

[28] *Praire Farmer*, XLV (Feb. 28, 1874), 71; Lincoln *Herald*, July 23, 1874. In 1876 Sullivant announced that he had "come to the conclusion that I monopolize more territory" than he should and was ready to sell 20,000 acres (*Indiana Farmer*, XI [Sept. 9, 1876], 1). See also *Piatt County Herald* (Monticello, Ill.), Feb. 13, 1878.

[29] Paxton *Record*, Feb. 6, 1879.

Although the local press had commented approvingly when Sullivant first came to Ford and Livingston counties to develop Burr Oaks,[30] it soon changed its tune. When he was forced to sell part of his land, and later when Burr Oaks was divided into small tenant holdings, the newspapers expressed gratification. These counties already had a very high percentage of land cultivated by tenants or hired laborers, much of which was absentee owned, and the disposal of the Sullivant interest, coming at the same time that the Jacob Bunn estate in Livingston County was being liquidated, was regarded as a step in the right direction.[31] In Monticello, the *Piatt County Herald* called large land holdings "a great drawback" to a region since the majority of the owners were land-poor, unable to pay their debts, and kept out small farmers who were much more desirable.[32]

Somewhat reluctantly, it appears, Hiram Sibley, principal creditor of Sullivant, took over the larger part of Burr Oaks, now renamed Sibley Farms. Already experienced in large farming operations on his Howland Island estate in Cayuga County, New York, Sibley threw aside the whole Sullivant plan of operations and began anew. The 40,000-acre estate being considered too unwieldly for efficient administration, one-half was offered for sale in 1879, part being sold in large tracts and part being divided into small holdings.[33] Sibley reserved 17,640 acres that he divided into 146 tenant farms ranging in size from 80 to 320 acres. In the short space of four years he built on Burr Oaks 134 houses and barns in which were established as many tenant families, who were now largely displacing the migratory labor that Sullivant had employed. All the houses, barns, ditching, tiling, fencing, and other improvements were put on the land

[30] *Ibid.*, Sept 8, 1866.

[31] Pontiac *Sentinel*, Jan. 9, 1878, March 19, 1879; Gibson *Courier*, in *ibid.*, Nov. 6, 1878.

[32] *Piatt County Herald*, Sept. 13, 1876; Pontiac *Sentinel*, June 9, 1880.

[33] Paxton *Record*, Sept. 18, 1879.

by Sibley and they seem to have compared well with other tenant improvements in the same area.

Sibley struck immediately at the drainage question, determined to have most of his land cultivated. Where his predecessor had left the wetter parts in permanent pasture with native grasses, Sibley began an elaborate program of ditch construction.[34] Very soon he learned, as most owners of prairie farms did, that ditching was not a satisfactory solution; only tile draining would make possible the successful cultivation of wet areas. By 1887, 376 miles of tile had been laid on Burr Oaks, in itself no small investment.[35]

As was common practice, the Sibley lands were rented on a share basis. At the town of Sibley huge corncribs and warehouses for small grains were erected to receive the landlord's share of the crops. A practical and efficient system of supervision was established on the estate, including the employment of a general manager, a superintendent and executive officer, an overseer of hands, two overseers of tenants, an overseer of teams, and a foreman of repairs. In line with good farm practice it was the Sibley policy to feed the grain on the farms, and purebred beef and dairy cattle were introduced by the landlord. In 1879, 500 purebred calves were shipped to Burr Oaks from Sibley's New York farm.[36] The system of rotation and the farm practices to be employed by the tenants were closely prescribed. The lease in use on the Sibley farms was undoubtedly the result of long experience gained in reconciling the divergent views of landlord and tenant. It prescribes among other things how corn is to be planted and how frequently it is to be cultivated, the methods of dividing the crops, the care of the ditches, and the elimination of burrs and weeds, and even states that when mechanical corn

[34] Paxton *Record*, Nov. 6, 1879.   [35] Paxton *Record*, Feb. 3, 17, 1887.

[36] Paxton *Record*, Dec. 4, 1879. A detailed sketch of the history and development of Burr Oaks under Sullivant and Sibley, the information in which seems to have been supplied by Hiram Sibley, is in *Agricultural Review*, II (Aug. 1882), 76–89, and is reprinted in part in Hiram Sibley & Co., *Farmers' Almanac* (1883), 28–37.

pickers are used the tenant "shall glean the field picking up all the ears missed, when requested. . . ." The enlightened policy of a modern landlord and perhaps the greatest justification for tenancy may be seen in the following statement of principle that is included in the livestock and grain lease of the Sibley estate:

One major way in which maximum profit in farming . . . can be obtained is by maintaining a balanced, all-year program which includes livestock as well as grain production thereby helping to maintain soil fertility and to secure large crop yields. Good soil, adequate buildings and fences combined with a system which includes limestone, legumes and livestock can produce the maximum profit through the co-operation of all parties concerned.

The fact that Sibley was rapidly improving his estate and settling tenants upon it who would have, in the ordinary course of events, higher incomes and more purchasing power than the laborers formerly employed by Sullivant won for him commendation in the local press. Sibley succeeded where Sullivant had failed; his system of rotation and diversification not only built up or conserved soil qualities, but made for better results, on the average, than Sullivant's system with its heavy dependence upon corn as a crop. A rich section of Ford County which previously had had but slight development, now, under the benevolent management of Hiram Sibley and his representatives and tenants, became a prosperous and thriving area. By 1887, when the pressure for rent lands was heavy in Illinois and when the Sibley policy of providing relatively attractive improvements and giving fair treatment to tenants had become well known, it was reported that "a great many applicants" for rents were being turned away.[37] Since that time the Sibley family sold a part of the estate and encouraged tenants to enlarge the size of their tracts until by the 1940s the 13,600 acres remaining to it were

[37] Paxton *Record*, Feb. 17, 1887. A visit with Mr. Rohrer, manager of the Sibley farms, was most helpful in studying the relations between the landlord and the tenants.

divided into forty-three farms ranging from 160 to 960 acres. The red barns and rusty yellow houses, the great fields of hybrid corn, the herds of Brown Swiss milking cattle and Hereford steers were familiar sights to residents of east-central Illinois.

Sullivant's chief rival to fame as the farmer of vast tracts of land was John T. Alexander, who took over Broadlands in 1866. Like Isaac Funk and Samuel Allerton, whose extensive operations are mentioned above, Alexander was chiefly interested in the buying and fattening of cattle for market. On his 5,000 acre estate in Morgan County he pastured great droves of cattle that were bought in Texas and Kansas. The possession of Broadlands, which he enlarged to 26,500 acres, permitted him to increase his operations to such an extent that he was pasturing 5,000 cattle in addition to 500 hogs and many draft animals on his two farms, and was planning to double his herds of cattle.[38] Five thousand acres were planted in corn and 660 acres in other grains. Alexander continued Sullivant's policy of managing Broadlands as a single farm divided into large operating units, the labor being provided by Scandinavians under the charge of overseers. Dwelling houses were kept at a minimum and were found by an observer to be in dilapidated condition.[39] Mortgages in excess of $153,000 and a debt to the Illinois Central Railroad of $89,000 so heavily encumbered the farm that, despite his good fortune in some years, the interest burden, together with management problems, defeated Alexander as it was defeating Sullivant on Burr Oaks. In 1871 the trustees to whom the property was assigned sold two sections to Charles Ridgely, and the remainder was deeded to the principal creditor, Augustus E. Ayers, a banker of Jacksonville.[40] Ayers managed

[38] *Transactions of the Illinois State Agricultural Society* (Springfield, 1870), VII, 135–136.

[39] *Prairie Farmer*, XL (Aug. 7, 1869), 249.

[40] 23 Deed Records, Champaign County, 552.

Broadlands for some time, but he had no such grandiose ideas as Sullivant and Alexander, and only waited for an opportunity to unload without sustaining any loss. In 1875 it was reported that Ayers had sold 10,000 acres to 100 farmers and two years later it was said that 1,000 people were living on Broadlands. Even then, some of the land remained available for rent or sale.[41]

While the large-scale farming operations of Sullivant, Alexander, and other owners of big farms who relied on hired labor delayed the introduction of tenancy for a short time, they assured its widespread adoption, once the estates were broken up, for by then land values had risen so high that few immigrants could do other than rent. Tenancy came earlier on estates which the landlord did not choose to farm himself through hired laborers, but elected to rent instead. Much information on the beginning of tenancy in the Corn Belt may be gleaned from the story of the land business of Matthew T. Scott, Jr.

The Scott family had been prominent in the annals of early Lexington, Kentucky, and it was to leave its mark upon the development of Illinois.[42] Matthew T. Scott, Sr., president of the Northern Bank of Kentucky, with his five sons, Isaac, Joseph, John, Matthew T., Jr., and William, and his four daughters, Mary, Margaret, Winnie, and Lucy, for themselves and others with whom they were associated, purchased a total of 54,876 acres of land, mostly in Livingston, Grundy, McLean, Piatt and Vermilion counties in the years from 1836 to 1855, in addition to 5,600 acres in western Iowa. For years the investment remained dormant, the owners waiting until increasing settlement made possible either sale or rental of the land. Proper attention seems to have been given to the investment for, unlike

[41] Lincoln *Herald*, July 23, 1874; *Piatt Republican* (Monticello, Ill.), Nov. 4, 1875; Pontiac *Sentinel*, Sept. 5, 1877.

[42] George W. Ranck, *History of Lexington, Kentucky* (Cincinnati, 1872), 382.

many other such estates, the Scott holdings did not become involved in tax titles and squatter claims. Eventually Isaac Scott came to Piatt County to develop a number of thousand acres in that section. He settled tenants upon his land, built them homes "better than tenants usually have," constructed an elevator in Bement to house the share grain he received, and became one of the influential men in the community.[43]

After some experience in Ohio managing the family's lands, Matthew T. Scott, Jr., came to Illinois in 1852 to enter land, and three years later to settle. In the midst of a large block of the family land in southern Livingston and eastern McLean counties, he selected a site on the Chicago and Alton Railroad which was planned as a center of operations for his extensive farm business, and on it he laid out the town of Chenoa. In an advertisement calling attention to the "Great Sale of Lots in the Town of Chenoa," Scott related numerous advantages the site held, promised a credit of two years to lot buyers with remission of interest to those who within six months would build houses worth $400 or $500, offered to take a quarter-interest in a steam mill and to furnish one-half the money to build it. Inducements were also offered to attract mechanics.[44]

These were the usual efforts made by the town platters on the frontier, but Scott could add to them the construction of great corncribs and warehouses to receive the quantity of produce he was shortly to get from his numerous share tenants. Although Chenoa was too close to Bloomington to become an important city, it did become a considerable agricultural center. It was soon apparent that real estate values in Chenoa would always be

[43] Emma C. Piatt, *History of Piatt County* (Chicago, ca. 1883), 393–394.

[44] Bloomington *Pantagraph*, April 30, 1856. Several visits with Mrs. Carl Vrooman, daughter of Matthew Scott, with her husband, Carl Vrooman, and with her sister, Mrs. Letitia Bromwell, were most helpful in tracing the story of the Scott-Vrooman-Bromwell land business. Mrs. Vrooman graciously gave to Cornell University the papers of the land business of her father and mother and of Lewis G. Stevenson, who with Carl Vrooman managed the lands at different times.

modest; Scott, more hardheaded and practical than many western landlords, turned his attention to the development, sale, and rental of the large family estate in wild land.

Matthew Scott planned to make the estate in his care a permanent and profitable investment. To accomplish this without undue delay it was necessary to attract settlers by constructing tenant houses, barns, and fences, and by draining wet areas. The cost of such improvements was to be met by selling those portions of the family's holdings, improved or unimproved, for which there was a ready demand. The income from sales, judiciously invested in additional improvements, would raise the rental or the sales value of the remaining land, and would thereby assure a steadily rising income of a permanent character.

The Scott land was not pushed on the market; distress sales were avoided; and only when prices were satisfactory were tracts sold. Study of the deed records shows that a minimum of $6 or $7 was maintained and few tracts were sold for less than $10 an acre. Nor did Scott have to wait long for acceptable prices. The prosperity of the years 1855, 1856, and 1857 and of the Civil War years sent land values up at an unparalleled rate and well-located tracts with only slight improvements brought good returns. In the sixties most sales were made for $10, $11, and $12 an acre and in the seventies for $20 and $25 an acre. Thereafter the price rose to $30, $40, and $50 in the eighties, and to $60 to $90 in the nineties. One tract of 160 acres was sold in 1909 for $200 an acre. A tabulation of Scott's land sales, exclusive of town lots, in the four counties of Ford, Livingston, Logan, and McLean, shows 13,289 acres for which $265,367 were received. These prices, of course, include improvements put upon the land by Scott or his tenants. Funds derived from these sales, together with some capital he brought with him from Kentucky to Illinois, made it possible for Scott to finance extensive improvements on the land he planned to retain.

Both to attract immigrants to his land, either as purchasers or tenants and to aid them in getting farming operations under way the first year, Scott undertook to build modest, inexpensive "cottage houses" upon the forty- or eighty-acre tracts into which he was dividing his land and to break the prairie preparatory to the first crop. During his first year in Illinois he built ten or a dozen such houses and broke up and seeded to wheat and corn more than a thousand acres.[45] Since his improvements were in a part of McLean and Livingston counties that was still quite untouched by settlers and unused by cattlemen, he did not find it necessary to start fencing at the outset. In 1856 Scott was advertising for "Farmers, Prairie Breakers and Laborers" to aid in developing the twenty quarter-sections that were already considerably improved.[46] Thereafter, Scott rapidly enlarged his land operations and agricultural improvements, building between 160 and 200 tenant houses, setting out 275 miles of hedge, digging 250 miles of ditching, and tiling 5,000 acres.[47]

Without fanfare Scott put into operation a plan which was to aid in bridging the gap between the buyer and seller of land and to provide in theory, if not in practice, a ladder from tenancy to ownership. The plan called for contracts whereby Scott agreed to deed a piece of land in six, seven, eight, or nine years in return for one-half the crops for that period. An examination of forty contracts, embracing 3,500 acres, reveals a common pattern in the conditions of the sale with, however, wide variations in terms. In general, Scott provided housing accommodations, although in some instances the buyer had either to erect his own house or to provide the labor or its equivalent for construction; taxes were to be paid by the buyer who was to drain all wet areas, at least share in the cost and labor of fencing,

[45] The Bloomington *Pantagraph* watched with much approval the vigorous way in which Scott applied himself to the task of improving his land and the success he had in bringing in settlers, and urged other large landowners to follow his example (May 2, Oct. 3, 1855; May 15, 1856).

[46] *Ibid.*, April 16, 1856.

[47] George B. Pickett, *A Short Sketch of the Life and Character of Matthew Thompson Scott* (Bloomington, Ill., 1891), 8.

exterminate noxious weeds, bring one-half the land in cultivation the first year and the remainder the second year, and keep all buildings and fences in good condition. Scott allowed the buyer to retain all the first or sod crop, but thereafter required that his half should be hauled by the tenant to his cribs at Chenoa or other focal points.

The crop sharing system required close supervision at harvest time and did not prove entirely satisfactory to Scott, so in many of the contracts a clause was substituted that worked something like a cash rent. Instead of requiring one-half the crops, Scott commuted his share to sixteen bushels of corn per acre, multiplied that by the number of years the contract was to run, and allowed the purchaser to make payments toward the total quantity as fast as he desired. For example, Stephen Casey contracted in 1866 for the S½ SW ¼, Sec. 16, T 26 N, R 4 E in McLean County, of which seventy acres were to be planted to corn. One thousand one hundred and twenty bushels of number-one corn were to be delivered to Scott yearly from 1868 through 1875, and one-half of eight crops of timothy hay—which was to be raised on the remaining ten acres—was to be baled and delivered to Scott. Payments in excess of the required 1,120 bushels would be credited toward the total of 8,960 bushels for which the contract called, thereby making it possible to hasten final deeding of the property.[48] Another contract, made with James L. Sheppard for 160 acres in Sec. 30, T 29 N, R 7 E in Livingston County in 1864, called for one-half of six crops of corn, rye, oats, flax, and timothy hay; when the aggregate of the crops grown on 477 acres had been delivered to Scott the property would be deeded to Sheppard.[49]

Under Scott's system of making sales on what amounted to a rental basis, most of the risk was born by the purchaser. Scott, it is true, provided the materials and sometimes the labor for the houses, set out part of the fencing, paid for part of the cost

[48] 61 Deed Records, McLean County, 169.
[49] 5 Deed Records, Livingston County, 133.

of ditching and breaking the prairie, and tiled some of his land, but much of the labor involved in these improvements was provided by the purchaser or tenant. All such improvements added to the value of the land, whether held for sale or rent, and in case the tenant failed to fulfill the terms of the contract everything reverted to Scott. The interests of the landlord were also carefully safeguarded by stipulations requiring that his share of the crops should be assured to him through a lien on all crops and property of the tenant. Some of the contracts did state that full payment of the landlord's share for one or more years would entitle the buyer to a fraction of the land if he did not wish to farm the entire tract any longer. Furthermore, it should be pointed out that the buyer was not held for the high rate of interest on delayed payments that was required of frontier debtors, and that he was not encouraged to borrow from others because of the difficulty of providing collateral, his interest in the land being neither assignable nor subject to mortgage. On the other hand, when there was a poor harvest and the landlord exacted his share despite the smallness of the crop, or in lieu thereof extended the period of the contract to compensate for the failure, the tenant or buyer might have inadequate supplies to carry him to the next harvest, or he might become discouraged at successive failures and throw up his equity. A succession of poor crops or low prices, accompanied by marketing difficulties, put many of Scott's tenants into a frame of mind that induced them to abandon the struggle to acquire title to their farms.

That many of the settlers on Scott's land failed to fulfill their contracts is evident from a study of the deed records. Some gave up the first year, one piece of land having three successive settlers in as many years, while others clung tenaciously to their tracts for a number of years despite drought, poor crops, and low prices, only to lose their homes at a later time. A considerable number succeeded in meeting the terms of their agreement and in securing title to their homes, but the high rate of turnover among settlers and the frequent releases of contracts show that the terms were difficult for many to meet. This was also the experience of numerous buyers of Illinois Central land who struggled in vain to fulfill their contracts. There is no evidence that Scott was harsh in his treatment of settlers, whose welfare and success meant much to him. Yet when settlers were forced by circumstances to give up their homes he found it easy to sell or rent at higher prices than were previously obtainable, for the improvements put upon the land with the labor of former tenants had definitely made it more attractive. In this way Scott established a successful land business which became highly productive and could be counted on to net good rents or to bring attractive prices at sale. In 1862, only seven years after he had first undertaken the development of his land, Scott sold a part of the corn and wheat he had reecived on fourteen contracts, amounting to 20,000 and 2,000 bushels respectively, for $3,500—a net return of more than $2 an acre. Meantime, the unfortunate settler whose contract had been voided for failure to fulfill its terms found that land values in Illinois had gone far beyond his capacity to purchase and the choice of tenancy or trying life anew in central Kansas or Nebraska, to which the great tide of immigration was now flowing, alone remained to him.

Equally long-lasting and somewhat more successful than the Scott estate is that of Clifton H. Moore of Clinton, Illinois, who was a partner in numerous land transactions with David Davis of Bloomington. By purchase from the government, the Illinois Central Railroad, and the counties that had ownership of great areas of swamplands, and through loans and foreclosures, they built up holdings of more than 70,000 acres in Illinois, Iowa, Missouri, Kansas, and Nabraska. Moore and Davis sold some of their land when they could obtain a substantial profit on it to aid in carrying the balance, but from the outset it was their intention to retain the greater portion and develop it through tenants. At first Moore, who managed his own and the jointly owned land, left improvements except fencing to the tenants, but he gradually swung over to employing them to make improvements as rent and later to shift from cash rent to share (grain) rent. As early as 1852, Moore and Davis were renting parts of their Illinois land, and on January 20, 1854, Moore wrote that he had plenty of applications for farms to rent but he was not pleased with the class of men applying. By 1876 all but two of their farms were rented to eighty-four tenants, though how successfully the rents were collected is not clear, for thirty of the tenants were not sufficiently good risks to get credit at stores. Both men died multimillionaires. Davis' farms have been divided and subdivided among his heirs, and there is little evidence that much of the land has passed out of their possession. The Moore-Warner estate (Moore's only surviving child, a daughter, married Vespasian Warner) by the will of Clifton Moore was to be held in trust for twenty years after the last grandchild had died. This kept the estate intact until well into the twentieth century. In 1925 the hundred farms containing 36,000 acres were then valued at more than $3,000,000. Gross income from the farms in the twentieth century has ranged from $75,000 in 1933 to $378,000 in 1945; the net was little in 1933 but ten years later was sufficient to permit distribution of $248,000 to the heirs.[50]

Outranking all other estates of Illinois in acreage, in value, and in the public attention it attracted, was the Scully estate, which was first established in 1850 but enlarged at a later time. No frontier landlord in the entire country caused as much unrest among his tenants and was the object of as much ill feeling and

---

[50] The heirs of both Clifton Warner and David David were kind enough to permit me to work through their relevant papers. The very detailed probate reports of the trust since 1901, in the courthouse in Clinton, are amazingly valuable. The marriage of Winifred Moore with Vespasian Warner united the holdings of two great landlords of DeWitt County—Clifton H. Moore and John Warner. The estate is deserving of more attention. Some detail is given in Maurice Graham Porter, "Portrait of a Prairie Lawyer, Clifton H. Moore, 1851–1861 and 1870–1880: A Comparative Study," J.S.D. thesis, University of Illinois 1960.

political agitation as William Scully. Few men of the time were as harshly condemned and as ruthlessly caricatured as he was during 1887, when the campaign against him was at its height. Sullivant, Sibley, Scott, and Alexander generally enjoyed a favorable press, but Scully was belabored in this country and in Ireland. His difficulty was that his career as an Irish landlord had been unhappy, to say the least, and that he introduced into America some highly unpopular features of the Irish land system just at the time when they were being modified in Ireland.

Scully was a member of a prominent landowning and "moneyed" family of Tipperary and Kilkenny counties, Ireland, which in 1875 was found by a British parliamentary commission to own or hold an long-term lease 15,449 acres with a rental value well in excess of £11,499. William Scully himself held at that time 3,344 acres with a rental value of £1,933.[51] His dislike of developments in Ireland since 1849 had contributed to the partial liquidation of his Irish property.

The term Scullyism, as used by historians of nineteenth-century Ireland, meant rack renting, or extortionate rents, and evictions of tenants without due cause, frequently under distressing circumstances. In the 1860s a series of clashes between Scully and thirty tenants on his Ballycohey estate culminated in a murderous assault on the former when he was attempting to

---

[51] A. M. Sullivan, *New Ireland* (London, 1877), I, 328. Information on the land holdings of various members of the Scully family for 1875 may be found in "Return of Owners of land of One Acre and Upwards in the Several Counties, Counties of Cities, and Counties of Towns in Ireland," *British Parliamentary Papers*, Session of 1876, LXXX, 109, 170. Around 1866, Scully appears to have recovered by purchase earlier family holdings in Ballycohey, on which he rigorously applied his policy of evicting a portion of the tenants in order to provide for larger farm units. In this messy process he was indicted and given a sentence of a year in jail, but whether he served I know not. Thereafter occurred the explosion at Ballycohey elsewhere alluded to and a rising tide of opposition to Scully as an Irish landholder in which other landlords and the London *Times* joined. The upshot of it was that Scully was induced to sell his Ballycohey lands. I have borrowed here heavily from the London *Times* Aug. 15, 17, 18, 19, 21, Sept. 5, 7, 28, Nov. 6, 1868; and Sullivan, *New Ireland*, *passim*.

serve eviction notices. This desperate action resulted in the wounding of Scully and the deaths of the bailiff and and constable who accompanied him. Condemnation of the murders was immediate, but the accounts, even in the London *Times,* showed that the guilty parties had been driven to such extremes by Scully's brutal treatment of his tenants.[52] One historian maintained that Scully's "despotism," which arrayed against him "every voice" including "his brother landlords and magistrates" and which was condemned by the coroner's jury, provided the "decided impulse to public opinion" that led to the Irish land

[52] Sullivan, *New Ireland,* II, 350–371; James Godkin, *The Land-War in Ireland* (London, 1870), 350–351; London *Times,* Aug. 17, 19, Sept. 5, 7, 1868. Many years later, when Scully was concerned about his image, he prepared or had prepared a long obituary in which he explained that the causes of his unpopularity and the attacks upon him and his policies in both Ireland and the United States were the result of misunderstanding of his efforts to practice on his estate the best and most efficient use of the land. The small holdings in Ireland could not be made to produce sufficient for the tenants or an economic rent to him; consequently he decided not to renew the leases and to consolidate the small tracts into larger farms for grazing. The attacks upon him by the press and the clergy for his evictions were caused by a complete misunderstanding of his motives. He did not import into the United States the worst features of Irish tenancy but was compelled by his own inadequate resources to leave to tenants the construction of improvements on his lands, other than draining through ditching and tiling. The obituary denied that he had been "in any sense a rack-renter, being always satisfied with a return . . . of 3 per cent on the capital." Scully's efforts to induce, if not to compel, his tenants to introduce and maintain alfafa growing as a part of efforts to retain soil quality and production were a most constructive step. It was admitted that owners of large estates were not popular, but "more successful farmers" in Illinois, Kansas, and Nebraska have "received their start in life upon the lands of William Scully in those states than of all the other holders of land . . . and if this is true he cannot have been a hard landlord, and his ownership altogether an evil" (Lincoln *Times-Courier,* Oct. 19, 1906). Like most of the specious arguments in the statement the 3 percent interest statement is incredible. For example, on the 4,141 acres of Sangamon County land bought of the Hamilton heirs in 1877, rents of three dollars per acre were charged, or 5.7 percent on the cost (Lincoln *Herald,* Oct. 4, 1877). Management costs would have to be deducted from this, but there should be added the rising value of the land which was to reach four, five, and six times the original cost.

act of 1870.[53] Among other reforms, this act sought to make evictions more difficult and to require that ousted tenants be compensated for their improvements. Though land reformers were aware of the weakness of the measure and that it accomplished little, it was the first of a series of reform measures which transformed the insecure, downtrodden, and thoroughly discontented tenant population of Ireland into a class of peasant proprietors.[54] While Irish tenancy was, therefore, slowly to diminish, Illinois tenancy gradually, if not rapidly, increased, and William Scully was an important factor in this development.

It may be that Scully's entrance into the western land business was an indirect result of an act of Parliament of 1849 which provided for the creation of the encumbered estates court. Passed to permit the sale of encumbered estates, the act led to the transfer of some three thousand estates worth £25,000,000. Within a year after the adoption of this act Scully journeyed to America where, after some preliminary inquiries, he proceeded to Illinois. Here, according to the oft-told story, he made a tour of the prairies, taking with him a famous spade with which he dug into the tough prairie sod to determine the nature of the soil. How extensive his search was it is impossible to say, but that it bore fruit in wise selection of land none can deny. Having satisfied himself that the prairie soils of Logan County were rich and potentially valuable, Scully appeared at the federal land office in Springfield on October 11, 1850, and located with Mexican bounty land warrants of the act of 1847, 54 quarter-sections. Between then and July 5 of the following year, he located 133 additional quarters of which two were later suspended because of a conflict. In 1852 Scully located in the Chicago land office 55 quarter-sections in Grundy County,

[53] *The Economist*, XXVI (Aug. 22, 1868), 957; Sullivan, *New Ireland*, II, 364–365.

[54] A. M. Sullivan, *The Story of Ireland . . . Continued to the Present Time* by James Luby (Providence, R.I., 1886), 625–626; John E. Pomfret, *The Struggle for Land in Ireland* (Princeton, N.J., 1930), 44 ff.

thereby bringing his total acquisitions to approximately 38,000 acres. By using bounty warrants Scully acquired a large acreage for a very modest sum. For 792 additional acres in Logan County that were bought from private individuals between 1852 and 1857, he had to pay an average of $6.43 an acre.

It was Scully's plan to keep these lands permanently and to lease them to tenants in much the same way that he and his family had owned and rented lands in Ireland. Possibly, at the outset, he contemplated using part of the land for a large stock farm as Sullivant, Alexander, and others were doing. There is an intriguing advertisement in the Bloomington *Plantagraph* for August 8, 1855, which lends support to this supposition. Circumstances, whether economic necessity or the death of his wife is not clear, led to an alteration in Scully's plans, for in the advertisement he offered 1,200 sheep and 30 head of cattle for sale. He was also busy selling land.

The terms of Scully's sales contract remind one of the Scott contracts. A cash payment of $1 an acre was required to bind the bargain, the balance being due in equal payments at the end of the third and fifth years. Improvements worth $100 or $200 were to be put upon the land within the first two years or the contract would be voided and the advance payment would be regarded as rent for the land, not subject to return to the settler. Interest on the amount due ranged between 8 and 10 percent and taxes from the time of purchase were to be paid by the buyer. For persons fully paying for the land in one transaction, of course, no such terms were included.

The sale in the fifties of 6,200 acres for an average price of better than $9 an acre with 8 or 10 percent interest on delayed payments—land that had been acquired for $.70 an acre five or seven years earlier—provided quick returns that might have satisfied the most greedy speculator. True, fifteen of the forty settlers to whom Scully made sales in this period failed to meet their payments and their contracts were forfeited, but Scully had at least collected the $1 an acre advance payment which was

Scully Land in Logan County, Illinois

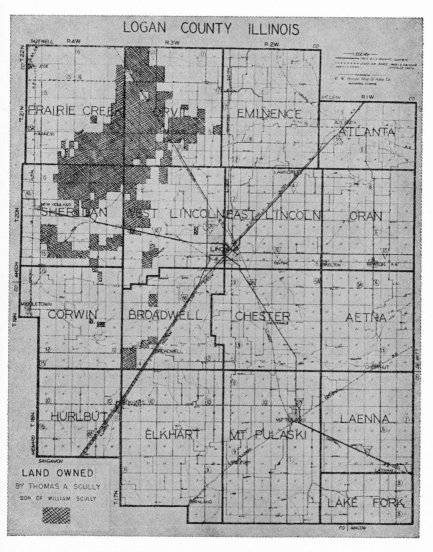

Adapted from W. W. Hixson & Co., *Plat Book of Logan County, Illinois* (Rockford, Ill., c. 1916–1924).

sufficient rent for a couple of years. Furthermore, the improvements the purchasers made added to the attractiveness of Scully's land and were shortly to make it possible for him to rent tracts for $1 an acre. These sales, together with a few tracts sold in the sixties and one piece of 152 acres sold in 1888 for $50 an acre, amounted in all to some 4,000 acres, part of which, it is interesting to note, Scully was to buy back at many times the price for which he sold it.

It is unlikely that Scully ever intended to dispose of all his land. Probably the sales of the fifties were for the purpose of tiding him over until paying tenants could be secured. During the Civil War he leased tracts for $1 an acre and soon after he were able to secure tenants for all his land. These rents were shortly to provide Scully with a net income of $80,000 and more, which, contrary to the statements made by some of his detractors, was not to be spent entirely abroad but was largely invested in additional land purchases.

Another source of funds for these purchases was the income from rents and from the liquidation of a part, at least, of the Irish estates. In 1868, the year of the Ballycohey tragedy when public opinion in Ireland was running strongly against Scully, pressure was brought to bear to induce him to sell that estate, on which were settled twenty-two tenant families. When, therefore, a local landlord offered to purchase Ballycohey for its "improved value," Scully agreed to sell. In the words of the London *Times* of September 28, 1868, this was a "welcome deliverance for the people." Irish landlordism was coming more heavily under attack at this time, partly because of the excesses to which some owners went in increasing rents and in making evictions, and thoughtful people were beginning to feel that reform was necessary, whereby tenant rights of fixity (or security) of tenure, fair rent, and free sale (the right to sell improvements put upon the land should be guaranteed by the government. In 1870, Parliament passed a land act which took the first halting steps in this direction, thereby making landlordism in that distracted country less attractive. Scully was doubtless distressed at the success of the reformers in pushing through Parliament the act of 1870, as were most Irish landlords, and, with funds now well in hand, he turned away from his own country and began investing in a larger measure than before in America where the laws gave all the traditional protection to property rights that was characteristic of England.

Only in Kansas and Nebraska were there still available for purchase public lands that were at all comparable to the Logan and Grundy County land. Consequently, Scully turned to these states for investment. In June, 1870, he purchased at the Beatrice, Nebraska land office 41,420 acres in Nuckolls County which is in the southern tier of counties about 130 miles west of the Missouri River. The following month Scully purchased of the federal government 14,060 acres in Marion County, Kansas, and 1,160 acres in Dickinson County, Kansas, being located about 150 miles from the Missouri River. These purchases of Scully's were among the last of the large acquisitions of farming land by individuals or companies. By 1870 the unrestricted public lands that were still open to private entry were about gone, except for some rich tracts of timberland in the Lake States, the Gulf States, and California, and an area of grazing land that was subsequently to be sold in Colorado. Henceforth, any additional tract that Scully might want would have to be bought from land-grant railroads, from large speculators who had seized upon the agricultural college scrip of the states to acquire tracts of great size, or from pioneer settlers who were having difficulty in meeting mortgage payments or were too restless to stay anywhere for long.

By now the Illinois rents and the liquidation of the Irish estates were producing sums sufficient to make possible a rapid expansion of land buying, and for the next decade Scully's agents were scouring Kansas, Nebraska, Missouri, and Illinois in one of the largest individual land buying campaigns in American history.

The greatest volume of purchases being made by Scully's agents was in Marion County, Kansas. Here land was bought from persons living as far away as Waterford and New York City; Lenawee County, Michigan; Grant County, Wisconsin; Umatilla County, Oregon; Skowhegan, Maine; Ouray County, Colorado; Brown County, Texas; and Ontario, Canada. Scully bought of John Williams, a well-known banker, railroad promoter, and land speculator of Springfield, Illinois, 9,440 acres in Marion County, Kansas, for $2 an acre. These lands had been purchased by Williams at the Junction City land office a little earlier for the government minimum price. From the Sante Fe Railroad, which in this transaction as well as in others showed no disinclination to sell to speculators and large buyers, were acquired 8,622 acres for $38,008. A part of the famous Christie ranch, consisting of 2,560 acres, was bought at forced sale for $13,240, which was about two-thirds of the appraised value. In forty-one other transactions Scully acquired 19,824 acres for $90,048. Finally, 960 acres of tax-delinquent land were purchased for $621. Altogether, Scully acquired 55,666 acres in Marion County at a cost of $179,197. In Butler County, just to the south of Marion, he bought in the eighties 8,605 acres for $77,410.

In 1881 Scully turned his attention to two fertile counties just north and south of the Kansas-Nebraska line. In Gage County, Nebraska, he acquired 22,288 acres for $290,254, and in Marshall County, Kansas, he acquired 5,115 acres for $55,252. Of the 63 persons from whom the land in Gage County was bought only 19 were residents of the county, while 18 were residents of Illinois and 9 were residents of Ohio. In both of these states, but especially in Illinois, were numerous individuals who had accumulated small fortunes from the rise in land values of the fifties and sixties, and who, in the late sixties, began investing heavily in Kansas and Nebraska lands. Illustrations of individuals who carried their land business westward as the frontier advanced from Illinois into Kansas and Nebraska are John and Robert Niccolls, Asahel Gridley, E. B. Munsell, and John Williams.

The price paid by Scully for tracts in Kansas and Nebraska indicates that a considerable proportion of them were improved.

A summary of the land he acquired there between 1870 and 1886 is shown in the following tabulation.

Location	Acres	Cost
Marion	55,666	$179,197
Dickinson	1,120	1,400
Butler	8,605	77,410
Marshall	5,115	55,252
Gage	22,288	290,254
Nuckolls	41,420	51,775
Total	134,214	$655,288

About the same time 42,000 acres were acquired in Bates County, Missouri, which probably cost about $200,000. In 1941 the Bates County land was sold to the Farm Security Administration for $1,078,000.

Most profitable among Scully's many investments were his Illinois lands, and naturally he was ready to purchase more of them. Money invested in Illinois, however, acquired much smaller acreages, so rapidly did land values rise in the twenty years following the Civil War. Where attractive land in Kansas and Nebraska could be acquired for $5, $10, and at the most $20 an acre, it was necessary to pay from $30 to $50 an acre for prime land in Illinois. Thus in 1875, a depression year, Scully paid $47 an acre for 824 acres in Logan County. The following tabulation shows his purchases in this county together with the number of persons from whom the land was bought and the price paid.

Year	Number of sellers	Acres	Amount paid	Average price per acre
1875	4	824	$39,082	$47.73
1877	2	263	10,303	39.17
1878	10	1,662	67,750	40.16
1879	3	751	25,000	33.28
1880	1	160	6,200	38.75
1883	1	80	3,600	45.00
1885	1	188	4,938	26.26
1886	1	114	4,290	37.71
Total	23	4,042	$161,163	$39.88

In Sangamon County, Scully made but one purchase, but it called for the largest payment and one of the highest per acre prices of any of his contracts. The purchase included 4,161 acres in two townships that had been entered in May, 1836, by John Berry of Bath County, Kentucky, for the estate of Archibald Hamilton in the great speculative boom of the middle thirties. The land remained in the hands of Berry until 1876 when the court ordered that it be conveyed to the Hamilton heirs with reasonable expenses to the Berrys for their management during the preceding forty years. A year later, in 1877, James C. and George H. Hamilton sold the land to Scully for a total price of $215,297.40, or an average of $51.75 an acre.[55] This was a depression year, when the price of land, as well as of commodities, was abnormally low.

About the same time Scully pushed into Livingston County, which, in the fifties, had a larger proportion of its area in the hands of speculators than any other Illinois county. Here Solomon Sturges had acquired 40,000 acres, Alexander Campbell 11,000 acres, Bronson Murray 8,120 acres, and Michael Sullivant 13,920 acres. In addition the 70,000 acres of Illinois Central land, the 27,000 acres of canal land and the 39,360 acres of "swamp" land had been in part acquired by speculators. Many of these large owners, like Murray, Sullivant, Jacob Bunn, William H. Osborn, and Matthew T. Scott, were developing their tracts either with hired labor or through tenants, and there early appeared a high proportion of tenancy in the county. The breakup of the Sturges, Campbell, and Osborn estates was favorably regarded by the residents of the county, and the financial embarrassment of Sullivant and the sale of his Livingston County land were locally approved. When, however, Scully began buying in the county in 1876, his action was subjected to unfriendly criticism. Only two important purchases were made: one in 1876, when section fourteen in Round Grove Township was

[55] 43 Mortgage Records, Sangamon County, 563; 61 Deed Records, Sangamon County, 11.

bought for $17,920, and the other in 1887, when the Cayuga lands, amounting to 1,500 acres, were acquired for $45 an acre. One negotiation that Scully failed to consummate—why is not clear—was the purchase of a portion of Burr Oaks. Rumor had it that his agent had succeeded in negotiating for the purchase in April, 1878, of either 15,000 or 30,000 acres at $30 an acre. Much alarm was aroused in Ford and Iroquois counties, but to the relief of the local people the deal was not consummated.[56]

This constitutes the whole of Scully's land purchases aside from 27,000 acres in Louisiana [57] which do not appear to have been bought as farming land, and some tracts in Grundy and Logan counties which he had sold and which he later repurchased, paying in some instances five times what he had sold them for. In the four states of Illinois, Missouri, Kansas, and Nebraska, Scully had amassed an empire of land amounting to 220,000 acres at a cost to him of $1,350,000.

Scully's rental policy, while differing sharply from that of most frontier landlords, did not embody the worst features of the Irish system, as was later charged.[58] Historians generally are in agreement that one of the chief causes of Ireland's misery was that, outside of Ulster, tenants had no right in improvements on the land. When evicted they had nothing to sell, nothing for

[56] 65 Deed Records, Livingston County, 414; 90 Deed Records, Livingston County 257; Pontiac *Sentinel*, April 17, 1878; Lincoln *Herald*, April 18, 1878.

[57] Chicago *Tribune*, Aug. 15, 1937. My efforts to gain access to the records of the Scully land business, which was centered in Lincoln, Illinois, were quite unsuccessful, but in three of the district offices I was given an opportunity to work through records and was taken around to visit some of the Scully farms.

[58] It is not the common practice to record leases as deeds and mortgages are recorded, and yet in the Miscellaneous Records and sometimes in the Deed Records of western countries may be found scattered leases that for one reason or another have been recorded. For examples of Scully leases in 1863, 1884, 1921, and 1932, see the following: I Miscellaneous Record, Logan Country, 209; F Miscellaneous Record, Gage County, 610; 133 Grundy Deeds, 56, 19 Miscellaneous Record, Logan County, 172.

which to claim compensation. Hence they abused the land through improper farm practices and erected the very poorest hovels in which to live. Scully even tore down tenant homes as part of the process of making evictions on his Tipperary estates, and his tenants had no legal redress.[59] From the very beginning of his leasing in America, however, Scully provided that improvements, such as fences, houses, barns, and other buildings, were to be constructed by the tenant and, more important, that they were to be subject to removal or sale by the tenant. The concession of tenant-right was probably necessary in America in order to attract settlers, but Scully's refusal to aid them in getting started, as Scott, Sibley, and other landlords were doing, had the effect of delaying settlement of his land for a decade. It was to farms already somewhat improved or on which the landlord would provide part of the cost of building and fencing that the first persons looking for rents naturally went. Isaac Funk, David Davis, Asahel Gridley, and Jesse Fell were accumulating and improving their thousands of acres of prairie land through hired laborers and tenants, and scores of smaller owners were also improving and offering for rent 80- and 160-acre farms on a share rent basis. In the fifties, "For Rent" advertisements were becoming common in the prairie newspapers, and once in a while there also appeared such advertisements as: "Wanted. Farm for Rent." [60] Landlords with improved farms were having little difficulty in securing tenants, but Scully's policy of using his available funds for the purchase of land and not for improvements, while permitting him to buy a large acreage, delayed the expected income from the land and explains why the Scully improvements were among the poorest in the West.

Scully's policy with regard to security of tenure was more liberal than was the custom in Ireland. The concession of what amounted to tenant-right encouraged tenant improvements and

[59] Sullivan, *New Ireland*, I, 255–256.
[60] Bloomington *Pantagraph*, Feb. 8, 1854, Nov. 5, 1856; *Prairie Chieftain* (Monticello, Ind.), Dec. 23, 1852.

made for more contentment on the part of the renter, who, so long as he farmed his land properly, paid his rent and taxes at the appropriate time, and did nothing to antagonize Scully or his agents, would be assured of the right of continued occupation. Nevertheless, the exacting rents combined with poor times in the seventies and in the eighties made for restlessness among tenants and frequent moves, and a series of threatened uprisings and rent strikes.

Taxes on the Scully farms were the obligation of tenants. In practice they were paid by the landlord, added to the cash rent, and collected at the same time. In this way any danger that the titles would be placed in jeopardy through non-payment of taxes was avoided. There was reason for Scully's tax policy. With such a large group of tenants as he was to have, it would have been possible for them to vote, in local tax districts, heavy appropriations for roads, schools, and other public buildings and as loans for local railroads, and to have the burden carried by the landlord. It is only necessary to read frontier newspapers of the time to realize that this was common practice in states like Illinois, Iowa, Kansas, and Nebraska, where large quantities of land were owned by absentees. For example, an advocate of township subsidies to aid railroad construction in Piatt County urged that such a subscription "compels the lordly speculator, who holds thousands of acres of land in our county at such prices as to prevent its settlement and improvement, to bear his just proportion of the burden of building the road. . . . In no other way can these speculators be reached; they have already induced our Legislature to shield them from the burden of school tax, and I say now tax their land to build the Railroad." [61] Another observer, writing from Thayer County, Nebraska, said: "The speculators are getting tired of building school houses, so that they are offering their lands for sale very low and on reasonable terms." [62] By requiring that the tenants should pay the taxes and

[61] *Piatt Independent* (Monticello, Ill.), March 21, 1866.
[62] *Piatt Republican* (Monticello), Feb. 5, 1874.

all local assessments, Scully not only made certain that they would, as a group, be cautious in voting for expensive buildings or road construction programs but that they would constantly exert a moderating influence to keep costs of local government and taxes at the lowest possible level. This tended to produce within the Scully area poorer roads and inferior school facilities than were being provided elsewhere.

The later farm-management practices in operation on the Scully farms generally were enlightened and progressive. Requirements that clover should be planted on every part of the land once in four years, that alfalfa should be included on portions of the farms, that corn should not be planted more than two years in succession, and that a proper system of rotation should be followed to make sure that soil depletion did not occur are well known. The supervision given to the tenants doubtless assured better farm practices than were generally followed on owner-operated farms, though there is no evidence of encouragement for the raising of livestock. Such controls irked the tenants, but they worked to the mutual advantage of landlord and tenant. Had Scully attempted to include such requirements in his early leases and to enforce them he would have been laughed to scorn by frontier farmers who had no idea that the prairie soils of Illinois could be exhausted by planting them to corn year after year. Nor was it expedient for Scully to prescribe in the early period, as was done later, that "all burrs, thistles and other weeds and willow bushes" shall be destroyed. Good practice required that farmers, whether tenants or owners, do these things, but experience was to show that tenants were inclined to neglect them.

The appearance of weeds and brush in the fields as well as in the hedgerows was characteristic of tenant farms. A Livingston County paper complained that there was such a high turnover among tenants on the neighboring farms that the burrs were rarely eradicated. It urged that a law be adopted to compel the owners to have weeds destroyed.[63] A campaign for compulsory weed eradication was directed at tenant-operated farms, particularly the Scully farms. It was stated:

> Rented farms can always be identified by the dilapidated state of the buildings, the tumble-down fences, the mammoth crop of weeds, the unthrifty general appearance—the air of desolation and destruction . . . all too flagrant not to be observed. The rented farm is free to be plucked in every possible manner. . . . The whole object too, is to secure the utmost drain on the soil—getting everything off without returning any of the fertilizers to make it productive.[64]

It was argued that Scully's policies attracted to his land "the very poorest of farmers, who only take Scully's land with a view of leaving it just as soon as they can" after skimming the cream and leaving the land much depreciated.[65]

In Logan County it was pointed out that the practice of planting corn on the Scully land year after year without any rotation and the continued neglect of weeds were not only impoverishing the land, which was overrun with weeds, but were having a deplorable effect upon surrounding farms. On few farms in Illinois in the nineteenth century could it be said that careful methods of cultivation and husbandry were employed, and Scully's tenants and their farm practices were probably little worse than those on most other rented farms. But attention was focused upon Scully because of the size of his holdings, the fact that the farms were grouped together and were more obvious than scattered units, the unpopularity of his cash rent policy, the liens he slapped on tenant crops, the evictions of grumbling and discontented tenants, the social gap that he and his sons made clear existed between them and the tenants, and finally the fact that he was an alien who was contributing little to the

---

[63] Pontiac *Free Trader*, Jan. 10, 1879; Pontiac *Sentinel*, Sept. 2, 1881.

[64] *Farm, Herd and Home*, quoted in Pontiac *Free Trader and Observer*, Nov. 23, 1883.

[65] Pontiac *Free Trader and Observer*, April 8, 1887.

development of the state. Although cash rents were not unknown on the frontier, share or grain rents were more usual. Some landlords, Matthew Scott for example, rented for a stipulated amount of wheat or corn per acre. More common and certainly more thoroughly approved was the share rent, which, according to the *Vermilion County Press* of July 28, 1858, was generally based on one of three fairly standard rates: the proprietor who furnished all the stock, seed, and equipment and paid the taxes received two-thirds of the produce, the tenant who furnished everything likewise received two-thirds, and if the stock was jointly owned and other expenses were equally divided the landlord and tenant divided the crops equally.

A principal advantage of the share rent was that, unlike the cash rent, it did not have to be adjusted upward or downward with fluctuating prices and rising land values. On a cash rent basis land generally brought $1 an acre in the fifties and sixties, $2 and $3 an acre in the seventies, up to $4 an acre in the eighties and nineties, and $8 and $10 an acre in the twentieth century. When land values were rising fairly rapidly, upward adjustments were to be expected, but they almost inevitably led to cries of rack-renting when instituted by Scully. Furthermore, Scully was not inclined to be lenient when crops were poor or prices low. Later, the Scully agents made abatements and reduced the cash rent on occasion, but only under great pressure and the threat of tenant strikes.

Somewhat less supervision is necessary under the cash rent system than under the share rent, and perhaps it avoids some of the suspicion and ill will that has characterized landlord-tenant relations in certain areas. But to make certain that he received his rent, Scully found it advisable to require rent payments before the crop was sold a—demand certain to involve the tenant in great hardship, especially as he could not borrow on his crop because of the lien Scully slapped on it. He informed shippers and buyers in the vicinity of his land that his lien on the crop of his tenants came first under the terms of the lease and under the tenant laws and that he could and would recover damages from anyone who bought grain before his rent was paid.[66]

No feature of the landlords' policies in the seventies and eighties was more disliked than the cash rent. The drop in agricultural prices after 1873 was not reflected in land values to the same degree and was not followed by rent adjustments. Not only were prices low but weather conditions were unfavorable for corn in 1876, 1877, and 1878 in much of the prairie section, and there were partial crop failures or light crops. Farmers were caught between the upper millstone of rigid costs, such as taxes, freight rates, rent, or interest, and the nether millstone of diminishing income. Share renters and mortgaged owners, of course, were seriously affected. Many mortgages were foreclosed and the previous owners either depressed into tenancy or forced to emigrate elsewhere. The cash tenants at the same time were actually being asked to pay higher rents, despite the trying times. In the neighboring state of Indiana it was said that work in cities was so scare that laborers were anxiously looking for farms to rent, even though the "extortionate and heartless" landlords were charging as high as $4 and $5 an acre.[67] Such rents, while high, were not unknown in Illinois.[68]

Discontent and unrest began to appear among tenant farmers and were reflected in the rural press. For example, in 1876 the Farmer City *Journal* published a "pitiful story" of two cash renters who had leased a farm for $700, did their best to make

---

[66] Chicago *Tribune*, in Bloomington *Pantagraph*, March 21, 1887.

[67] *Indiana Farmer*, II (June 3, 1876), 5; *Edinburgh Scotsman*, in *Indiana Farmer*, XII (Sept. 8, 1877), 6.

[68] In 1870 the University of Illinois, which had come into possession of the Griggs farm, was renting seven tracts at prices ranging from $2.80 to $5.00 an acre (*Third Annual Report of the Board of Trustees of the Illinois Industrial University* [Springfield, 1870], 115, The McFee farm near Bloomington was advertised for rent in 1876 for a cash rent of $5 an acre (Bloomington *Pantagraph*, Feb. 8, 1876).

a success of it, but, failing, were faced with the loss of their crops, horses, and farm utensils. Finally a compromise was reached by which they paid $200 and gave up their entire crops for the year. The writer said:

What a sad comment this and similar cases is upon the cash rent system in such a variable climate as central Illniois. Paying $200 for the privilege of toiling all season with three teams, the wear and tear of farm machinery, board and incidental expenses, then to crown all, donate the crop and have nothing left.[69]

The Pontiac *Sentinel* of August 10,1876, warned that few renters were able to meet the terms of their leases without beggaring themselves and their families and many of them were abandoning their farms. Tension between landlords and tenants reached serious proportions. In one case a landlord was attacked and badly mauled by an outraged and disillusioned tenant and in another squabble between a landlord and a tenant the latter was shot to death.[70] Scully, whose three hundred-odd Illinois farms were now tenanted on a cash rent basis, came under attack perhaps for the first time in his experience in America. The Chicago *Times* wrote of his "very exacting terms and high rates" which were being continued despite the lightness of the crops in recent years and the arrears into which tenants had fallen. When Scully announced that he would "allow no tenant to sell any of his crop of this year until the rent has been paid up in full," the tenants became highly indignant. They held a protest meeting at which a committee was appointed to visit the Governor to ask him to intercede for them. "Scully's actions savor much of the tyranny of the absentee landlords of Ireland," said the Chicago *Times*. "All over central Illinois a strong feeling is growing up against such immense estates, especially when operated by persons outside the State." [71] Another mass meeting of renters was

---

[69] Quoted in the *Piatt County Herald*, Nov. 29, 1876.
[70] Pontiac *Sentinel*, Oct. 31, 1877; Lincoln *Herald*, Jan. 2, 1879.
[71] Quoted in Pontiac *Free Trader*, Dec. 20, 1878.

held at Saybrook in February, 1879, at which resolutions were adopted declaring cash rent unjust and discriminating in favor of the landlord. The participants pledged themselves to pay grain or share rent only, unless the landlords would lease their farms for a "cash rent of $2.00 per acre and that only for cultivated lands." [72]

At a meeting of two hundred Scully tenants at a schoolhouse in Emden in December, 1879, "great excitement among the leasers" was exhibited at the notice to grain buyers that Scully held a landlord's lien on his tenants' crops for back rents and warning the buyers of swift action against them if they bought such grain. The tenants appointed a committee to wait upon Scully and his agent, who, according to the Republican Lincoln *Herald* of December 12 and 19, 1879, reported back that instead of requiring back rents in full, Scully would take a third of the proceeds of small grain, half of corn, and "some small amounts on arrearages." It was about this time that a measure was introduced into the Illinois legislature at the request of those who found Scullyism repugnant to American principles, to impose an extraordinary tax on absentee and alien owners of land.[73]

The tenant unrest in the prairie counties of Illinois, which came to a head in the late seventies, failed to win political attention for the problems of the renter. Illinois was immensely stirred by agrarian unrest that was directed against the malpractices of the railroads and the deflationary policies of the federal government. But Grangerism was a landowners' movement and did not concern itself with the problems of the tenant. Being the poorest educated and most foreign of the rural population, the tenants were unable to dramatize their grievances sufficiently to win the attention of the agrarian parties. In fact, tenants were dealt an additional blow during the height of their unrest by the action of the legislature in authorizing landlords, under certain circumstances, to "institute proceedings by distress" be-

[72] Pontiac *Sentinel*, Feb. 12, 1879.
[73] *History of Logan County, Illinois* (Chicago, 1886), 368.

fore rent was due.[74] This legalized a practice which Scully in effect had required his tenants to sanction. Their cries being ignored, the tenants had an outlet still open to them: to abandon their farms or, in the case of the Scully tenants, to try to sell their improvements on a declining market and to migrate to the new frontier in central and western Kansas and Nebraska.

When the discontent of the tenant farmers was at its height, the Burlington Railroad seized the occasion to advertise its Nebraska land in the papers of central Illinois.[75] Young men were urged not to rent in Illinois when they could own in Nebraska; "Life is too short," the advertisement stated, "to be wasted on a rented farm." About the same time the Sante Fe Railroad, in calling attention to its Kansas land, claimed that there were "no lands owned by speculations" in the area of its grant, in contrast to the huge acreage of speculator-owned land in Illinois.[76] This, it should be noted, was not true, for in Morris, Chase, Dickinson, Marion, and Butler counties were numerous large speculative holdings, and in Marion County, Scully was at that very time buying some of these holdings and was later to purchase of the Santa Fe 8,600 acres. The advertisement was correct, however, for that portion of the railroad west of Marion, Butler, and Dickinson counties. Discontent and the attractions of a newly developing frontier induced many thousands of tenants, as well as unsuccessful owners, to join the western trek, including a number of Scully tenants who were locally called exodusters. Farmers operating tracts of less than a hundred acres were finding it difficult to compete with those working larger units of land, and in the decade of the eighties seventeen thousand of them were forced to give up their homes to their more successful competitors.[77] In Ford County, where tenancy and

[74] Act of May 21, 1877, *Laws of Illinois*, 1877, 129.

[75] Pontiac *Sentinel*, May 21, 1879.

[76] *Piatt Republican* (Monticello, Ill.), Feb. 5, 1874.

[77] The census of 1890 reported 17,037 fewer farms of less than a hundred acres than were reported for 1880 (*United States Census, 1890: Statistics of Agriculture*, 116; Lincoln *Times*, Feb. 10, 1881).

large scale farms predominated more than in any other county in the state, a series of meetings was being held as early as 1872 by a group which was organized as a homestead colony and was planning to move westward.[78] Six years later another group of 121 people was organized, consisting mostly of renters from Ford and Vermilion counties, who were going as a colony to Kansas with their seventeen carloads of freight.[79]

Throughout the prairie counties a similar movement of population was under way. Renters, dispossessed owners who had been unable to meet the high interest charges on their mortgages, and agricultural laborers who had failed to get the much desired piece of land, all were moving, the goal being Kansas, Nebraska, Iowa, and Missouri. In the decade of the seventies 175,000 people who were born in Illinois migrated to these four states in addition to many thousands of others who came to Illinois from the East or from Europe and then moved farther west in search of land. Many were to succeed in the new country, but others were to find conditions in the younger states not materially different save in degree from those in Illinois. If they tried life anew in Marion, Butler, Marshall, or Dickinson counties, Kansas, or in Nuckolls and Gage counties, Nebraska, they found the best land in private hands, owned by the railroads, which were advertising for purchasers, or held by William Scully and other large landlords, who were looking for tenants on the same conditions as applied in Illinois though at lower rents. Emigrants from Illinois, arriving in the humid section of Kansas, were faced with notices: "Wanted: Farms to Rent," indicating that their search for land was again to be frustrated.[80] Frequently it was the experience of these landseekers that no matter how far they proceeded in their search they were certain to be anticipated by the railroad, the speculator, or the frontier landlord. When the futility of their search for land became ap-

[78] Paxton *Record*, Aug. 1, 1872.
[79] Paxton *Weekly Standard*, Feb. 9, 1878.
[80] Peabody (Kan.) *Gazette*, July 21, 1876.

parent, their feelings were crystallized into keen resentment against those who had forestalled them.

Western attitudes toward large-scale land speculation and frontier landlords were not always consistent. Absentee owners were thoroughly disapproved of but the resident owner generally escaped criticism. "You are a curse to our country," said an indignant writer of nonresident landowners of Livingston County.[81] Careless cropping methods, the one-crop system, poor housing accommodations, inadequate fences, the existence of weeds and brush, and poor roads and school facilities were all blamed on the absentee owner, not on the renter.

William Scully was not only an absentee landlord but also an alien who had no intention of settling in Illinois or in any part of the United States, until 1895, when he deemed it wise to establish a residence in Washington, D.C., and in 1900 to take out American citizenship. As if that were not enough of a challenge to frontier mores, Scully refused to improve his own land but waited for tenants to do that, and the nature and quality of their improvements were not to win for him good feeling. A fourth count against Scully was his system of cash renting, that seemed to many who were accustomed to share renting an alien institution. Finally, at a time when powerful monopolies were extending their control over many fields in America, it was natural that the huge land-buying program of Scully should arouse indignation. One of his purchases, 1,500 acres in Livingston County, acquired in 1887, was particularly ill-timed, coming as it did when anti-Scully feeling was strong in Illinois and Kansas. It was called "very unfortunate" for the community which was certain to be "injured" by it.[82]

Resentment against the Scully leasing policies accomplished

81 Pontiac *Sentinel*, Jan. 15, 1886.
82 Pontiac *Free Trader and Observer*, April 8, 1887; Lincoln *Times-Courier*, Oct. 19, 1906.

little in the seventies, but a decade later it had become deeper
and more dangerous in all four states in which the Scully farm
lands were located. Journalistic vituperation of the rankest kind
was heaped upon Scully, anti-alien landowner bills directed at
him were passed by three of the states, and in the legislatures of
these states and in Washington Scullyism became a major issue,
the principal question being how best to strike at it.

Westerners were troubled that Scully was deriving a hand-
some income from their area and paying no taxes, since his
leases required his tenants to assume this obligation. Had it been
argued that the total rates charged tenants were determined in
part by the productivity of the land and in part by the demand
for rent land, and that Scully's rents plus taxes could not have
been materially higher than those other landlords were charging,
the westerners would not have been convinced. In their opinion
Scully was evading taxation by requiring his tenants to pay
assessments for him, thereby adding to their burdens. The people
of Logan County became so incensed against Scully that they
tried to tax his rent roll. This tactic he met by contending that
the rent roll was owned in England, and, therefore, was not
taxable in Illinois.[83] On somewhat different grounds the state
Supreme Court invalidated the tax.[84]

Failing in their efforts to tax Scully's income or rent rolls, the
anti-Scully forces united in a move to make alien ownership of
land illegal. From 1883 to 1888 small-town newspapers of the
prairie counties published editorial after editorial condemning
alien and absentee ownership of land and demanding either that
future alien acquisitions should be made illegal or that all alien-
owned land should be forfeited to the states. Successive purchases of land by Scully, who kept doggedly at his task of increasing his domain, were given wide publicity and added fuel
to the fire. Soon the Bloomington *Pantagraph,* the Chicago *Tri-*

[83] Pontiac *Free Trader,* Feb. 10, 1882.
[84] *Scully* v. *The People,* 104 Ill. 350.

bune, and other influential papers—even the New York *Times*—joined in the cry against Scully.[85] In Kansas and Nebraska similar journalistic campaigns were under way, the principal differences being that in these two states they were marked by a greater degree of scurrility.[86] Papers that were slow to join the hue and cry were called Scully organs. They soon found that few issues were more popular at the time than the attack upon William Scully and the demand for legislation to curb or end alien ownership, and before long they, too, were making pointed remarks about the undemocratic character of tenancy and the danger of land monopoly.

The newspaper attacks followed a common pattern in their onslaught on Scullyism and alien ownership. Stress was laid on the un-American character of tenancy—despite the fact that numerous westerners owned large tracts of land they were renting to tenants, on the fact that taxes had to be paid by tenants, and above all on the cash rent feature. The term "rack renting" was frequently bandied about, though there is no important evidence to show that Scully's rents were higher than those of other landlords. The safeguards that Scully included in his leases to make sure that his tenants paid their rents were called outrageous. That they were comprehensive and were sometimes harshly enforced is doubtless true, but any person who reads a lease of yesterday or today will be struck by the realization that it was designed—like the modern installment contract—to protect the landlord or the vendor, not the renter or the purchaser. The Scully tenants were described as ignorant foreigners, Bohemians, Scandinavians, and Poles who "are not a class who are

---

[85] Chicago *Tribune,* March 11, 1887; Chicago *Inter Ocean,* Feb. 16, 1887; Bloomington *Pantagraph,* March 21, April 2, May 26, 1887; Lincoln *Herald,* March 24, April 7, June 9, 1887; Paxton *Record,* April 21, 1887; Pontiac *Free Trader and Observer,* April 8, 1887; Princeton *Republican* in Pontiac *Sentinel,* May 13, 1887; New York *Times,* April 18, 1887.

[86] Leadership in the fight against Scully in Kansas was provided by the Marion *Register,* published in Marion, and in Nebraska by the *Gage County Democrat* of Beatrice.

desirable neighbors," a "dreary and woebegone" lot of "scare-crow tenants" who "are in a state of absolute serfdom under his heartless alien rule, mostly transients raising nothing but corn, year after year, from the same ground." The Scully lands were described as the "most forlorn-looking estate in Illinois" with dwellings that were "a miserable lot of shanties"—mere sheds, bearing no paint and having little glass. Constant crop-ping of corn had so impoverished the land, it was argued, "that it breeds burrs and weeds, the seeds of which are carried to sur-rounding farms." The poverty-stricken tenants were unable to meet their taxes, and public improvements on "Scully land," it was said, were the worst to be found in the entire state of Illi-nois; roads were execrable, schoolhouses were as poor as the tenant dwellings and the school term was limited to five months.[87]

That there was a good deal of truth to these accusations cannot be denied, but neither can it be denied that somewhat the same kind of thing could be said of tenancy on other estates. True, efforts were made to distinguish between "bad" landlords and "good" landlords who had "good" tenants that employed "good" farm practices, had "good" improvements, and enjoyed "good" treatment, and were prosperous. Among these good landlords were John D. Gillett, whose 16,000-acre estate in Logan and Sangamon counties entitled him to rank among the leading frontier landlords; David Littler, who had some twenty or more farms in Logan, Sangamon, and Piatt counties; Bronson Murray, whose 10,000-acre estate in Livingston and LaSalle counties, now somewhat reduced, was said to have "an excellent lot of tenants"; and Bernard Stuvé, the famous historian of Illinois, on whose estate in Piatt County were said to be built "the model tenant houses of the county." [88] Likewise, the tenant

---

[87] Chicago *Tribune*, March 11, 1887; Lincoln *Herald*, March 24, 1887; Bloomington *Pantagraph*, March 21, 1887; Pontiac *Free Trader and Ob-server*, April 8, 1887; *History of Logan County*, 369. The touch of xeno-phobia is evident.

[88] Pontiac *Sentinel*, Aug. 22, 1877; Piatt, *History of Piatt County*, 452.

policies on the Sibley and Funk farms were generally approved, but the Jacob Bunn farm of 2,500 acres, the Buckingham farm of 2,000 acres, and the Oliver farm of 3,000 acres in Livingston County were unfavorably regarded.[89] The landlord who built homes for tenants, fenced and drained the land, and used the income from it for further improvements, or who lived in the neighborhood of his estate won commendation. That Scully instituted an elaborate and comprehensive system of tile drainage on his Grundy County lands in the eighties seemed to make no difference to residents in the neighborhood. He was an alien who spent his income elsewhere, extorted rack rents from his tenants, and kept them in poverty while casting a blighting influence over the counties in which his land was located. "The Lord Scully tribe of aliens will have to go—so far as Illinois is concerned," said the Princeton *Republican*, while the Pontiac *Free Trader and Observer* urged that speedy action be taken to prevent Scully from buying any more land in the United States. The Indianapolis *News* charged that Scully "galled and gored his tenants, squeezed the last attainable drop of rent from them and did the land as much good as a visitation of grasshoppers," while the Watseka *Republican* called Scully a "brutal crank," an "exaggerated Legree," whose land was being "literally skinned." [90]

[89] Pontiac *Sentinel*, Jan. 9, 1879.

[90] Princeton *Republican*, in Pontiac *Sentinel*, May 13, 1887; Pontiac *Free Trader and Observer*, April 8, 1887. Even conservative Republican papers found it good business to join in the hue and cry against Scully. See especially the Lincoln *Herald*, March 24, 1887. The Scully agent in charge of the Lincoln office, F. C. M. Koehnle, attempted a reply to the anti-Scully criticisms in a detailed letter of February, 1886, apparently first published in the *Anzeiger des Westens* (St. Louis) and reprinted in the Lincoln *Herald*, March 11, 1886. No "drunkards, gluttons, or disturbers of the peace" were accepted as tenants; Scully brought with him in 1849 and 1850 an "Irish Colony" to develop the land, but business reverses and dissension forced its abandonment, and Scully had to take back most of the land he had sold; Scully had expended nearly $100,000 in draining his land, nearly one half of which was paid to tenants for work they did on the land, and most of the $25,000 spent on hedging the land had similarly gone to tenants. Koehnle denied that

The campaign against alien landlords was associated with the demand for the forfeiture of unearned railroad land grants and for the withdrawal of the public lands from large-scale purchasing. As early as 1884 all national parties had joined in the fight against alien landlordism, the clearest statement being made by the Union Labor Party in 1888:

We believe the earth was made for the people, and not to enable an idle aristocracy to subsist, through rents, upon the toil of the industrious, and that corners in land are as bad as corners in food, and that those who are not residents or citizens should not be allowed to own lands in the United States.[91]

Until into the nineties the cry against alien landlordism as well as unearned railroad land grants was taken up by all agrarian parties, and the demand for confiscation of alien lands and for forfeiture of land grants was vigorously pressed. The platforms of the Farmers' Alliance and the People's or Populist Party stressed these two issues as much as the silver question, the Northern Alliance in 1889 actually giving first place to them. Despite this condemnation of alien ownership and the demand for its end, and the flurry of legislation that it precipitated, historians of agrarian movements, without exception, have neglected it and centered their theme around that of silver and the malpractices of railroads. They fail to recognize that fundamentally, but not very clearly, this western discontent was directed at the forces which were making for tenancy and the disappearance of many small farm owners.

The campaign against alien landlords reached its climax in 1887 when the farmers of the West were aflame with hatred

---

Scully had resorted to the courts to compel collections and evictions, but this and other defenses were shown to be so largely false as to deserve no repetition. For the vigorous and generally effective reply see the Chicago *Tribune,* March 13, 1886, in the Lincoln *Times,* March 25, 1886.

[91] *Marshall County Democrat* (Marysville, Kan., Sept. 8, 1887); Indianapolis *News,* quoted in *Public Opinion,* VIII (Jan. 11, 1890), 345; Watseka *Republican,* Feb. 10, 1886.

of Scullyism, "land monopoly," absentee and alien ownership of land, and the land-grant railroads. In the newspapers, the state legislatures, and farmers' meetings, William Scully was held up to excoriation as the archetype of alien landlord whose rental policies made mere serfs of his tenants. A barrage of legislation directed chiefly at Scully was adopted. On June 16, two such measures received the approval of the Governor of Illinois and became law. The first prohibited nonresident aliens from acquiring real estate though it did not and could not require, as the most bitter opponents of Scully demanded, that alien-owned lands should be forfeited to the state. The second act was designed to prevent alien landlords from requiring tenants to pay the taxes assessed upon the land they rented.[92] At the same time the anti-Scully agitation in Kansas and Nebraska produced results. The Nebraska act prohibiting aliens from acquiring land was similar to that of Illinois. Kansas, where the most violent feelings were aroused against Scully, contented itself after considerable legislative maneuverings, with proposing an amendment to the state constitution that would permit legislation to prohibit alien ownership of land. Wisconsin, Minnesota, and Colorado likewise adopted laws to prevent alien ownership. Similar laws were adopted by Iowa in 1888, Idaho in 1891, and Missouri in 1895.[93]

To shut Scully and other nonresident aliens out of the territories, Congress in 1887 adopted an act "to restrict the ownership of real estate in the Territories to American citizens." [94] The most vigorous supporter of the anti-alien landowning bill was Lewis E. Payson, representative in Congress of a number of the prairie counties of Illinois including Livingston, where Scully at the very moment was engaged in enlarging his hold-

[92] *Laws of Illinois*, 1887, 4–8.

[93] *Session Laws of Nebraska*, 1887, 568; *Session Laws of Kansas*, 1887, 340; *Session Laws of Wisconsin*, 1887, 536; *Session Laws of Minnesota*, 1887, 323; *Session Laws of Colorado*, 1887, 24; *Session Laws of Iowa*, 1888, 125, *Session Laws of Idaho*, 1891, 108; *Session Laws of Missouri*, 1895, 207.

[94] *U.S. Statutes at Large*, XXIV: 476.

ings. Payson was given active aid by the Pontiac *Sentinel,* which called the bill of "vital importance" to the country.[95] Never before in American history had such a barrage of legislation been directed so largely at one man as were the acts of nine states (including Indiana, whose law of 1885 anticipated the others) and the federal government.[96]

Cynics there were, at the time, who took pleasure in deriding the agrarian radicals and reformers who were sponsoring both the anti-alien landowning legislation and a comprehensive and thorough reform of the entire public land system. They called the reformers demagogues, accused them of seizing upon a popular issue like Scullyism and riding it for all it was worth while neglecting more fundamental issues. They pointed out that the western radicals were proposing to close the public domain to speculators when the last of the desirable land was gone and to stop alien purchases of land when foreign capital was already tending to go elsewhere. They showed that while the radicals were demanding the forfeiture of the Scully lands, none of the bills that were being seriously considered and had a chance of passage threatened any such drastic action. All the legislation was likely to accomplish at this late date was to stop further

[95] Pontiac *Sentinel,* May 28, June 4, 1886.

[96] The federal act of March 3, 1887, was clearly the result of anti-Scully agitation in Illinois, Nebraska, and Kansas and the feeling in other plains states that the great volume of land then being acquired by British cattle interests was dangerous for America. In 1886, when the anti-alien landowning bill was being considered by the House Committee on the Judiciary, it was first reported unfavorably with, however, a minority report urging its adoption in which it was said if enacted it would "prevent any more such abuses as that of Mr. Scully, who resides in England, and is a subject of the Queen, but owns 90,000 acres in the State of Illinois, occupied by hundreds of tenants, mostly ignorant foreigners, from whom he receives, as rent, $200,000 per annum. . . . This alien non-resident ownership will . . . lead to a system of landlordism incompatible with the best interests and free institutions of the United States. . . . A considerable number of the immigrants arriving in this country are to become tenants and herdsmen on the vast possessions of these foreign lords under contracts made and entered into before they sail for our shores" (*House Report,* No. 1951, 49 Cong., 1 Sess., April 27, 1886).

purchasing by Scully, and then only if he failed to become an American citizen.

One of the most effective of these cynics was a Scottish alien —George Campbell—who objected to the measures being considered by the Illinois legislature on the ground that they did not strike at the real causes of tenant unrest. "If Scullyism exists it exists because it is not inconsistent with existing laws, and there is no proposal now being made to modify the laws in any way, beyond this Alien Land Bill." If the legislature was in earnest in wishing to end Scullyism and rack renting, argued Campbell, it should adopt reforms similar to those that Gladstone was introducing into Ireland which provided for fair rent, freedom to sell tenant-made improvements, and security of tenure.[97]

Another criticism that was made of the anti-alien landowning bills was that they could easily be evaded by the foreign owners' taking out American citizenship. What was needed, the *Bureau County Republican* argued, was an amendment to the constitution that would "positively prohibit any one man from holding over one thousand acres of tillable soil." [98] In Illinois no one seriously pushed such proposals. The legislature was in no mood to deal with tenancy in a constructive way but was blindly striking at Scully, possibly to soothe its conscience for its failure to solve the problems of the tenants. Dozens of landlords had by 1887 attained a state of great affluence in Illinois, among them the governor, Richard J. Oglesby, and David Littler, a prominent member of the legislature. Another, David Davis, who had died just the preceding year, had been justice of the United

[97] Paxton *Record*, May 26, 1887. In 1881, when feelings against Scully had somewhat subsided for the moment, a ball was held on St. Patrick's Day, in Lincoln, the center of the extensive farm operations of William Scully, in behalf of the Michael Davitt Land League, at which $125 was netted. It is interesting to read of a considerable outpouring of funds and sympathy elsewhere in the Middle West for oppressed tenants in Ireland (Lincoln *Herald*, March 24, 1881).

[98] Quoted in Pontiac Sentinel, March 5, 1886.

States Supreme Court, senator from Illinois, and prominently considered for the presidency. The interests of the landlords were not to be disturbed.

The attack upon Scully had its effect, however, in bringing to an end the purchasing of land by him in Illinois, as well as in Kansas and Nebraska. To meet the provisions of the anti-alien landowning acts, which denied aliens the right of permanently holding land they acquired by inheritance, Scully took out citizenship in the United States so that his heirs who likewise would be citizens could retain his estate intact. This action was taken in the national capital, and there is no evidence that he contemplated establishing a permanent residence in Illinois or in any other state where his lands were located. The Illinois act to prevent landlords from requiring tenants to pay taxes, of course, made necessary revising the terms of the leases, but it may be doubted that it resulted in any reduction in the total cost of the land to the tenant. It did, however, serve to remove from Illinois one of the major grievances that the public had against Scully.

For better or for worse, landlordism and tenancy were well established in Illinois and in parts of Missouri, Kansas, Nebraska, and Iowa by 1890. Contributing heavily to this end were the land speculators like Riggs, Sturges, and Grigg, and the frontier landlords like Sullivant, Alexander, Scott, Allerton, Sibley, and Scully. In the counties where their holdings were concentrated, were found the highest percentage of farms operated by tenants. Ford County, which contained the Sullivant, later the Sibley estate, had the highest proportion of farms operated by tenants, 54 percent as compared with the state average of 34 percent. Logan County, in which Scully had 225 farms and where many more were owned by Gillett, Littler, and others, had 52 percent of its farms tenant-operated. Mason County, where the McHarry and Herget estates—containing respectively 5,000 and 9,200 acres—were situated, had one-half of its farms in tenant hands. The county fourth highest in tenant-operated farms was Christian, where the 22,000-acre Malhiot estate lay, much of which was by 1890 in the hands of the Vandeveer famliy. Next came Piatt County, where the Allerton and Scott estates were located, and Grundy County, where Scully owned 70 or 80 farms, the Collins family 30 to 35 farms, the Holderman family 16 farms, and where the Hoge family and other large owners had many more.

Other substantial landed estates, established for the most part during the early development of central Illinois, that were in the 1930s and 1940s being farmed by tenants are here listed. The list, with holdings, is by no means complete, because the lands owned by individuals are widely scattered, and only when probate records fully exist, as with the Moore-Warner estate, can one be satisfied he has the full story.[99] Where the number of tenants is not given, one may reasonably estimate it by dividing the holdings by 160 to 320 acres.[100]

It may be argued that landlordism and tenancy were necessary frontier institutions in the prairie counties where the costs of beginning farming were so much higher than in wooded areas farther east. Certain it is that the capital required to buy land, especially from speculators or from land grant railroads, import

[99] It is a matter of serious complaint that no agency—Bureau of the Census or the United States or state departments of agriculture—has ever undertaken to compile information about estate, family, and individual farm holdings. Like income tax reports, this information seems sacred, not to be shared with the inquisitive historian. Some estate owners and managers have been generous in sharing such information, but others curtly refuse to answer enquiries or blandly reply with a mass of meaningless verbiage.

[100] The table has been compiled from platbooks, assessment and probate records of the counties, and interviews with owners or farm managers, all for the 1930s and 1940s. The Park-Lawrence-Lowrie estate is of particular interest because of substantial gifts the owners made to Park College of Parkville, Missouri, and Knox College of Galesburg, Illinois, and because George A. Lawrence, son-in-law of George Park, the founder of the estate, after managing it for many years, left in his will one hundred dollars to each of the eleven tenants who had been on the land for five years or more (747 La Salle County Miscellaneous Records, 22).

Name	Acres owned	Tenants	Location of holdings
Babson Farms	7,847		DeKalb, Ogle, Kane
Bevan, Rowena	1,687		McLean
Brass, E. E.	3,225		Menard
Burnside, W. T.	5,737		Douglas, Edgar
Cummings, C. R.	14,200	62	Adams, Tazewell
Diller, W. H.	4,849		Logan, Morgan, Sangamon
England, C. E.	6,000	30	Piatt, Macon, Christian
Ennis, W. H.	5,900	26	Macon, Moultrie, Piatt
Hill sisters	1,409		Douglas, Macon, Moultrie
Leimbach, M.	1,338		Logan
Lowden, F. O.	4,517		Ogle
McQueen, J.	2,703		De Kalb
McWilliams, N.	1,495		Livingston, Grundy
Marbold, B. F.	2,171		Menard
Mueth, J.	2,077		Sangamon
Oughton, J. R., Trust	5,041		Livingston, Grundy
Park-Lawrence, Lowrie	4,000		Putnam, La Salle
Passfield, G.	3,174		Sangamon, Clinton, Logan, Christian
Powers, O.	6,000	26	Macon
Proctor Endowment	5,311		
Raymond, C. W.	3,224		Iroquois
Roll, W.	1,947		Edgar
Rothwell, J. M.	2,835		Macon, Logan Sangamon
Ryan, M.	3,522		Livingston, McLean
Solon brothers	3,342		Champaign, Macon, Piatt, Douglas
Stoddard family	9,400		Piatt, Livingston, Woodford, Lee, Marshall
Swigart, C.	1,746		DeWitt, McLean
Ulrich-Stevenson-Ewing-Bumstead	4,280		Moultrie, Shelby, Douglas
Watts, E.	4,300		Menard, Sangamon

lumber for buildings, erect or set out fences, ditch, drain, and later tile the wet areas, break the tough prairie sod and seed it to corn, and purchase supplies until the first harvest was ready, together with the high interest rates charged on borrowed capital on the frontier, made it difficult for many settlers to start as actual owners without accumulating a heavy debt. Funk, Scott, Sibley, and Allerton, with their ample resources, could accomplish what poor settlers could not, at least not without long delays. That they were influential in bringing the prairie into cultivation somewhat earlier than small owners could was their service to the state, but tenancy was the result and the cost.

On the other hand, on the Scully estates, where the landlord made few or no improvements except for tiling and that only after the land had already been tenanted, the renters had to provide their own capital for buildings, fences, prairie breaking, and early ditching. True, their improvements were wretchedly poor as were tenants themselves, but the fact remains that here was a substantial group of settlers who brought some 38,000 acres into cultivation with the investment of what little capital they may have brought with them. The only thing they did not have to provide was the $200 with which to buy the quarter section from the government or a larger sum to make a down payment on speculator- or railroad-owned tract. Does this suggest that small-farm development by owner-operators might have occurred in the prairies had not the large speculators and frontier landlords anticipated them and got possession of most of the prairie land? It cannot, of course, be claimed that tenancy would thereby have been kept out of the prairies.

The swift rise of tenancy is one of the most striking features of this history of the American prairies. Careful observers had no occasion to be shocked in 1880 at the publication of the first census statistics showing that this rise of tenancy dated almost from the beginning of white settlement. A government land policy that permitted large-scale purchasing by speculators bears its responsibility for this early appearance and rapid growth of tenancy. The rise in land values that set in during and after the Civil War, and, of course, the increasing rents, made it difficult for laborers and tenants to acquire ownership, while the increasing capital demands of prairie agriculture and the unfavorable prices that produce brought in the seventies and again in the early nineties tended to depress many farm owners into the tenant class. The agricultural ladder from laborer through tenant to owner doubtless worked for many, as evidenced by the biographical sketches that appear in the numerous county histories of Illinois. But it must be remembered that these sketches are generally of those residents who had succeeded, who were now proudly describing their accumulations of property despite all adversity. At a later time the ladder seemed to work among children of owner-operators who started as laborers and worked up to the stage of mortgaged owners. On the other hand, the ladder worked in reverse for many others who, unable to meet the mortgage interest, lost their farms to the banker, the insurance company, or the local money lender.

Nowhere in America at the end of the century was tenancy more deeply rooted than in the prairies. While critics in the twentieth century were to find that prairie landlordism frequently provided expert farm management and the best of farm practices that were not always found on owner-operated farms, they were to confess that the old dream of owning one's farm was coming to be practically unattainable by large numbers of prairie residents.

William Scully, the greatest American landlord, has been the object of two studies: Homer E. Socolofsky's "The Scully Land System in Marion County," *Kansas Historical Quarterly*, XVIII (November, 1950), 338–375, adds materially to our knowledge; Russell L. Berry's *The Scully Estate and Its Cash Leasing System in the Midwest* (Brookings, South Dakota, 1966), is an economic study of Scully's large estate. Yasuo Okada, *Public Lands and Pioneer Farmers: Gage County, Nebraska, 1850–1900* (Tokyo, Japan, 1971), analyzes the operation of the public land system in an eastern Nebraska County and offers information on the management of the Scully lands in that county. Margaret Beattie Bogue has a case study of Matthew T. Scott's business in land development in *Patterns from the Sod: Land Use and Tenure in the Grand Prairie, 1850–1900*

(Springfield, Illinois, 1959), and of the management of the Scott lands in the twentieth century in "The Scott Farms in a New Agriculture, 1900–1919," in David M. Ellis, editor, *The Frontier in American Development* (Ithaca, N.Y., 1969), 217–248.

Hiram M. Drache, *The Day Of the Bonanza: A History Of Bonanza Farming in the Red River Valley of the North* (Fargo, North Dakota, 1964), expands upon this spectacular farming operation resulting from the exchange of depreciated bonds of the Northern Pacific Railroad for its lands. Morton Rothstein provides a detailed examination of the operations of a bonanza farm in "A British Investment in Bonanza Farming, 1879–1910," *Agricultural History* XXXIII (April, 1959), 72–78. Jacob van der Zee's *The British In Northwestern Iowa* (Iowa City, 1922), remains the only account of the extensive settlement promotion and land development work of the Close Brothers in Northwestern Iowa.

Efforts to halt further alien ownership of public lands are dealt with in Roger C. Clement's "British Investment and American Restrictive Legislation in the Trans-Mississippi West. 1880–1900," *Mississippi Valley Historical Review*, XLII (September, 1955), 208–228.

Margaret I. Snyder, in *The Chosen Valley* (New York, 1948), has shown how the acquisitive instinct and sharp bargaining of J. C. Easton made it possible for him to create a large landed estate on the Minnesota frontier.

Willard L. King, *Lincoln's Manager: David Davis* (Cambridge, Massachusetts, 1960), is a fine biographical study, but it barely mentions the way the millionaire justice of the Supreme Court and United States senator built up his extensive holding of Illinois prairie farms. Also, like all studies of Davis, it fails to show how he blunted the extreme efforts of Justice Stephen J. Field to stretch to the utmost property rights in Mexican land claims.

9. Frontier Estate Builders and Farm Laborers

To the simple democratic society of the American frontier consisting mostly of small farmers, as Frederick Jackson Turner described it, should be added two types, the one common, the other small in numbers but profoundly important in shaping landownership patterns, political action, and the beginnings of a cultured society. The first of these types includes the farm laborers, some of whom became farm tenants. The other type is the capitalist estate builder who took with him a "seemingly endless appetite for power and for land," as Arthur Moore put it.[1] It was these capitalist estate builders, whether cattle barons, land speculators turned developers, or men who went West with the set purpose of creating great plantations operated by tenants or hired hands, who made posible the employment of thousands of laborers.

The capitalist developer, big and little, was first revealed indirectly in 1860 when the Bureau of the Census presented statistics showing the number of farm laborers—statistics as noteworthy in their way as those showing the extent of farm tenancy in 1880 or the statement of the superintendent of the census in 1890 that the frontier was gone. Nothwithstanding America's much-boasted opportunities, its seemingly limitless supply of public lands, its ever expanding and newly opening frontier, the farm laborer, ordinarily a landless person whose economic status was less secure than that of the European peas-

[1] Arthur Moore, *The Farmer and Rest of Us* (Boston, 1945), 131.

[303]

ant, was shown to exist in large numbers, not only in the older and well-developed communities, but in the new states and middle border territories.

Consider for a moment Iowa, only fourteen years a state, still but lightly touched by settlement, not able to boast two people to the square mile, with less than a third of its land in farms but the bulk of its public lands already in private ownership. Despite the slight development of this state, largely concentrated in the eastern counties, its obvious frontier status, its abundance of raw unimproved prairie, Iowa in 1860 reported 40,827 farm laborers—6 percent of its population. More to the point, out of every hundred persons engaged in agriculture, twenty-three were farm laborers. Or look at Kansas, which had neither attained the dignity of statehood nor acquired anything but a thin veneer of settlement along its eastern border in the six years since it had become a territory. Census enumerators found here 10,400 farms and, surprisingly, 3,660 farm laborers. Nineteen out of every hundred persons engaged in agriculture were farm laborers. For the states of the Old Northwest the percentage of farm laborers among the total number of people engaged in agriculture ranged from 20 to 28.

Throughout the rest of the century, the number of farm laborers grew rapidly in the newer states of the Upper Mississippi Valley, while in the old states it fluctuated up and down and took a violent upward turn in the last decade. In proportion to the total number of persons engaged in agriculture, the number of farm laborers reached a high point in 1870. The census for that year shows that the percentage of farm laborers in the total number of persons engaged in agriculture was 30 in Minnesota, 32 in Nebraska, 33 in Wisconsin, 34 in Kansas, and 37 in Iowa. All these states had fairly stable and well-developed areas by 1870; but all except Iowa also had portions not yet out of the frontier stage. With so many farm laborers in new as well as old communities, no picture of the West can be considered complete without attention to their social and economic background, the reasons why they existed in such numbers. But western historians have not been concerned about them. The stereotype of the mortgaged farmer is familiar to all students of western lore, but the farm laborer has not been the subject of rowdy ballads, he does not appear in the fiction of the frontier, nor is he to be found in the works of Turner, Paxson, Riegel, or Billington.

Statistics of farm labor for these years in new states and territories are so startling that it seems desirable to look into their compilation to determine just who in the opinion of the census enumerators fitted into this category. Analysis of the original census schedules shows that older boys of farm familes who were over fifteen years of age and were living at home were not infrequently listed as farm laboreres. Undoubtedly they performed heavy routine work on the farm, but I have not thought of them as laborers, since they rarely drew wages and since they could expect to inherit a share of the farm some time in the future. Offsetting this factor was the exclusion of migratory workers who were employed for the harvest season but were not at the time of enumeration living with the farmers who had previously engaged them or were thereafter to do so. Clearly, the timing of the census was important in the matter of enumerating farm laborers. The first of June, the date for which information was collected, was not the busiest time for farmers in the Corn Belt, because crops were already in, haying had not begun, and wheat was not yet ready for harvest. A month or six weeks later, enumerators would have found greater numbers of hired hands to list.[2]

By 1870 the census takers were collecting information respect-

2 Information on the use of migratory laborers is meager, but the Davenport (Iowa) *Gazette*, published in an important river port, is helpful in its issues of July 13 to 18, 1868. Daily mention is made of the demand for farm hands, for which as much as $3 and $4 per day was being paid. A stampede of city workers was reported which so depleted the community that construction projects could not be carried on. On the 18th, the steamer Dubuque was reported as bringing in 75 field hands, who within thirty minutes after arrival were engaged at $3.50 to $3.75 a day. Later reports of the movement north of wheat harvesters indicate that migratory labor was a major feature of agriculture in Illinois, Iowa, Wisconsin, and Minnesota.

ing the value of compensation, including board paid hired hands the previous year. True, this information was not processed and published, but a sample study of Poweshiek County in central Iowa shows that of 1,634 farmers owning land, 932 paid out for labor the previous year sums ranging from $5 to $2,000, the average being over $150. In nine townships in this county, payments to farm laborers, including the value of their board, amounted to $234,000.[3]

The census schedules also furnish information on the emergence of farm tenancy, a midway step from laborer to farm owner, information which is particularly valuable since we have no specific data on tenancy as such until 1880. Years ago, in a colloquy on land speculation, Joseph Schafer, superintendent of the State Historical Society of Wisconsin, who in his studies of pioneering in Wisconsin gave much attention to land speculation and its profits and losses, scoffed at the suggestion that owners of land in the pioneer period might have collected rents from their holdings. Tenancy could not exist on the frontier, he declared.[4] Yet newspaper advertisements, probate records, and even manuscript census schedules clearly reveal scattered evidence of the renting of farms and that in frontier Wisconsin in the fifties it was not uncommon, and it does have to be taken into account in any consideration of the frontier process. In the absence of de-

[3] The original census schedules of Iowa and Wisconsin are in the Iowa State Department of History and Archives, Des Moines, and the State Historical Society of Wisconsin, Madison.

[4] For his study of the land speculation of Charles Augustus Murray, who bought 20,000 acres in Grant and LaFayette Counties, Wisconsin, in 1836, Schafer used the conveyance records at the county seats to determine when the various parcels of land were sold and at what prices. He concluded that Murray had not done as well as if the money had been invested in gilt-edge securities. Since leases ordinary were not recorded, he had no way of knowing whether any of the land had been rented, as some had been, or what income might have come from rents. In regard to farm tenancy in 1880, these two counties ranked close to the top among Wisconsin counties. The state figure for 1880 is 9 percent; figures for Grant and LaFayette are 14 and 18 percent. For Schafer's treatment see his *The Wisconsin Lead Region* (Madison, 1932), 148–154.

tailed census compilations, we can learn much about tenancy from earlier census schedules, the county deed records, local newspaper advertisements, and correspondence of land dealers and landlords.[5]

The censuses of 1850, 1860, and 1870 show a sharp increase in the number of farms in excess of five hundred acres, the expanding volume of hired hands previously alluded to, and numerous "farmers" and farm laborers who owned no real or landed property but did have personal property such as horses, mules, oxen, milch or beef cattle, and hogs. Some of these "farmers" and farm laborers may have been attempting to buy farms they were operating, but whether they were or not, they were at the time tenants. Analysis of the 1870 census listings of farmers and farm laborers in two lightly developed western Iowa townships and one well settled central Iowa township shows that of 184 persons (excluding children) listed as engaged in agriculture, 96 owned land and 88 owned no real property, but 57 of these latter owned personal property and were presumably tenants. Thirty-one "farmers" and farm laborers listed no property of any kind. Of the agricultural population of these three townships (Belvedere, Ashton, and Shiloh), 53 percent owned farms and 47 percent owned no land.

Farm land was being rented to tenants in Ohio, Indiana, and Illinois as early as the 1820s, but the practice did not become common for nearly a generation.[6] After the frenzy of land speculation in the thirties, many investors, caught with heavy obliga-

[5] Notices of Wisconsin farms for rent in the fifties were found in the Janesville *Gazette*, the Janesville *Democratic Standard*, the Baraboo *Sauk County Standard*, and the Eau Claire *Free Press*. The papers of Catlin and Williamson, Cyrus Woodman, and J. Richardson & Co. in the Wisconsin State Historical Society and of Allen Hamilton and George W. Ewing in the Indiana State Library are useful.

[6] Solon J. Buck, *Pioneer Letters of Gershom Flagg* (Springfield, Ill., 1912), 22–46; *Indiana Oracle and Dearborn Gazette* (Lawrence, Ind.), Oct. 4, 1823. Nicholas Longworth had 27 tenants on his farms near Cincinnati in 1850 (Ophia D. Smith, *The Life and Times of Giles Richards, 1820–1860*, Ohio Historical Collections, VI [Columbus, 1936]), 45.

tions in a falling market, with interest and tax costs growing, offered to rent their land to squatters or newly arriving immigrants too poor to buy, partly to protect their property but also to get at least the taxes out of them.[7] As early as 1842, Solon Robinson, the well-known agricultural writer, in describing the attractions of the flat lands of northwestern Indiana to immigrants, said: "No matter if you have no money, you can rent land very low, and will soon be in a condition to let land instead of hiring it." By the middle of the century, tenancy was emerging everywhere in the prairies of Indiana, Illinois, and eastern Iowa and a little more slowly in Wisconsin. From northern and eastern Indiana, the Military Tract and the central prairie counties of Illinois, and the eastern counties of Iowa came many reports of persons renting land who lacked the means to buy. Renting was so common in La Salle County, Illinois, in 1854 that the local newspaper in its price current listed farms as renting from $1.25 to $1.50 an acre. Fred Gerhard wrote in 1856, in *Illinois as It Is*, the most detailed account of the economic opportunities the prairie state offered, that almost everywhere land was available for rent, while James Caird, the eminent English agricultural authority who was employed to aid the sale of the Illinois Central lands, found in 1858 that tenancy was "very common in Illinois." He maintained that English agricultural laborers "possessed of the requisite skill and prudence" would be assured of success as tenants or farm owners. There is nothing in Gerhard's or Caird's writing that points with alarm at tenancy.[8]

Tenancy came slightly later to Iowa, but in 1852 a dealer was offering 13 farms in the eastern counties for rent at $1.00 and $2.00 an acre. Elsewhere newspapers discussed the growing practice of share renting.[9]

[7] See Chapter 8, above.

[8] Herbert A. Kellar, ed., *Solon Robinson, Pioneer and Agriculturist*, Indiana Historical Collections, XXI (Indianapolis, 1936), I, 351; La Salle (Ill.) *Independent*, March 4, 1854; Fred Gerhard, *Illinois as It Is: Its History*, . . .(Chicago, 1857), 404; James Caird, *Prairie Farming in America: With Notes by the Way on Canada and the United States* (New York, 1859), 93–94.

[9] Letter of J. W. Schreyer, June 22, 1846, in *Indiana Magazine of His-*

In mid-century Indiana, a move to define the rights of land-lords and tenants developed into a major political battle. Bills to give landlords a lien on crops raised by their tenants had the support of legislators from the prairie counties, where landlord-ism flourish, but were opposed by the Democratic representatives from the small-farm counties of southern Indiana. Opponents, perhaps not aware of how far landlordism had already devel-oped in the richer counties of the north, said that any such mea-sure would stimulate landlords to enlarge their domain, "in-crease their subordinate tenancies," and strike at "our true policy to encourage every man to become a land owner." It was legis-lation "in favor of capital, the rich, and against labor, the poor." Another Hoosier opponent of the measure proposed an amend-ment to give landlords liens on the furniture, the wife, and the children of the tenant! Session after session of the legislature gave consideration to the question from 1857 to 1881, but not until the latter year was action completed.[10]

The growth of tenancy was stimulated by the granting of lands to railroads to aid in their construction. Two early bene-ficiary railroads—the Illinois Central and the Burlington and Missouri River—after making their selections, found squatters on them who could not easily be dispossessed without creating ill feeling, but who were not in a position to pay the price asked for their claims. The Burlington officials found that the easiest policy to follow in such cases was to rent the land to the squatters for one to three years at a nominal price of 20¢ an acre with the

---

tory, XL (Sept., 1944), 294; Anon., *A True Picture of Emigration: Of Four-teen Years in the Interior of North America* (London, 1838), 60; Florence E. Janson, *The Background of Swedish Immigration, 1840–1930* (Chicago, 1931), 141–142; Harvey L. Carter, "Rural Indiana in Transition, 1850–1860," *Agricultural History*, XX (April, 1946), 114; G. C. Beman, Croton, Lee Co., Iowa, Jan. 12, 1853, to D. Kilbourne, (Kilbourne MSS., Iowa State Depart-ment of History and Archives; Davenport *Gazette*, Jan. 29, Nov. 25, 1852, Oct. 6, 1853, March 26, May 5, 1858; Sioux City (Iowa) *Register*, March 17, 1860, March 15, 1862.

[10] *Brevier Legislative Reports*, 1852, 1857, 1859, 1861, 1865, 1881; *Laws of Indiana General Assembly*, 1881, p. 565; *Indianapolis State Sentinel*, Jan. 14, 23, 1857; Monticello *Herald*, April 1, 1875.

hope that such improvements as the squatters made would enable the land to bring a good price when the lease expired and that legal action might be taken to evict, if necessary. In 1878, the Burlington was renting Nebraska land which had been farmed during the past year for $1 an acre and idle lands for fifty cents an acre; its land in Iowa was then being rented for as much as $1.25 to $2 an acre. Railroad land-grant policy, like the government policy of permitting—and, indeed, encouraging—extensive speculation in Western lands, hastened the coming of tenancy to the West.[11]

The rapid alienation of public land and swiftly rising land values helped to accelerate the renting of land in the sixties and seventies. In 1880, when statistics of tenancy were compiled, the figures for the public-land states, particularly those which still contained land available for homestead, alarmed land reformers. In Illinois 31 percent and in Iowa 23 percent of all the farms were tenant operated. The counties of greater land values and higher productivity had tenancy rates ranging into the high 30's and 40's. More surprising was the swift emergence of tenancy in the border counties of Kansas and Nebraska, where the land had been in private ownership no more than twenty-three years, much of it less than fourteen years. Here the tenancy figures ranged from 25 to 40 percent. In the states of the Upper Mississippi Valley, the percentage of people engaged in agriculture who were either tenants or farm laborers ranged from 32 in Minnesota to 53 in Illinois.[12]

[11] Peter Daggy, Land Department, Illinois Central Railroad, Nov. 30, 1865, to C. E. Perkins; J. M. King, Clarinda, Iowa, June 21, 1865, to Perkins; J. D. McFarland, Lincoln, Neb., Nov. 25, 1868, to A. E. Touzalin; W. W. Baldwin, Land Commissioner, Burlington and Missouri, Aug. 23, 1879, to R. A. Crippen, Burlington Archives, Newberry Library, Chicago. The correspondence of Edward Hayes of Oak, T. S. Goddard of Hastings, R. A. Crippen of Corning, Iowa, land agents of the B & M, contains allusions to numerous instances of the roalroad's leasing to tenants on a cash or share-rent basis.

[12] To arrive at these percentages I added the number of tenant farms (presumably farmed each by one tenant) to the number of farm laborers and

The early appearance of tenancy and agricultural labor in the amount that has been shown in or close to frontier areas, together with their rapid increase, provides convincing evidence that government land policy was not producing the results it defenders claimed. In view of the oft-repeated objective of American land policy—to assure a nation of freeholders—how is it possible to account for the early appearance of farm laborers and tenants in frontier communities?

Paradoxically, the fact that cheap, and finally free, land was to be had in the American West has a direct bearing on the appearance of farm laborers and tenants in that section. Government land prices were progressively reduced from $2.00 an acre in 1800 ($1.64 for cash) to $1.25 in 1820, to $.60 to $1.00 by the use of military bounty land warrants of 1847–1855, to as little as $.125 in 1854, until finally, in 1862, free land could be obtained. European peasants and debt-ridden farmers in older sections of America were lured west by the vision of cheap or free farms that they confused with cheap or free raw land.

Nor was it sufficiently noted that the cost of farm making was increasing as settlers moved into the tough-sodded, poorly drained, and timberless prairies, where in competition with construction and railroad building they either had to pay high wages for custom work such as breaking, harvesting, and threshing or buy expensive labor-saving equipment. Custom plowmen, using the heavy breaking plow pulled by a number of yoke of oxen, charged $2 and $3 an acre for breaking prairie. Lumber for the house, fencing, and perhaps a barn could no longer be "hooked" from neighboring government- or absentee-owned tracts and had to be brought in at heavy expense from the Mississippi River mill towns or Chicago. A yoke of oxen, wagon, plow, stove, chains, ax, shovel, grindstone, scythe or cradle, together with seed, funds to maintain the family until the first crop came in,

---

computed what percentage that total was of the number of people engaged in agriculture. The figures are from the *Tenth Census, Agriculture* (Washington, 1883), *passim*.

fees for filing land-office papers, or money to make the down payment on a railroad tract, brought the amount needed to start farming to $500 at the minimum; safer estimates were two or three times that much. Land agents and representatives of the land-grant railroads warned prospective emigrants in the East and in Europe that they should bring some capital with them to the West.[13]

Notwithstanding these well-meant warnings, immigrants continued to reach the outer edge of settlement destitute, unable to start farm making. We need not probe their disillusionment when their scant resources proved insufficient to enable them to take advantage of the government's free homestead policy. They could still cherish the dream of owning a farm while they worked for others.

Immigrants newly arriving in the West soon learned that unless they quickly established a claim to land, their chances of making good selections would be minimized, perhaps lost to other more foresighted settlers or to speculators. The settler and the speculator were catching up with the surveyor, especially in Iowa, Kansas, and Nebraska, and land when offered or opened to entry was quickly snatched up. Consequently, a first step toward farm ownership was to select a tract, establish a claim upon it, and hope that it could be held for two or three years without cost even though the claimant was not actually living upon it or abiding by the provision of the pre-emption or homestead acts. Frontiersmen moving early into newly opened communities found they could sell their claims with but slight im-

[13] *Guide to the Lands of the Northern Pacific Railroad in Minnesota* (New York, 1872), 22; Arthur F. Bentley, *The Condition of the Western Farmer as Illustrated by the Economic History of a Nebraska Township*, Johns Hopkins University Studies in Historical and Political Science, 11th Series, No. 7 (July, 1893), 28; Clarence H. Danhof, "Farm Making Costs and the 'Safety Valve': 1850–1860," *Journal of Political Economy*, XLVI (June, 1941), 317 ff.; Paul W. Gates, *Fifty Million Acres: Conflict Over Kansas Land Policy, 1854–1890* (Ithaca, 1954), 223.

provements for $50 to $100 to later comers and then go a little farther west and make another selection. Claim making, a species of land speculation, was indulged in by many who gradually acquired a little livestock and equipment through sales of claims or through outside earnings and were ready in a few years for more permanent farm making. A combination of claim specunation and temporary work on railroad construction jobs or building projects in growing urban centers was common. That many immigrants also took agricultural jobs as hired hands in areas close to, if not right in, the frontier is not as well known.

Some students and readers of fiction relating to western pioneer life have entertained the notion that western farmers never really prospered but were in a more or less chronic state of depression that was aggravated by periods of unusually low prices and near crop failures with resulting acute distress. Perhaps more attention has been directed to the agrarian reaction to such distress and the causes thereof than to periods of favorable prices and bountiful crops that brought early prosperity to many. Certain it is that in no comparable period did such large numbers of immigrants to a new region gain ownership of the farms they were improving and live well upon those farms as in the fifty-year period from 1850 to 1900 in the Mississippi Valley. Boomer literature of the time tells of numerous cases of individuals in Illinois, Kansas, or Nebraska who made enough on one good crop to pay for their land and equipment. That there were such cases cannot be denied, but whether they were typical it is impossible to say. We do know that industrious, skillful farmers favored by good fortune did succeed not only in subduing the usual 80- to 160-acre tract of wild land to grain production and livestock use, but in many instances in developing even larger farms. This was accomplished not alone by the head of the family and his children, but with the aid of hired men.

The census schedules of 1870 reveal thousands of instances of farmers with no more than 160 acres employing one or two laborers.[14] These farmers did not attract the attention of journalists or travelers of the time, and, consequently, their operations are more difficult to reconstruct than those of the larger capitalist farmers, whose operations were on a much bigger scale and who individually employed numerous farm hands.

The American West proved attractive not only to poor immigrants but also to men of means interested in developing not single family farms but estates of thousands of acres worked by laborers and tenants. Large capitalistic enterprises in the pioneer West are not unknown to historians, but most attention has been centered on the bonanza wheat farms of the Red River Valley of Minnesota and Dakota and on cattle ranching in the Great Plains. Carried out on a grand scale and with a dramatic flourish, they drew the attention of journalists and other commentators of the time and consequently found their way into most histories of the West.[15] Their day was short, their long-range influence not great, and they deserve a mere footnote in history compared with the quieter, more pervasive, and longer-lasting investments by masterful and aggressive capitalists in the Corn Belt, who came not merely to speculate nor to develop a bonanza farm but to create rent-producing estates composed of numerous farms operated either by hired hands or by tenants.

These estate builders were to be found in practically every portion, one can almost say in every county, of the Corn Belt. Their homes, in highly stereotyped and stilted engravings, the number of acres they owned, and the moral qualities of the owners, all are presented in the numerous county atlases and biographical volumes that were the rage in the Gilded Age.

[14] Paul S. Taylor, "The American Hired Man: His Rise and Decline," *Land Policy Review*, VI (Spring, 1943), 3–17; LaWanda F. Cox, "The American Agricultural Wage Earner, 1865–1900: The Emergence of a Modern Labor Problem," *Agricultural History*, XXII (April, 1949), 94–114.

[15] Harold E. Briggs, *Frontiers of the Northwest* (New York, 1940), 509–522; Fred A. Shannon, *The Farmer's Last Frontier, Agriculture, 1860–1897* (*The Economic History of the United States*, Henry David, Harold Faulkner, Louis Hacker, *et al.*, eds. V [New York, 1945]), 154–161.

Their investments ranged from a few thousand to hundreds of thousands of dollars and, for a score or more, to one or two millions.[16] That is not to say that they brought capital in this amount with them when they first ventured into the West. Much of their capital was made in the West.

The cattle ranchers and drovers who flourished in Indiana and Illinois in the forties, fifties, and sixties and in Iowa and Missouri a little later dominated great areas of the prairies for a time. They built upon their first investments by shrewdly buying the surplus stock of neighbors, fattening them on the prairie bluestem with the addition of a little grain, and then driving them to Chicago, Indianapolis, or the East, wherever they could get favorable prices. Later they brought in cattle from Missouri and Texas. Their profits were invested in land when it could be bought "dirt-cheap" to assure an abundance of grass and grain for their operations. Slowly, they turned to grain feeding and grain production and improved livestock, using meantime an increasing number of hands. By mid-century the operations of the successful cattle kings were being conducted on a huge scale, with herds of cattle numbering in the thousands, fields of corn covering thousands of acres, and scores of hands to carry on the business. Their holdings in land increased to 5,000, 10,000, 20,000, even 40,000 acres.[17] For every giant farm of this size

---

[16] In Illinois alone a compiler found in 1892 the following "millionaires" whose wealth was largely made in farm lands: Matthew T. Scott, Orlando Powers, L. B. Casner, Estate of John Shaw Hayward, John C. Proctor, George Pasfield, Horatio M. Vandeveer, William H. Ennis, W. H. Bradley. In Missouri the outstanding millionaire landowners were David Rankin and five heirs of Milton Tootle; in Nebraska, Stephen Miles; in Minnesota, J. A. Willard and A. H. Wilder; in Indiana, William H. English and the estate of Moses Fowler. Other identifiable millionaires in these states added materially to their wealth through farming operations and land improvements (*American Millionaires: The Tribune's List of Persons Reputed to be Worth a Million or More* [June, 1892], reprinted in Sidney Ratner, *New Light on the History of Great American Fortunes: American Millionaires of 1892 and 1902* [New York, 1953]).

[17] See Chapters 6, 7, and 8, above.

there were a score or more of smaller operators with holdings ranging from one to four thousand acres.[18]

These bonanza farms, located as they were in Corn Belt counties with high land values, soon became as outmoded as the sickle and cradle. Farm workers proved irresponsible when hired at low wages. They were careless with tools, they slighted their tasks, overworked or abused the draft animals, drank heavily, and often engaged in fisticuffs. On slight provocation they quit their jobs knowing that equally good opportunities were available elsewhere, and they demanded high wages when the peak of employment was reached in the harvest season. Old Isaac Funk, who accumulated a fortune of two million dollars in his land and cattle business in McLean County, Illinois, said in 1861 that no one could afford to hire men to grow and market grain at prices then prevailing. Their wages were too high and they worked too little, thought Funk. Another Illinois landlord, in deploring the wage of two dollars a day being paid to harvest hands in 1862, held that "cheap farm laborers" were essential for the winning of the Civil War.[19] The best agricultural laborers wanted to become tenants or owners and would remain in employment only as long as was necessary for them to accumulate the resources for starting on their own.

Continuing immigration into the prairies with its resulting pressure upon the supply of land, skyrocketing values, taxes, and assessments forced more intensive land use. Ranches with grain as a side issue could no longer be economically justified, and for a time the bonanza farms became grain farms with cattle as a side issue. Before long, central administration of the land was abandoned. The big farms were divided into small holdings and assigned to tenants. Though the workers might prove poor farm

[18] The Census of 1880 shows 2,916 farms in excess of a thousand acres in the ten states of the Upper Mississippi Valley.

[19] New York *Tribune*, July 30, 1861, Aug. 11, 1861; C. H. Moore to Dr. John Warner, July 21, 1862, Moore-Warner MSS., Clinton, Ill.; *Country Gentleman*, XXIII (March 10, May 5, 1864), 164, 292; XXVI (Aug. 17, 1865), 116.

hands, it was seen that, given a share in the returns from farming, they were more responsible, more willing to exert themselves,
more careful with their tools, horses, and oxen, and with their
housing accommodations. In the transition to full tenancy the
landlord might provide everything but maintenance for the
operator and pay him eight or ten cents a bushel for the corn he
produced. In 1870, a tenant who furnished his own team was
paid fifteen cents for each bushel of corn, fifty cents for each
bushel of wheat, and twenty-five cents for each bushel of oats he
produced. A more common practice was for the tenant to pay
the landlord one-third to one-half of the crops or a cash rent for
each acre of cultivable land.[20]

The day of the Corn Belt cattle kings was short, as was their
career as bonanza farmers. As entrepreneurs developing their
estates they made jobs available for many workers who later
were permitted, if not encouraged, to become tenants. In the
tenant stage of land development some of the landlords continued to expend their surplus from rents in additional improvements, so that their constructive period lasted throughout the
first generation and, indeed, well into the second. In the process
of change, some land was sold; more, through inheritance dif-
fusion, passed to a larger number of landlords. Analysis of the
assessment records or the current platbooks of Corn Belt counties reveals a century later how tenaciously third- and fourth-
generation descendants of the old cattle kings clung to their
possessions.

Side by side with these modern holdings are other equally

---

[20] Columbus (Ohio) *State Journal*, in Davenport (Iowa) *Gazette*, Aug 12,
1855; 1 Miscellaneous Record, 434, Logan County Recorder's Office, Lincoln,
Ill.; James MacDonald, *Food from the Far West* (London, 1878), 142–148;
Appendix, "Agricultural Interests Commission, Reports of the Assistant Com-
missioner" (London, 1880), *Parliamentary Papers*, 1880, XVIII, 18, 38–39;
Bloomington (Ill.) *Bulletin*, March 4, 1887. On the Fowler lands in
Indiana, in return for breaking land and putting it in corn, tenants were
paid $.25 a bushel for the corn they raised in the first five crop years (Benton
Review, June 11, 1885).

large estates which sprang from another type of investment on the frontier, that of the capitalists who came West to create permanent estates, like that of the Wadsworth family in the Genesee country of New York, by buying and developing extensive areas. Some of these capitalists concentrated their attention entirely upon farm making, while others bought and sold real estate, acted as agents for eastern capitalists wishing to invest in the growing West, or perhaps ran a bank and made loans to squatters. Profits and fees they invested in land improvements. A number took construction contracts on railroads, receiving land instead of cash in payment. They were careful to keep their titles clear, to pay the taxes before liens were issued, and to protect their timber against the prevalent custom of "hooking." With all these side isues, they kept before them the goal of land development.

Extensive improvement of their holdings required these estate builders to seek out workers to break the prairie, fence, erect tenant houses for the families of workers and barracklike constructions for single men, to seed, cultivate, harvest, shuck, thrash, and haul the grain to market. To assure themselves an adequate labor supply, and subsequently to attract tenants, these entrepreneurs had at times to advertise, distribute handbills in eastern communities, and in a number of instances publish pamphlets describing the opportunities their lands provided to immigrants.[21] Workers could not save much from the low wages paid them, but many pioneers did make their start by accumulating small funds from such earnings and investing them, per-

[21] Sioux City *Register*, Jan. 12, 1861; Margaret Ruth Beattie, "Matthew Scott, Pioneer Landlord-Gentleman Farmer, 1855–1891" M. A. Thesis, Cornell University, 1947, 58 ff.; Jacob Van Der Zee, *The British in Iowa* (Iowa City, 1922), 57 ff. Illustrative of these who entered land for settlers, using military land warrants, then were forced to retain possession of the land because of the settlers' defaults and to keep the unsuccessful settlers on the land as tenants, is the career of Jason C. Easton, of the firm of Gilbert & Easton of Chatfield, Minnesota. Easton owned as a result of his share in these operations thirty farms (Rodney C. Loehr, "Jason C. Easton, Territorial Banker," *Minnesota History*, XXIX [Sept., 1948], 223).

haps while still holding the farm job, in nearby land on which they might at the same time make some improvements.

For the western immigrant who was anxious to have a farm of his own but who lacked the means to acquire it, it was distinctly better to be a tenant than a farm laborer. He could, when he attained this status, feel he was moving toward his goal. Now he shared with the capitalist proprietor the profits from farming, but he also shared the losses. Furthermore, he was usually required by his lease to make capital improvements upon the rented land, with the cost deductible from the rent. Every improvement he made raised the value of the land and pushed farther away the possibility of his buying it. If he paid cash rent, continued improvement of the land was certain to be followed by a higher rent charge; if he paid share rent, the landlord might—and in the eighties did—exact a larger portion of the grain. Tenancy was no happy choice to the immigrant looking for the free or cheap land about which he had heard so much, but unless he was willing to go far beyond the railroad into areas lacking social facilities and market opportunities, there was no other alternative.

Some landlords were willing to pay for much of the cost of breaking and fencing, to provide machines and even credit to carry their tenants through harvest. Others insisted on the tenants' making all the improvements, which they then might own or at least have the right to sell to other tenants, subject to the approval of the landlord. Advertisements for tenants were increasingly common in the prairie newspapers, but more ominous from the point of view of the tenant were advertisements of renters looking for land.[22] Eviction for sloth, failure to make

[22] The Champaign (Ill.) *Gazette*, clipped in the Bloomington (Ill.) *Pantagraph*, Jan. 23, 1879, reported, "The demand for farms to rent far exceeds the supply, and men are compelled to seek other localities to get places." See also the Monticello (Ind.) *Prairie Chieftain*, Nov. 4, 1852; Bloomington *Pantagraph*, Feb. 8, 1854, Nov. 5, 1856; Watseka (Ill.) *Iroquois County Times*, Oct. 21, 1875; Malvern (Iowa) *Leader*, Feb. 8, 1883, Feb. 26, March 5, 1885.

required improvements, poor farming, and cheating the landlord increased as hordes of new immigrants looking for land to
rent came in from central Europe. The pressure for places to
rent made it possible for the landlord to exact more and to allow
the tenant less. Farmers of older American stock found the role
of tenant increasingly unbearable. Disillusioned by their meager
returns and unwilling to compete with the new wave of European immigrants, they abandoned their rented places in Illinois
and Iowa by the thousands in the seventies and eighties for a
new try at ownership in western Kansas or Nebraska, or per-
chance in the Dakota country. It was this emigration of older
American tenants from the Corn Belt that was responsible for
the increasingly conservative character of agrarian politics in
Illinois and Iowa. These disillusioned and frequently angry
tenants who emigrated farther west carried their resentment
with them and made the area in which they settled fertile ground
for the Populist agitator.[23]

Meantime, the capitalist estate builders, having divided their
holdings into small tenant farms, were emerging as farm managers. Where they had erected tenant homes, set out fences, and
established orchards they needed to protect their investment by
making certain that proper care and maintenance were provided.
They naturally wanted for their tenancies good farmers who
would keep the weeds down, get their crops in and harvested at
the right time, protect the timber if any, and pay their cash rent
promptly or turn in a fair landlord's share of the grain. Good
tenants assured better yields and hence more share rent. Both
landlords and tenants were driven to exploit the land by their
need for high returns to meet costs of farm improvements, new
implements, and perhaps livestock. Rotation, the use of alfalfa
or clover, prevention of erosion were all subordinated to the
production of grain, wtih declining fertility the natural—though

[23] Chester McArthur Destler, "Agricultural Readjustment and Agrarian
Unrest in Illinois, 1880–1893," *Agricultural History*, XXI (April, 1947),
104–116; Gates, *Fifty Million Acres*, 244 ff.

not immediately apparent—result. Much the same thing can be said of farm owners who were struggling to raise funds out of their crops to purchase new equipment, to fence additional land, to drain the low places, or to enlarge their original two- or three-room houses to accommodate growing families. Economic circumstances were largely responsible for a pattern of land use that disregarded the lessons of the past in older states and was exploitative and destructive of values. In defense of the capitalist estate builders, it should be added that some of them early showed concern for proper land management by insisting upon rotation of crops; the use of alfalfa, clover, and lime; the elimination of weeds; and careful use of pastures.

The operations of capitalist estate builders, whose individual and family holdings rans as high as 60,000 acres and in one case to 200,000 acres, have been described elsewhere. Few of these "feudal lords," as George Ade called them, would sell unless faced with disaster.[24] They instilled in their children a deep respect for the land they had improved and sought by every possible legal device to restrict the right of alienation. Because of their great success in retaining ownership of their many farms, the names of Scully, Moore, Davis, Vandeveer, Ennis, Funk, Fowler, Wearin, Rankin and Lawrence-Lowrie are as familiar today to the residents of the prairie states as were the names of the great planters of South Carolina and Georgia to the ante-bellum residents of those states.

With all the plethora of information the Bureau of Census had gathered the problem of multiple ownership of tenant farms received no attention until 1900. Something of the concentration of ownership of tenant farms, the heritage of the capitalist estate builder in the nineteenth century, may be seen in the census data of that year. The figures are not complete and are made less useful by the fact that they are compiled on the basis of residence of owner; but in the absence of anything better we

[24] George Ade, "Prairie Kings of Yesterday," *Saturday Evening Post*, CCIV July 4, 1931), 14.

must use them. For the states of the Upper Mississippi Valley, 3,800 landlords appear as owning 32,646 farms. Five hundred and fifty-one of these landlords had an average of 12.8 farms each, and 122 owners had an average of 35.5 farms each. In Illinois, 34 landlords are shown owning 1,115 farms, or an average of 32 each.[25] The following tabulation gives additional data about the ownership of tenant farms by owners living in the Upper Mississippi Valley in 1900.

Farms owned	Number of owners	Total farms owned
1	419,900	419,900
2	39,124	78,248
3–4	12,070	39,831
5–9	3,127	21,263
10–19	551	7,052
20–	122	4,331
Total (plural ownership)	54,994	150,725

Since one landlord owned 322 farms in Illinois and an additional 845 farms in Missouri, Kansas, and Nebraska but had his residence in the District of Columbia, it is easy to see how deceptive, how inadequate, the census data is.

The estate builder brought much-needed funds to the West, developed substantial areas, and provided early employment and housing facilities for many newly arrived immigrants who lacked means to begin on their own. He aided others in getting started by lending them funds to commence farming as a tenant or owner; by furnishing them the necessary farming implements, seed, and food until harvest; and by providing livestock on a partnership basis. Much of the risk in these operations was his. Frequently, he undertook such investments with borrowed capital on which he paid 10 to 15 percent interest. Taxes bore heavily on him, as the residents of his community seeking better

---

[25] *Census of 1900, Agriculture*, Part I, lxxxviii; Howard A. Turner, *The Ownership of Tenant Farms in the North Central States*, United States Department of Agriculture, *Bulletin*, No. 1433 (Sept., 1926), 10.

schools and roads raised his assessments on tangibles that could not be hidden. Poor crops or low prices or, worse still, a combination of both might so reduce his income as to make it impossible for him to meet his obligations. One bad year he could take, perhaps two, but a larger combination of bad years was disastrous. The late seventies marked the final defeat of a number of large farm operators, and this was the result of poor prices, unfavorable weather, high interest rates, and perhaps poor management.

Society on the frontier and in areas a generation beyond the frontier stage was more complex, had a wider range of economic well-being, than Frederick Jackson Turner thought. The early appearance of farm laborers and tenants, many of whom were never to rise to farm-ownership status, and of great landed estates, whose owners brought wealth with them and added much to it, did not make for a "fundamental unity in its [frontier's] social structure and its democratic ideals." Concepts of the homogeneity of frontier society, similarity of frontier outlook, common addiction to democratic principles, may well be questioned.

Ante-bellum Democratic senators of the Upper Mississippi Valley appeared to be more concerned with their own land speculation schemes or the welfare of fur, lumber, mining, and railroad companies than with the fortunes of their farmer constituents; they did little to loosen the reactionary control southern slave owners had over their party. The land-owning aristocracy early moved into politics via the Whig and Republican parties and fought as vigorously for privilege as did eastern conservatives. It was a combination of prairie landlords—Isaac Funk, Jesse Fell, Asahel Gridley, and David Davis—who had an important share in bringing the Republican nomination to Lincoln in 1860. Their activities contributed to fasten protection, the gold standard, land subsidies to railroads, and an incongruous land system upon the country. When the Democratic party in the Middle West recovered from its debacle, it was in the hands of Bourbons no more liberal in their outlook than the Republican officeholders they sought to displace.

The appearance of the Greenback and Populist parties seemed for a time to offer promise of effective agrarian leadership, but a combination of upper-class landowning families that directed the Greenback and Granger parties and a will-o'-the-wisp search for a magic commodity price formula by the Populist party offered no aid to the farm laborer searching for a route to ownership or to tenants struggling to retain their step on the ownership ladder. While western newspapers were bewailing the fate of Irish tenants, they gave no heed to the emergence of the tenant class at home whose rights were less secure, whose plight was as serious. The landlords and successful farmers and their urban allies were in the saddle politically, and though they might erupt in condemnation of financial lords of the East, railroad magnates, or tariff-minded manufacturers, they did nothing to assure fixity of tenure, fair rent, and compensation for improvements to tenants; in Illinois they joined together to beat down levels of wages paid to farm workers.[26]

At the close of the nineteenth century the agricultural laborers and tenants outnumbered full owner-operators of farms in five of the states we have studied, and in all the Upper Mississippi Valley the numbers of farm laborers and tenants were fast growing. Agrarian reform movements offered nothing to improve their lot. It was not until the twentieth century that the status of the tenant was bettered with his gradual accumulation of livestock, equipment, and investment in improvements, which has made him a substantial farmer with an equity worth thousands of dollars.

[26] A Farmers Union meeting in Mason County, Illinois, in 1885 resolved "not to exceed fifteen dollars per month, by the year, for the best farm labor, . . . that for the limit of six months, the limit of wages be eighteen dollars per month . . . that we pay no more than $1.50 per day for driving header wagon in harvest; $1.50 per day for labor in haying, and from 50¢ to $1.00 for common labor, to be regulated by time and circumstances" (*Mason County Democrat*, Jan. 16, Feb. 6, 20, 1885).

Merle Curti and a group of associates undertook a study of pioneer life in a relatively uncommercialized agricultural county of Wisconsin to test Turner's generalizations concerning democracy and the West. Employing the microscopic approach of Joseph Schafer, through detailed statistical computations of census, tax, assessment, and deed records, under the innovative guidance of Curti they produced a great landmark in historical studies that points the way for similar studies of other areas: *The Making of an American Community: A Case Study in a Frontier County* (Stanford, California, 1959).

Paul Schuster Taylor has written extensively on agricultural labor in the twentieth century. His "Migratory Laborers in the Wheat Belt: Second Half of the Nineteenth Century" (1957), in *Hearings before the Subcommittee on Migratory Labor of the Senate Committee on Labor and Public Welfare on "Migrant and Seasonal Farmworker Powerlessness,"* 91 Cong., 1 and 2 Sess., 1970, pp. 6258–6298, is an important work on an earlier period.

Index

*Landlords and Tenants
on the Prairie Frontier*

Designed by R. E. Rosenbaum.
Composed by Vail-Ballou Press, Inc.,
in 11½ point linotype Caslon O.F., 2 points leaded,
with display lines in Caslon Old Style.
Printed letterpress from type by Vail-Ballou Press
on Warren's 1854 text, 60 pound basis,
with the Cornell University Press watermark.
Bound by Vail-Ballou Press
in Columbia book cloth
and stamped in All Purpose foil.

Library of Congress Cataloging in Publication Data
(For library cataloging purposes only)

Gates, Paul Wallace, date.
  Landlords and tenants on the prairie frontier.

  Includes bibliographical references.
  CONTENTS: Tenants of the log cabin.—The role of the land speculator
in western development.—Southern investments in northern lands before the
Civil War. [etc]
    1. Land tenure—Middle West—History. 2. Middle West—Public lands—
History. I. Title.
HD210.M53G37   333.3'23'0977   72-12403
ISBN 0-8014-0763-X